A Soul came into
IRELAND

THOMAS DAVIS, 1814-1845:

A Biography

John Neylon Molony

GEOGRAPHY PUBLICATIONS

Published in Ireland by
Geography Publications,
Templeogue, Dublin 6W

ISBN 0 906602 65 3

Cover design by Christy Nolan
Typesetting by Phototype-Set Ltd., Dublin
Printed by Colour Books, Dublin

List of Illustrations

Contents

Thomas Davis, from the drawing by Frederic William Burton
(courtesy of National Gallery of Ireland).

The frontispiece and photograph on page 227 are reproduced courtesy of the National Gallery of Ireland. I am grateful to Marie McFeely and Adrian La Harivel of the National Gallery for their help. Photographs on pages 3, 9, 22, 44, 65, 85, 126, 147, 168, 189, 212, 218 and 298 are reproduced courtesy of the National Library of Ireland. The prints on which these are based are referenced in *Catalogue of Irish Topographical Prints and Original Drawings* by Rosalind M. Elmes, new edition revised and enlarged by Michael Hewson (Dublin, 1975). Captions and reference numbers are from this Catalogue. I wish to thank Eugene Hogan of the National Library for photographing these prints.

Thanks to Joe Brady, University College Dublin for providing the map for page 158. The photograph on page 199 is reproduced courtesy of the Office of Public Works. Photographs on pages 104 and 136 are based on the *Nation* newspaper in the archives of the Royal Irish Academy. I wish to thank Paul Mitchell and Siobhán O'Rafferty for facilitating access and Sarah Cully, Audio-Visual Centre, UCD, for taking the photographs. The illustration on page 281 is reproduced courtesy of the National Museum of Ireland. I wish to acknowledge the assistance given by Michael Kenny in locating the uniform in the National Museum's collection. Selections from Davis's work on pages 202, 232, 260, 322 and 374 are from *The Spirit of the Nation or Ballads and Songs by the Writers of the Nation* (Dublin, 1901). The illustration on page 237 is reproduced from the *Journal of the County Kildare and District Archaeological Society*, volume vi, (1911). Thanks to Dr Con Costelloe and Ms Mary Coughlan, County Library, Kildare for alerting me to this source. Mr J. C. Miller helped locate the grave of Annie Hutton.

Acknowledgements

My colleagues at University College Dublin (1990-1993) were ceaseless in their encouragement and friendship while I combined my teaching with research on Thomas Davis. The years I spent with them will remain among the finest of my life and their enrichment was enhanced by the times we had in the Common Room. In that place, the company of Con Ó Cléirigh, scholar, true Irishman and beloved friend to so many, will always live in my memory.

The two rich lodes in Ireland for Thomas Davis material are the Royal Irish Academy and the National Library of Ireland. I thank all those who helped me in both places. The debt to Dinny and Justine, who were with me in the happy times in the Glebe at University College, remains, as always, unpaid. On my return home to take up a post at the Signadou Campus of the Australian Catholic University in Canberra, I was welcomed and spurred on to write by the unstinting devotion to their own tasks of my colleagues. I am deeply grateful to Chris Gray and Robert Fitzgerald for their patience and good humour as they coaxed me through a maze of advanced computership.

I am very appreciative of the special help given to me by Maurice Bric, Art and Emer Cosgrove, Maura Cronin, John Crotty, Michael Laffin, Gerard Long, Gerry Lyne, James Maguire, Donal McCartney, Bede Nairn, Maurice O'Connell, Dick O'Neill, Tim O'Neill, Seamus Ó Riain, Ríonach uí Ógáin and Alison Pilger. My publisher, Willie Nolan, threatened, in his own words, to be my 'worst enemy' as he steered me through the final drafts. In him, I only found one to whom I now say, "Thanks, mate".

Preface

Thomas Osborne Davis died in 1845, a few weeks short of his thirty-first birthday. The brevity of his life should simplify the task of his biographer. Yet, there is only one full biography of Davis. His close friend and fellow worker on the *Nation*, Charles Gavan Duffy, looked back over almost fifty years to when he first met Davis in Dublin in 1842. Throughout those years, despite his own complete involvement as journalist, member of Parliament at Westminster and, later, as the premier of the colony of Victoria, Australia, the memory of Davis had never faded for Duffy. He collected all the available material and, in retirement at Nice, wrote the biography which came out in 1890.

The title running through the pages of Duffy's book is 'Memoir of Thomas Davis'. Duffy remembered Davis with much love, indeed veneration, and time had sharpened, rather than faded, the memories. However, Duffy was too good a journalist and historian, although an amateur one, to write mere hagiography, but he found it hard to stand back and look impartially at the lost patriot. The problem for Duffy was to see Davis as the sower of seeds that would bear their fruits in the future. In the person of Davis, Duffy saw blighted hope, unfulfilled promise, Ireland's destiny thwarted, a group of ardent spirits dispersed and the deeds of the dead threaded into the fabric of a futile past. Small wonder then that Duffy's memoir is one in which sadness marches with despair, bitterness with suppressed anger, pride with love.

Duffy could not see a future Ireland, even though a divided Ireland, with its own literature, art, theatre, fine and all-embracing education system, myriad institutions of higher learning, legal order, in some measure its own language, flag, anthem, parliament, diplomatic corps, army and all the other institutions of an independent state. He could not see the day when the thing Davis had longed for so desperately had come about. To the question 'What is your nationality?', the simple answer of his countrymen in the Republic today is the one word 'Irish'. These were the things that Davis, Duffy, Dillon, MacNevin, and that group of young men who came to be known as Young Ireland, dreamt about, sang about, worked and prayed for. In their own day, however, as Duffy wrote mournfully, 'Young Ireland was routed and scattered almost to the last man. They bore away with them from Ireland the stigma of a lost cause, and the reproach of an ignominious failure. To scornful enemies they were pipers of sonnets and spouters of orations, who had mistaken themselves for men of action.' In 1862, Dillon, from

Dublin, wrote to Duffy in Australia, 'I rejoice that you are not here to witness the wreck of all the high hopes we have cherished.'

The distance of 150 years makes it possible to look back and see that the high hopes were not all wrecked and that the cause was not all lost. Thus, it is not as painful for another to write of the life and death of Davis as it was for Duffy. With Duffy there was another reason to mourn the death of Davis besides the loss of a beloved friend. Davis was the one who held the men of Young Ireland together, inspired them, gripped them with his enthusiasm and fired them with his vision of the Ireland they would help to create. At the apex of that vision lay independence and the flowering of the nation. The way to achieve that goal and make it fruitful was education. To Davis, education was not a sterile process of merely imparting knowledge. Education included all that made the good citizen. The past and the present, the arts and the economy, the familial and civic virtues, loyalty, sobriety, courage, determination and love of country, all these things and more were in Davis's mind when he said, time and time again, 'Educate that you may be free.' Through education, the people would learn how to be confident in taking responsibility for their own lives and for the well-being of the community they made up. To Davis, democracy began long before it took shape in the legislative process of an independent parliament. Democracy was born day by day in the individual citizen, and mass political movements, unless they went hand by hand with education, tended to inhibit, rather than foster, its growth.

The dominant passion in the heart of the Protestant, Trinity College graduate, Thomas Davis was an unbounded and unfettered love for Ireland. By Ireland, Davis did not simply mean a land mass. Unquestionably, he loved the Ireland of rivers, seas, mountains, rain and mists, valleys, colours and sounds, villages and cities. Yet, above all, he loved the Ireland of its people, the Ireland of all its people, those whose ancestors who had been there for countless generations and the newcomers who had come but yesterday. For Davis it was too painful, indeed unthinkable, to accept that the people of Ireland would continue to be divided on the basis of differing religious traditions. He did not want those traditions to be merged, lost or even muted. That each would be united at the summit of their Founder's message to love each other as neighbours was his hope and prayer. His happiness at the pursuit of peace was unbounded and the last words he addressed to his Protestant brethren of the north fell little short of a prayer. That he spoke to the men of the north perhaps indicates that he knew the women in their hearts longed for peace and unity,

Surely our Protestant brethren cannot shut their eyes to the honour it would confer on them and us if we gave up old brawls and bitterness, and came together in love like Christians, in feeling like countrymen, in policy like men having common interests. Can they – ah tell us, dear countrymen! can you harden your hearts at the thought of looking on Irishmen joined in commerce, agriculture, art, justice, government, wealth, and glory?

To read the names in these pages is to go far to explain how Davis became Ireland's son and why Yeats could say that he wanted to be one with Mangan, Davis and Ferguson. The names of O'Connell, O'Brien, Dillon, Duffy, Mitchel, Carleton, Hogan, MacManus, Wilde, Burton, Petrie, O'Donovan, O'Curry and many more are there, as they are on the scroll of Ireland's illustrious dead. To be in Dublin in the 1830s and 1840s, to meet, work with and learn from those men was truly to be alive. Davis knew it to be so, took from them what they gave, and gave back to them in even fuller measure. When he went from them they all grieved, because they knew what they owed to him. The people of rural Ireland, in their homes and villages throughout the land, gave him much also. To them he gave back his songs and much of his life.

The years of Davis's public activity were few, but almost every moment of them was given to the development of the single, motivating idea of his lifetime. He expressed it in the one word nationality. To him, nationality meant the acceptance, by all those who lived in Ireland, of a vital and dependent relationship with each other and with the land they lived in. That acceptance made them Irish. Without it, they were not Irish. It was a simple idea that Davis wove throughout everything he wrote and upon which he based his striving. Its simplicity was the reason for the remarkable success of the *Nation* and why, for over a century after his death, the name of Davis remained revered. That so much for which Davis worked has been achieved only means that his teaching on nationality is as appropriate today as it was in the 1840s because, like democracy, nationality is always in the making.

Davis was principally a thinker rather than a doer, so that his thought must be found in his words rather than in his deeds. At the same time, to write, for Davis, was to do. Indeed, in some way it was to reach the pinnacle of action because what was written remained, but what was done proved so often to be of the passing moment. Fortunately, whether in the pages of the *Nation* or in other publications, in his correspondence and in the writings of his contemporaries, the sources for Davis's thought are rich. The years of his early manhood are veiled in privacy so that, in large measure, the Davis we know today is the man of a short seven years. Into those years he poured the wholeness of his being and, in the end, he was spent. Famine loomed across the land as he lay dying. Perhaps it was as well for him that he went before it stalked. Like Daniel O'Connell's, his great heart could not have borne it.

It had to be that there are others who are met with in these pages in respect of whom silence would have been better. They do not include O'Connell and, had they, Davis would not want to be here either because he revered the Leader to the end. Many of his contemporaries recognised publicly that, in Davis, a soul had come into Ireland. Few perhaps could see how much his giving of himself had cost him. His life fleshed out in its totality the meaning of his own chosen word – nationality. Without peace and unity, Davis knew that Irish nationality was barren.

Chapter 1

The making of a patriot

On the west coast of Ireland, the Beara and Iveragh peninsulas stretch into the Atlantic between Dingle Bay and Bantry Bay. Kenmare stands at the entrance to the peninsulas where the river of that name enters the sea. With cliff and mountain, sea and rock, foam and fog, that whole place ranks among the finest of all natural creation. Near to Kenmare, in the 1830s, stood the ruins of Dunkerron Castle which had been the seat of the hospitable and ancient O'Sullivan family. The O'Sullivans had come to that part of Ireland from Tipperary where, in the thirteenth century, Daniel had ten sons, eight of whom, together with their father, were killed and their lands lost under the Anglo-Norman Conquest. One surviving son took up almost half of the Barony of Beare and Bantry and settled at Dunkerron, where his descendants held on to the language, traditions and religion of the Catholic, Gaelic Irish through five hundred years.[1]

The headship of the family finally came down to Morty Oge O'Sullivan towards the end of the seventeenth century and it was to his family that Thomas Davis traced his Irish origins. Morty Oge had proved to be a constant irritant to the English authorities who ruled the land. In the end he was betrayed by a retainer named Scully, who accused him of plotting treason, and he was shot dead by the soldiers sent out to arrest him. Morty Oge's family was scattered, much decayed as a lineage, and its memories as a noble family largely lost. Some little ember remained alight however and there was an English version of a lament his family and followers had sung in Irish. The first verse ran,

> The sun on Ivera no longer shines brightly,
> The voice of her music no longer is sprightly,
> No more to her maidens the light dance is dear,
> Since the death of our darling, O'Sullivan Bear (sic).[2]

A few miles along from Kenmare another family had enjoyed a measure of moderate prosperity since at least 1770. They managed to hold on to some of their land by exploiting its isolation, and they 'also maintained a profitable French connexion, a trade in priests and soldiers as well as brandy, silks and others luxurious contraband.' By the 1830s, Daniel O'Connell, Member of Parliament, held extensive land with his seat at Derrynane, near the ruins of the ancient Abbey of that name. He had inherited all he held from his uncle, 'Hunting cap' Maurice O'Connell and, like Morty Oge, he had become entwined with the land from which he sprang, but he knew nothing of dispossession and ruin. Wherever he went in life he held his head high because Daniel O'Connell knew that he was one with those who never ceased to regard themselves as the rightful inheritors of the land. A sense of their further right to control their own destinies, their pride in, and love for, their religion and their memory of the long attempt by their conquerors to degrade them lived on among the O'Sullivans to some degree, but fully among the O'Connells. As neighbouring Catholic families, they had intermingled and intermarried so that the blood of the one ran in the blood of the other.[3]

A child in whom that blood ran was born on 14 October 1814 at Mallow in county Cork as the last son of James Thomas Davis and Mary Atkins. Like his two brothers and one sister before him, the infant was baptised into the Church of Ireland in the medieval church of St Anne on 27 October where he was given the family names of Thomas Osborne.[4] Unlike Daniel O'Connell, Thomas Davis was destined to spend the rest of his life searching to answer the question of his being. To O'Connell, 'Being Irish was merely being himself; and totally assured and at ease in his national identity, he could extend this identity large-heartedly to all the inhabitants of his island.'[5] That sense of assurance could not, however, be found in Davis and those like him, who, wanting to be Irish, had to constantly ask the question, 'Who am I?'

The quest of Thomas Davis began hesitatingly because the boy never knew his father. James Thomas Davis was of a Buckinghamshire family of Welsh origin who considered themselves totally English. He became a surgeon in the Royal Artillery, took up a posting in Ireland and while on duty at the garrison in the town of Mallow in County Cork he met Mary Atkins and married her on 8 July 1802 at St Peter's Church, Cork. James duly received promotion and eventually he became head of the military hospital at Islandbridge in Dublin. Nonetheless, it was to the Atkins home in the main street of Mallow, now number 73 Davis Street, that Mary returned for the birth of their four children, John Nicholas, 1803, James Robert, 1806, Charlotte Mary, 1810, and Thomas Osborne, 1814 when Mary was aged forty. During the latter stages of the Napoleonic wars, in September 1814, James Thomas Davis left Woolwich for Exeter on his way to Portugal. He had

Davis Street, Mallow.

been appointed acting director of military hospitals on the Peninsula and duty had to prevail over family necessity. James never reached Portugal, dying at Exeter on 27 September where he was buried.[6]

Mary Atkins was born of a family which traced its lineage back to the English-Norman House of Howard. Davis later wrote that, in the seventeenth century, an Atkins became 'a Cromwellian settler whose descendants, though they occasionally intermarried with Irish families, continued Protestants, and in the English interest, and suffered for it in 1688 by the loss of some of their lands. For their loyalty and service to the Crown some members of the family were knighted.'[7] An intermarriage between the new settlers and the old Irish took place in 1728 when Davis's great-grandfather, Robert Atkins, married Anne O'Sullivan, daughter of the O'Sullivan Beare. Their only issue was a son, John, who took, as was often the custom, the Protestant religion of his father rather than the Catholic religion of his mother. John inherited the modest lands of his father at Fountainville, Ballyandrew, County Cork, and married a kinswoman, also Mary Atkins. Their daughter was the Mary who married James Thomas Davis and bore him the son Thomas Osborne.[8] Through his mother, Thomas thus shared in the blood of the distant ancestor who had come to Ireland for spoil in the wake of Cromwell. Through his great-grandmother, Anne O'Sullivan, he was said to carry the blood of the fabled Milesians, who, legend says, came into Ireland across the seas from the south. Throughout his adult life it was to the ancient Celtic and Catholic family of O'Sullivan Beare that Thomas Davis looked as the guarantor of his Irish origin.

Mary Atkins spent the first four years of her widowhood with her family in Mallow, where Thomas passed his early childhood. He always looked back with pride to the place and county of his birth, although no clear impression of Mallow with its gracious surroundings on the Blackwater River could have been made on him. Certainly he was never to rejoice, or share, in Mallow's reputation as the stamping ground of the young blades sung of in 'The Rakes of Mallow', nor in its claim to be the place where the first recorded steeplechase occurred. He never showed an interest in such matters. Perhaps in order to ensure the education and prospects of her children, Mary left Mallow at Christmas 1818 and moved to a dwelling at 7 Warrington Street, Dublin. In due course Thomas was enrolled in Mr Mungan's school in Lower Mount Street, which was a short walk from his home.[9]

Mungan's establishment was an institution of some repute scholastic-ally, which possibly accounted for Mary's choice of it for her youngest son who was said to be a dreamer and a slow learner. The former could account for the latter in that those whose thoughts are elsewhere find difficulty in concentrating on the text before them, and the learning of the day was much by rote. Thomas, furthermore, was 'never any good at handball or hurling', and his disinterest in economic matters was evident for 'he knew no more than a fool how to take care of the little money his father left him.' Things that spoke to the heart, as well as to the head, gripped him and he was easily moved by music of any kind so that a relative sometimes observed him, in postures that remained for life, 'in tears listening to a common country fellow playing old airs on a fiddle, or sitting in a drawing-room as if he were in a dream when other young people were enjoying themselves.'[10]

Davis's childhood was secure and happy in the warmth of a home where moderate means and a loving mother ensured that neither material nor emotional needs went unfulfilled. When Mary Davis died at the age of 79 her son John wrote, 'My own ever darling Mother ... How I loved her.'[11] There is every indication that Thomas and her other children loved Mary with the same tender intensity. Shielded as he was from the misery of the Dublin poor and from the anxiety of those of the middle classes whose economic base had been struck a blow with the loss of Parliament to the city after 1800, there is no indication that an awareness of his own comfort caused Davis unease or the evidence of want about him guilt. In his holidays he returned to Mallow or to Templederry in Tipperary where his aunt was wife of the Church of Ireland rector, the Reverend Hastings Atkins, and where the old people later frequently remembered him among them.

Monaquill, the Atkins's home in Templederry, was a gentle haven from city life for the Davis children and on his walks in the surrounding hills Thomas often heard the Irish language in speech or song. The memories of 1798 remained vivid and bitter among many people in those parts and, during the Rising, the parish priest of Templederry was arrested and his parishioners were 'bullied and tortured'. At nearby Silvermines the Protestant minister, Henry Fulton, for his alleged role among the rebels there, was transported to Australia.[12] Of the men of Tipperary, Davis later wrote,

> Tall in his form, his heart is warm
> His spirit light as any fairy
> His wrath is fearful as the storm
> That sweeps the hills of Tipperary.[13]

During his last year at school the family moved to an unpretentious but substantial terraced house in the Georgian style at 61 Baggot Street Lower. Thomas, his mother, James Robert, the second son who became a solicitor and Charlotte, together with several servants, including a manservant named Neville, lived in the house. John, the eldest, had left

Davis's Home, 67, Lower Baggot Street, Dublin (from Arthur Griffith, ed. *Thomas Davis: The Thinker and Teacher* (Fourth impression, Dublin, 1922)).

home to follow in the footsteps of his father as a surgeon in the Royal Artillery. The house was of three storeys with a basement for servants' quarters and stood within a hundred yards of that artery of commerce and travel, the Grand Canal.[14] No record survives of Davis's recreations or of his schooling in its customary classical and mathematical components, but he took his first steps in the precious and, in his case, lasting virtue of tolerance under the guidance of Mr Mungan. In the school Davis learnt, without distinction as to creed, 'to know, and, knowing, to love my countrymen.'[15] Although it was not unusual for boys from the middle class to be educated in private schools that admitted adherents of varying religious traditions, tolerance was a high virtue in the Ireland of the late 1820s and early 1830s. It was a period that had seen and suffered the setback for some, and the apparent triumph for many, of Catholic Emancipation in 1829. To tolerance Davis added perforce patience and forbearance because, throughout his youth, he was physically weak and unable, or perhaps unwilling, to participate in the games his companions played. With time, however, his frame became more robust and his health improved so that he became a normal Dublin schoolboy, even if the study and the library remained more his arena than the street or the playing field.

During the eighteenth century Dublin was, for a time, the second city of the British Empire and the presence of an Irish Parliament at College Green had done much to make its growth possible. The population was 233,000 in 1841, by which time Glasgow had outgrown it. As the city of his childhood and youth, Dublin had become Davis's landscape with its sights and sounds, its long darkness and soft dampness. Yet the time came when the buds broke, the skies cleared and a gentleness flowed over the city during its all too brief summers, to be followed by the fading colours of autumn. Clothed in its Georgian elegance, the city possessed its own gracious loveliness which Davis grew to treasure. Visitors to it often remarked on its splendour, the charming affability of its inhabitants, as well as its beggars, destitute but often happy poor and the filth of some of its suburbs. With its mingling of straight and curved streets and the Liffey dividing north from south, its core or central plan in the early nineteenth century was much as it is today. Engels said that Dublin Bay with its harbour was 'the most beautiful' in the whole British Kingdom, although the entrance to the port was difficult due to silting in the Bay. Nonetheless, it was the busiest port in the country with exports and imports amounting to £2,529,000 and £4,300,000 respectively in 1836. The suburbs beyond the canals, such as Ballsbridge and Donnybrook, were growing and Rathmines and Sandymount were, in effect, connected to the city. At the same time, there was little in Dublin that recorded the Gaelic past or present except the name. Founded by Norsemen, the Anglo-Irish had given it the character which Davis knew and which in large measure it has retained.[16]

Thus, while his holidays at Mallow and Templederry may have been part of his dreaming, Dublin was Davis's substance and he was, and remained, an urbanite. Yet in a sense the urbanity of Dublin, capital city of an island, was truncated because its political life was conducted at one remove with its home across the Irish sea at Westminster, if one discounted the doings of the Dublin Corporation which remained unreformed and representative only of the Protestant minority. The Latin Davis learnt at Mr Mungan's was enough for him to translate with ease the motto of his city, which told him that the happiness of everyone in Dublin would be ensured provided its citizens remained obedient, rather than that happiness would flow from harmony. He knew full well to whom that obedience had to be extended because in Dublin Castle the representative of the united Crown of England, Scotland, Wales and Ireland held the highest authority in the land. There is no evidence that he ever entered its portals.

Davis was, as yet, unaware of the social contradictions in which Ireland abounded, or of the anomalous position of the class to which he belonged. The population was moving towards 8,000,000, of whom almost half were completely illiterate. They lived on an island which abounded in natural resources, an abundance of good soil, plentiful water, an equitable climate admirably suited for growth of both crops and livestock, an improving transport system with roads and canals, and some social developments in health and education, which the Union with England had seen fostered. The effects of the Industrial Revolution were widespread in industry, transport, banking and economic organisation and by the 1830s there was an abundance of available capital. Much of the capital flowed to England due to a lack of local prospects for profits in a climate which, for example, saw the Irish textile industry hard hit by English competition, with the result that it supplied only 14 per cent of home needs as compared to the previous century. In both urban and rural areas there was much misery, a good deal of it abject, especially since the boom years 1793-1815 when exports rose by 40 per cent, due principally to the Napoleonic Wars. The economy had slowed markedly after 1815, there was famine in 1819-20 and a severe depression in 1825-6, so that within some Protestant and most Catholic circles there was a tendency to link recession with the Union and a Protestant author wrote that, among those who lived by their hands or their wits, 'there is a strong feeling of dissatisfaction at the invisible decay in every branch of trade, commerce, and manufactures, under an always absentee government.' In Dublin, the poor lived in

Library of Trinity College, 1859.

degrading conditions and a concentration of wealth intermingled with great poverty, high unemployment and frequent outbreaks of smallpox. Living in the midst of a family without an interest in either commerce or agriculture, it is unlikely that such matters impinged on young Davis in the quiet atmosphere of Baggot Street Lower.[17]

By the summer of 1831 Davis was ready to enter university. In this matter he had no choice were he to remain in Ireland because there was only one university on the island, founded for the education of the clergy of the Church of Ireland by Elizabeth I in 1592. It still remained their nursery in Davis's time. The site, with its buildings, as well as extensive land holdings, had formerly belonged to the Augustinian monastery of All Hallows and were granted to the city of Dublin when the monasteries were dissolved in the early 1540s. Davis, confident in his background, standing and intellectual formation, happily found his way from home to Dublin University with its one college, Trinity where, aged sixteen, he enrolled on 4 July 1831 under the tutorship of Thomas Luby.[18] From his home it was a brisk walk along Baggot Street into Merrion Row and then down Kildare Street with its imposing edifices of the wealthy, as well as the former town residence of the Duke of Leinster that now housed the Royal Dublin Society. Once across Nassau Street, he was able to walk along the wall thrown up around Trinity and thence through its entrance on College Green.

The physical Trinity Davis entered remains much today as he saw it, with some later additions and modifications. The resemblance ends there. Entry depended upon an examination in the Latin and Greek classics, as well as the languages in which they were written because translations were considered undesirable. The undergraduate course was four years of classics, philosophy, mathematics and physics taken by all the students, who were required to sit quarterly oral examinations. Chapel was at six a.m. and again at four p.m. and external students, the majority, were required to attend chapel four times weekly. Lectures were spasmodic and spartan events with a science lecture daily at seven a.m. and Greek three times a week at eight or nine a.m. Students could be externs with no requirement to ever attend the university, except for the examinations. The professor of Modern History never lectured and alongside the classes given by tutors, a system of private tuition was the norm with grinders of all kinds available to help the students prepare for examinations. Except for divinity there were no professional courses and no law school as such, although a rudimentary medical school had begun to organise itself. The famous Long Room was gradually filling up with about 75,000 volumes, but the undergraduates were refused entry to the library and they had to use a rudimentary form of lending system or buy their own books. No organised sport or other leisure activity existed, leaving the students, who were all males, to find ways of filling in their spare time, which, being students, they were not slow to do in ways of which their masters invariably disapproved.

Of the roughly 1,700 students in 1831, whose average age was seventeen and a half at entry, about 92 per cent were born in Ireland. Since 1793, when Catholics and Dissenters were permitted to enter the university, their numbers had fluctuated at about five per cent for the Catholics and two percent for the others. Thus Trinity was, as its founder intended, a Protestant university which comfortably continued to represent about ten percent of the Irish population by enrolling ninety percent of its students from the one denomination, the Church of Ireland. The senior academic staff was mostly clerical and a large proportion of the students were destined for the cloth. Sincere in its evangelical sectarianism, Trinity had become the springboard for the last concerted effort to convert the Irish people to Protestantism and many of the students underwent 'a personal conversion' while in college. Many others 'regarded it as natural to devote a large part of their leisure to Sunday school and Bible classes.'[19]

Davis, like the majority of students, was enrolled as a pensioner, which meant that he was recognised as coming from a family of moderate means. His mother paid a fixed annual sum for his tuition, initially under the direction of Mr Luby. He thus ranked above a sizar who was allowed free education in consideration of undertaking prescribed duties, at one time menial, and below a fellow-commoner who paid double fees, but enjoyed special privileges such as taking his degree six months before a pensioner. The highest rank, noblemen, paid four times the set fee but could take their degree in two years. Daniel O'Connell considered it 'unpleasant to a young gentleman to be a pensioner' and enrolled his sons John and Maurice as fellow-commoners, but Davis never gave any indication of having suffered from discrimination due to rank.[20] Nonetheless, Trinity preserved the hierarchical levels of society that prevailed among the middling Protestant Ascendancy, but Davis bordered on the fringes of that society because his people were neither of the aristocracy of birth or wealth, nor were they landholders. They were, in sum, Protestant, genteel, respectable, of moderate means and, above all, staunch defenders of the Union with England that had welded the western isle to the Kingdom across the waters into a seemingly indissoluble oneness in 1801.

With all its faults Trinity already had a long tradition of thought, and sometimes action, that was ill-prepared to remain within the accepted norms of conformity, whether in literature, religion or politics. Thus, in 1831, no place in Ireland was likely to be richer in the development of individual inquiry, questioning the conventional and flying in the face of established ideas. The very names of Swift, entered 1682, Berkeley (1699), Burke (1744), Goldsmith (1745), Tone (1781), Emmett (1793) Moore (1794), and many others who had departed from the path

11

marked down by prudence and tradition, or who had lifted their minds to higher thought in literature and theology, had already entered the consciousness of Ireland in their varying ways. Thus, were the power of example to mean anything to a young man, Trinity offered much. Furthermore, Davis was fortunate in that his student days coincided with the reforming provostship of Bartholomew Lloyd (1831-7) who, as a mathematician and then a physicist, was the inspirational drive behind the great Dublin school in those disciplines. As a reformer, but scarcely a Whig, Lloyd breathed life into an institution in danger of decay. During his time the academic year was organised into three terms of roughly equal length and vacations were rationalised, academic salaries were increased, a chair of Political Economy, all the rage at the time, was endowed and some outmoded traditions were changed, including restoring the time of evensong to nine p.m. The most important development was the introduction of an honour's system into the first degree in 1833, accompanied by a partial reform of the creaky examination system. In order to qualify for honour's, called moderatorships, candidates had to pass the ordinary examination with distinction and then take further examinations requiring specialised reading. Senior and Junior Moderatorships were awarded according to the percentage who sat, but the most valuable facet of the reform was that the teaching system, especially regarding tutorials, improved considerably.[21]

One of the most endearing and remarked upon characteristics of Davis was his ability to make friends, and for those friendships, never lightly embarked upon, to endure for life. Yet in the early years it was not easy for others to penetrate the mask of his shyness and aloofness, both of which were mostly a defence mechanism ensuring that he could pursue his primary purpose of acquiring the knowledge he knew to be the prerequisite of a life of thought and action. Thus he became known as a dull fellow, whose life revolved around books and manuscripts, but his solitude and his unrelenting application to study were fundamental to his intellectual and moral formation. He was rapidly becoming that rare phenomenon of a thinker who imbibed all he could from the available past and living sources, but who came to his conclusions and formed his judgements based on his own knowledge and character, rather than allowing himself to be shaped by others.

Thomas Charles Wallis was the only person who claimed to have had a decisive influence on the intellectual shaping of Davis. Born in Dublin in 1811, his father died before his son entered Trinity in 1829. Given the poverty of his family, Thomas Charles was enrolled as a sizar and graduated in 1836. He lived in a garret at the College and styled himself 'Professor of Things in general, and Patriotism in particular', although he never held a teaching position, or indeed any recognised role except perhaps as a grinder helping students prepare for examinations. A man of undoubted intellectual quality, Wallis failed to achieve any lasting status as a scholar and Charles Gavan Duffy, who observed him closely, later wrote, 'his faculties were not his servants; the sinews of his will were so relaxed that he could never count on employing them on a given work on any given occasion.' Nonetheless, his influence on the young men in the circle in which Davis soon began to mix was unquestionably strong and, in particular, he helped to turn their minds to Ireland as an entity in itself, rather than as a mere appendage to England. Furthermore, Wallis was always brimful of new ideas which he expressed in a great flow of flamboyant language and Davis never denied the effects of his thoughts and personality on him in his student days. However, Davis's contemporary and intimate associate, John O'Hagan, asserted that Wallis had little to do with the shaping of the young scholar and that Davis was uniquely responsible for his own development.[22]

Patrick Robert Webb was at Mr Mungan's with Davis and they met again at Trinity, remaining the closest of friends. James Clarence Mangan, later author of 'Dark Rosaleen' and a contributor to the *Nation*, was never a university student, but he 'was given compassionate employment in the library', where, says John Mitchel, he 'laboured mechanically, and dreamed, roosting on a ladder.'[23] Apart from Francis Kearney who died at the age of twenty, others of the Trinity world with whom Davis formed close bonds of friendship which endured were a group of Protestant students, all of whom made their mark on Ireland in various ways later. They were Torrens McCullagh, William Elliott Hudson, James O'Hea, John Mitchel and John Martin. Given the times and the minuscule proportion of Catholics at Trinity, more remarkable was the way in which Davis moved easily and intimately in a circle of Catholics. At Trinity, and after they had graduated and gone out into the wider world, his Catholic and Protestants friends seeemed to revolve around him as the bond that endured among them and, of the whole group, eleven contributed later to the *Nation*. The Catholics, like the Protestants, also made their mark on Ireland. They were John Edward Pigot, Denny Lane, John Blake Dillon, John O'Hagan, Thomas MacNevin, William Keogh, Colmen O'Loghlen, Denis Florence MacCarthy, Thomas Devin Reilly, and Richard O'Gorman.[24]

Among the reasons why this group stood out at Trinity was the fact that, whether Protestant or Catholic, none of them was destined for the Church in an institution that still preserved strongly the reasons for its foundation. That is not to say that they wore their religion lightly. It merely says that they were, at heart, laymen whose lives were to be lived in and for the world. Another strong bond between them was their essential seriousness, shown especially in the way in which they all regarded the intellectual life, and the work necessary to foster it, as of fundamental importance. A final reason for the ease with which this close companionship was established, and perhaps also for the way in which a sense of nationality was able to grow up among them, lay in the feeling they all shared, whether Protestants or Catholics, of being second-rate citizens in their own country. That astute judge of human affairs, Alexis de Tocqueville, visited Trinity College in 1835 when Davis was still a student there. He wrote in his diary for 9 July of that year,

> This university was founded by Elizabeth with the estates confiscated from Catholics, the fathers of those whom we had just seen wallowing in their mud at the poorhouse! This establishment contains 1500 students. Very few belong to rich Irish families. Not only do the Irish nobility live abroad; not only do they spend abroad the money it produces, [but] they rear their children in England, for fear undoubtedly that the vague instinct of patriotism and youthful memories might bind them one day to Ireland. If you wish to know what the spirit of conquest, religious hatred, combined with all the abuses of aristocracy without any of its advantages, can produce, come to Ireland.[25]

Despite the bonds he formed with his friends, Davis was never able to cast off his innate aloofness or to share their sense of humour which the circumstances of undergraduate life heightened, frequently as a reaction to the many absurdities they were expected to endure in the academic sphere. Those who remembered him well in later life were able to describe his strong frame, his slightly stooped posture, his ready smile and especially the seemingly unfathomable depths of his brown eyes. Very few, however, admitted that they knew him well at Trinity for the essence of the man had yet to be revealed. One particular gift he had that marked him off was his sense of the appropriate, combined with a thirst for the beautiful in thought and matter so that in music, art, literature, appreciation of the landscape and architecture, in conversation or in his relations with his family and friends he strove for balance and a quest for the truth. It was a solitary road he travelled as he learnt that truth comes in many guises and that the beautiful reveals itself to few.

Davis's years at Trinity passed uneventfully. He remained his own man, refused to turn to a grinder for help in preparing for examinations, and never sought academic distinctions for their own sake. Above all, he read. Paley, Butler, Wordsworth, Byron, the Utilitarians, especially Bentham, Bolinbroke and Burke and many others were all there. He acquired a useful knowledge of French, German and Italian and read widely in authors in those languages. Reading Jeremy Taylor helped to confirm him in a liberal attitude to religion, but he appeared at the time to remain a firm believer in Christianity according to the teachings of the Church of Ireland. History, in particular Irish history, drew him constantly to its source but in it, as in much else, his reading was undirected and undertaken only 'from pure thirst for knowledge, with a spirit of moral enthusiasm akin to a brave mariner, like Cook, voyaging to seek new countries.'[26] Yet his time at Trinity was precious also because he knew that those whom he grew to love there had helped to shape him and that the College itself had a role in forming Ireland's greatest patriots. Later he recalled 'the days when he wore (Trinity's) gown as the sweetest of his life ... We formed in it friendships which the grave has rather sanctified than destroyed; friendships unchanged by time or death or ambition as they originated without respect to creed or rank or race. Trinity College too is associated with the names of our greatest ...'.[27] Those gifts from Trinity he was able to add to the simple parchment bearing testimony to the incidental learning he gained in its halls.

On 16 February 1836 Davis graduated B.A. on the same day as John Mitchel. He was examined in physics, ethics, philosophy, Greek and Latin and, having passed at a satisfactory level, he took further examinations in logics and ethics, Brown's lectures on the Philosophy of the Mind, a further study of Butler's sermons, Smith on the Ancient Moral Systems, some elements of Bacon and all of Paley's Evidences. He gained a Junior Moderatorship, placing him low in the top fifteen of a class of 196.[28] Thus his degree was undistinguished which was a source of no concern to him as he had never intended to remain on at Trinity or try to achieve an academic position there. Once graduated, he kept himself busy with incessant reading. Wallis records that in the summer of 1837 he was one day sitting at the Long Table in the library at Trinity reading Shelley. Davis looked over his shoulder and said that he too had been 'a rapturous admirer of Shelley'. Wallis became 'wrathful' because Davis, 'by common consent the tamest and prosiest of all our society' was 'a political economist in the Ricardo model, a disciple of Scotch philosophy, a theoretical utilitarian and a Whig in practise' and yet here he was 'daring to appreciate Shelley'. Wallis, furthermore, could see little in him then that would attract anyone's attention as his conversation, though varied, lacked sparkle and his character and ideas seemed narrow, although he had a great store of knowledge. While admitting that Davis showed him an 'unaccountable partiality', which inclined Wallis to judge him kindly, the older man looked upon Davis as a dry and boring young man of little consequence at the time, and less promise in the future.[29]

Were it the case that others shared Wallis's impression of his young friend, their judgement would not have been enhanced by Davis funding the publication of a forty-page pamphlet he wrote in 1837 under the title *The Reform of the Lords*. There is no evidence that anyone except his closest friends read it and, as Duffy observed, oblivion is normally the fate of self-published work.[30] Given his background in a Unionist family it is unremarkable that Davis accepted the official structures of government and saw his country as part of a wider imperial whole. As a result, it would have been unrealistic to expect that he would propose other than reform of the higher institutions of the imperial state, including the House of Lords, rather than their abolition. Nonetheless, the pamphlet began with Burke's 'All men possessed of an uncontrolled discretionary power, leading to the aggrandisement of their own body, have always *abused* it.' Seemingly, Davis had concluded that the House of Lords was both uncontrolled and prone to abuse, and he went as far as to say that 'the Lords have been the perennial perpetrators of wrong', which suggests that he had already moved into a realm of critical and radical thought that marked him off from his peers.

Although by birth Davis stood on the lower rungs of the Irish ascendancy, he rejected its claim that only the Protestants were the Irish nation. Thus he refused to call the Catholics and Dissenters aliens in their own land and he wanted to see them all embraced as part of the nation. He drew the line at the Orangemen, with whom he refused to have any truck, categorising them in Stanley's words as 'the miserable remnant of an expiring faction' and declaring, 'to that irreclaimable body we say nothing. Reason or prudence, principle or common sense, would be alike thrown away on them ...'. To the Unionists he said that, unless the Imperial Parliament put its full confidence in the Irish people, the Union itself would never be confirmed in its power over Ireland. Of the Federalists, who wanted an Irish Parliament to sit in Dublin that would deal only with strictly Irish affairs, he asked what chance they had 'of a peaceable success with the existing state of the Peers?" More pointedly, he warned those who wanted to break the Union by Repeal that there would be scarce hope of 'peace or prosperity', especially if the Irish Parliament were to offend the unreformed and irresponsible Lords by attempting to abolish the Church establishment and to reform the corporations.

Davis had concluded that Emancipation was achieved by 'personal intrigue' or 'bought' and that the delay in granting it was an act of 'criminal injustice', while 'the unprincipled manner of yielding it made the passing of the Emancipation Bill the craven cry of defeated violence; and instead of adding confidence in English intention to fear of English power, it *augmented distrust* ...'. The Reform Bill was the same in that it was yielded to only under great distress, while a new Coercion Bill, directed at Ireland, rivalled Stanley's ferocious behaviour to the Irish and yet the Lords, persistent in being wrong, passed the Bill. Despite his membership of the Church of Ireland, Davis rejected outright the system by which his Church was financially supported by demanding 'the whole pound of flesh from the peasants'. 'No reasonable politician, no true Christian, can wish to compel a man to assist in supporting what he believes in his conscience to be false and injurious' and yet the Lords had done such an 'evil act' in the last twelve months, while at the same time they had continued to champion 'the self-elected' municipal corporations and remained steadfast against open municipal government, rather than questioning 'the loathsome impurity, the complete exclusiveness of the old municipalities'.

After this forthright statement of his specific grievance against the House of Lords, Davis passed to a more detailed analysis. Using Bailey's *Rationale of Representation* he argued that a government responsible to no one but itself was 'monstrous' and that 'the only just form of government' stemmed from representation by election. The Lords were completely irresponsible and could even reject money bills, while the right of the Commons to create peers was useless as the newly created soon became as corrupt as their predecessors. Furthermore, no peer had to be admired or respected to gain admission to the Lords, where he wielded 'judicial and legislative power.' All he had to do was attain the age of twenty-one, 'an achievement commonly within the reach of the debilitated and debauched', which led Davis to conclude that hereditary rank 'should be unhesitatingly swept away', although he refrained from applying that principle to the concept of an hereditary monarchy.

At a recent dinner in Glasgow, Peel had argued that the Lords were not responsible in the same way as the Commons who relied on an electorate, but that they were 'responsible to God, their conscience, and public opinion'. Davis thought such reasoning was arrant nonsense because Nero, Czar Nicholas and 'the tyrant princes and the despotic councils, in every age and nation,' were similarly responsible and no one had to be reminded of their legacy of infamy. In that vein, he saw some point in reminding his readers of the reigns of George III and George IV. The former was a tyrant, the latter contemptible, and both were *'extravagant'*. Nonetheless, mass action could be taken too far in remedying wrongs and the doctrines of the English radicals were unsocial in that they struck at the essence of the social order, which was the mainstay of peace and prosperity. Davis thought that the English, as a nation, had become accustomed to having and using some measure of civil rights, because they had grown up 'in the possession of tolerable liberty'. Therefore, unlike the Irish, who had no such rights, they did not need years of practice in developing their political capacities. The Irish could only look to their distant past when those who now lived in the cabins of the peasant had been chieftains in the land, but, too often, it was on their past that the Irish dwelt as a form of escape from 'every present misery'. He could only plead with the English to trust the Irish in the hope that by so doing things would get better.

Davis held firmly that a reformed House of Lords should retain the power to reject bills and he asked the Whigs to bring in radical bills on tithes and on the corporations, which he was certain that the Lords would reject, thus leading to a dissolution of Parliament. The next parliament could then begin the task of setting up a system of an elected peerage that would gradually make the House of Lords responsible to the people. His ending seemed insipid and weak and indeed Gavan Duffy, when writing the life of his friend fifty years later, said that the pamphlet was tame in style, had an unconvincing tone, and contained no suggestions for reform inconsistent with 'the more generous Whig opinions of the time'. Duffy seems to have overlooked the fact that the essential radicalism of the work consisted in Davis using the need for reform of the Lords to expose the resentment of many of the Irish, including some Protestant Irish, to British rule. Davis also wanted to highlight the general political immaturity of the majority of the Irish, which stemmed from their continued civic repression. In *The Reform of the Lords* the framework for future thought and action was laid down when Davis was not yet twenty-three. He thus took a first decisive step on the road he was to pursue for the remainder of his life.[31]

References
1. For the O'Sullivans see John Nicholas Croft Atkins Davis, 'Pedigrees' vols. 1-16 Mss 380-400, 404-5, especially vol. 16. Ms. 396 p. 100. Genealogical Office, Dublin. Atkins Davis said that the O'Sullivans were accepted as 'the eldest branch of the Milesians'. John Atkins Davis, eldest brother of Thomas Davis, added the Atkins in later life, after his mother died in 1859. A note on the 'Pedigrees' by an unknown hand, signed T.U.S., says that Atkins Davis was a reliable genealogist and that his system was to 'write in *backways*' any

information which he thought was not proved. See vol. 1, introductory page, Ms 405. J. F. Fuller said that Atkins-Davis, 'brother of Thomas Davis the poet', was 'a very great genealogist and from his intimate knowledge of the family history of *everybody* who was anybody, was known in Dublin society as "Who's who".' Fuller also said that he was a 'rabid Conservative' who, like his father, became Deputy Inspector General of Army Hospitals. See Fuller's handwritten note on the fly leaf of a copy of Sir Charles Gavan Duffy's, *Thomas Davis, the memory of an Irish patriot* 1840-1846 (London, 1890), presented by Fuller to the Royal Irish Academy. [Cited henceforth as Duffy, *Davis* and Royal Irish Academy abbreviated to RIA.]

2. See Mr and Mrs S. C. Hall, *Ireland: its scenery, character, etc.* 3 vols (London, 1841, 42, 43), vol. 1, pp 178, 229.

3. For O'Connell and his family see Oliver MacDonagh, *The Life of Daniel O'Connell* 1775-1847 (London, 1991), pp 1-14 [Henceforth cited as MacDonagh, *O'Connell*]. For the relationship between the O'Sullivans and the O'Connells see Atkins Davis 'Pedigrees', vol. 16, Ms 396, pp 120-21, 155. Atkins Davis has a reference to John O'Sullivan of Coulagh, Co. Cork, who died in the mid-1780s. John was of the O'Sullivan branch from whom the Davises descended and Atkins Davis adds the words after his name 'Maurice Connell of Darinane (sic) Co Kerry Gent his uncle'. The reference is written in normal script so it was a relationship of which Atkins Davis was certain. The O'Connells had dropped the O in the eighteenth century but restored it later. When I said that I had come across this reference to Professor Maurice O'Connell, direct descendant of Daniel O'Connell, in an interview with him in Dublin on 27 May 1993, he told me that there was a tradition in the O'Connell family that the O'Sullivans and O'Connells were kinsmen and that Maurice O'Connell of Tarmons, Co. Kerry had married Morty Oge O'Sullivan's sister. The relationship is further attested to in MacDonagh, *O'Connell*, p. 9 where the male O'Sullivans of Couliagh (sic) are accepted as nephews of 'Hunting Cap' O'Connell. The spelling Darrynane for the O'Connell home was the constant usage of O'Connell himself and of those who wrote to him. The modern spelling, Derrynane, came into use in 1946.

4. The date on the baptismal certificate of Thomas Davis is 27 October 1814. See entry in Baptismal Register, Mallow, no. 2. p. 89. The ruins of St Anne's are behind the new church, which dates from 1824. The inscription on the family tomb in Mt. Jerome Cemetery has 24 October 1814 for Davis's birthdate and one, near contemporary, source agrees with that date. See Samuel Ferguson, 'Our portrait gallery Thomas Davis' in *The Dublin University Magazine,* vol. xxix (Dublin, January-June, 1847), p. 198. In the centenary year of his birth, 1914, *Essays Literary and Historical by Thomas Davis*, was republished in Dublin. In the preface, at p. vii, the statement is made that, rather than the generally accepted 14 October, he was born on 24 October 1814 because that is the date on his tombstone. I am strongly inclined to accept 14 October because I am unable to believe that Charles Gavan Duffy, his intimate friend and close collaborator, was mistaken when he wrote, 'By a curious coincidence the arrangements [for the first edition of the *Nation*] were completed on Davis's twenty-eighth birthday, and next morning the journal was flying through the city.' The first number came out on 15 October 1842. See Duffy, *Davis,* pp 88-9. It was not uncommon for mistakes to be made when dates were cut into a tombstone and, in this case, it is likely that all the family details were entered after the death of Thomas Davis's brother, James Robert Davis, in 1891. By that time Thomas was dead for forty-six years and his eldest brother, John Atkins

Davis, who would have known the exact date of Thomas's birth, had died in 1879.

5.   MacDonagh, *O'Connell*, pp 3-4.

6.   See Atkins Davis 'Pedigrees' vols. 10 and 15, Mss 390, 395, p. 10 and p. 121. For death notice of James Thomas Davis see Sylvanus Urban, *The Gentleman's Magazine*, vol. lxxxiv (London, 1814), p. 505.

7.   See Davis in Duffy, *Davis*, p. 3. See also Atkins Davis, vol. 11, Ms 391, p. 53 where he proves that the Atkins had resided in Ireland since the seventeenth century.

8.   The information on the marriages and other relevant material is in Atkins Davis, vol. 16, Ms 396, pp 120-21.

9.   For the move from Mallow to Dublin, see press cutting June 1912 in 'Thomas Davis Cuttings and Notes' compiled by R.D. Walshe, Ms 14056, National Library of Ireland [henceforth NLI]; *The treble Almanack for the year 1825* (Dublin, 1824), p. 22 in a list entiled 'Nobility and Gentry' has Mrs Davis living at 7 Warrington Place.

10.   For Mungan see George Dames Burtchaell and Thomas Ulick Sadlier, eds., *Alumni Dublinensis* (London, 1924), p. 215. The name is spelt Mungan, not Mongan or Morgan. For the recollections of a kinswoman of Davis see Duffy, *Davis*, p. 4.

11.   See Atkins Davis, vol. 10, Ms 390, p. 10.

12.   See K. J. Cable, 'Fulton, Henry (1761-1840) in Douglas Pike (ed.), *Australian Dictionary of Biography*, vol. 1 (Melbourne, 1966), pp 421-2. See also Marjorie Quarton, *Renegade* (London, 1991), an historical novel based on the life of Henry Fulton.

13.   *Thomas Davis: Essays and Poems with a centenary memoir 1845-1945* (Dublin, 1945), p. 3, and Dermot F. Gleeson, 'Father John Kenyon and Young Ireland' in *Studies*, vol. xxxv (Dublin, 1946), pp 100-1. Kenyon served at Templederry from 1842 until his death in 1869. Gleeson says that the memory of Davis's visits there lived long among the old people. Monaquill House was demolished in 1888 and a new residence built close to the original site by the Boland family. The entrance gate and gate lodge of the original house are still extant. I am grateful to Séamus Ó Riain for this information.

14.   The family had moved to 61 Baggot Street Lower by 1831. See Pettigrew and Oulton *Directory* (Dublin, 1831), p. 194. The street numbering was later changed so that 61 became 67 and remains such today. The house is now used as offices by an engineering company, the members of which have no knowledge of the former plan of the house and thus of the room in which Davis died. There is a plaque in honour of Davis on the outside wall.

15.   The recollection by Davis of his days at Mr Mungan's is in the *Nation*, 31 May 1845.

16.   See Fergus D'Arcy, 'An age of distress and reform' in Art Cosgrove (ed.), *Dublin through the ages* (Dublin, 1988) pp 93-112; T. W. Freeman, *Pre-famine Ireland* (Manchester, 1957) pp 157-167; J. C. Beckett, *The Anglo-Irish tradition* (London 1976), p. 66.

17.   See L. M. Cullen, *An economic history of Ireland since 1660* (London, 1978), pp 90, 91, 100-101, 105-7, 129; J. G. V. Porter, *Ireland*, 3rd ed. (London, 1844), p. ix; Mary E. Daly, *Dublin, the deposed capital. A social and economic history 1860-1914* (Cork, 1984), passim; David Dickson (ed.) *The gorgeous mask: Dublin 1700-1850* (Dublin, 1987), p. vii; Of Ireland, Disraeli said, 'a starving population, an absentee aristocracy, an alien Church and the weakest executive in the world

– this was the Irish question'. See James Bryce, *Two centuries of Irish history* (London, 1888), p. 392.

18.   For Davis's entry to Trinity see Burtchaell and Sadlier, *Alumni*, p. 215. Thomas Luby later became a Fellow of Trinity. He was an uncle of the Fenian leader, Thomas Clarke Luby. See T. F. O'Sullivan, *The Young Irelanders* (Tralee, 1944), fn., p. 217.

19.   R. B. McDowell and D. A. Webb, *Trinity College Dublin 1592-1952: an academic history* (Cambridge, 1982), pp 113-151. On Trinity see also G. Maxwell, *A history of Trinity College Dublin, 1591-1892* (Dublin, 1946).

20.   McDowell and Webb, *Trinity*, p. 114; For John and Maurice's entry to Trinity see Burtchaell and Sadlier, *Alumni*, pp 629-30.

21.   McDowell and Webb, *Trinity*, pp 153-74. The number awarded Senior Moderatorships was fixed at two and a half percent of those sitting and they were rewarded with a Gold Medal. Junior Moderatorships were set at five per cent and they received a Silver Medal.

22.   Burtchaell and Sadlier (eds.), *Alumni*, p. 852; Duffy, *Davis*, pp 11-12; John O'Hagan, 'Thomas Davis', *The Irish Monthly*, vol. 19 (Dublin, 1891), p. 3. O'Hagan died in 1890 but his article, which was his last, was published in *The Contemporary Review* in October of that year. For Duffy on Wallis see O'Sullivan, *The Young Irelanders*, p. 369.

23.   Ibid., pp 278-284.

24.   See ibid., pp 326, 380, 315, 407, 278, 218, 131, 358, 320, 301, for Hudson, Lane, McCarthy, MacNevin, Mangan, Martin, Mitchel, O'Gorman, Pigot and Reilly.

25.   Emmet Larkin (ed.), *Alexis de Tocqueville's journey in Ireland between July and August, 1835* (Dublin, 1990), pp 25-26.

26.   See Daniel Owen Madden in the recollections of Davis he sent to Duffy a decade after Davis's death. Duffy, *Davis*, p. 23. Madden changed his name to Maddyn on his conversion to Protestantism. I decided to remain with Madden because he continued to use that form of spelling on his publications.

27.   Undated document in Davis's hand, probably 1845. Ms 10862 (7). NLI.

28.   See *Dublin University Calendar*, 1836 and 1837 (Dublin, 1836, 1837), pp 60-62.

29.   See article by T. W. (clearly Wallis) in *Nation*, 20 October, 1849.

30.   *The Reform of the Lords by a graduate of the Dublin University* (Dublin, 1837); Duffy, *Davis*, p. 29.

31.   For all references in the foregoing see *The Reform of the Lords*, pp 1-5, 8-10, 12, 18-23, 26-29, 31, 33. For Duffy see *Davis* p. 28.

Hogan's statue of Thomas Davis (Lawrence Print, NLI).

Chapter 2

Fruits of reflection

While still at Trinity, Davis had begun to address the Dublin Historical Society which met at the Dorset Institute in Upper Sackville Street from 1836 to 1838.[1] Made up of a handful of law students, the Society, of which Davis became president, disappeared without a trace, but Davis gave two lectures at it that have survived in manuscript form.[2] The lectures prove conclusively that Davis had become a convinced Irish nationalist by the time of his graduation. Several of his contemporaries stated that he suddenly revealed himself as an Irish nationalist in 1840 and that his 'conversion' was abrupt and inexplicable. Madden speaks of him before that date as 'a hearty Liberal', certainly not a radical, and said that he was 'not particularly devoted to Irish affairs', but more of an 'Imperialist', who had not even considered nationality as an alternative because 'the option was not fairly presented to him.'[3] Wallis went even further and wrote of 'the extraordinary discrepancy that existed between Davis's early tastes, opinions and character ... (with) those by which he afterwards won the sympathy and co-operation of the brave and ardent youths who enlisted themselves under his banner'. To Wallis, 'the apostle of Irish nationality began public life as an Imperialist and a Whig', so that the youth of Ireland who continued in the late 1840s to share similar sentiments need not despair because, like Davis, they too could suffer conversion. What completely astonished Wallis was the physical and mental change that Davis underwent, which even revealed itself in his temperament. The problem with this Damascene *volte face* by Davis was clear to Wallis who was surely familiar with the conversion of Paul, although he did not draw an analogy. 'I know no phenomenon in biography more rare; no problem in psychology more deserving of attentive study.'[4]

Wallis would assuredly have been correct, and the problem for a biographer acute, had there been any foundation for such assertions. The fact is that Davis was a thorough-going Irish nationalist by 1838 at the latest, and his addresses to the Society clearly prove the voluminous reading he had undertaken over several years to reach his conclusions. The only possible explanation for the attitudes of Madden,

Wallis and Duffy is that they preferred to see other elements at work in Davis than a natural growth based on reading and reflection. In their eyes, no pure act of the intellect and will could result in the creation of an Irish nationalist and Madden, ever cyncial of idealism, was never able to share fully the ideas of Irish nationality elaborated by Davis. Given the erratic and unsuccessful path of his own life and probably needing the stimulus arising from the thought that he had helped shape the life of another, Wallis preferred to think that a good deal of Davis's conversion stemmed from his own influence upon him. On the other hand, Duffy was content to observe the flowering of Davis the nationalist in the days when he himself was reaching the same stage immediately before the foundation of the *Nation* in late 1842. By that time Davis had been a confirmed nationalist for at least five years.

While Davis's pamphlet on the Lords clearly showed that his ideas of Irish nationality were already well formed, it nonetheless reveals that he had not yet thought through the practical steps that needed to be taken to achieve Irish independence. It is not surprising that Davis was reticent to enunciate his views, even in the esoteric and closed circle of his Trinity friends. Wallis said that Davis often upbraided him for not entering public life and that in Davis's own case such a step had been one of 'the purest self-sacrifice'. He left it, unkindly perhaps, to a future biographer to dwell on 'the private reasons' which made the public act one of such sacrifice, but he was writing at a time when Thomas's mother was still alive in Dublin. Mary Davis never hid the fact that there was much love for Thomas in the family home, but also complete rejection of his adherence to Irish nationality. Indeed, it was a rejection that almost bordered on abhorrence and was shared by his mother and brothers, especially John, although Thomas's convictions met with greater understanding and acceptance from his sister, Charlotte. Thus the road he trod to nationality was a lonely one, but that very fact forced him to make certain that his ideas were ones of substance based on convictions and wide reading. He was prepared to admit only enough sentiment to make his conclusions appeal to the hearts, as well as to the intellects, of those whose minds were not entirely closed on the matter of nationality.[5]

Another reason for misjudging Davis's development as a patriot stemmed from the notion that he had spent a good deal of time in the late 1830s travelling on the continent. There, he allegedly imbibed elements of romanticism, especially of the German variety, which converted him to a kind of romantic nationalism based on emotion rather than on rationality. It is unclear from what source this error, both of fact and interpretation, took its origins, but it was already established in the early 1930s and has since gained momentum to the extent that it has been said 'in the development of modern Irish nationalism, the most critical single event seems to have been Thomas Davis's visit to Germany in 1839-40', where he 'underwent an evangelical-like conversion' to German Romanticism.[6] The fact is that, apart from keeping terms in London and a walking tour of Wales in 1838, there is no evidence whatever that Davis ever again left Ireland and his residence there can be accounted for throughout the years 1836 to 1840 and, after that date, no one would ever assert that he was outside Ireland. None of his contemporaries ever said that Davis had visited the continent, nor is there any reference to his visiting Germany or anywhere else on the continent in his correspondence or in his published material. Duffy, who knew him intimately, is absolutely emphatic that Davis 'had never travelled' and it would be perverse to think that Duffy had a reason to hide Davis's travels had they ever taken place. Furthermore, Duffy said that Davis decided to give up writing for the *Nation* in August 1844 in order to visit the continent so as 'to obtain the practical acquaintance with races and institutions, and with art and political geography, which travel alone supplies'. Other more pressing matters arose and the visit was postponed indefinitely.[7]

The most reasonable explanation for the widespread acceptance of Davis's dependence on foreign, and especially, romantic ideas on nationalism lies in an understanding of the inferences that have been drawn from the fable. To pin him down as an ardent but impractical youth whose emotions ruled his intellect and, at the same time, see him as the progenitor of 'modern Irish nationalism', as understood by its critics, is an effective way of reaching two objectives. Davis is thereby disposed of as a serious thinker and portrayed as a romantic dreamer who is overshadowed in the sweep of recent Irish history by men of practical wisdom, foremost of whom in his own period was Daniel O'Connell. More importantly, the form of romantic nationalism that Davis is said to have introduced into Ireland is seen as a range of unworthy concepts and emotions, attractive only to those who let their hearts run away with their heads. The resultant caricature of Davis and his ideas thereby gains validity, even at the price of the historical record.

In fact, Davis's writings reveal no evidence that he relied for the development of his ideas about nationality on continental sources of romantic nationalism any more than would be expected to be found in the writings of his contemporaries on the subjects Davis treated. R. F. Foster thought that the ideology espoused by Davis and his friends may have borne 'a superficial resemblance to European romantic nationalism' that had been filtered through Carlyle rather than Herder. However, to the degree that such nationalism depended on language for its expression there was no way it could be fostered in Ireland with the increasing loss of Irish, even though Davis did his best to help to revive the language.[8] Nonetheless, the stereotype has become official to the extent that the section of the Irish National Museum devoted to Davis and the men who stood with him in their attempt to give a new vitality to Ireland and its people goes under the banner 'Repeal of the Union and Romantic Nationalism', with the Young Irelanders said to have been 'stirred by romantic nationalism'.

A combination of factors had provided the opportunity to develop an idea of nationality and Davis was quick to grasp the moment. Internationalism had died since the Reformation because it was no longer possible to feel unity within a greater whole, and democracy had grown in the wake of the French Revolution. The powers of monarchy had waned, education was more available and, with it, the means of knowing the past were increasingly provided, which was important to Davis's purpose. The Irish had to be taught about their past because they were 'a people who have no clear idea who they are or what history they spring from' and, as MacDonagh says, they were regarded by many of those who ruled them as 'a subject and inherently inferior people, occidental orientals in fact'.[9] Furthermore, when the Gaelic Society of Dublin was founded in 1807, it declared that 'an opportunity is now, at length, offered to the learned of Ireland, to retrieve their character among the Nations of Europe, and shew that their History and Antiquities are not fitted to be consigned to eternal oblivion.' In 1786 the Royal Irish Academy had been founded and other bodies followed, such as the Irish Record Commission in 1810, so that the means were already at hand to Davis to study the Irish past and decide to diffuse knowledge of that past more widely among the people.[10]

What Davis wanted was that the past be continued but transformed, based on the nation that had been there before Conquest, and that in the refounded nation all the inhabitants of Ireland would find a place, irrespective of race or religion. Thus, he was reacting essentially to the present rather than to a 'romantic past' except he recognised that, in the past, there had been loss of land, of language, of, in part, religion and, most importantly, of self-respect as a people. To have told Davis, or O'Connell, that there had never been an Irish nation would have been to enunciate a nonsense, although O'Connell saw the nation still fully in being, while Davis wanted to breathe back life into it. They took for granted the reality of an Irish consciousness giving a sense of belonging to a community and a place wider than the locality of the immediate grouping. They accepted that the Irish language and Irish law had been basic to communal existence throughout Ireland, and that the bards and poets had sung of the communal past, even if they had exaggerated the extent of resistance to the invader. Without any difficulty they would have recognised that the nation was a collective distinct from the state and that an Irish nation had existed for many centuries, even though it had never achieved Irish statehood.[11]

As a first and tentative step in sharing the knowledge he had gained by study, Davis, in 1837, gave the first of his two addresses to the Dublin Historical Society, which he claimed was 'the only Historical Institute in Ireland'. His growing dedication to Irish nationality was clearly known to his friends because a well-wisher had warned him not to touch on that 'distasteful theme' but to deal with a 'topic whose remoteness from your country would attract your zeal'. He ignored the warning and made it plain that he intended to deal with Irish history. Calling his audience 'Irishmen', and confident that they would live true to both name and country, he told them that they must know their past if they were to influence the future. He foresaw that his address would cause debate and perhaps disagreement, but welcomed both because 'frequent discussion is fatal not even so much to error as to intolerance.' He was convinced that, although sentiment could lie behind both action and virtue, 'reason is our *only* instrument for the *discovery* of truth', while those who resorted to mere authority for their statements did so simply to flee into 'the asylum of detected ignorance'.[12]

Davis began with a strong recommendation to the Committee to select Irish topics for discussion and to set up 'a section for the peculiar study of Irish history'. He noted that, in practically every debate they held, Irish topics tended to creep in, often in an irrelevant way. Furthermore, they were introduced without purpose or seriousness which led to 'condensed and extravagant declamation' and 'a fierce and ignorant reply.' He pleaded for a more responsible approach, 'Believe me the man who deals in passing with the generalities of Irish party feeling and derives his inspiration from newspapers, not histories, is the most dangerous foe to your peace and instruction.' On the other hand, were they to debate the past based on thorough study, the very act of struggling through its intricacies, 'would dilute its fervour, declamation would soon become more discriminating, zeal more learned, and therefore more reasonable', and, at the very least, they would learn to be tolerant.[13] These sentiments were scarcely likely to come from one who, already, or soon afterwards, would prove susceptible to the embrace of German or any other form of sheer romanticism.

He had decided to avoid modern Irish history because of the difficulty of being 'impartial', and, were he to tell the truth, it would almost result in his being charged with treason. Instead, he would deal first with the periods of Stafford and Cromwell and, in the second address, with the Treaty of Limerick and thus remain confined to the seventeenth century. Davis listed several contemporary and earlier authors from whom he drew material, including Augustin Thierry, 'one of the best historians', Sir John Davies and John Curry. Others were Edmund Campion and Edmund Spenser 'who participated in the cruelty and shared the plunders of the Elizabethan wars'. Of the latter he said, "Tis sad to see the poet's laurels stained."[14] He began, "Tis vain, 'tis puerile to deny that Ireland was conquered', but 'the conquered were valiant and faithful.' He reminded those present that some of them were of the blood of the vanquished, while all were heirs to their country, but that none of them should blush, whether descended from either the conquerors or the conquered. Nevertheless, they should 'think *who* fought for *home and country*, who for 'conquest and supremacy' and then ponder the 'noble maxim, "better to lament a defeat than blush for victory."' If they were only able to triumph over their prejudices, and thus quell the dissension among them, their triumph 'would do you more honour, your country more good than all the victories of the lately landed over the long settled vales of Ireland'.[15]

One of the central themes of Davis's thought was then formulated when he said that division among her people had been fatal to Ireland since the first English invasion. As proof, he instanced how large bodies of Irish troops had co-operated with the foreigner from the twelth century 'down to 1798 when the Irish republic after a brief existence perished in the mountains of Leinster'. In any event, what did the Irish know of their own history? Indeed, what could they know when Irish history was always told 'by the servants and priests and comrades of [our] deadly foes'. In his judgement, Irish history was consequently 'told falsely' which was 'a characteristic we never after lose'. A long section on the development of the Pale was followed by a comparison between the situation in Ireland and that in India. As in Ireland, the British government spent large amounts of revenue on the salaries of public servants and on the maintenance of the army in India while very little was spent to improve the country itself. Yet the situation in Ireland had been much worse arising from the decision to exterminate large segments of the native population and he compared the brutality of the English to that of the Turks and of the Boers who had done the same with the African natives.[16]

The Fitzgeralds were a family whom Davis admired because, besides having been granted the appellation 'more Irish than the Irish themselves (*Ipsis Hibernicis Hiberniores*) they were so often seen as *almost* saving because *almost* uniting Ireland but they ever failed. She is yet to be saved because she is yet to be united.' Often through the centuries some of the leaders of the Irish, 'then as now', were bribed to be false to their people but many nobles and priests rejected the options that were offered to them 'at the point of an English sword'. Even if his youthful opinions had elements of exaggeration in them, they show that Davis was beginning to realise that, through the retention of the Catholic religion, many of the Irish had also been able to retain elements of Irish nationality during the long occupation by the English. Drawing on the works of 'one of the most impartial historians alive', he concluded that 'England was guilty of every grade of persecution from meanness the most petty to cruelty the most ferocious.' If she could behave that way at home 'in the garden of liberty as its panegyricists say and its histories disprove' what then would prevent England from being bloody in all her behaviour in Ireland?[17] In that passionate vein Davis allowed himself to indulge in an unworthy reference to Elizabeth I, even though Elizabeth's record in respect of Ireland was decidedly more damaging than any remark Davis could pass about her physical appearance. He admitted she was 'bold' but said she was an overrated woman 'whose vanity was such that were he to call her ugly her bones would rattle in her grave'.[18] A serious scholar, who seems to be the only one to have commented on Davis's address, chose this remark to sum up its totality as 'silly abuse' which prevented any worthwhile attention being paid to the central themes Davis was presenting.[19]

The second address, also given in 1837, was entitled 'The Insurrection of 1641, its causes, character and fate'. It was about as long as the first, probably taking 100 minutes to deliver. Davis only went as far as 1640, by which time he concluded that he had said enough to be able to ask the audience whether they, in similar circumstances, would not also have engaged in insurrection. He claimed the lecture was based on '*original* authorities' both English and Irish, and he asked his hearers to study the same sources. Some of his authors were Cox, Warner, Leland whom he despised, Hume, Hallam whom he regarded as 'a dupe, not a tool', Semple, Borlase, Clarendon and other 'more original liars', L'Estrange, Curry and Cambrensis who was 'wonderful in calumniating' the Irish. From them they would learn how the rebels had been the victims of English ferocity and their rebellions positively fomented in order for the victors to obtain estates by forfeiture. As a result of their designed and concerted behaviour, the English noble families in Ireland had become 'thieves and murderers'.[20]

The question of English behaviour in Ireland and its intentions has been strongly argued in more recent times, but Davis can now be judged only on the sources he read and the use he made of them. On that basis he concluded that England's behaviour was constantly both treacherous and perfidious and an analysis of his address explains why he took that stand. A study of his subsequent thought and behaviour from 1838 to 1845 will answer the question whether the position he took in the late 1830s remained consistent, or whether he departed from it later when further reading, political experience and the advice and guidance of those whom he trusted had worked their effects upon him. If there is any truth in the assertion that much of Irish nationality as a concept was shaped by Davis, and that many of those who later attempted to develop that concept in practice looked back to him as a source of inspiration, the thoughts and judgements of the young Davis are important, not merely as relics of the past but also as motivators of later historical events.

He began with a cascade of flowing rhetoric summing up his first lecture in which he had narrated the 'savage and treacherous assaults of the English on these scanty tribes'. The explanation for their behaviour was that 'unscrupulous appetite for power and plunder which has in every age marked the conduct of that mixed Norman and Saxon race living East of the Severn and South of the Tweed'. That race had called itself English but 'A petty German tribe has given its chance name to this haughty corporation of adventurers who have taken a flower from Asia and a beast from Africa for their national symbol to signify I suppose their piratical origin and predatory habits and to forewarn the world that no country be safe from their devastations, uninvaded by their conquest, undergraded by their morals or uncalumniated by their scribblers.' Davis then came to his main point. Were his hearers to accept his analysis as correct, they could either blame the system the English had set up in Ireland or the men who ran it. 'Justify the nation and you make the conduct of its greatest men in Ireland the most atrocious in the annals of crime. Condemn the whole system of the English in Ireland as treacherous and savage and you very much, as I think, lessen the weight of censure on these famous men and this last is, I confess, my own humble opinion.' Perhaps his distinction stemmed from his judgement of two men who ran the 'system' in Ireland in his own time and who attempted to make it less 'savage'. They were Lord Morpeth, chief secretary, and Thomas Drummond, undersecretary. They were English and both 'remote kinsmen' of Davis, which fact perhaps swayed his judgement. However, it has been said of Drummond that, as undersecretary 1835 to 1840, Ireland was administered 'in a spirit of justice, humanity, and enlightenment, without parallel in Irish history'.[24]

The distinction between a system and its agents was a neat one, but begged the question in that every system has its human origins and makes real the intentions of those who devise it. However, Davis sidestepped the issue of responsibility by not excusing one set of men, the kings James I and James II and Charles II. They either took control by 'force and fraud' or they were 'selfish, mean and contemptible, faithless and despotic' by turn. Their minions, Cromwell the 'sovereign protector' of England, Stafford and Wentworth, got off lightly by comparison. The most despised set of men to Davis were those whose whole prosperity and long past lay in Ireland, but who had turned their backs on her. He called them 'West Britons' and they were, he fondly and vainly hoped, 'a race of animals becoming rare and wonderful'.[22]

It was not so much his condemnation of the English that made Davis distinctive because even the harshest instrument of criticism is blunted unless it can be used positively. Theobald Wolfe Tone, especially, had seen the need for unity among all the Irish, including the Catholics, to whom he turned for support. Davis revered Tone for his life and work, but he went deeper and further than Tone had done by trying to understand why the Catholics were different, why they thought as they did and why the majority of them reacted so strongly to the English presence. Unlike so many others, then and since, he did not look only to the material and single out the loss of land by the Catholics as the main cause. To him the principal reason was the way their religion had been treated and themselves persecuted because of their general refusal to renounce it. He saw the Acts of Supremacy and Uniformity under James and Charles as 'odious and absurd' and, although he thought that Catholics 'misjudged' the truth of their religion, he was sure 'their fidelity to it was an act of unsurpassed virtue.' The lyricist in him came out as he contemplated the fate of the old religion in Ireland. 'As it sank in the estimation of the powerful they loved it more. Poor was their church, persecuted it wooed them with haggard eye and ragged garment and meagre force. They clung to its embrace.'[23]

To Davis the 'ancient Irish nation' were the Catholics who still remained the original people of Ireland. He saw the Norman settlers and their 'fellow-followers of the old Catholic faith' as one with the old nation because they lived 'in communion with the Church of Rome'. They were attached to their priests who lived among them as friends and brethren and although the clergy 'had *not always* much learning, they generally seem to have had much virtue'. On the other hand, their bishops were 'men of exalted learning and piety and, as their fate proved, zeal'. The Catholic bishops of the old Church were 'stripped of their cures by a tyrannous and plundering act of a half-packed and half-intimidated parliament. They were proclaimed, were outlawed, were sometimes slain or exiled and usually even when left alive in Ireland, they were exposed to a harassing system of espionage by the men who had plundered them.'[24] In his enthusiasm, or lack of knowledge, Davis overlooked the fact that, while the bishops were frequently treated in the manner he outlined, execution was extremely rare. The great burden of English persecution fell on the simple clergy and the laity, which explains why it was long remembered.

When he turned to the 'band of Puritanical Bishops' who had replaced the Catholic ones, Davis was scathing in condemnation of them. With one exception they 'most cordially agreed in their contempt for the Irish people and a furious hatred of the Catholic religion'. They were equally firm in either compelling 'the Irish to change their faith or to make it an expensive luxury for them by filling their own pockets with penalties on their flocks'. After all this it was no surprise to Davis that the feelings of nationality the Catholics had nurtured in the past still lived on among them, but they were now changed into those of an 'oppressed nationality', thereby making them even stronger. He saw the phenomenon of religious oppression as being particularly evident when people in power 'forget virtue and country for creed and churches'. Plainly, Davis had already formulated a hierarchy of values in which credal confessions stood below 'virtue and country'. He did not deny the freedom of individuals to worship God as their conscience directed, but no profession of faith relieved them of the obligation to be virtuous and patriotic.[25]

Davis then turned to his audience and asked them to think about where they stood, because it was more than likely that anti-Catholic prejudices had been handed down to them by their ancestors. It was even probable that their clergy had 'fostered vices which served their interest, their pride and their taste'. He challenged the young men present by asking, 'Do you never indulge one feeling of sectarian bitterness, never sacrifice an opportunity of serving your country to the dogmas of a doubtful theology or the bigotry of a favourite sect?' They were strong words, and he directed them particularly at his largely Protestant audience, but he would not have wanted any Catholic or Dissenter present to ignore them. As a temporal value, service to Ireland should be embraced by them all, irrespective of their religion.[26]

It cannot be supposed that Davis as a boy, at Trinity, or in the short time since his graduation had been exposed personally to virulent forms of Catholic propaganda that had led him to adopt such a strong attitude to the past. That he had read very extensively in the sources of Irish history, and the commentaries on them, is clear. His conclusions, therefore, had to be consequent upon that reading. He had thought them through himself and his decision to enunciate them to a small, but a generally hostile, public audience whom he had to win over by reasoning, indicates his courageous stand on firm principles, interwoven with scholarship. Yet in none of his criticism was there the slightest hint that he remained other than a member of the very Church whose ministers in a past period he so berated. Nor was there any indication that he was tempted to convert. In effect, Davis was already his own man, in religion and in all else.

In his conclusion Davis set down a charter of national rights from which he never wavered. They are sufficient evidence of his maturity and prove that in his earliest manhood he already stood at the forefront of Irish thinking on nationality, and that any role he adopted later, or mantle he wore as a leader of nationalist thought, was both thoroughly prepared for and deserved. He had undergone no sudden conversion, but he would not have wanted to plead that his nationality was 'bred in the bone', except insofar as he could harken back to Morty Oge O'Sullivan and others who had stood upright for a time in 'the sun of Ivera'. To Davis it was enough that he stood with them now and was able to say,

> The rights of undisturbed property and of political and religious liberty are, I presume, the principal rights of every people which native or foreigner, magistrate nor faction, should neither take away or infringe. And if any of these rights are violated, the people for their own, for their nation's, for mankind's sake should resist the oppression and take security against its occurrence. This effort for redress should, if the times and institutions admit, be peaceable and moral. The people should not resort to physical force unless the oppression is great and the danger imminent, or unless their peaceable struggles are suppressed by physical force, and if they are, resistance becomes a duty, the time a matter of prudence, and the best tactician becomes the best patriot. Such are my canons of popular rights and securities.[27]

At the very beginning of his public career Davis spelt out his conviction on the use of physical and moral force. That he did not hold to the principle of 'peaceable and moral' force as the only means a people may use when its rights are violated is clear. Only circumstances could dictate when 'resistance becomes a duty' but, once the circumstances existed, he had no doubt but that physical force was imperative. In that way the principles of active nationality in defence of the people's rights were firmly laid in the fibres of another Irish patriot. Time was yet needed for their application, but time was a precious commodity for the youthful Davis.

Be it the case that Davis was mindful that time was pressing, it must have certainly occurred to his family and friends that as yet he had given no clear indication on what he proposed to do in life. His academic results were not such that the thought of devoting himself to teaching at Trinity, or elsewhere, would have come naturally and he had shown no inclination to do other than research and write on topics that were neither academic in the strict sense, nor popular in the wider. He had no close acquaintances in the world of Dublin journalism and, given his lack of interest, business was out of the question. Politics was a world apart from him because he owed no allegiance to any political group or party. In the event it was almost natural that he would opt for Law and seek admission to the Bar.

In turning to Law, Davis followed the example of many young men of means and leisure who, nevertheless, had neither the intention nor desire to follow a legal career. It was a respectable step to take and it required little effort. Some moderate degree of application to study was demanded to take out a degree at Trinity, but no such drudgery was required of those wanting to be admitted to the Bar, although Davis did some desultory reading in legal matters, as his diaries prove.[28] A witness to a Committee of the House of Commons, set up in 1843 to look into the state of the Irish Bar, said that no education of any kind was required for admission provided the applicant could sign his name and keep terms at King's Inns in Dublin, or at one of the Inns of Court in London. The latter procedure was fulfilled by attending a minimum number of dinners, which were primitive affairs where the food was coarse, the cutlery chained to the table and the surroundings dirty. The regulations regarding 'keeping terms' were introduced in 1542 and abolished in 1885, even though the Law Society had been founded in Dublin in 1830. The statute of 1689 restricting the legal profession to Protestants was repealed in 1792 and the first Catholic judge was appointed in 1835.[29]

Davis decided to keep terms in London, visited the House of Commons and toured Wales, but failed to record his reaction to the dinners to which his fastidious gastronomic inclinations were subjected. He was duly called to the Irish Bar in Michaelmas term in 1838. Madden wrote from London congratulating him on having donned the *toga virilis* and hoping that his bag would be as crammed with briefs 'as your head is stored with encyclopaedic information'.[30] For the rest of his life Davis scarcely ever looked at a prospective brief and certainly never accepted one. In a sense, his admission to the Bar was ill-advised or ill-judged, being one of the very few things he did which was not true to his character. The Bar remained nothing to him, but his admission meant that others could hold out the legal profession to him as an honourable and indeed desirable career to which, once admitted, he ought to devote himself, and especially were it ever the case that his economic circumstances became straitened. The fact that he refused to do so was sometimes seen later as a failure on his part.

References

1. See Duffy, *Davis*, pp 13, 29. I have preferred to follow Duffy's account of the Dublin Historical Society than that given by T. W. Moody, *Thomas Davis, 1814-45: a centenaly address* (Dublin, 1945), p. 20.

2. The papers are found in Ms 3199, NLI. That Duffy had the opportunity to read them is clear from his attached note, 'Materials for the Life of Thomas Davis'. The manuscript totals 120 pages and, in parts, it is difficult to read. Duffy, inexplicably, made no use of it in his biography of Davis.

3. See Madden in Duffy, *Davis*, p. 21 and Duffy on the Society, p. 29.

4. Wallis in the *Nation*, 20 October 1849.

5. Ibid., and Mrs Davis to ex-Repeal Wardens, 1 November 1845, Ms 5756.

6. See Oliver MacDonagh, *Ireland: the Union and its aftermath* (London, 1977), pp 152-3. This reference to Davis in Germany is repeated in Oliver MacDonagh, 'Ideas and institutions', in W. Vaughan (ed.) *New History of Ireland* (Oxford, 1989), vol. 5, ch. ix, pp 198-99. The source from which MacDonagh seems to have drawn this information was J. S. Kelly, 'The political, intellectual and social background to the Irish literary revival to 1901' Ph. D. thesis (Cambridge, 1972). The first reference I could find to Davis in Germany was J. M. Hone, *Thomas Davis* (Dublin, 1934), p. 25 followed by Moody, *Davis*, p. 20 and Leslie Stephen and Sidney Lee (eds.), *The Dictionary of National Biography*, vol. v (London, 1959-60) pp 621-22. The latter source says bluntly that, from 1836-1838, Davis spent much time in London and on the continent, so that there is even a degree of understandable confusion as to exactly when Davis was exposing his mind to German romanticism.

7. Duffy, *Davis*, p. 211. R. F. Foster, *Modern Ireland 1600-1972* (London, 1989), p. 311, said that 'there is no evidence that Davis ever visited Germany.'

8. Ibid., pp 311-12. For European romanticism see H. G. Schenk, *The mind of the European romantics* (London, 1966); J. L. Talmon, *Romanticism and revolt: Europe 1815-1848* (London, 1967). For Davis see Michael P. Hickey, 'Nationality according to Thomas Davis' in *The New Ireland Review* (Dublin, May, 1898) and Mary G. Buckley, 'Thomas Davis: a study in nationalist philosophy', Ph.D. University College Cork, 1980, passim. Hickey and Buckley see no dependence between Davis's ideas on nationality and those of European romanticism.

9. See Desmond Fennell, *The revision of Irish nationalism* (Exeter, 1989), p. 90; Oliver MacDonagh, 'Ambiguity in nationalism in the case of Ireland' in *Historical Studies*, vol. 19, no. 76 (London, 1981), p. 338.

10. R. F. Foster, 'History and the Irish Question' in *Transactions of the Royal Historical Society* (London, 5th series, no. 33, 1983), pp 171-73.

11. Some of the varying attitudes to an Irish nation, ranging from denial to affirmation of its previous existence, can be seen in Thomas Bartlett, *The fall and rise of the Irish nation: the Catholic question, 1690-1830* (Dublin, 1992); Seán Cronin, *Irish nationalism: a history of its roots and ideology* (Dublin, 1980); Thomas E. Hachey and Lawrence J. McCaffrey, *Perspectives on Irish nationalism* (Kentucky, 1989); Donnchadh Ó Corráin, 'Nationality and kingship in pre-Norman Ireland' in *Historical Studies*, vol. xi (Belfast, 1978), pp 1-35, R. Dudley Edwards, 'The contribution of Young Ireland to the development of the national idea' in Seamus Pender (ed.), *Feilscribhinn* Toma (Cork, 1947), pp 115-133; C. G. Kiernan, 'The emergence of a nation' in C. H. E. Philpin, *Nationalism and popular protest in Ireland* (Cambridge, 1987), pp 16-49; Michelle O'Riordan, *The Gaelic mind and the collapse of the Gaelic world* (Cork, 1990); Owen Dudley Edwards, Gwynfor Evans, Joan Rhys, Hugh MacDiarmid, *Celtic nationalism* (London, 1968).

12. Davis, Ms 3199, pp 1-2, NLI. The emphasis is that of Davis who wanted to stress the underlined words in his delivery.
13. Ibid., pp 2, 3-4.
14. Ibid, pp 14-15 and 45.
15. Ibid., pp 5-6. The use of 'T'is' or 'Tis was both distinctive and constant throughout Davis's writing and helps the identification of his authorship of some anonymous contributions to the *Nation* and elsewhere.
16. Ibid., pp 7-9; 14-15.
17. Ibid., pp 31-33, 34.
18. Ibid., p. 34.
19. See the otherwise excellent study by Buckley, 'Thomas Davis', p.18.
20. Thomas Davis, 'The Insurrection of 1641, its causes, character and fate.', Ms 3199, pp 3, 7, 17, 32.
21. Ibid., pp 2-5; Duffy, *Davis*, p. 28; Moody, *Davis*, p. 15.
22. See Thomas Davis, 'The Insurrection', pp 7-9.
23. Ibid., p. 11.
24. Ibid., p. 16.
25. Ibid., p. 17.
26. Ibid., pp 17-21.
27. Ibid., p. 22.
28. See Davis's diaries in Ms 12, p. 19 (12 b) RIA, where there are scraps of legal notes, including some on the law of property in regard to husband and wife.
29. See Daire Hogan, *The legal profession in Ireland 1789-1922* (Naas, 1986), pp 3, 7, 14, 106-7.
30. Madden to Davis, London, 11 December 1838, Ms 2644, NLI.

Chapter 3

An ideology of nationality

By 1839 Davis was twenty-five and still unclear as to his future prospects. His family enjoyed moderate financial independence, which meant that he did not have to work provided he remained at his mother's home in Baggot Street where his wants were slender, apart from buying books. The indifferent health he had been subject to as a child had given way to a robustness that matched his habitual spiritual and intellectual powers. His strength was developed by his main recreation as an inveterate walker in and about Dublin itself, and especially in the Phoenix Park, on the Howth peninsula or in the Dublin mountains. He was not part of that upper element of Irish society, in which, for many, idleness was marked by riding to hounds in the winter and trips on the continent in the summer, so as to help stave off the boredom of an existence without purpose.[1] Already, Davis had made it plain that such a world meant little to him and that he was determined to serve the idea of nationality that he had begun to shape in an embryonic form. It was a question of fleshing out the idea and giving it reality by action.

Daniel Owen Madden had come to know him well and said that, although Davis was 'as delightful a young man as it was possible to meet in any country', he did not have many companions, except for his 'faithful loving friend' Patrick Robert Webb. Madden thought that they were brothers, such was their closeness, but Webb had been a friend of Davis since their schooldays at Mr Mungan's and followed Davis in his development of liberal and national views. Duffy also left a description of Davis in that period. He was 'of middle stature, strongly built ...' and 'a great walker', to whom 'habitual temperance gave a healthy glow'. He remarked on the fact that his 'carriage was not good: a peculiar habit of leaning towards you in familiar conversation, arising from the eagerness of his nature, gave him the appearance of a stoop, and he dressed and walked as carelessly as a student is apt to do.' He had a 'broad brow and strong jaw' which spoke of a powerful character but his main characteristics were that 'his glance was frank and direct as a sunbeam, he had a cordial and winning laugh, the prevailing expression on his face was open and genial, and his voice had tones of sympathy which went straight to the heart.'[2]

Despite the closeness of his immediate circle Davis began to move on to a wider public stage and his 1837 pamphlet on the Lords had brought him to the attention of a few readers, including Madden. The small group of friends who had heard his addresses on Irish history now knew he was no mere pedant, as the pamphlet might have suggested. As auditor [president] of the Dublin Historical Society, to his intimates at least, his attitude to nationality was already well known. Madden begged him from London to start admitting graduates of English universities to the Society, as not to do so would be 'unIrish for impoliteness' and against Davis's high concept of the *'national character'*.[3] In fact the Society had become little more than a boisterous debating club in which banter and invective were the main weapons, while the serious-minded rarely attended. Its reform was thus imperative, were it to have a useful future. Davis, 'by mutual nomination of conservatives and liberals', of which there were ten of each, became an original member of the new Society which met in Francis Kearney's rooms for the first time on 14 March 1839 and was constituted as such on 29 March.[4]

The new body, named simply the Historical Society, had a distinguished lineage, despite the several names it had gone under. Edmund Burke had founded it as a debating club, Wolfe Tone had been its president and a host of Irish names notable in the annals of the country had been associated with it.[5] Davis read two papers to the Society. The first was in June 1839 when he closed the session by giving one on 'The constitutions of England and America' and he then opened the next session in November with 'Some parts of the constitution of the United States'.[6] He was clearly determined to ensure that the Society wore its new mantle of seriousness and high purpose with honour, so that, as the outgoing president, 26 June 1840, he marked his relinquishing of office with an address on 'The utility of debating societies in remedying the defects of a university education'. The title was sufficiently innocuous as to lull his hearers into a sense that they were to be treated to a purely pragmatic discourse of passing moment. In fact, its contents marked a decisive moment in the early development of Irish nationality and it was the true beginning of the public career of Thomas Davis as an Irish patriot. John Dillon was in the chair as incoming president while Wallis moved the vote of thanks and then moved that the address be published. The pamphlet was dedicated to Francis Kearney whose death had occurred a few months previously. In his dedication to his late friend, Davis said that, before his death Kearney concurred with 'most of the opinions' put forward in the Address.[7]

To dwell on the estimate Davis made of his Alma Mater in his Address is useful provided it is not done to denigrate an institution which was assuredly no worse than Oxford or Cambridge before the general reform of university education at those places. Furthermore, Trinity had begun to undertake its own reform, even if in a rudimentary manner. To see the attitude adopted by Davis can only be useful as an illustration of the gravity of mind of a young man who felt both determined and obliged to speak with bluntness mixed with rashness. The perceptiveness of his judgement and the resoluteness of will by which he surmounted the difficulties which stood in the path of his own education and development are also illustrated. The fact that he wrote a preface to the Address over three months later, in which he recanted nothing but gave even greater stress to his convictions, indicates that, in the matters with which he dealt, he stood firm. On the title page he prudently reminded his hearers of Lessing's 'Think wrongly if you will, but think for yourselves', perhaps to remind them that he, Davis, could also be fallible. He then went on, 'You who are called the upper classes in Ireland possess no institutions for any sort of instruction worthy of you. Nay, more, so strong are the bigotry, interest, and laziness that you will get none. You must found your own institutes, you must conduct your own affairs.'[8]

That Davis was uncertain as to how to proceed and nervous about the outcome is plain from some of the hesitant notes he made to open his address, 'Gentleman, my usual place has been as arguer and debater, if you will as gladiator. I now appear under a different character as preacher of your duties and adviser of your conduct, but for one night only and you will bear with me.'[9] Those words were not used in the final address, but they indicate that he felt he was embarking on unchartered waters. Tone had a different and wider audience when he appealed to his countrymen to rally to the cause of Ireland but, in the quiet cloisters of Trinity and its surroundings, Davis was about to cast his seed on to untilled ground held by young men to whom 1798 and all those other rebellions of the Irish were the unspoken past, while the Union with England was the reality to which, in the great majority, they held tenaciously. Perhaps for this reason Davis came as preacher and moralist rather than gladiator in that he thought the time had come for an appeal to the heart as well as to the head.

Davis made it plain that his quarrel was not with Trinity itself, but with its methods of education, although he made an honourable exception of the medical school which he regarded highly. He was also happy to state that he had no 'sad or angry reminiscence of old Trinity', which he called a 'merry monastery' where he had made many friends. Nonetheless, those amiable feelings towards his friends, some of whom were in his audience, did not serve to lessen his criticism of Trinity as an institution of higher learning. He was pleased that the National Schools, 'the first bold attempt to regenerate Ireland', were working well but he warned his hearers that from them would come forth 'peasant boys' bent on acquiring an education, who, before they would accept that Trinity graduates were entitled to be their leaders, would ask for proof of their intellectual prowess. For him, the question was how such prowess could be acquired in an institution 'from whose offices seven-eighths of the Irish people are excluded by religion, from whose porch many, not disqualified by religion, are repelled by the comparative dearness, the reputed bigotry, and pervading dullness of the consecrated spot.' In his judgement, 'The people think it better not to devote all their spare cash to a university, so many of whose favourite alumni are distinguished by their adroit and malignant calumnies on the character, and inveterate hostility to the good of that people with whose land and money they are endowed.'[10]

Davis listed Trinity's failings in mathematics, natural philosophy and natural history, all of which he thought were better taught in the Mechanics' Institutes. He felt there was some hope for moral philosophy, given that such authors as Bacon, Butler and Locke were read, but theology was so rent by superstition and bigotry that it was worse than useless. After an aside proclaiming his belief that capital punishment was unChristian and brutal, he declared that it was better to read a good translation of a classical author well than to stumble through the original. The reason was that classical learning was a shaft into 'the richest mines of thought which time has deposited'. Nonetheless, his main concern was that so many students spent the best years of their lives on the classical past. As a consequence they knew nothing of the past 1700 years, whether of modern history, modern languages or of English, French, and German literature and 'perhaps I should add, Irish literature'.

In case his hearers may have concluded that some of his criticism of Trinity was exaggerated he asked them to look around them and they would 'see the native abilities of hundreds of young men ruined in our college'. With that introduction, he launched into a vigorous attack on Trinity 'as the laughing stock of the literary world, and an obstacle to the nation's march; its inaccessible library, "the mausoleum of literature", and effete system of instruction, render it ridiculous abroad; add its unaccounted funds, and its bigot laws, and know why it is hated.' In his view, voluntary associations entered into to cultivate the intellect would help mitigate the worst effects of Trinity on its scholars and he felt that the Lyceum system, embodied in the Historical Society, was better than that employed in the university. He pleaded for the formation of an Irish Lyceum concentrating on history, language, natural history, literature and statistics.[11]

Davis had taken pains to prove that he had not spent his own years at Trinity idly by quoting from, or alluding to, some fifty authors whose works he had read, ranging from the classics through to Sismondi and De Tocqueville. With some justification he was able to plead that study done of one's own free will is always done earnestly and he asserted that the Historical Society had great value in that 'it teaches things which a citizen should know.' Some of those things were politics, local and central government, the forms of democracy, the problem of social equality, a free press, the jury system and a penal code. Furthermore, there should be knowledge gained of the agricultural and manufacturing systems, the Poor and Corn Laws, absenteeism, finance, supply and demand, wages, rent, capital and taxation. In that way he strove to impress on his hearers that practical knowledge about their country was absolutely necessary were they to serve it, and in so doing gave further proof that he had not been converted to romanticism.[12]

As president, he fittingly spelt out to the Society his own philosophy of history. The study of history was not undertaken merely to record facts, but so that the facts would be examined 'as parts of political and social institutions, as manifestations of human nature', after which they could be applied to the present. History was also a teacher of the 'head and heart' and helped to prevent the aristocracy from repeating their ways of vice and the people from shedding blood in revenge. This was a clear reference to some lessons that ought to be drawn from the French Revolution, as well as from the Irish past and indeed present with the then prevalence of so-called Secret Societies. Then he made a statement which went with him into practice for the rest of his days. 'With rare exceptions *national history* does dramatic justice, alien history is the inspiration of a traitor.' In a footnote he applied that remark to most of the histories of Ireland written by *'hostile strangers'* whom, he said, should be refuted and then forgotten. To Davis, Irish historians were wanting in that they did not go to the original sources of their history and they sinned because 'too many of them *receive* and *propagate* on Irish affairs "quidquid *Anglia* mendax in historia audet".' [whatever historical lies England dares to tell.] Thus it was especially necessary that the Irish study and write their own history because 'The history of a nation is the birth-right of her sons – who strips them of that "takes that which not enriches him, but makes them poor indeed".' Davis, together with his contemporaries and most historians until the recent past, was content to stress the 'Titans of our race' as the foremost object of history. Thus the obscure and the unrepresented, especially women, were those upon whom history acted.[13]

After a lengthy discourse on oratory, Davis exhorted his hearers to acquire the virtue of civic zeal which he saw, with De Tocqueville, as absolutely necessary to purify the morals and warm the faith of the people in order to make democracy work effectively. The morality of laws and the religion of 'sects' could not suffice because they may not touch true morality and true faith. Every citizen had to be educated in the heart and strengthened in the intellect and, in that regard, the privileged and educated had a special duty through their action and their influence. He cried out for their patriotism for the 'country of our birth, our education, of our recollections, ancestral, personal, national; the country of our loves, our friendships, our hopes, our country.' He warned his young hearers that, were they 'eloquent and strong thinking, threats and bribes will be held out to you. You will be solicited to become the barking misleaders of a faction, or the gazehounds of a minister.' In those circumstances he begged them, if tempted, to turn to poetry, 'the instructor of the heart and fancy', but above all to nature which would restore their 'native nobility'.[14]

He ended with a powerful plea for the primacy of Ireland in the endeavours of the men of Trinity and his appeal was remarkable both for the strength of its conviction and the cogency of its argument. What was even more striking was the speaker and his audience. Were it taken that Trinity was the bastion of Protestant privilege on the level of higher education in Ireland, and that Davis himself had been shaped in a strong Tory and Unionist household, the enunciation of his thoughts, so vibrant with an appeal to nationality, was little short of revolutionary. That its members decided to print his Address indicates how far Davis had misjudged the likely reception they would give to his words, even though they dealt with an argument seemingly barely related to the purposes for which the Society had been established. He pleaded that his thoughts were not inconsiderate and rash, but were *'the best I had'.*[15]

He began his peroration by asking his hearers to consecrate their total endeavours to Ireland and to do so with conviction. Without foreign friends to aid her, she could only turn to her own people. Around them were the poor and the starving because Ireland had been wasted by the 'stranger from without, by means of the traitor within'. In her sufferings, at the foot of the scaffold and on the battlefield, she had been 'chastened for some great future'. He prayed that her sons, 'like the leaves of the Shamrock', would unite, despite their divided sects, and give to all the people their 'full share of the earth and the sky'. He did not ask them to look back to the ancient and glorious past of Ireland but only to sixty years before, in the days of Grattan, whence a pure example and inspiration could be drawn from a struggle which had resulted in constitutional concessions and at least a small measure of independence to the Irish Parliament. To those who could not be stirred by either the present or the past Davis appealed to a future in which they would make their 'country not behind at least in the progress of the nations'. Education, knowledge and virtue were the keys to that progress. In a footnote, written later for the last page, Davis admitted that he had not spoken his final paragraph in a hopeful mood but that he had thereby underrated the generosity of his hearers and misjudged their expectations of him because, 'they heard my lay sermon kindly, attentively, and with no cold or critical minds.'[16]

With the exception of those few of his audience who were close to him, the rest were unaware of the bent that Davis's thinking had taken. His growth towards a formulation of Irish nationality went back to the end of his student days, but he had refrained from making his sentiments public until they had become fully matured in his own mind and he felt secure in that he was not alone in holding to them. Within the immediate circle of his family he would not have been able to enunciate such opinions without pain to those to whom he was closest, none of whom shared either his attachment to Ireland or his rejection of British rule. It was within the unlikely circle of Trinity that such opinions had matured and it was fitting that his thoughts were given voice there.

Wallis admitted that Davis's address 'excited surprise and admiration even of those who knew him best, and won the respect of numbers who, from political or personal prejudices, had been originally most unwilling to admit his worth'. He went further to assert that, 'So signal a victory over long-continued neglect and obstinate prejudice as he had at length obtained, has never come under my observation, and I believe it to be unexampled. There is no assurance of greatness so unmistakable as this.'[17] To Wallis, the character of Davis was formed at exactly the moment when the time for action had come. Davis himself later claimed, justly, that the idea of a nationality, 'indifferent to sect and independent of party' was formed 'in the historical societies of Dublin and belongs to Trinity College Protestants and a few Roman Catholics of T.C.D.'[18] Thus Trinity, with all its contemporary intellectual failings, was the seed bed wherein matured the most powerful, cogent and developed ideal of modern Ireland. Assuredly, when Davis sat down that night, he knew that he had given a hostage to fortune which his own future would either redeem or betray.

A desire for assurance from a higher level probably motivated Davis to send a copy of his Address to the English writer William Savage Landor and to Wordsworth. Davis had drawn much on an intellectual and emotional level from the works of both men and that he had the

View of the Four Courts looking down the River Liffey, 1818.

courage to write to them indicates that he was not reticent to expose his thoughts to literary figures whose criticism he valued. The Wordsworth correspondence has not survived but Davis told a friend that Wordsworth praised the Address while stressing that there was 'too much insular patriotism' in it. Landor, a prolific poet and prose writer of considerable contemporary standing, replied from Bath on 15 December, 1840. He hoped the Address 'may conduce to the cultivation of the national mind' and he foresaw a bright future for Ireland with the advent of steam and the work done for temperance by Father Mathew, whom he praised extravagantly. Mindful certainly of the power of O'Connell, Landor preferred to see the Irish turn to leaders like Mathew 'than to expose their heads to the dangerous flourishes of declamatory demagogues'. The latter remark may have been an oblique warning to Davis not to follow in O'Connell's footsteps. Davis wrote back and concurred in the praise of Mathew, who had 'taken away a degrading and impoverishing vice from the hearts and habits of three millions of the people in a couple of years ...'[19] He disagreed with Landor's critical reference to O'Connell and asked him to consider the circumstances under which the Irish struggled. Were he to do so, Landor would 'forgive the exciting speeches, and perchance sympathise with the exertions of men who think that a domestic Government can alone unite and animate all our people'. Finally, he begged Landor to accept that 'the desire of nationality is not ungenerous, nor ... strange in the Irish (looking to their history) nor ... is the expectation of it very wild'.[20] Davis was correct in his evaluation of nationality as a worthy and reasonable objective, but wide of the mark when he expected it to be attainable without great opposition.

During the period of his last presidency of the Historical Society Davis started contributing to a magazine called the *Citizen* that had been established in 1839 by his friend Torrens McCullagh and which Wallis edited for a time. The financial burden of publication, given that the magazine ran at a constant loss, fell mainly on the shoulders of another close friend, William Elliot Hudson, whom Davis regarded as the finest flower of the Irish in his time. Hudson's interests covered Irish archeology, history, literature, art and music. His home in Upper Fitzwilliam Street became a mecca for the young men who met the intelligentsia of Dublin there and his exertions in the cause of nationality never ceased.[21] McCullagh had met Davis in the Historical Society and, in the same desultory manner as Davis, he had also studied law without any intention of practising it. The magazine was Whig in tone with elements of Irish nationality, to the latter of which Davis contributed.[22]

His first article was entitled 'Emigration – No Remedy'. The article was unsigned, but the reference to Norway and the consistent stand Davis later took in the *Nation* against emigration forced by social circumstances make it plain that he was the writer. Davis's basic premise was that Ireland needed her people in order to prosper and to illustrate his meaning Davis held up the example of Norway which he was then studying in regard to its land tenure system. Edward Gibbon Wakefield's ideas on systematic colonisation had been published in his *A letter from Sydney* in 1829 and he was one of the principal backers of settlement in South Australia, founded in 1836, which was modelled on his ideas. Davis found the plan for the settlement of South Australia repugnant because emigration that was 'directly or indirectly promoted by compulsion', was 'mischievous and indefensible', whereas 'free, gradual, unstimulated, but unhindered emigration, is a safe and beneficial function of society.'[23] With a population then standing at just over eight million, many of whom were living in poverty, it was an attitude scarcely likely to meet the approval of Irish economic rationalists, but Davis never pretended to be an economic rationalist.[24]

In February 1840, the *Citizen* contained an article on another country Davis was also studying. It was entitled 'India – Her Own – And Another's'. The 'Another' was England whom Davis condemned for her butchery in France and America, and for her desire for conquest that, in his eyes, was the act of 'taking from another that which he lawfully hath'.[25] He continued this topic in later volumes and in March he wrote a long review article on the two-volume work by Gustave De Beaumont on Ireland, which had been published in Paris in the previous year. On two visits in 1835 and 1837 De Beaumont had seen people starving in 'that poor Ireland desolated by such great misery'. De Beaumont forthrightly rejected the 'injustice' to which Ireland had been subjected and the way it had been rent by 'upheaval and discord'. Indeed, he thought that the sufferings of the Irish were in themselves a menace to the aristocracy of England. He finally claimed that the questions he raised were eternal ones that went to the heart of 'humanity and morality'.[26]

In this vein De Beaumont dealt with the Irish question for 759 pages and Davis read them with keen interest, thereby awakening his own consciousness to the misery about him that had not previously seemed so intense. He also strengthened his resolve to condemn the aristocrats who fattened on Irish lands and on the fruits of peasant labour, while so many of them lived abroad in abundance and idleness. Nonetheless, he looked to a time in which the social convulsions would cease, but he was convinced that such a day would not dawn for Ireland until she 'shall have attained the grandeur of a nation'. In its own way the reading of De Beaumont was a consolidating epiphany for Davis because, through the eyes of a foreigner, he saw more clearly that Ireland's lack of independence lay at the heart of her woes and that only through the process of bringing the people to a realisation of their belonging to Ireland, and being responsible for and dependent upon each other, would a future state of independence be achieved.[27]

From late 1839 a series of events took place in Ireland which helped Davis to formulate more fully his concept of the rights of nationality and pushed him on to a wider public stage. A rumour had begun to circulate in Dublin towards the end of 1839 that the position of Irish chancellor, then held by the Irish Lord Plunket, was to be given to a Scottish judge, Sir John Campbell. Plunket, an orator of great fame, a patriot who had resisted the Union and had been pro-Emancipation, came from an ancient Anglo-Norman family and was eminently worthy of his post. He was first appointed in 1830 but had to resign in 1834 when the Tories sent an English judge to replace him. With the return of the Whigs in 1835 he resumed the office from which he was now about to be removed once again, and on 18 June 1841 the removal duly took place. In response to the original rumour Davis noted bluntly that the Irish had 'put up with this sort of thing for too long and there must be an end to it'. He followed up this broadside with a scathing article in which he rejected assimilation of the Irish with the English, calling it a 'pickpocket', and asserted that the firmly-held differences in faith and thought by the Irish were the reasons why they were subject to humiliation. He was indifferent to his critics because, belonging as he did to 'the party of the nation', he was writing for the people to whom alone he owed his 'allegiance', and if the government opposed the people they therein became 'our adversaries'.[28]

Davis did not object to the appointment by Westminster of worthy men from Britain but he rejected the system, which was a virtual monopoly, whereby men who had no knowledge of Ireland were appointed to high office while Irish candidates were passed over. For such responsibilities, 'knowledge of a country in the unteachable intricacies of its feelings, thoughts, habits, and opinions' was indispensable and only one born in the country, or long a resident there, was so equipped, although he acknowledged an exception to the general rule in Thomas Drummond who had admirably served Ireland as under-secretary. The argument that good came to Ireland through English appointments because such men could be impartial was 'cant' because 'we know their ill-conceived contempt and hatred of the land, upon whose misappropriated revenues they are battening.' Thus Ireland had been 'trepanned' by the Union into a 'dishonest bargain' and it was senseless to argue that they all lived in a united

Empire and were 'one people'. The Irish were totally different in their blood, faith, opinions, social habits, sentiments and traditions. Society in England was structured around the aristocracy, the Church and the mercantile class while in Ireland the aristocracy was 'daily more alien', the Church was maintained by 'absolute force' and the commercial classes had almost ceased to exist. He was emphatic in wanting no favours from England but 'mere justice' because 'the giving away of Irish offices of trust and honour, from Irishmen, is a gross and unpardonable offence to the dignity and the interests of Ireland'.[29]

When the blow finally fell and Plunket was removed, Davis was back on the attack both in print and in action. He acknowledged that Plunket had made mistakes but rejected the deliberate insult to Ireland. He called for the overthrow of 'Every trace of the accursed system of anti-Irish rule' and rejoiced that the widespread reaction by some sections of the press and public revealed 'the dawn of a brighter future'. When the Bar met on 22 June 1841, a few days after Plunket had made it plain that his resignation was forced, Davis was present with 150 others to hear Torrens McCullagh make a 'great national speech' and Davis suggested to the Father of the Bar, Thomas Dickson, that an address be sent to the Queen protesting Campbell's appointment. The senior members of the Bar were against such a step, as was O'Connell who allegedly detested Plunket and feared the Whigs would suffer politically by the protest, but it duly went ahead and Dickson signed it. The outcome of the opposition, nonetheless, was that the address was meekly put and it simply argued that the members of the Irish Bar should have the same privileges as the English Bar in such appointments. The whole affair came to nothing. This had been the usual outcome of questions for which the liberals fought unless O'Connell supported them and it was a lesson that Davis quickly learned. He nonetheless poured scorn on those who had acquiesced in the government's action. 'Such men are fit slaves of despotism – they bow before its insolence. But thank God! all Irishmen are not like unto them.' He was yet to learn how few would stand upright when England stood firm.[30]

Davis was not alone in his stand on Plunket. The *Dublin Evening Post* was cleverly and carefully written and contained an extraordinary combination of pro-Dublin Castle, strongly Whig and mildly pro-Catholic views. Nonetheless, it was appalled at Plunket's enforced resignation by a Whig government, especially because it would put a weapon into the hands of the Tories. It recalled that Plunket had been rejected by the English Bar when he had been made Master of the Rolls there, and hoped that Campbell would be similarly rejected in Ireland. Yet its strongest argument was directed against 'this remnant of the most besotted bigotry' whereby, under the law, a Catholic could not be appointed chancellor. To the editor, even were an Irish chancellor appointed, it would not be for the benefit of the nation but only for the Protestant portion of it and thus, until the Bar argued for the removal of the Penal law, the question would remain *'not national but sectarian'*.[31] It was an argument that Davis had not taken up, perhaps because he could see no good coming of it, despite the fact that there was a perfectly acceptable Irish, Catholic candidate in the person of Sir Michael O'Loghlen. It is possible also that he was not at ease taking up an argument by a paper that pursued an editorial line of subservience to England that he totally rejected. Finally, he may have concluded that the most important factor was nationality and the question of religion could take care of itself later.

Meanwhile from 1839 until late 1842, he kept up a steady stream of articles for the *Citizen*, which continued under various titles, and in it he developed constantly his theme of nationality. In 1839 Henry Grattan wrote a life of his father which Davis reviewed at length. Davis, while full of praise for Grattan, saw clearly that the gains won by him in the Irish parliament of 1782 were rapidly lost and that neither the Irish nor Grattan himself did anything to consolidate them. 'Never was freedom, once won, so weakly forfeited', wrote Davis. He spoke of 'The Revolution of 1782' as 'a thing complete in itself', 'a national act in which all men united; but they never united again' because of divisions, brought about by 'jealousy, corruption, selfishness'. Davis concluded that England had unmercifully pirated the Irish economy after 1782 and he blamed Grattan for his 'Anglo mania' that caused him to treat Britain's reluctant concessions as favours and to accept her promises as security. He thought that Grattan, great orator that he certainly was, lacked the quality of a statesman. However, to Davis, Grattan was always Irish, which largely forgave the weakness and lack of vision that allowed the victory to be squandered. Although Davis revered the year of 'freedom' of 1782, he knew fully that the gain turned to loss because the English would not accept the existence of a free Parliament in Ireland. In that way, the power of Dublin Castle was strengthened and, through patronage and subtle bribery, many of the weaker members of Grattan's parliament were rendered ineffective. In the event, the control of Ireland by England was heightened so that in the aftermath of the Rising of 1798, with almost startling rapidity, Ireland lost all autonomy by being united to England.[32]

In other articles, the way in which many Irish landlords, especially since the Union, absented themselves from their properties was regarded by Davis as 'The real Grievance', 'intolerable' and 'the lameness of our nation.' He recalled how repeatedly Swift had denounced the practice and how all genuine Irishmen agreed that it dishonoured Ireland. From his reading he had concluded that there was no such thing as absenteeism in Norway and also no beggars there, because there was no law of entails and no 'iniquity of primogeniture'. He warned England not to permit her avarice to provoke a 'social war' in Ireland, a 'war of the pauper many against the gorged and gluttonous few'. Experience elsewhere had proved that ideas condemning the ownership of landed property were 'fearfully contagious' and were they to take hold in Ireland the results would be disastrous for English landlords.

It seems that Davis was 'chided' for his two articles on absenteeism which moved him to remind his critics that the *Citizen* had been founded to uphold the 'whole rights of the whole people' and he refused to become more 'docile or genteel'. To him tenancy was 'the heart-scald of the people', but eventually the large estates would be broken up and sold, and a better day for Ireland would dawn because the land would then be owned by industrious Irishmen living on, and cultivating, their own farms.[33] He placed great hope in the passing of the Corporate Reform Bill, which reformed the scandalous and irregular state of local government in Ireland to some extent. That reform would bring together men of good will who were united in a common purpose for the good of their own municipalities. Accordingly, party spirit would be mitigated, prejudices lessened and a local public opinion would grow up, 'divested of sectarian bitterness, and, to use the eloquent expression of the late Chief Baron Woulfe, be "racy of the soil"'. On the same grounds of Irish institutions being necessary for the development of an Irish nationality he berated the system whereby law students had to serve their terms in London which 'would be ludicrous for its absurdity, if it were not a monstrous inconvenience and expense, an irreparable loss of valuable time, and a badge of subjection insufferably offensive'. Thus he called for the setting up of a Law Institute in Ireland 'to displace a system so utterly ruinous and absurd'.[34]

Davis made a substantial contribution to the *Citizen* in 1842 with two articles entitled 'Norway and Ireland – Udalism and Feudalism'.[35] He was aware that, despite the widespread rejoicing engendered by 1829, Catholic Emancipation had brought little benefit in the material sense to the Irish people, and particularly to the peasantry. He decided to address himself to the land question, which he thought was funda-mental to Irish economic, social and political development. His basic premise came from the French historian, Jean Charles Sismondi, 'The social order in Ireland is essentially bad, and must be changed from top to bottom.' To Davis, 'Ireland exists, and her millions toil for an alien aristocracy ... while the people rot upon their native land.' He thought it a madness and a crime 'to talk of prosperity from railroads, and poor laws, and manufacturing societies, while the very land, ay, *Ireland itself, belongs not to the people, is not tilled for the people.*'[36]

Basing himself on a long list of authors, including Sismondi and Augustin Thierry for France, Carlyle for England, Henry Hallam, author of *A view of the state of Europe during the Middle Ages* (1818) and *Constitutional History of England* (1827), for the Middle Ages and De Beaumont for Ireland, Davis gave an historical explanation for land tenure in Europe where he held Norway up as a model in which a system he called udalism prevailed. Under such a system, the land belonged to the people through small, independent proprietorship. However, ownership was not of the kind that permitted each proprietor to do exactly as he pleased with his land because it was a type of ownership which involved the local community, but the state had no right to interfere in his property. Davis then contrasted udalism with feudalism which was imposed by force on small proprietors and made them subject to their overlords with their rights in and to the land lost.

He next set about revealing and deploring the state of land tenure in Ireland where the land was owned by landlords who wanted to rationalise their estates by enforced emigration and ejection. Paradoxically, given his own partial origins in mercenaries who had come to Ireland and whom he was prepared to defend insofar as property rights were concerned, he saw as the cause of Ireland's woes the fact that the real power of the aristocracy lay in its origins at a time when it had been reinforced by 'British regiments, recruited by inconsiderate Irishmen.'[37] What made it impossible to better the state of Ireland was the fact that those same landlords held a different 'creed' to that of their peasantry. As a result, there could be no peace or respect between them, given that the landlords 'despise the people, the people hate them'. Thus, any attempts to assimilate 'us to England are worthless' because all the plans of emigration, poor laws and attempts at economic development are 'all meant to be so many precursors of Anglicanism'. With a touch of youthful romanticism Davis refused to see Irish morals, manners, or passions assimilated to those of any people on earth and least of all did he wish 'to change the faithful, pure, natural, affectionate Irishman into that animal John Bull'.[38]

Any plan of the landlords to 'clear' the people from the land in order to consolidate their estates would be rejected by the majority of the Irish and all the forces the English could muster would never suffice to achieve that aim. He quoted from De Beaumont's *L'Irlande* where the case was made that the state of the aristocracy in Ireland was its ultimate condemnation because it was no more now than 'the bloody phantom of a government'. To De Beaumont, it was 'not enough to destroy the Protestant aristocracy; it is necessary to abolish the principle of aristocracy in Ireland'.[39] As for emigration, Davis asked, why was it necessary? Ireland exported annually vast quantities of food, the land was as good or better than that of Belgium where there was over twice the population, and enforced emigration would be vigorously resisted by the people in any case. Furthermore, what could the people do were they to remain in Ireland, but not on its land? Here Davis renewed his innate distrust of industrialisation by painting a powerful but partly exaggerated picture of the English worker, which would be outrageous were it not backed up by many contemporaries. 'That withered, blotched thing, querulous as a sick noble, or desperately calm, stunned with noisy mill-work; filled to the top of his mind with cranks and yarns; trembling lest fashion, or the exchange of trade, or the competition of some wretch more desperate than himself, may end his hiring, and bring him to the workhouse.' The workhouse, to Davis, was *the prison for poverty'* and he pleaded that the Irish not be asked 'to copy English vice, and darkness, and misery, and impiety; give us the worst wigwam in Ireland and a dry potato rather than Anglicise us.' In so pleading Davis was going no further than Dean Swift who held that everything English should be burnt, with the exception of its coal.[40]

Despite his inclination to utopianism Davis was prepared to recognise that home manufacturers were a partial remedy for unemployment. Yet he would have none of the argument for large farms because on them the labourer worked for hire without any direct interest in, or involvement with, his work. In England, where the aristocrats were not 'aliens in religion and language', the labourers were content in some degree. Such could never be the case in Ireland where a rental system prevailed under which the tenant generally paid two-thirds or three-fourths of his produce as rackrent, which Sismondi called 'rente torturee'. Davis could not understand how his compatriots bore with such a system. He thought their industrious habits were wonderful and their patience 'miraculous' and could only conclude that they had not become savages because they were 'one of the most religious and least sensual people on earth'.[41]

Arguing strongly for small proprietorship, Davis arrived at a principle which he enunciated crisply as, *'Make a man's interest in his labour perfect and permanent, and you do the best to ensure his industry and wisdom as a labourer. That is, make him proprietor of the land he tills.'* How that principle was to be applied without largescale and enforced ejection of the landlords, even with compensation, he was not prepared to venture but he was sure that 'the devices of a subtle policy will delay success.' Some were arguing that land reform should await a resolution to the matter of nationality but Davis disagreed because 'tenure is a question of life or death with the people.' He did not want the national question postponed, but he wanted action on land tenure to run jointly with it and 'Of this we are sure, that unless they are fools or cowards, eight millions will not wish in vain.'[42]

That, within the few years 1845 to 1851, the whole matter would take on a different aspect with the reduction of the population from 8,200,000 to 6,000,000 as a result of starvation, disease and emigration was unknown to Davis.[43] Nonetheless, had he known it, he would not have changed his argument one whit because he was convinced that Ireland could support a still higher population, although he did not address himself to the level at which such a population would be forced to exist. He was unable to reconcile himself to largescale manufacturing given its effects on the workforce in England and in forthright, if simplistic terms, he saw land tenure as a key to the future of the Irish people. Essentially, by his article, he proved that he was much more than a dreamer or revolutionary who wanted the English hold on Ireland broken simply for its own sake. The dignity, prosperity and future of the Irish people were bound up in land tenure and to that he had addressed himself with substance and in terminology that brooked little argument except by those who persisted in seeing the Irish people as incapable of managing their own affairs. How many, if any, of the Irish, landed aristocrats he would win to the cause of Irish nationality, which could not be divorced from the question of land tenure, is another matter.

The final contribution, in prose at least, by Davis to the *Citizen* in 1842 was a series of five articles on the war in Afghanistan. As always, his interest was essentially Irish so that the title of the first article was 'Who are the Afghans? And why should Irishmen fight with them?' His consideration of the situation of the Afghans, once 'freemen' and now fighting to expel foreign invaders, led him into an emotional transport. Their example made 'our pulse beat quicker, visions pass before us, heroic memory whispers (low, low, for our tyrants may hear) ... and our whole soul melts with sympathy for "the old cause" and – yes, it must out – we heave a sigh to think that Ireland is calm – calm as the grave.' He quoted at length from Lamennais who said in his *Paroles d'un croyant* that 'enslaved nations' had to unite in their struggle for freedom. Davis agreed and thought that another enslaved nation such as Ireland had to either unite with the Afghans or at least refuse to assist in suppressing the liberties of nations struggling for independence; otherwise, 'there can be no hope for nations'. Thus Irish foreign policy had to be based on having good relations with small, free states and 'with the provinces which, like ourselves, are trying by arms and agitation to get free'. As far as he was concerned it was 'a bloody patricide for the Irish slave of England to smite the Afghan foe of England'.

He then left the high ground and proceeded to a thorough examination of the history of the Afghans and the social and political conditions which led to their present crises. He had read widely, referenced his sources and used them with proper discrimination and concluded that 'England had acquired by every variety of valour and treachery ... by diplomacy, bribery, intelligence, and infamy her sway over India'. He thought that English fear of Russia was the real reason for the war but asked whether that gave England a right to break a solemn treaty, 'to invade and plunder her allies, and overrun and tyrannise neutral states?' Surely she was not permitted thus to throw off all moral restraint based on her interest, 'real or imagined', which could not be 'superior to the laws of God and of nations'. In the end he was left wondering whether the 'brutal crusade' of the English against the Afghans would end in victory or retreat, but in any case he had made his point very firmly as to where Ireland should stand in such matters.[44]

Interwoven with the articles Davis contributed to the *Citizen* were a number of poems. Later, when he began to contribute verse to the *Nation* at the end of 1842, much was made of the fact that he had never previously published any, which implied that he needed the impetus of his new association with the *Nation* and his involvement with Repeal to awaken the spark of the poet in him. All subsequent writers on Davis have followed Duffy's judgement that he made Davis aware that he could write verse, but whether Davis himself fostered the idea that he had never published any is impossible to judge. The last scholar to sum up this impression was T. W. Moody who said, 'The idea of making original verse a feature of the *Nation* led Gavan Duffy to discover in Davis a hitherto unsuspected faculty of versification'.[45] In fact, under the initials D. or T.C.D., he began to do so in December 1840 by contributing verses to the *Citizen*. A love poem of no merit was followed by a slightly better effort entitled 'The Meed of the Minstrel', in which he spoke of the 'Land of my home and heart', lamented that his fingers fell 'Weakly upon thy lyre' and mentioned the 'elder or the younger Geraldine'. By July 1841 he had begun to achieve some degree of rhythm and theme with 'To the Harp', one verse of which ran,

> God made us *free*, and our country a *nation* –
> Despots have marr'd the Almighty's decree;
> But Erin is proudly regaining her station –
> First in the lists of the happy and free,

In September he touched on his own tendency to innate sadness in 'Stanzas'. It was a theme he often went back to both in verse and conversation in later years,

> But alas! in the dark will my destiny cast,
> Where the soul in Hope's sepulchre lives –
> To fear for the future and sigh for the past,
> Is all that reality gives.

He returned to the theme of nationality and his authorship is clear from his own copy of the magazine, now in the Royal Irish Academy, in which in his hand he crossed out the word 'nations' in the first line and substituted 'spirits',

> In the soarings of thought, let all nations unite –
> Let national mind assert national right –
> And thus – monumental, through wandering time,
> Shall Erin be free, yet unsullied by crime.

The reason he gave for Ireland becoming free without recourse to crime was that she heard 'a blessed voice' and

> It bids us *be free* – but no weapon to wield –
> Save that of the will to no master to yield.

In the October 1842 issue of the *Citizen*, he contributed a poem entitled 'The Geraldine's Daughter'. The Fitzgeralds were a family he held in great esteem given the manner in which they had become totally Irish and the devotion they had shown to their country through several centuries, although Ireland may have been to them simply a symbol for their loyalty to family. The poem is redolent of both the plaintive style and content of so much that he later wrote and it deserves to be recorded in full.

> Speak low – speak low – the beansige is crying
> Hark! hark to the Echo! – she's dying! 'she's dying,'
> What shadow flits dark'ning the face of the water,
> 'Tis the swan of the lake – 'Tis *the Geraldine's Daughter*
>
> Hush, hush! have you heard what the beansige said?
> Oh! list to the Echo! she's dead! 'she's dead';
> No shadow now dims the face of the water,
> Gone, gone is the wraith of *the Geraldine's Daughter*

The step of yon train is heavy and slow
There's wringing of hands, there's breathing of woe;
What melody rolls over mountains and water
'Tis the funeral chant for *the Geraldine's Daughter*

The requiem sounds like the plaintive moan
Which the wind makes over the sepulchre's stone;
'Oh, why did she die? our hearts blood had bought her!
Oh, why did she die? *the Geraldine's Daughter*'

The thistle-beard floats – the wild roses wave
With the blast that sweeps over the newly made grave;
The stars dimly twinkle, and hoarse falls the water,
While night birds are wailing *the Geraldine's Daughter*.[46]

His contributions to the *Citizen* had served a useful purpose for Davis in that he had honed his ideas on nationality and given them greater practical shape. He had mixed in a circle where his ideas could be disputed and hammered into a coherent form by opposition and encouraged by acceptance. Despite that, the world of the *Citizen* was narrow and did not extend beyond the boundaries of Trinity students, former students and a few others of the Dublin intelligentsia. The next step had to be on to the public stage. It was not a step to be taken lightly because Davis was conscious that his family, apart from his sister Charlotte who loved and admired him and in whom the consciousness of nationality was awakening under his influence, was united in opposition to his ideas and indeed grieved at his promotion of them. The moral and spiritual sustenance that Davis so sorely needed, given the gentility of his own nature and his unwillingness to cause pain to those whom he loved, meant that he had to look elsewhere for strength. He was fortunate that a source was at hand.

References
1. For an account of the behaviour of one set of the upper class, see Matthias M'Donnell Bodkin, 'The Lord Lieutenant's Adventure' in Donal Ó Siodhacháin (ed.) *Glimpses of old Ireland* (Cork, 1990), pp 32-37. An account of idleness spent to other purposes in the form of balls and riding to hounds, is contained in *Seventy years young: memories of Elizabeth Countess of Fingall*, told to Pamela Hinkson (London, 1937, Dublin, 1991).
2. For Madden's recollections see Duffy, *Davis*, pp 15-25; For Duffy see Moody, *Davis*, pp 27-8.
3. Madden to Davis, 11 December, 1838 in Ms 2644, NLI.
4. Wallis to Davis, 13 March 1839, in ibid.
5. Moody, *Davis*, pp 9-10.

6. Ibid., p. 21. No trace of the papers on the constitutions can be found.
7. See Thomas Davis, *An address read before the Historical Society, Dublin, on the 26th of June, 1840* (Dublin, 1840). See original edition of 48 pages in Halliday Collection, RIA, Box 1784, no. 6. The Address is also contained in T. W. Rolleston (ed. with intro.) *Prose writings of Thomas Davis* (London, 1889), pp 1-43.
8. The preface was written from 61 Baggot Street and dated 12 October, 1841. See pp i-vii and p. 2.
9. See Notes by Davis in Book of Autographs, Ms 12 P 19 (12b), RIA.
10. See Rolleston, *Prose writings*, pp 20 and 6-7. I have used Rolleston's edition of 1889 for the main body of the Address.
11. Ibid., pp 8-23.
12. Ibid., pp 23-5.
13. Ibid., pp 25-9.
14. Ibid., pp 39-40.
15. Ibid., p. 43.
16. Ibid., pp 41-3.
17. Wallis in Duffy, *Davis*, pp 30-31.
18. See Davis in Moody, *Davis*, p. 9. Moody quoted from Gavan Duffy, *Young Ireland: a fragment of Irish history 1840-1845* (London, 1880), p. 527. The version I used of Duffy was the Irish People's edition in two parts (Dublin) 1884.
19. On the remarkable Father Mathew see Colm Kerrigan, *Father Mathew and the Irish temperance movement* (Cork, 1992). As an example of his success, in the town of Kilrush, county Clare, £30,000 were spent on spirits in 1836. The sum was reduced to £1,200 in 1842. Father Mathew claimed that he had five million members in his movement by late 1842. See pp 56, 82.
20. Landor and Davis are in Duffy, *Davis,* pp 40-41. For Landor, see A. W. Ward & A. R. Waller (eds.), *The Cambridge history of English literature* (New York, 1932), vol. xii, pp 226-44.
21. For Hudson (1796-1853) see O'Sullivan, *The Young Irelanders*, pp 326-9.
22. *Citizen* began publication in November 1839. In a desperate bid to survive it added *A Monthly Journal of Politics, Literature and Art* to its title in February 1840. It changed to the *Citizen*, or *Dublin Monthly Magazine* throughout 1841, called itself *The Dublin Monthly Magazine*: being a new series of the *Citizen* in 1842 and, in its death throes, settled for *The Dublin Monthly Magazine*, January to April 1843. See NLI and RIA for holdings. Referred to henceforth as the *Citizen*.
23. *Citizen*, vol. 1, no. 2, December, 1839, pp 74, 75-6, 83.
24. See Graeme L. Pretty, 'Wakefield, Edward Gibbon, 1796-1862' in D. Pike (ed.) *Australian Dictionary of Biography*, vol. 2 (Melbourne, 1967), pp 559-562.
25. 'India – Her Own – And Another's in *Citizen*, no. iv, vol. 1, February, 1840, pp 255-63; no. vi, April, pp 418-33; no. ix, vol. 2, July pp 120-29; no. xii, pp 325-35.
26. Gustave De Beaumont, *L'Irlande sociale, politique et religieuse*, 2 vols (Paris, 1839), pp i, v, vii.
27. For the review see *Citizen*, no. v, vol. 1, March, 1840, pp 326, 328, 330, 332.
28. See 'The Chancellorship' in *Citizen*, no. ii, vol. 1, December 1839, p. 141; 'Irish Men for Irish Offices' no. ix, vol. 11, July 1840, pp 73-9.
29. Ibid.
30. See Ibid., p. 103. See also Duffy, *Davis*, pp 45-6 and *Morning Register*, 19, 21, 23, 25 June, 1841.
31. *Dublin Evening Post*, 19, 24 June 1841.

32. Ibid., vol. i, no. iii, January, 1840, pp 154-65; vol. i, no. xxii, Aug 1841, pp 53-62; vol. i, no. xxiii, September, 1841, pp 145-52. Thomas McCullagh kept Davis up to the mark with his overdue review on Grattan. See McCullagh to Davis, 12 August, 1841, Ms 12 P 19 (12b), RIA. See also the excellent pioneering work on Grattan's Parliament by James Kelly, *Prelude to Union: Anglo-Irish politics in the 1780s* (Cork, 1992) and the review of same by Kevin Whelan, 'Opening the doors on Grattan's Parliament', *Irish Times*, 10 April 1993.

33. *Citizen*, vol. ii, no. xi, Sept. 1840, pp 223-33; vol. ii, no. xii, Oct, 1840, pp 297-307; vol. ii, no. xiv, Dec 1840, pp 44-8.

34. Ibid., vol. ii, no. xiii, Nov 1840, pp 370-86, 431-44.

35. See *Citizen*, no. i, March and April, 1842, pp 218-37; 293-315. The articles were reproduced in the 1899 edition of Rolleston (ed.) *Prose Writings* but dropped from the 1914 edition. I have used Rolleston.

36. Ibid., p. 55.

37. Ibid., p. 53.

38. Ibid., p. 57.

39. Ibid., pp 58-60.

40. Ibid., pp 62-3.

41. Ibid., pp 63-6.

42. Ibid., pp 71-5.

43. See Foster, *Modern Ireland*, pp 323, 331.

44. *Citizen*, March, June, July, August, September, 1842, pp 216-37; 439-52; 19-48, 96-109; 169-77.

45. See Duffy, *Davis*, p. 93, Moody, *Davis*, p. 34.

46. *Citizen*, vol. vii, no. xiv, Dec. 1840, p. 439; vol. 3, no. xvii, March, 1841, p. 173; vol. i, no. xxi, July, 1841, p. 16; vol. i, no. xxii, Sept. 1841, pp 122, 152; vol. ii, no. xxxiv, October 1842, p. 75. The reference to the wraith of the Geraldine's daughter as a swan over the lake is obviously taken from the Children of Lir legend.

Chapter 4

A public stage

John Blake Dillon was an early member of the newly formed College Historical Society and he became its president after Davis. During that time the two men had formed a close friendship and a working relationship centred around a mutual desire to take their ideas on nationality to a wider public. Dillon, born on 5 May 1814, was a few months older than Davis. His birthplace at Ballaghaderreen then in county Mayo in east Connacht, caused him to be reared among 'the most abject and oppressed population of Europe', while the circumstances of his Catholic birth meant that he went to a hedge school. Only in that did he conform to the pattern of life of his contemporaries because his father, Luke, was a prosperous farmer and merchant from whom he possibly learnt something of nationality, but little of privation. At the urging of his mother, Dillon entered Maynooth in 1830 to test his vocation to the priesthood. After two years he realised that he had no vocation so, with the blessing of the ecclesiastical authorities, he returned home but always preserved 'an affectionate remembrance' of Maynooth. Dillon began at Trinity in 1834, graduated with a prize in political economy in 1841 and was also called to the Irish Bar. He was of immense dignity and his aquiline but striking features stamped him among others as reserved and even aloof, especially as he always dressed in 'sombre black'. Davis, and those few with whom he shared his friendship, knew him as warm, noble in spirit and as one who had an 'instinct in common with Swift; the villainies of mankind made his blood boil'.[1]

Davis had already begun to devote a great deal of his time to writing and the further opportunity to do so offered itself in the *Morning Register*, published by Michael Staunton in Dublin. The paper was strongly Catholic with reports of such activities as the collection for the Propagation of the Faith. Although it was regarded as a complaisant mouthpiece for the imperial authorities in the Castle, it also printed the proceedings of O'Connell's Loyal National Repeal Association. Staunton, who believed that the freedom of the press demanded that he maintain his right to be critical, had not proclaimed himself as a

Repealer. Known widely as the Liberator, O'Connell was never one to be content with anything less than full adhesion to his cause and he publicly expressed the hope that Staunton would join the ranks and thus line up with the editors of the two Repeal papers, the *Pilot* and *Freeman's Journal*. In the meantime he had to be content with editorial and other support by the *Register*.[2]

Dillon was acquainted with Staunton and, for whatever reason, Staunton decided, in early 1841, that he would permit the two young men to use his paper to put forward their ideas on nationality. Thus, the paper began to take on an entirely new tone. Davis began with an editorial on 30 January 1841 which reiterated his arguments against the 'panacea' of migration and scorned those who were worried they would be smothered unless they could regularly ship off a good bulk of the population to Australia. He hoped that by 1861 the Irish would have increased by another two million and saw the drainage and cultivation of spare land in Ireland as the solution to the problem of overpopulation.[2] It was naïve and optimistic to imagine that Ireland's population problem could be so readily solved, but it was probably 'more practicable than the policy which Malthus and Ricardo contemplated'.[3]

The fact was that the Irish population had risen by four-fifths in the previous forty years and the 'pre famine exodus was unparalleled', with nearly 2,500,000 emigrants leaving between 1801-1845. Forty per cent of all families lived in one room cabins, often with no beds, and over 2,000,000 people were below the poverty line. Nonetheless, with turf for warmth and the potato, 'the only single cheap food that can support human life when fed as a *sole* article of diet', commonly available, the population continued to rise, to peak at about 8,200,000 in 1845. Despite the growth in consumption based on a rising population, agricultural output had increased by over 80 per cent since the Union, making Ireland a 'granary' for England and the road system made transport of goods relatively easy.[4] However, the peasantry and farm labourers reaped little benefit from agricultural prosperity. There were about 10,000 landlords receiving £12,000,000 in rent annually, 700,000 farms, mostly minuscule in acreage, carved up the arable land and the density of rural population was five to six times higher than it is today. The gross disproportion in landownership was well illustrated in the Barony of Ballybritt, King's County, where 74 landowners held as much land as the remaining 1,008. Such a situation would seem conducive to revolution but 'property relations were not radically questioned', which must say a good deal for the social control exercised by the Catholic clergy, and for the decency of some large landholders who treated their tenants with humanity. Although brewing was an exception, as well as linen around Belfast which generally remained prosperous due to manufacturing, the decline in industry, unprotected from English competition since 1824, kept pace with the rise in agriculture which was more attractive to capital, given the proximity of the English market. The premature withdrawal of duties after the Union had helped to pull the Irish economy back, and the drain on capital due to absenteeism worsened matters. All in all, the situation was not one that any responsible government could contemplate or confront with ease. Indeed, the Devon Commission's extensive enquiry on the land question from 1843 to 1845, although focussed on the evidence of the ruling elite, reported that, 'We cannot forbear from expressing our strong sense of the patience and endurance which the labouring classes have generally exhibited under sufferings greater we believe, than the people of any other country in Europe have to sustain.'[5]

In the *Morning Register*, Davis followed up with an editorial directed at the Tory leader, Lord Stanley, whom he accused of harbouring 'a pique' against Ireland so that, 'Headlong, rash, and unreflecting, he rushes upon his object, careless of what he may overturn in his mad career.' Davis demanded a widening of the Irish franchise, pointing out that only 10 per cent of the potential electorate could vote, while 50 per cent could do so in England. Were the Tories returned it would be up to every 'true friend of the liberties of Ireland' to become Repealers, at which stage Stanley and his followers would either have to grant Repeal or suppress it by force. Davis thought the former would not be done but 'the latter, we are persuaded, they *could* not do.' The reason was that Stanley's National Schools, together with Father Mathew's crusade against alcoholic drink had combined to make the Irish 'sober and full of reflection'. Indeed, Stanley did not even know what he had achieved because he had put books into the hands of the Irish and 'books teach wisdom ... wisdom points to union and united millions cannot be conquered'. The next week O'Connell was praised for his defiance of the Tories, but he too was warned in a way that must have given pause for thought to the Liberator had his attention been drawn to one sentence Davis wrote. 'The people of Ireland go far beyond him in this respect. They are too strong to tolerate the hated ascendancy ... These are times that call forth bold words and fearless hearts.'[6]

This heady stuff was followed by a sober article on the economic state of Ireland, deploring the fact that in 1790 the Irish had made their own cloth, which they now imported from England, but rejoiced that the current edition of the paper was set in a 'beautiful specimen of new type' which had been made in Ireland at a new foundry in Liffey Street. Thus, 'We long to see a literature native in spirit, native in execution, in everything native.' This was a further development of the idea of nationality by extending it to the physical and cultural levels and the conclusion was reached that Ireland could never prosper while she was mortgaged to England because 'our debt *by* and *for* the aristocracy of *England* is eight hundred millions'. Citing De Beaumont, Davis asserted that the African tribes endured less hardship than the Irish peasants and he accused the English of treating Ireland as 'their farm, and its people as their serfs and bondsmen'. To some degree, therefore, he had already departed from his simplistic opposition to manufacturing, possibly based on the hope that, in an Ireland governed by the Irish, manufacturing would show a more humane face. Davis was convinced that the Irish would defend both themselves and the English if either were attacked by France or America, but that they would do so only for 'so long as the Irish are governed constitutionally and justly'. However, a different situation could prevail were the Tories returned in the forthcoming election and Stanley was warned to leave the Whigs in office and thus *to keep something between you and the Irish nation*'. Seemingly, Davis had already conceived a loathing of Toryism and he feared intensely its return to office. To him, the Tories were unchanged in their ferocity, they were 'still thirsty for blood' and the Irish ought not be reminded 'that the debt of vengeance is yet unpaid' because 'Six hundred years of unmitigated suffering have not satisfied their [the English] malignant hatred of the Irish people; they would still persecute – they would still torment her.' Despite this concentration on the Union with England the new editors ranged widely and on 20 February there was an editorial on the 'Abomination of slavery' but it is unclear whether Davis or Dillon wrote it. Nonetheless, it is plain that they both condemned slavery outright. They repeated their arguments against it in another editorial a week later.[7]

Both in Dublin Castle, where the new departure was being watched with something like incredulity, and among the small readership of the *Morning Register* who had not experienced anything like they were now being served at breakfast, it must have come as something of a relief when Davis turned his guns on a matter of more practical local interest. The occasion was the threatened withdrawal of the parliamentary grant to the Royal Dublin Society. The Society had been set up by the old Irish Parliament over a century earlier to promote the arts and sciences and further the development of Ireland's natural resources. It had done some fine work in developing statistical information and gave some promise of continuing and developing its work further. The last Irish Parliament in 1800 voted it £15,500 which, under the Union, had been reduced by 1840 to £5,300. In that year the British Museum received £85,803. However, in its composition the Society resembled a wealthy, private club with high subscriptions and a membership, mostly of the landed gentry, who enjoyed a reading room which had become 'a very agreeable lounge for a number of idle gentlemen'. It went its way without hindrance or criticism until after Emancipation when, on 26 November 1835, Daniel Murray, Catholic Archbishop of Dublin and widely respected even in the Castle, was blackballed for membership, which occasioned much criticism even in the least expected quarters.[8] In 1836 the Whig government fruitlessly suggested that the Society reform itself and in 1840 threatened to withdraw the grant unless reform occurred. The Society replied that it had done its best to conform with the wishes of the government, but the grant was withdrawn thereby causing much satisfaction in Irish liberal and reforming circles, whether Protestant or Catholic. The *Dublin Evening Post* led the charge against the Society.[9]

Davis and Dillon, consistent with their idea of nationality, thought differently. To Davis, what had happened was a blatant act of interference in the affairs of a body that had been set up by the representatives of the Irish people. In the past it had done, and was still doing, much excellent work and it deserved to be fostered. He saw the act of Parliament as a denial of a basic principle of nationality in that it denied the right of the Irish to decide for themselves how to govern their own institutions. All of this he set down in an editorial on 25 February 1841. To him, the Society was 'a great national body' put in jeopardy in a way that no French or English government would place such institutions of their own. 'Verily we are provincials', Davis said in a summary of the situation. Nonetheless, he censured the Society for its rejection of Murray, that 'venerated prelate, who united all that endears the man with all that ennobles the public character', and who was 'rejected from political, or worse, from sectarian feeling'. At the same time he denied that there was any connection with that act done in past years and the retribution being exacted on the Society now. In any event he was not prepared to 'look on quietly and see such a body insulted, threatened and trampled on', when it should be treated with 'respect and patience'. He asked the public not to stand back and watch 'this *old*, useful, *Irish* institution sacrificed to the rashness or caprice of an English minister'. He also asked the members of the Society to remember that it was created by 'the native legislature' while 'its assailant has been an imperial government' and thus to realise that 'its only firm reliance can be on the national sympathy of the Irish people'.[10]

All this caused much consternation in Dublin Castle and almost apoplexy to F. W. Conway, the editor of the *Post*, when the editorial was put on his desk. He thought it had come from an Orange journal but, in his view, even the Orange *Evening Mail* was less offensive. He judged the author of the piece as a 'puny whipster' and the like of his 'wordy and furious' column had not been seen since 'the *ruffianing* days'. The worst aspect of it was that Staunton's trust had been abused 'by a treacherous attempt to wound infamously the principles he supported and the party he has espoused' which apparently meant that Davis had refused to follow the pro-Castle and pro-government line that Staunton normally put forward. The most 'positively amazing' aspect of Davis's writing was his preposterous notion that Irish conservatives, who were vigorously anti-Catholic, could be expected to take a pro-Irish stance and support the nationality of the Catholics. This was a 'new and strange doctrine' and the conservatives could be relied upon to never change from 'their appetite for plunder'. As for 'Nationality! But, really, the thing is too ridiculous.'[11]

During the attack by the *Post*, Davis was absent from Dublin on a business visit to county Meath, the nature of which is not known but, given his ineptitude with money, it could scarcely have involved financial transactions. Dillon responded in the *Morning Register* with a hard hitting article reiterating the points made by Davis and refuting the charge of the *Post* that Davis's article was 'personally offensive'; that the *Morning Register* was 'a vehicle of slander' and that the paper's owner, Staunton, regarded by many as the father of the Irish press, had been 'infamously used'. Dillon made it plain that they would not be mere hacks and scribblers, constrained by party loyalties, despite their opposition to the Tories. He wrote, 'Whatever party be in office – Whig, Tory, or Radical – if we see it acting arbitrarily or using unjustly its Imperial strength against an *Irish* institution, we shall oppose it independently and decisively. Will any man be so base as to say that we ought to do less?'[12] When Davis saw the articles in the *Post*, he wrote in a calm vein to Webb and spelt out even more clearly his dream for the future in which there would be 'a better understanding between Tories and Radicals who have any claim to be Irishmen'.[13]

Thus Davis was not prepared to use loyalty to party against an ideal of nationality that he was determined should be shared even by those who differed in politics. He wrote, 'When a great national institution is injured or slighted, we shall forget our party politics, and remember only that we are Irishmen.' This idea of nationality, which appealed to the Protestant ascendancy to also defend Irish institutions, was new, although it had elements of Wolfe Tone in it that had long been forgotten in Dublin. Not only was it new but it was forceful, clearly put and cogent. The Royal Dublin Society was eventually saved and Davis was happy that he and Dillon had written for 'justice', 'peace' and 'nationality'.[14] Indeed, the success of the foray was such that the normally prudent Staunton, whose own sense of nationality had been

Provost's House, Trinity College Dublin.

considerably clarified by his exposure to the thoughts of Davis and Dillon, agreed to an arrangement whereby the two young men would take over the *Register* for a period as an experiment in a decidedly new form of journalism.

Dillon had put 'our project' to Staunton, using as bait the fact that the *Freeman's Journal* wanted him and Davis to contribute to it, which hugely impressed Staunton. Indeed, Staunton was so taken with the *Freeman's* offer that he wanted its former editor to take over his paper, but Dillon told him that he would not be involved were such the case. The result was that an unfettered offer was made by Staunton to Dillon and Davis. He was a remarkably open-minded individual who taught young journalists that 'the freedom of the press could be maintained only while the newspaper retains its liberty to criticise the policies, not only of its antagonists, but also of the interests it wishes to support.' Perhaps he did not realise, nor even care, that he was dealing with young men whose zeal and impetuosity had not yet been tempered by experience. Davis was a firmly committed campaigner for an Ireland yet to be born, while Dillon burnt with the desire to uplift the Irish people from their degradation and poverty. Together they were an explosive combination, likely to turn the *Register* into a radical mouthpiece of Irish nationality.[15]

Davis quickly concluded whatever it was detained him in county Meath and was back in Dublin to take up the cudgels in his new role as a joint editor. The political atmosphere was increasingly unstable with the Whigs hanging on to power precariously, but refusing to resign. Their foremost ally in Ireland was O'Connell who was uncertain of his Dublin seat and anxious about his ability to sustain an electoral battle in which he and his sons, Maurice, John and Daniel, who were all standing, would require financial support. His Loyal National Repeal Association was making little impression on the public and even less on the bishops and clergy who were the indispensable element required for a successful political campaign. He was convinced that the only way to keep the Tories out of power was to combine a Repeal campaign in Ireland with a reform movement in England, but he was fairly sure that the Tories were 'on the very verge of office'.[16] In short, it was a situation in which any allies had to be favourably accepted, even those as young, clearly fractious and possibly rebellious, as Davis and Dillon decidedly were.

Even before they took up their editorship on 5 March the future course was made plain with an editorial on 2 March. It stated that there was no desire to recall the past uselessly or to call for vengeance but that, 'Six hundred years are enough – too much. Six hundred dreary years of degradation and suffering. They are at an end – our pilgrimage is done. We shall no longer be the whipped slave of England. She may be our friend: she *shall* not be our mistress'.[17] For the next sixteen weeks the paper rang with clarification, denunciation, pleading, examination and opposition. The greater part of the work was done by Davis, but Dillon wrote a long series of articles on land rights, a question which, in part due to his upbringing, was of great interest to him. As for Davis, he began to enunciate attitudes to a whole range of subjects that he developed later, but which had already become part of his mental and moral being. Thus, well before Davis started to write for a Repeal paper, or in a formal sense had committed himself to the influence of O'Connell, he had revealed publicly that his concept of Irish nationality, in almost all the facets that later became synonymous with his name, was developed.

Among the subjects treated in the *Register* were the economic problems besetting Ireland. An editorial said it was a mistake to concentrate on Irish agriculture alone, given that the profits went to the landlords who were often absentees, and the readers were reminded of Drummond's words, 'Property has its duties as well as its rights.' In a *volte face* from Davis's earlier attitude to manufacturing in England, and as an indication that his strain of utopianism was already diminishing as he gained experience, he said that to rely overheavily on agriculture would keep Ireland poor, but that great encouragement had to be given to manufacturing also, which would help agriculture. It was 'absurd to say Ireland is essentially an agricultural country' and the claim was made that it had been humbugged into accepting that its only role was to produce primary products for the English market. A following editorial on the Corn Laws claimed that, '*Vast quantities of food are exported every year from this country, and the people are starving*', which summed up 'the evils of Ireland'. The landlords wanted the retention of the Corn Laws, which imposed duties on foreign corn, so as to ensure that the farm labourers should pay more for their food and thus enable the farmers to pay their landlords higher rents and 'a greater piece of robbery was never perpetrated on any people ... The corn laws are one of the pillars of the rotten system [of landlordism]: their removal should be regarded as the prelude to its demolition.'

The constant agrarian outrages were no surprise to the young editors because oppression was their true cause. 'As long as the people feel that the laws are not made for them they will never respect the laws ... When a people are goaded to madness, they do not exercise much discrimination in selecting the objects of their vengeance.' Nonetheless, there was no outright justification of the outrages but a condemnation of 'the unhappy wretches who are driven to commit them' with a reminder to the readers that 'a large share of the guilt belongs to those who, knowing the remedy, are doing all they can to prevent its adoption.' A look across the Irish sea at the disturbances in the neighbouring island did not lead to a condemnation of the Chartists 'as fools or criminals' simply because they 'chattered some nonsense about physical force at a time when they had no chance of succeeding in it'. The Chartists had survived 'the imbecility of their leaders' and, in the future, they would be in 'the position of a successful democracy'.

As in England, taxation in Ireland was crippling and it was proved to be so with long lists of statistics claiming that such a 'mortgage' had to be removed from Ireland; otherwise 'real or substantial prosperity' would be '*utterly* impossible', with Irish debt standing at thirty times what it was at the time of the Union. The state of the Irish linen industry, in which prices had fallen from 2/6d. a yard in 1800 to 10d. a yard in 1830, claimed particular attention and Irish readers were begged to buy Irish-made products, as Henry Grattan had done in 1782 to much effect.[18] This idea that Ireland was in any way mortgaged to England sent Conway back on the warpath. He was tempted to call such a proposition many things but satisfied himself with, 'It is unique – unparalleled.' He also had come to the conclusion that there was no Catholicism in the *Register*, but that it had become straight radicalism going well beyond Repeal and tending towards rebellion.[19]

In his editorials Davis dealt with many of the topics that had already claimed his interest and about which he read and thought deeply. Capital punishment was 'cruel' and 'barbaric'; the principle of free trade was not applicable to the medical profession because 'Human life is a thing of too much importance to be made a subject of experiment'; England was committing a 'crime' in China with its 'opium war' and the situation in the Punjab, the Sind plains, Egypt and Turkey all had to be looked at in the light of powerful nations oppressing weaker ones. He regarded the Kirk in Scotland as 'democratic' and thus it was unlike the Anglican Church, although he was careful not to be critical of the hierarchical nature of the Catholic Church. He thought that separation of Church and State in Scotland would be excellent, both as a solution in that place and as an example in Ireland.

The role of the Irish in the British forces had already become a constant source of study to Davis, perhaps stemming from the life-long involvement of his father with those forces. He said that two-thirds of the British at St Vincent and Trafalgar had been Irish Catholics who returned to their homes to find 'decay and ruin' because England in her gratitude to them had used her laws and her system of Orange colonisation to 'make a desert', after which, in the manner of the Romans, they 'called it peace'. He asked Wellington to remember the bravery of the Irish soldiers and to 'let Ireland alone' because what happened before 1798 may happen again so that, were the English to 'resort to force, their overthrow will be more rapid, though not more sure, than if opposed by the *now* untrained millions'. He also mocked the British Parliament debating hotly whether to allow £8,000 annually to be spent on the education of the Irish Catholic clergy whose people were seven-eighths of the population. 'How dare these people talk of Popish intolerance' and 'what proof is there that Irish Catholics would persecute their Protestant fellow-countrymen if they had the power to do so?', as was being alleged by detractors. Finally, he was appalled at the 'humbug' of the Tories in their anti-slavery stand and he went to their own past utterances to prove the humbug, while stressing his own condemnation of slavery.[20]

Davis was constantly prepared to defend the Catholic Church and its adherents because Catholicism was the religion of the native Irish and, by far, the religion of the greater portion of the population. He showed no interest in the dogmatic content of Catholicism, or indeed in that of any Christian body. To him, they were all sects and he saw the tendency of his own Church of Ireland to become increasingly defensive as proof of the 'madness of sects' which 'generally increases as their power declines'. He was capable of a direct and forthright attack on Protestantism in Ireland such as, 'For almost two hundred years the people of Ireland were proscribed, and hunted, and slaughtered, and they were taught that all this was necessary for the safety and spread of Protestantism ... They were excluded from parliament for the safety of Protestantism. They are still refused the privileges which are their due, lest Protestantism be endangered ...'.

Nonetheless, Davis refused to accept that Protestantism should be made 'odious' by presenting it as a body which shielded 'public plunder' and snatched food from the 'mouths of famished men' and he called upon those 'who love Protestant truth' to 'maintain the civil and religious liberty which we have inherited from our forefathers'. At the same time he thought that the Protestant Association, with its pamphlets and handbills deriding popery and Catholicism generally, was a deplorable body; the 'Orange outrage' at Carlow, when innocent citizens were fired upon in June, was seen as 'a foretaste of the blessings we are to enjoy' were the Tories returned to power and he was appalled at the way the Tory press vilified the Irish, calling them 'villainous perjurers', 'frieze-coated ruffians' and a 'Romanist rabble', while their priests were portrayed as 'surpliced ruffians' and their monks as 'hooded incendiaries.'[21]

The fear that the Tories would regain the treasury benches in London was foremost in the minds of those who looked towards a continuation of some minimal form of just government in Ireland. Davis had long since accepted that the Whigs, with all their faults, were preferable as a government, but not simply because he saw them as a lesser evil. Essentially, he linked gaining Irish independence to the existence of a Whig government and thus the repeal of the Union as the first step was also dependent on its acceptance, gracefully or otherwise, by the Whigs. Until 6 June 1841, when they lost a motion of no confidence in them by one vote, the Whigs remained in office although it had become increasingly apparent for some months that their days were numbered. In such circumstances it is not surprising that the young editors would use the *Morning Register* to the fullest in campaigning against the Tories. The important aspect of their campaign however was that it became more a cry for Repeal than for the retention of the Whigs.

The London journals, especially the *Spectator* and the *Times*, drove Davis to fury so that from his pen flowed invective, pleading and much sense. 'Union for Ireland' was his constant cry, but there would be no 'premature insurrection' to gain it. His early conviction was that 'should Ireland be openly united for Repeal, England would quietly yield.' By May he had become resigned to the inevitability of the return of the Tories to power but he tried to console his readers with 'Freedom is the gift of God to man, and independence is the right of nations; we shall be free and our country independent, spite of fraud-spite of force.' He had praised O'Connell for his 'peaceable, moral, and determined agitation' in March, but now he was telling the Liberator, with a degree of youthful enthusiasm, that he had to look to 'that patient, hardy, numerous, martial and enthusiastic race' of peasants who, belonging to the 'native soil, are *always* patriots'. With an idealism that outstripped reality, but based on his conviction that a Tory victory would result in a direct and physical contest, Davis wanted the peasants organised into one strong body, because the Irish would not accept 'the degrading alternative of abject subjection'. With his own forthright interpretation of 1798, he was certain that the outcome would not be the same again. In 1798, 'tortures and degradation' had forced a premature reaction with the consequent decimation of 'our gallant peasantry' who were 'the ill-guided martyrs of a noble cause'. In the aftermath, exhausted and dispirited, the Irish were forced into an 'infamous Union' but this time, were force resorted to, the English would be overthrown because they would be opposed by 'the *now* untrained millions'. It was heady stuff indeed, but scarcely likely to cause any anxiety in Dublin Castle.[22]

On 14 May an anti-Tory meeting took place at the Royal Exchange in Dublin. That morning Davis appealed in the *Register* to all those citizens of Dublin who loved Ireland and valued liberty to be present and even Conway had begun to see some value in the support Davis was giving to the Whig cause. He was also anti-Corn Laws and was delighted with the meeting protesting against a Tory advent to power. Davis insisted that the election was momentous because they had to ask themselves whether they were to have the privileges of 'free subjects', or to be 'treated as citizens or slaves'. If the latter, Ireland would be involved in 'turbulence and anarchy, and perhaps rebellion'. The meeting took place with Davis, Dillon, Staunton, Thomas Hutton, John O'Hagan, Dr Gray of the *Freeman's Journal*, Thomas Mathew Ray, secretary of O'Connell's recently formed Repeal Association and others on the stage. They passed motions in support of the present ministry, but to little avail and Davis bewailed the way in which so many of the Irish preferred 'English parties to Irish interests, old feuds to common country, and (worst of all) the miserable, canting ferocity of sects to charity and mutual service'. While the civic society of Ireland continued to be thus rent, Ireland 'might be despaired of', because 'no effort could save her'. Finally, he sounded a note of warning, entirely based on militarism. 'Military strength and military resources are necessary to a *nation*', were it to avoid becoming a province and a Tory victory may make it '*necessary* for the nation to know her strength, and to *make it known*'.[23]

The acceptance of a Whig defeat meant the need to spell out in some detail an alternative course of action on the part of those in Ireland who had relied on their support for the furtherance of Irish causes. To O'Connell the campaign for Repeal had become a political weapon which would temper the actions of the Tories in controlling Ireland, but to Davis it was an end in itself. Nonetheless, he praised O'Connell in urging Repeal agitation, 'without adjournment or compromise', and he hoped that it would mean an end to any truck with English factions or English parties. Thus he urged 'the national cause' based on 'national principles' and he spelt out his idea of nationality more fully than he had done previously.

> To have Irish laws made by Irishmen – Irish offices administered by Irishmen – to have everything in Ireland, of and for Ireland, from our food to our literature; from the goods in our stores to the flag on our towers; from the centre of our isle to the sea, aye, to the ships which guard its shores, to have each and all Irish – this is the craving of patriotism – this is the meaning of nationality – this is the resolve of Ireland.
>
> We have done with the cry for justice – we ceased long ago to expect it ... We have done with the demand for assimilation; at the best it would have been an allayed good, which assimilated our

institutions to those of aristocracy-ridden, gold-worshipping, heartless England, which would have drawn into too close proximity our pure, generous, social peasantry with the selfish clodpoles or the corrupted factory-men of England.[24]

While the theory was easily enough spelt out, how was Repeal to be carried? Time was the key and the first thing was to get rid of the Tories because they would bring against Repeal, and 'against agitating it, military force, which should be met, by all but wretches and slaves, with force'. Thus, to defeat the Tories was the principal objective and this was the duty of all who wanted Ireland to become a nation, without suffering the exhaustion of a war in becoming so. Nevertheless war, 'be its horrors what they may, they are better than the impoverishment, the degradation, the madness of slavery'.[25]

Amid all this Davis could still find time to applaud Trinity, 'hitherto an unnatural nursling of unnatural prejudices', for having started both an Irish Archaeological Society and an Irish History Society and to protest that the Art Union proposed to spend £1,000 for an engraving 'by an *English* artist'. He considered the sum too large but it was an 'outrage' to spend it out of Ireland because the objective of the Art Union should be 'to encourage *national art*'. He carried on the campaign against Plunket's enforced resignation, urged Dubliners to pay their taxes so as to be able to vote, and gave explicit instructions to them how to organise the elections. Meanwhile, he reviewed books and magazines, signed petitions and attended meetings while, at the same time, continuing to write extensively for the *Citizen*.

After four short, but full, months the experiment with the *Morning Register*, suggested with some enthusiasm by its owner, was over. In his letter to Davis of 24 July 1841, Michael Staunton terminated the arrangement with gentility and wrote, 'There is, I am sorry to say, no dividend to be computed, our condition having been the opposite of one in advance.' Davis was paid £32 for his efforts, the young editors packed their pens and pencils and departed. The diet served up daily to the already dwindling readers, in which an odd report on horse racing results was mingled with the strong stuff of nationality, had proved too much. There is no indication that Davis or Dillon showed any regret at the cessation of their remarkable venture into journalism that had so astounded their readers, although Davis later acknowledged that his and Dillon's impatience helped to spoil the prospect of making the *Morning Register* into a national paper.[26]

At some stage during those crucial few weeks in March and April 1841 the two friends must have decided that they would remain powerless unless they allied themselves with a wider and more powerful group. It had become evident to them that to turn to the generality of Protestants and to the Conservatives as allies was useless. Such people could never hope to win the allegiance of the Irish people and they were only a cohesive force in their general opposition to the growth of Irish nationality and in their support, even if grudging at times, for the Union. The Catholics were another matter. There was much less difficulty in fanning the latent embers of nationality amongst them because they were in some measure united. They had a powerful leader in the person of O'Connell and the Repeal Association, although structurally and numerically still weak, was a reality. Yet for Davis and Dillon to turn to O'Connell and his Association would be to deprive themselves of the great weapon of impartiality that could only be preserved provided they remained independent from taking a party political role. Only desperation or a lack of experience and vision could have led them to contemplate such a step. For Dillon, it could be said to have been a natural step given his religion, his sympathies and his background. For Davis it was unnatural, injudicious and fatal, although the latter two elements would take time to reveal themselves.

It was obvious to O'Connell that, when a change in government came about, new tactics would be necessary in Ireland. He had set about the founding of the Loyal Repeal Association, with headquarters at the Corn Exchange, on 18 April 1840, as a kind of warning that the only 'good government' that would ultimately be found in Ireland would be an Irish one. He remained loyal to the Whigs, stood ready to do his best for them electorally but, ever the realist, he knew that the evil day of Tory rule would return. All he could do was to strive to put it off and ready himself and his followers to meet it when it came. In the north of the country both the Presbyterians and that minority of the old Protestant Ascendancy, who had shown support for Wolfe Tone, were now in general content with the Union which had brought them much benefit, while Catholic antagonism to the Union had only served to awaken the Orange Lodges to a new form of activity that was in essence anti-Catholic.

On the other hand, under the Whigs, the Catholics in some measure had been lulled into a sense of security. The wealthier ones among them saw no point in further agitation for a goal that in any case had never been spelt out. They had been presented by O'Connell with essentially vague notions of a national parliament in an Ireland that would in some sense remain tied to England. The very person of Victoria, young and gracious still, had seemed to fulfil the promise of her coronation when many Catholics had rejoiced with other Irish loyalists at her coming to the throne. Indeed, it was customary to honour the loyal toast at public gatherings and the Repeal Association itself continued to do so and thereby demonstrate its adhesion to the loyalty expressed in its title.

The result was that in Ireland in 1841 there was little warmth for Repeal and a good measure of solid and determined opposition. England, and certainly an England under Tory government, was not going to break imperial unity short of force and O'Connell was solemnly bound by his own choice to eschew the use of force. It was therefore entirely premature to imagine that Repeal could be achieved by agitation of a peaceful variety and the history of past revolt could scarcely make a bloody uprising attractive, except to extreme hotheads. Moreover, were it the case that the long and difficult process of awakening the generality of the Irish people to an appreciation of their nationality could only be achieved through the inculcation of education and higher virtues, in some measure made more possible by the work of Father Mathew on temperance, such a process could only suffer harm by uniting or blending it in with the Repeal movement which would make it immediately sectarian and partisan.

At all events, during those turbulent days on the *Morning Register* Davis took the most decisive step in his short life. On 19 April 1841, he accompanied Dillon to the Corn Exchange on the Liffey quays where they both became members of O'Connell's Repeal Association.[27] Fifty years later Gavan Duffy, in retirement at Nice, looked back on the moment almost with awe. He compared Davis's step to that of the 'son of a Roman centurion who left the retinue of Caesar to associate with the obscure Hebrews gathered around Saul of Tarsus' and thought that Davis 'scarcely made a more surprising or significant choice'. It was wide of the mark to see Davis with such a lineage or association because he claimed no rank, nor was he ever close to Caesar as embodied in Dublin Castle.[28]

In all probability, unlike Staunton, Davis had little room left to manouevre in the Irish political spectrum once he had taken up the public stance on Repeal as evident in the *Morning Register* and by the public meetings he had attended. Either he was to remain on the sidelines, pen in hand, exhorting others to follow the Liberator, or he was to take his own place in the vanguard. To have adopted the former stance would have laid him open to the charge of double-dealing, of face-saving and perhaps even personal cowardice. It was not in his character to give grounds for such charges. Nonetheless, it is possible that the full implications of his action were not weighed in the heat of the moment with an election in the offing and with the day-to-day emotions that his journalistic activities stirred. Assuredly, at his home in Baggot Street there was refined and restrained disapproval on the part of his mother and probably more outspoken opposition by his brother John, a Tory and a conservative to his bootstraps. Perhaps the blood of the Western Celts, which Davis shared with O'Connell, made the step inevitable. For both of them it marked the beginning of the end.

Until now Davis had stood aloof from both party and sect. He had set down as a principle that his new thrust towards nationality had Ireland and Irishness as its objective and his stands on the Royal Dublin Society and on Plunket's enforced retirement had made it plain that he was nobody's man. The path he had foreshadowed for himself and others who wanted to follow was difficult but clear-cut. By diffusing among the Irish people an awareness of the uniqueness of their nationality through education and not mere exhortation, Davis hoped that all the diverse segments of Irish society would, in sufficient measure, unite so as to throw off eventually the dominion held over them and their land by a foreign power. Difficult such a goal may have been to attain, but it was limpid in its simplicity and it contained no element of force or division based on sect or party.

Davis had begun his active career with important and vital attributes of background and character which fitted him admirably for his task. He was young, highly gifted, widely read, passionate, warm and hard working. Although of minor standing personally, he sprang from a ruling elite, even if its best days were over. His education at Trinity marked him out for a leadership role in society, were he to want to take it. He wore lightly his allegiance to the Church of Ireland and counted Catholics among his friends. He had no hankering to belong to that class of his compatriots to whom life in Ireland was a semi-exile because, to Davis, Ireland was home, his native place, and he had made her history his own. He had never been a party man in any active sense so that he could stand beyond and aloof from the party struggles around him. Although his immediate family neither understood nor accepted his determination to foster Irish nationality and throw off the English yoke, they did not oppose him to the extent of causing a rift and he continued to live comfortably in the warmth of his family home. All these things seemed to say of him that he could bring something new to Ireland had he remained his own man and built up his own following over a longer period of time.

In his very strengths there were also weaknesses. His modest means and lack of standing, in the sense of wielding authority, meant that he knew nothing of the fear of losing either wealth or power and, in any case, he showed little interest in possessing or managing money. He knew nothing of what it was to own land because he, and his immediate family, had none, and their very lack of it meant that they stood materially with the generality of the Irish people. What is more important, he knew nothing of what it was to yearn for land in a society in which the possession and enjoyment of one's own land had been paramount for long centuries. He could not share the bitterness of those who looked back to a time when, in their belief, they owned the land others now stood upon, nor could he share with those others the feeling that they were regarded still by many as usurpers. To them, the danger of the loss of their lands by violence or by legislation, or more pointedly, by impoverishment, was ever present.

If those were weaknesses, there was also a flaw in his thinking because he lacked an understanding of a fundamental aspect of the religion of Ireland. He would have been horrified to be regarded as less than a believing Christian but Christianity, although he was full of respect for it and its physical and literary remains, when he saw it expressed in 'sect', and even worse when those same sects seemed to lie at the heart of division in Ireland, left him perplexed and troubled. Perhaps his reading of Lamennais had brought him to conclude that religion was essentially an interior and private act between the individual and God. To Davis, both the Catholic Church and the Church of Ireland were sects, and the Dissenters were simply members of other sects. He was bent on the development of an Irish nationality that would remain 'indifferent to sect', as if the sects in Ireland were all of equal status. Yet the Church of Ireland regarded itself, and was still so regarded, as the official Church in the country while the Catholic Church, on both dogmatic and historical grounds, judged itself to be the true Church of the Irish people.

Furthermore, Davis seemed ignorant of the teaching of the Catholic Church that stemmed back to the Fourth Lateran Council, held in Rome in 1215, when it was decreed that outside the Church there could be no salvation. More strikingly, he seemed ignorant of, or chose to ignore, that strongly-held belief of the Irish clergy and their people in a one, true, holy, Catholic and apostolic Church that, to them, could only be the Church in communion with Rome. Assuredly, he was strongly in sympathy with the feelings of those who had suffered legal and other disabilities for the retention and practice of their Catholic faith but, in the end, the parson in his pulpit and the priest muttering the old cadences of the Latin Mass in his chapel were the same in that they were both ministers of the Christian religion. In his eyes, at the same time and in their own ways, because of their differences based on sect, they were destroying Irish unity and all decent values by, as Davis saw it, warring against each other.

Thus, in his attitude to the role of religion in Ireland it is not too much to say that Davis did not understand Ireland in a vital aspect of her past that flowed into the present, and the degree of his lack of understanding could only be tested in the future. For the while, he could embark on his task of fleshing out an all-embracing nationality and let others engage in theological debates about historical legitimacy in the religious sphere. All of that he regarded as of little moment except in its results in the shape of sectarian differences and animosities. Nonetheless, it is strange that seemingly none of his Catholic friends, and especially John Dillon, warned him that, were he to continue to regard the Catholic Church merely as one among several differing sects, he would meet trouble eventually. The option was not one of giving up his own religion. It was merely a matter of treading softly. Doubtless, given his great sense of tolerance and the generous impulses of his heart, time, with the wisdom to be gained and honed by experience, would have developed in him a finer sensitivity to religious beliefs and the passions they engendered. Unlike those closest him, time, for Davis, was becoming a fleeting moment.

Whatever the reasons Davis and Dillon had in joining the Repeal Association, O'Connell knew exactly what his own intentions were. He was immensely gratified at the acquisition of the two new recruits to his cause and especially that of Davis. There were too few Protestants in the ranks of the Repealers and perhaps Davis would be the first of many more. Yet O'Connell was long in experience in dealing with men and movements and he could not have been unaware of the flamboyant, if not outrageous, way in which the two young men had been pressing the case for nationality through their writings. The very idea itself was strange in the ears of O'Connell and his followers who had been content to spell out their objectives, such as Emancipation, in highly practical terms which were immediately intelligible both to those to whom they looked for redress and those upon whose support they counted. Davis could usefully have pondered the question whether O'Connell and his people at the Corn Exchange thought there was already a nation in Ireland and, if that was the case, whether they had decided who made it up.

On several occasions, Davis had made it plain that he would not baulk at the use of force if necessary to achieve the ultimate objective of freedom for Ireland. O'Connell may have been unclear what freedom for Ireland meant to his audience, or indeed to himself, but he was absolutely clear on the use of force and he had insisted that it never be used. It was necessary therefore to make immediately clear to the young men what the conditions of membership of the Association were and he took the first possible opportunity to do so. Among those conditions, even though never spelt out in explicit terms, was that there be one leader, the Liberator himself, to whom loyalty was due at all times. No chance could be allowed to the young men of lacking an understanding of that condition from the very beginning.

Davis and Dillon were not so naïve as to appear at the Corn Exchange on 19 April for the normal Monday meeting of the Association without making some preliminary arrangements. Thus O'Connell himself moved their admission and spoke glowingly of Davis as 'a gentleman who had distinguished himself by opposing the abuses of Trinity College'. Davis, he said, 'had already written his name on the pages of Irish history and he (Mr O'Connell) had no doubt that it would come out in bright and brilliant characters. (loud cheers)'.[29] O'Connell was not prepared, however, to let the occasion pass by lightly and he quickly decided that there was more on the agenda than a perfunctory welcome to the newcomers. Thus it was agreed that an extraordinary meeting of the Association be held on the following day and, as was usual, O'Connell 'entered the room amidst tumultuous applause'. He then moved that the chair be taken by 'Thomas Davis, Esq. Barrister-at-law' and proceeded to give Davis and Dillon a baptism in endurance. For the customary two hours of an O'Connell speech, the young men were subjected to rhetoric, high oratory, declamation, common sense and precise instructions for the campaign. Clearly, the Liberator had thought out what he wanted to say on this occasion, and he was determined that there be no possibility that it be misunderstood.

The landlord and tenant question had been sufficiently pressed in the *Morning Register* as to move O'Connell to make it clear that the question was also part and parcel of the present struggle and he spoke of 'that odious, reckless, rackrent system'. Moving to the crux of the matter O'Connell stated that 'here we are ready to bear the burthen and fight the battles of England, and all we ask in return is that justice be done to us'. The proof of justice being done would be England restoring an Irish Parliament in Dublin. In case anyone was unclear as to who were the Irish, and to dampen any ardour about unusual views of nationality, he said 'Ireland was a nation when I was born.' He was speaking of the days prior to 1801 and he was sure that, in the same sense, Ireland would become a nation again before he died. He did not spell out what such an idea entailed unless he meant that nationality consisted principally in having one's own legislature, which perhaps said much more about O'Connell the lawyer and politician than O'Connell the Liberator. In any case, it was a curiously formal and narrow attitude, and one which Davis regarded as little more than a beginning in the growth of nationality.

However, the essential point O'Connell wanted to make was that there were provisos to the achievement of freedom. He did so in unambiguous terms.

This freedom shall be won by moral combination; one drop of human blood shall never be shed in our struggle to obtain it ... One crime or aggression against the person or persons would be a price too high, in our estimation, to pay for liberty; and therefore no crime shall be committed by us in our struggle to obtain it. We will have peace, order, and morality established throughout society.

After an instruction to the wardens of the Association, who held responsibility for the implementation of its policies throughout Ireland, to do all they possibly could for Irish manufacturing, together with an appeal to the people to wear only Irish-made articles of clothing, O'Connell concluded his address with a series of seven resolutions. They contained the guidelines of the campaign for Repeal as he wanted it carried through and, as the leader, he had every right to put them forward and to expect compliance in essence with them. There can be no doubt that O'Connell saw a new opportunity for the Repeal movement with the joining of Davis and Dillon. Such a development was, however, to be entirely on his terms. His right to the title, the Liberator, had been won through the long, but eventually successful, campaign for Emancipation. In that struggle he had learnt a great deal and he saw no reason to ignore those lessons, or to depart from the methods that had been used to gain his first objective.

Nevertheless, O'Connell did not seem to be aware that things had changed with his insistence on Repeal. The hardline English Tories and the members of the old Irish ascendancy were not the only ones to see the granting of an Irish parliament as the first step to the dismemberment of the Empire. The great majority of the Whigs felt the same way as did those Irish, especially in the North, who saw themselves as essentially part of England and Empire before they were Irish. Repeal, therefore, was unthinkable in the minds of the vast majority of those who held power in England and Ireland and they were not prepared to concede it. Indeed, were matters to come to a head they would use force to prevent its achievement. There can be no doubt but that O'Connell had thought through the problem of whether to use or reject violence, even to the extent that he rejected any outside involvement, whether by America or France, in achieving his objective. Aware of it or not, his rejection of force meant his rejection of achieving Repeal. Whatever else it was that he hoped to achieve never became clear. The surprising thing is that no one asked him.

O'Connell's resolutions could have come as no surprise to Davis and Dillon because they had been reiterated time and time again. In summary, they stressed 'peaceful and legal means', used through political pressure lawfully exerted and 'within the principles of the constitution'. Success would depend exclusively upon the Irish people combined as a moral force through membership of the Repeal Association and nothing was to be served by bringing the measure to the British Parliament until the Irish showed their own will and determination. There could be only one solid basis for Repeal and it consisted in 'the perfect equality in the eye of the law of all sects and persuasions', together with the extension of the franchise 'to every householder and heads of families'. Finally, O'Connell wanted the 'total oblivion of by-gone distinctions, former feuds, and the perfect cooperation of all classes, sects and persuasions in the encouragement of the manufacturing, agricultural, and commercial interests of Ireland; and in securing the tranquillity, prosperity, and liberty of our native land'. Nothing was said by O'Connell about what was to be done were the authorities to threaten force to put down the peaceful means he demanded be used by his followers in his campaign for Repeal.

The meeting was then treated to a large dose of the normal blarney from Thomas Steele, the Liberator's trusted lieutenant, which must have bemused Davis and Dillon considerably more than anything O'Connell had said. Thomas Ray, formerly secretary of the National Trades Political Union in Dublin, who was assuredly the most competent and level-headed member of the Association, reported on the revival of the Irish Volunteers, to which Charles Gavan Duffy had been admitted the day before. Ray then took the unusual step, again probably for the benefit of the new members, of outlining the eleven ways in which the Repeal Rent would be used, all of which were perfectly legitimate within the objectives of the Association. At the end of the meeting a motion of thanks was moved to Davis as chairman, despite the fact that there was no report of his having said anything at all throughout the proceedings. The meeting was detailed at length in the *Pilot*, the leading Repeal organ which remained consistently loyal to O'Connell through its editor, Richard Barrett. The frequent symbols of acclamation by loud cheering and similar forms of approval or disapproval were not distinctive to the Association but were part and parcel of the Association's, and all similar organisations, proceedings at the time and thus given in any report in a newspaper.[30]

There is no record of what impression the meeting made on either of the young men. They had joined because they wanted Repeal and the Association was the only available vehicle with that as its objective. O'Connell had laid his cards down on the matter of force to the degree that acceptance of non-violence was at least a moral condition of membership. Neither Davis nor Dillon were fools or hypocrites. From now on they were bound to accept the ruling that they could not propose the use of violence as a means to achieve Repeal and, at the same time, remain members of the Association. Their decision to accept membership on those terms did not preclude a rethink, for them at least, were it the case that, even though the Association rejected violence, the British authorities proposed to use violence to suppress it, or proscribe as unlawful the peaceful means it used to achieve its objectives. It was a situation that neither they, nor O'Connell, as yet, had to face.

References

1. See Brendan Ó Cathaoir, *John Blake Dillon, Young Irelander* (Dublin, 1990), pp 4-7 and passim. For Duffy on Dillon see *Young Ireland*, part 1, pp 22-23. Edward Norman, in his *A history of modern Ireland* (London, 1971), p. 118, wrote that, at Maynooth, Dillon 'discovered that his vocation had evaporated; so he defected to Trinity College and became a barrister instead.' The words are worth recording in that they reveal the depths to which some of the critics of Young Ireland have chosen to descend.

2. *Morning Register*, 5, 11, 15, 20 January 1841.

3. Ibid., 30 January 1841.

4. R. D. Collison Black, *Economic thought and the Irish question 1817-1870* (Cambridge, 1960), p. 144. Collison thought that Ireland would have been better off under its own government, but that without emigration the population problem could never have been solved, p. 247.

5. For the economy of the period generally see Cormac Ó Gráda, *Ireland: a new economic history, 1780-1939* (Oxford, 1994); *Ireland before and after the famine; explorations in economic history, 1800-1925*, 2nd. ed. (Glasgow, 1993); Ó Gráda, chs. v and vii, 'Poverty, population, and agriculture, 1801-1845' and 'Industry and communication, 1801-45'; Oliver MacDonagh, ch. x, 'The economy and society, 1830-45' and T. W. Freeman, ch. xi, 'Land and people, *c.*1841'; in W. E. Vaughan, (ed) *A new history*, pp 108-57, 218-41, 242-271; Timothy P. O'Neill, *Life and tradition in rural Ireland* (London, 1977); Gearóid Ó Tuathaigh, *Ireland before the famine 1798-1848* (Dublin, 1990), pp 118, 120; Kevin Whelan, 'Pre and post-famine landscape change' in Cathal Poirtéir (ed.), *The great Irish famine* (Cork, 1995). For the judgement of an outsider on Ireland in the mid-1830s see Emmet Larkin (trans and ed.), *Alexis de Tocqueville's journey*, passim.

6. *Morning Register*, 30 January, 2, 9, February 1841.

7. Ibid., 13, 15, 17, 20, 24, 26 February 1841.

8. Terence de Vere White, *The story of the Royal Dublin Society* (Tralee, 1955), p. 92. Daniel O'Connell had been given the same treatment in 1811. Murray took his rejection well and asked the Society to forget him and get on with the work of 'national improvement'. Ibid.

9. See Duffy, *Davis*, pp 46-9 and the article 'Transactions of the Dublin Society, 1841' in the *Citizen*, March 1841, pp 204-18. In Davis's set of the magazine, now held at the Royal Irish Academy, this article is not claimed by Davis as having being written by him. See also *Dublin Evening Post*, 20, 23 February 1841. The *Freeman's Journal* was certain that the Irish people would support the Royal Dublin Society. *Freeman's Journal*, 28 November 1842.

10. *Morning Register*, 25 February 1841 and Duffy, *Davis*, pp 49-50. Duffy gives the impression that the editorial of 25 February, which he wrongly dates as

2 February, was the first contribution by Davis to the paper. Clearly, Duffy did not work from the paper itself but from a cutting of Davis's article and he was thus unaware of the previous contributions by Davis and Dillon.

11. *Dublin Evening Post*, 25, 27 February; 2, 4 March 1841.

12. *Morning Register*, 26 February 1841.

13. Davis to Webb, Oldcastle, 28 February 1841 in Duffy, *Davis,* p. 51. On p. 53 Duffy prints Dillon's letter to which Davis was replying. He misdates Dillon's letter to 17 February. Dillon assured Davis that Staunton, far from being dismayed, was 'staunch' and stood for Irish institutions 'whether they be Orange or Green'.

14. *Morning Register*, 5, 23 March 1841. Reform was slow in coming within the Society and by mid-1845 Davis was suggesting that it be undertaken forthwith. *Nation*, 17 May, 5 July 1845; Terence de Vere White, *Royal Dublin Society*, p. 111. A few years later the Society had so far forgotten its debt to Davis that his statue by John Hogan was removed from its halls on the occasion of the Queen's visit, lest she or her court be offended by the statue of such a notable radical being on display.

15. See Dillon to Davis, 27 February 1841, Ms 2644, NLI. Dillon asked Davis to start sending articles immediately were he to remain out of Dublin. Duffy, *Davis,* pp 53-4 reprints this letter but omits Dillon's uncharitable and uncharacteristic reference to Staunton as 'the old fool'. Perhaps Dillon's implication was that Staunton had no idea what the possible ramifications of his step were. In the event, the reference proved more appropriate than Dillon intended. On Staunton and freedom of the press see Brian Inglis, *The freedom of the press in Ireland 1784-1841* (London, 1954), p. 227. Inglis was of the opinion that O'Connell did not believe in an independent press and that his line had to be followed by 'liberal papers', p. 221.

16. See MacDonagh, *O'Connell,* pp 473-5.

17. *Morning Register*, 2 March 1841.

18. Ibid., 18, 19 March; 3, 17, 18, 26 April; 4, 6, 17 May; 1, 5 June 1841. It is difficult to be certain as to the authorship of these editorials, although Dillon was probably more interested at that time in the land question.

19. *Dublin Morning Post*, 9, 11 March 1841.

20. *Morning Register*, 5, 9, 11, 13, 20, 29, 30 March; 1, 12, 24 April; 18, 19 May 1841.

21. Ibid., 8 March; 14 April; 19 May; 29, 30 June 1841.

22. Ibid., 15 March; 7, 14, 28 April; 1, 4, 13, 19 May 1841.

23. Ibid., 14, 15, 18, 19 May 1841. *Dublin Evening Post*, 6, 18 May 1841.

24. Ibid., 22 May 1841.

25. Ibid., 8 June 1841.

26. Ibid., 6 May; 12, 15, 18, 19, 21, 22, 23, 25 June, 1841; Duffy, *Davis*, p. 57. For Davis's later regrets on the experiment with the *Register* see the manuscript 'Origin and Writers of the *Nation*', 30 April 1844. Ms 3199, NLI. Michael Staunton became lord mayor of Dublin in 1847. He died in 1870 and never lost the respect of the profession of journalism he had served so well.

27. Duffy, *Davis*, pp 63-4. Duffy got the correct date of 19 April. Four years later, when renewing Davis's membership in 1845, Thomas Ray gave 17 April as the date when Davis first joined. Davis's membership number was 3919 in 1841. See ticket of renewal in Ms 2644, NLI.

28. Duffy, *Davis*, p. 58.

29. *Pilot*, 21 April 1841.

30. Ibid.

Chapter 5

The Nation

By 1841, Davis had been thinking deeply for at least five years about what it was to be Irish. As he walked from his home to the Corn Exchange, or through other parts of Dublin, he perhaps observed that the lamentation of a generation earlier of John Keogh still bore a measure of truth. Keogh, forerunner of O'Connell as a leader, had said that a Catholic could be recognised in the street 'by his timid gait', while Duffy later wrote that 'the bulk of the national party were still Catholics who had not wholly outgrown the traditions of slavery.' Davis could see no symbol, whether in street name or statuary, that the city he walked in was Irish. The past had become a land inhabited by unclear memories and ghostly figures so that even the idea of being Irish as something distinctive was fading, except that among the people there still rankled an indefinable feeling that somehow in that past there had been vast disasters, flagrant injustices, dreadful defeats and shameful traitors, interspersed with a handful of mighty heroes and famous victories. Throughout the whole of Ireland almost all the responsible positions were in Protestant hands. They were the makers of public opinion and they presided over the few cultural societies that met in the capital. Their libraries contained little that spoke without prejudice of the Irish and in the national school system the children learnt as little of the history of their own people as they did of that of the Hottentot. The Irishman of stage or joke was a buffoon or a piteous simpleton, while in a more serious vein he was an untrustworthy savage who would bend to no law and his religion was shrouded in superstition and mummery. Of culture he was seen to possess none and the songs and music of his past had gone into the recesses of the cabins except for the ballad singers who still offered a popular fare in such places as the Liberties. In short, to be Irish was to be a figure of reproach and the road ahead for one who wanted that changed was long and hard.[1]

Without the same intensity of feeling as in his prime, or, perhaps even the same degree of perception because he had begun to grow physically but not mentally weary with the years, O'Connell still understood the feelings of those who followed him. His solution, Repeal, was at heart political and, despite any hesitation he may have had about the prudence of his new recruits, he made them welcome because they opened an avenue into a world that, largely, had been closed to him and to the causes for which he fought. He brought them immediately on to the general committee of the Repeal Association, as well as assigning duties to them on special sub-committees. He wanted them to look upon his work for Repeal as having only been temporarily in abeyance, due principally to a lack of funds to prosper it, and he assured Davis that he would personally see to the setting up of proper machinery in every parish to foster Repeal.[2] Looking back later, Duffy thought that the Repeal cause was at its lowest ebb in mid-1841 which is partially belied by the fact that even the Whig *Dublin Evening Post* had begun to report the proceedings of the Association. Undoubtedly the election fever bred its own necessities and allies had to be sought wherever they were on offer, which probably explained the temporary enthusiasm of the *Post*. Nonetheless, the air of urgency stirred some element of nationalist feeling given the probability of a Tory victory, so that Repeal took on an importance that it had not possessed since the early thirties when O'Connell had first worked for it with serious intent.[3]

Davis threw himself into the work of the Repeal Association with a will and in a few months he had become secretary to its Franchise Committee as well as to its Municipal Election Committee. He was even prepared to lend some of his own money to the latter Committee as an earnest of his serious intent in the election campaign.[4] At the same time he was undertaking some work in court on the matter of the Dublin Registry, although his lack of interest in legal matters made him less effective in that sphere. He tried to keep himself fit by walking eight Irish miles in two consecutive hours daily, but the fact that he was unable to take a holiday from what he referred to as the 'decayed metropolis' of Dublin did not help him. As well as his work for the Association and his writing for the *Citizen*, during the summer of 1841 he kept up a stream of correspondence, especially with his friend from childhood, Robert Webb, who was on holidays in Wales.[5]

He continued to read widely and it was perhaps during this period that he acquired a work on the formation of the human character that left a lasting impression on him.[6] His own tenacity of purpose he found supported by the words, 'The devout man exults in the indications of his being fixed and irretrievable. He feels this confirmed habit as the grasp of the hand of God, which will never let him go', but whether Davis applied the thought to matters of faith is not clear. In a long chapter entitled 'On decision of character', he became uneasy with the

Stephens Green North, Dublin, looking from the East.

insistence on the spiritual aspect of character, as if the human person were pure spirit and he made the note 'The char [sic] of the body lost sight of.' He was, however, taken with 'An infirm character practically confesses itself made for subjection, and passes, like a slave, from owner to owner', and he marked and underlined 'the habit of associating with *inferiors*, among whom a man can always, and therefore does always, take the lead, is very conducive to a subordinate kind of decision of character.'[7] Possibly Davis had already been struck with the way in which O'Connell was adulated in the ranks of the Association and that his inferiors in those ranks were generally of a calibre which made it easy for their leader to maintain his hold over them without obstacle or objection.

Meanwhile, the Whig campaign for re-election was proving unsuccessful, most significantly in Dublin. Nonetheless, the *Post* felt secure of a Whig victory and an increase in Whig members and its editor reminded his readers that 'The eyes of Europe are upon us' which bade fair to rank with the *Skibbereen Eagle's* famous words. He referred to the domination of the Orange faction and 'the blood-stained volumes of our history' which went back for seven hundred years and he warned of the peril to which religion, liberty, altar, and hearth would be all subjected were there a Tory victory. Surprisingly, he took up some of the themes of Davis and wrote, 'We can, if we choose it, be once more a nation.' Henry Grattan, son of the famous father, wrote to the paper to deplore the fact that the decrease in voters since 1835 had been over 20,000, so that only 84,000 out of eight million were enfranchised. As a result, no one could vote on class lines in an economic sense because those without financial means had no vote. In the event the two sitting members for Dublin, O'Connell and Robert Hutton, both standing as Whigs although Hutton was anti-Repeal, were beaten by two Orange members, Grogan and West, by less than 100 votes each in a poll of 12,000. It was a remarkable result given that O'Connell did not campaign in the capital. He stood for, and won, seats in both Cork and Meath but spent his time campaigning in Carlow where he was beaten, so he eventually chose to sit for Cork. The Tories came out with a comfortable majority of about sixty seats, but the Whig campaign in Ireland must have had some effect because the Tories only won six extra seats there, taking their total to thirty-eight out of 105.[8]

Nevertheless, Repeal, with its heartland in the Corn Exchange and among the 3,000 Irish priests and a few of the bishops, was not much more than talk and bombast at this stage. How far Davis was himself committed to Repeal as an objective rather than as a tactic is uncertain, but as soon as he knew that the election was lost he was thinking out other strategies. To that end he wrote to Robert Wyse on 10 July 1841. Wyse, MP for Waterford since 1835, had not joined the Association, although he wanted a separate but subordinate parliament in Dublin. He was a powerful and highly respected figure in Irish politics who had been lord of the treasury until the Whigs lost power. Davis wanted Wyse to be active in Parliament by pressing motions on each separate Irish grievance, which he enumerated: 'The Church, National education both in schools and colleges, the Franchise, the Debt, the expenditure, the absence of local authorities or councils, landlord or tenant, foreigners and bigots in Irish offices, municipal qualifications, powers, Poor Law, and yeomanry of bigots, no national militia.' The list was long and the grievances were real, but to Davis they were to be used as part of an overall strategy leading eventually to independence. He thought that, were sound statistical information provided and a cogent argument mounted on each motion, followed by two or three nights of vigorous debate, 'it would break down the ministry, give the opposition the force and progress of an attacking party, (and) accustom the English educated classes to see that we had hard, real grievances the redress of which could not be safely postponed ...' Furthermore, it could well be that 'the people of Ireland might be induced to consider the propriety of accepting federalism and a full equality instead of that independence which they otherwise can and will conquer for themselves'.[9]

While it is possible that Davis was cutting his cloth to suit Wyse's own lack of warmth for an independent Ireland, the fact that, within a few weeks of joining the Association, he was prepared to consider a federal system, in which the two countries would be equal, but remain united, while Ireland would have its own parliament to legislate on domestic matters, is remarkable. That it was a tactic to be used on the way to full independence is clear from his last remark containing his conviction that, were England to remain obdurate, then Ireland would 'conquer' its independence in a way that did not need elaboration. In effect, he wanted to give England its chance in regard to Ireland. What he was unable to recognise, or accept, at the time was the clear fact that any number of Irish grievances were of no greater moment to the politicians and bureaucrats in London than the normal difficulties they were accustomed to encounter in governing other subject peoples throughout the Empire. Such grievances could, and perhaps would, be taken care of in their own time, but it would not be up to the Irish to decide either the time or the manner. As for federalism, to say nothing of independence, both still languished in the realms of Irish fancy.

Davis gave a clearer indication of how his mind was working in a long letter to Webb in August, which put in better perspective his thoughts on relations with England and how they were to be conducted. Writing from his home, from which the other members of the family were apparently absent on a summer vacation, he began by begging Webb to keep writing to him from Wales because 'I am alone, and grow lonely; the weather is miserable, O'Connell is in low spirits; so write to me and rehumanize me.' He hoped that O'Connell's proposed book on Irish history 'would help to put thoughts into the mind of the country' and exclaimed, 'By heavens, 'tis maddening to see the land without arts or arms, literature or wealth.' Perhaps the loss in the elections and the lack of a positive response from the people made him impatient and caused him to write the next sentence which suggests at least that inwardly he was uneasy about O'Connell's strictures on force other than moral. 'I am for the sharp remedies' he wrote, and, harking back to Brian Boru and his victory over the Vikings in 1014, he continued, 'Oh for another Clontarf! the crowded hour and the worthy grave.'

After bewailing the spectacle of England and Anglicanism, both of which he deplored for their isolation and lack of originality, he asked what development there had been in civilisation in six hundred years apart from printing and gunpowder. He refused to accept that there could be 'no moral and intellectual progress in religion, and happiness, without a simultaneous growth of mechanics and material pursuits and condensed population', which was another way of saying that he rejected the utilitarianism of his age. Finally, he asked Webb, 'Do you feel any necessity for a creed to satisfy your feelings?' because, 'Unless one has something of the sort he is apt to grow inactive and uncomfortable.' It is not clear whether by creed he meant religious creed but, were it so, he was perhaps hinting that the form of Christianity in which he had been reared did not fulfil him. On the other hand, he may have already developed his idea of nationality to the degree that it had become his day-to-day creed on the secular level, without his necessarily rejecting a need for a concomitant spiritual one.[10]

Dillon was also away at his home in Roscommon and probably working on the address he had to give to the Historical Society as its auditor in November. He followed the same line set by Davis who had done the path-finding, even if somewhat stridently. As a consequence, Dillon could approach his subject, patriotism, in a more relaxed vein. Moreover, he had profited immensely by the experience he had gained on the *Morning Register* and his address was mainly a resumé of the thinking on nationality that the paper had contained. His audience contained several new members who would later leave their mark on Irish society, but Davis does not seem to have been present. In any case, it could be safely assumed that Davis was fully aware beforehand of what Dillon had to say. Thus Dillon was able to begin by praising Davis who had departed from talking about rhetoric to dealing with matters of 'far greater practical importance'. He thought that the very existence of the Society which, even though it was not yet a year old but showed every sign of a promising future, could be ascribed to the observations contained in Davis's address in the previous year.[12]

Dillon was convinced that the times make the men and that great patriots, like Demosthenes and the men of the French Revolution, spoke first from the heart wherein the sentiment or conviction of patriotism is engendered. He paused to praise, but also damn, the great orators of the Irish Parliament in Grattan's day whose speeches resounded louder than their deeds because their Parliament was a mockery in that it depended on the whim of the English legislature for the enforcement of its laws. To Dillon, Grattan's Parliament had let slip a great opportunity because 'they had the enemy completely at their mercy', which was exactly what Davis had said about the same Parliament. As far as Dillon was concerned, 'a Parliament is nothing more than a debating club, if it be not sustained by the sympathy, and, if need be, by the arms of the people.' He refrained from saying that Grattan's Parliament, entirely Protestant in composition, was not elected by, nor represented in any true sense, the great majority of the Irish people.

With thinly-veiled contempt for those Irish who looked to London as the source of their patriotism, Dillon fiercely denounced false cosmopolitanism which would empty the people of any genuine attachment to country. 'National patriotism is as much a part of our nature as filial or fraternal love,' and 'the patriot revels in a thousand pure delights, which the cold cosmopolite can never taste'. He asked his hearers to note that among the class to which they belonged, rather than among the 'humbler classes', the notion was gaining ground that 'the spirit of nationality is an unreasonable and mischievous prejudice', and that 'it were better to draw a veil over the past, and to obliterate it from their memory ...'. He rejected such an idea and reminded them that 'When cold and grovelling selfishness takes possession of the minds of a people, and draws them away from virtue and from honour, there is then a wound inflicted which festers at the heart, and which the centuries may not heal.' He flayed 'the patriotism of those men who exhaust the little stock of enthusiasm that nature has given them in admiring and praising a people, every page of whose history is stained with some villainous perfidy or savage atrocity practised on their country', which must have struck a negative response in the anglophiles who heard or read him. Rejecting mere sentiment, Dillon refused to ask the Irish to feed on the glories of their past while neglecting the material needs of the present and 'the physical wants of mankind', and concluded by stating that, if he had convinced his hearers to doubt those who told them that Ireland was 'unfit to enjoy, and unable to defend her freedom,' he would have attained his objective.

Dillon's words reinforced the convictions of those who had already been won over by Davis and led others to adopt a similar stand for nationality. Duffy said that the whole nature of the Historical Society had changed since the address by Davis and that its new membership consisted of young men whose seriousness was such that a call to public duty could not but evoke a positive response in them. John O'Hagan was among those who were stirred by the address, because later, when he had become an eminent Irish judge, he told Duffy, 'The night before I read Dillon's address I was a whig; next morning and ever after I was a nationalist.'[13] Others joined the ranks openly at about that time, or soon afterwards, so that, in the wake of Dillon's address, an understandable degree of euphoria prevailed in the small circle which revolved around Davis and Dillon. The fact, however, remains that they were all young Trinity men, whether Catholic or Protestant, none of whom came from the leading families of the old Ascendancy class. What is more important, none of them had established himself by making a mark on society and it was imprudent to imagine that they could do so on those who held power in Ireland by taking a stand which the upper classes rejected. Unless they could win converts from among the eminent and respected, the likelihood was that they would have to rely on the Catholic masses who were, as Dillon had admitted, of the 'humbler classes'. As a student of history, Davis had to be aware that the powerless masses had never achieved their objectives except through force and the outcome of force had been singularly fruitless in Ireland. Once the masses had power through the ballot box the matter was different, but the democratic process required conviction which came through intellectual formation and emotional stimulation. That task of education lay ahead, but the dilemma remained. There was no way to win the Catholic masses without O'Connell, but to win them with O'Connell was virtually to ensure that national unity would not be achieved. That situation prevailed despite the large-mindedness of O'Connell in whom there was no bigotry, but his championing of the Catholic masses had placed him and them in opposition to the interests of conservative Catholics as well as those of Irish Protestants. J. M. Hone put it well, 'O'Connell even continued the chief effects of the Union – namely, the diminution of the political influence of the gentry – and thus this advocate of Repeal did more (from the point of view of the propertied classes) than anyone else to render the Union a necessity!'[14] There is no indication that the young men were aware of that dilemma.

It was fortunate that, at exactly this time, a practical and more experienced person entered Davis's life when he met Charles Gavan Duffy. Duffy was born on 12 April 1816 in Monaghan, which made him twenty-five and therefore younger than both Davis and Dillon. The son of a well-to-do shopkeeper, he attended a Presbyterian school, but his Catholicism and nationalism blended to make him, as he boasted, the 'first Catholic emancipated in Ireland'. Like Davis, he was a voracious reader and his horizons expanded through his friendship with Matt Trimble, son of a British army officer, the painter Henry MacManus and Terence Bellew MacManus. The latter remained steadfast to the cause to which he pledged his life on Tara Hill, suffered imprisonment in Van Diemen's Land after the rising at Ballingarry in 1848 and died in exile in San Francisco in 1861.[15]

Duffy had started writing as a cadet journalist for a paper in Belfast and, in 1836, he obtained employment, still as a cadet, on the staff of Michael Staunton's *Morning Register* in Dublin. He was disappointed to find that, in the newspaper world, there was no enthusiasm for Repeal, which at the time was practically in abeyance as an objective to be striven for, rather than talked about. Despite the fact that, through overwork, he was ill throughout 1838, he kept busy educating himself so that in 1839 he was able to enrol as a law student at King's Inns in Dublin. In that same year he returned to Belfast as founding editor of the *Belfast Vindicator*, a new, Catholic, bi-weekly paper which he was able to buy in August. The paper was a consistent supporter of O'Connell and in it Duffy, together with others, including James Clarence Mangan, wrote to such effect that Repeal meetings were soon organised throughout the North and a branch of the Repeal Association was founded in Belfast.[16]

On a Saturday in early January 1841, O'Connell slipped unnoticed into Belfast. He put up at a hotel but was unable to attend Mass on Sunday because of the danger of assault. On Tuesday he spoke to an assembled crowd from the balcony of the hotel, but his words were drowned by the surrounding tumult. The mob tried to break into the office of the *Vindicator* and broke its windows. To an excited and overwrought crowd, the firebrand parson, Reverend Cooke, explained why Repeal had to be rejected. First, Protestant liberties would be put in jeopardy by the rise of a Catholic ascendancy. Secondly, the prosperity and industrial growth of Ulster stemmed from Protestant enterprise and, finally, the future of Ulster lay in its capacity to serve the markets of the Empire. They were arguments with a strong appeal to the worthy burghers of Belfast and their industrial labouring class but O'Connell, who had to be smuggled out of the city, and Duffy, who had grown up with the bitterness of sectarian hatreds all around him, each learned a lesson as to what kind of liberties Catholics could expect to enjoy in Ulster.[17]

In the spring of 1841 Duffy visited Dublin to continue his studies in law and he met Dillon at the office of the *Morning Register*. He was immediately drawn to him as a kindred spirit and as a fellow Catholic. On the next day Dillon took him to meet Davis in the committee room of the Repeal Association at the Corn Exchange. Duffy did not immediately warm to Davis whom he thought was inclined to self-esteem, an estimate which he admitted later was 'extremely unjust' because Davis was 'the greatest and best of his generation'. He was, however, forcibly struck by the vigour and freshness of the attitude to nationality of the two friends, given the prevailing cynicism he had encountered elsewhere but, because of the brevity of his stay in Dublin, he did not get past a first acquaintance. He also met Dr Gray, who had given up practising medicine to become the new proprietor of the *Freeman's Journal* and thereby the most powerful figure in Catholic journalism in the capital. Duffy wrote that Gray was then twenty-six, but 'looked barely twenty years of age'. The old world was already passing and the new one about to start. The men who would lead it were all in their twenties, with Dillon the oldest by a few months, followed by Davis who was to turn twenty-seven in October 1841.[18]

Despite his comparative youth, Duffy was already an experienced journalist wise in the ways of the newspaper world with a keen head for business, quality of writing, likely readership and circulation. Furthermore, Duffy was about to marry Emily McLoughlin,[19] whose father was a Belfast merchant of some means, he was ambitious and he knew that Dublin would hold out prospects both in journalism and in the legal profession that were lacking in Belfast. He could thus contribute qualities to a partnership which both Davis and Dillon lacked. Experience had also taught him that he could not run a paper single-handed if it was to be more than a mere provincial organ. He had few contacts in the capital and he was mindful that he lacked the standing that passing through Trinity seemed to give to its alumni, such as Davis and Dillon. At the time, however, the conviction that a new format was needed to take their thoughts and enthusiasm to the public had not formed in the minds of Davis and Dillon. Duffy, for his part, still had the pressing matter of running his own paper to keep himself busy so he returned to Belfast while the others continued their various pursuits in Dublin.

His increasing involvement with the *Citizen* took up a great deal of Davis's time in the first half of 1842 but it gave him a semi-public profile in the rarified world of his readers. Little, however, is known of his private life in that period except that he remained at home in his mother's house where he increasingly found a 'great ally' in his thoughts and actions on nationality in his sister Charlotte, 'a tiny, fiery woman'.[20] He would assuredly have caused considerable unease to his mother and to his brother, John, had he shared his thoughts at the dinner table on the current visit of the members of Dublin Corporation to Queen Victoria, the purpose of which was to invite her to Ireland. Davis thought that the visit was worse than a waste of time because they could offer nothing to her except 'kind hearts' and 'a little loyalty'. He pointed out that it was well to remember the expense of the visit of 'George the Fat', whose coming to Ireland in 1821 nearly ruined them financially, and that during the visit, 'the country seemed guilty of reverence to the vilest of men'. The Repeal of the Union would be a more practical way of enriching Dublin than any flying visit by 'the Imperial Magistrate' but, were she to come, she would be treated with respect and 'with the courtesy due to her station and sex'. His attitude both to the royal personage and the proposed visit was in marked contrast to that which O'Connell had shown twenty years previously when the newly-crowned George IV had visited Ireland. During that visit, O'Connell's servility was such that it even 'aroused disgust and contempt among the liberals of England'; Tom Moore berated him as 'preeminent in blarney and inconsistency' and Byron wrote of his 'welcome of tyrants'.[21]

Meanwhile, in Belfast, Duffy continued to write the greater part of the material for the *Vindicator* and laid down a format in it of editorials, correspondence, international news and comment on such places as China, India and Afghanistan, all interspersed with poetry and ballads. In that way he continued to refine his editorial methods, experimented with the paper's contents and satisfied himself, when the *Vindicator* went close to overhauling the circulation of his local rival, the ultra-Tory *Northern Whig*, that he had found a successful format. In May, he was prosecuted for libelling the system that held sway in Ulster of packing juries with Protestants and even the Tory press condemned the prosecution except for his rival, which would surely have wanted to see him out of the way. The jury in the case, itself totally Protestant, took only ten minutes to find him guilty so Duffy, unwilling to give comfort to his enemies and be constrained by a prison sentence, apologised for the words found to be in contempt of the administration of justice.[22]

In the spring of 1842, Duffy returned to Dublin and met Davis and

Dillon in the hall of the Four Courts where, as they were gowned, they were clearly involved in some form of legal activity. It probably had to do with the registers of voters as there is no indication that Davis, for his part, then or later, ever engaged in other forms of legal work. They disrobed and all three set off for a walk in the Phoenix Park. Duffy remembered that, 'sitting under a noble elm in the park, facing Kilmainham', he outlined to them his project for a weekly paper to meet the ends they held in common of raising up 'Ireland morally, socially and politically' so as to put 'the sceptre of self-government into her hands'. It is worth recalling that, of the three, Duffy was the only one with funds and the previous ventures in journalism of the other two had proved unsuccessful. Unsurprisingly, it was decided that Duffy would find the money and be the editor, while all three would work on getting contributors. Davis said he could rely on recruiting John Cornelius O'Callaghan whose *The Green Book*, a collection of mediocre poetry but with valuable historical notes, had achieved some distinction since its publication in the previous year.[23] Dillon spoke for John O'Hagan and John Pigot while Duffy offered Mangan, Terence McMahon Hughes, the London-based journalist who was Duffy's cousin and brother of his second wife Susan, and O'Neill Daunt, who had been secretary to O'Connell and who had already agreed with Duffy's plans. They parted on the understanding that they would meet again in the summer and launch the, as yet, unnamed journal in the autumn. It was not mere hyperbole when T. W. Moody, on the centenary of Davis's death in 1945, said in an address at Trinity College, 'Thus began what was to prove the most notable journalistic venture in Irish history.' It was also the most decisive in its effects over the next century.[24]

While Duffy was winding up his affairs in Belfast, Davis continued to mull over the prospective publication. He was especially hesitant about the prospects of a paper that would only come out once a week, and he had good reason to do so given the abundance of local papers circulating in Dublin at that time, as well as others, such as the *Times*, that arrived daily from London and elsewhere. There were eleven Dublin papers and, although their sales were mostly small, they each had an established readership which could prove hard to break into. At the end of the September quarter in 1843 the Dublin papers, their editorial bent and their circulation figures were, *Saunders News Letter* (daily, ultra-Tory, 2,314); *Evening Mail* (Orange, ultra-Tory, anti-Peel, 940); *Evening Packet* (government organ, moderate, 1,371); *Warder* (Orange, Sunday paper, 6,000); *Evening Post* (Whig, 2,769); *Freeman's Journal* (daily, Repeal, 1,293); *Evening Freeman,* (Repeal, 1,192); *Weekly Freeman,* (Repeal, 6,650); *World* (Repeal, 2,077); *Pilot* (Repeal, thrice weekly, 1,615) and *Weekly Register* (Repeal, 2,461). Thus, there were six Repeal papers in the capital, as well as five anti-Repeal, so that the field seemed saturated. Moreover, three of the papers, the *Warder*, the *Freeman* and the *Register* came out at the weekend and had a wide readership so that even that end of the market seemed captured.[25]

Davis was also subjected to advice from his old friends, Wallis and Madden. Wallis told him that the educated classes never read weeklies and warned him that, once established, the new paper would fall under the control of O'Connell and the other elders of the Repeal Association. According to Wallis, they already regarded Davis and Dillon with some derision given the failure of their venture with the *Morning Register*. Furthermore, was there room for a new Repeal paper alongside the *Pilot*, an O'Connellite organ, as well as the pro-Repeal *Freeman's Journal* which was a powerful and much-respected voice among Catholics? Perhaps it would be better to give up the idea of a paper and stick to that of a magazine of substance. As a result, Davis became increasingly cautious and even suggested that, to run alongside the new venture, they buy the *Evening Freeman* which at least came out twice a week, even though it was ailing. Gray refused to sell, bought the *Morning Register* which had struggled fitfully on since Davis and Dillon had almost brought it to ruin, amalgamated it with the *Freeman's Journal* and by his venture into rationalisation inadvertently opened a possible space for a new publication.[26]

However, the prospect that attracted Davis the most was one which appealed to his old loyalties and to his recognition that the *Citizen* had done valuable service in awakening a sense of nationality in a small but influential circle in Dublin, as well as giving him considerable scope as a writer. Wallis suggested that it would be better to put the money and manpower into the *Citizen* which, once strengthened, would serve to educate its readers further on the question of Irish nationality and help to win Protestants to the cause. He further argued that the local newspapers were not read by the people with means and education, thus rendering futile any addition to their number. Davis was so swayed with this idea that he pointed out to Duffy that, while he was not going to abandon the projected publication, the time he may have available beyond his services to the *Citizen* would be so limited that he would scarcely be of use.[27]

Amid all this vacillation Davis seems to have overlooked the fact that the newly-wed Duffy was the one who was prepared to give up a flourishing paper in Belfast and risk his means by putting them into the new project. He, nonetheless, completed his part of the bargain agreed upon in Phoenix Park by which he and Dillon would each write a prospectus for the new paper. Having done his best, he sent his draft to Dillon for perusal. He already knew that Dillon, with all his great qualities, sometimes lacked perseverance and that ill-health often made it difficult for him to fulfil his promises. In the event, when Dillon received Davis's letter which, as well as the prospectus, contained his plans regarding the *Citizen*, he came to the rescue with a sensible, straightforward return letter which clarified things considerably. He rejected alternatives to the new paper out of hand and made it plain that he would not join Davis in any attempt to invigorate the *Citizen*, much less join the group of young men whom Wallis had in mind to foster it. At the same time, Dillon, however, wished Davis well and hoped that the revamped *Citizen* would be a success, although he had no confidence that it would change from being a money-losing venture to a profitable one or that its readership would grow. Dillon was in a mood to be absolutely direct with Davis and told him that he was unenthusiastic about the prospectus which Davis had written, while admitting that, due to pressing concerns, he had been unable to write one himself. He sent Davis's original back in the hope that he would improve it, remarking, 'It would be highly desirable to have a good prospectus, and you have done first-rate things in that way.'[28]

Davis, who valued very highly both Dillon's close friendship and his keenness of judgement, must have felt more decided after Dillon's blunt refusal to cooperate because he told his old friend of Trinity days, Cadwallader Waddy, that he proposed to return to journalism in the autumn but in a way that would not take up the time he had given to the *Morning Register*. He thanked Waddy for a report he had sent him on children's employment, 'which is a most awful account of *Old* England or New England or whatever that triangle to the east of Ireland is called'. He asked him whether he had seen 'the very treasonable papers' he had been writing on the Afghan war in the *Citizen*, referred to the case against Duffy and thought the judge had 'damned himself past recovery'. He was confounded that, 'to keep the ball up', a printer in Drogheda was being prosecuted 'for publishing the *Shan Van Vocht*! Only think of such madness. Is it possible Peel sanctions this?' At least he was able to take some comfort from these episodes of Tory hostility and thank God 'for with a persecuting govt [sic] we need only be true to ourselves and Ireland will be ready whenever an opportunity offers to emancipate herself'. At the end, perhaps not wishing that anyone would have their attention drawn to his admission that his articles on the Afghan war were 'very treasonable', Davis asked Waddy to burn the letter.[29]

On the next day, 7 July 1842, Davis wrote to Madden bewailing the fact that his friend seemed to have withdrawn both in body and spirit 'from us Irishers' and begged him to write something 'for the twig you so richly nourished – the *Citizen*', which he and the others had decided to keep going for a time at least. He also said with evident happiness that, although he was in 'savage health', on the following Tuesday he would leave Dublin with Webb for a tour of the north, given that he had taken no holiday in the previous summer. They proposed to take in Down, Belfast, the Antrim cliffs, Derry and perhaps Donegal and return by the Fermanagh lakes. He said that he could be contacted through Duffy at the *Vindicator* office until the 25th and that on his return he would 'take another dash at the press here, but under better auspices than last time'. He thereby made it plain that he intended to embark fully on the new venture with Duffy and Dillon. Madden replied offering a contribution on Stephen Woulfe, the Catholic liberal lawyer who, after Emancipation, had become chief baron in Ireland. Davis wrote back from near Drogheda on the northern trip and said that he and Webb had been over the Boyne battleground, but had yet to visit Benburb and Belfast, so that it was clear he proposed to take as leisurely and as full a trip as possible.[30]

Despite the fact that he felt 'sun-stricken and plethoric', Davis nevertheless had embarked on an important and thoughtful analysis of the Irish situation to Madden, which helps to illustrate how his thoughts were developing. While admitting that the machinery then working for Repeal would not be successful under the present circumstances, he felt that 'within ten or fifteen years England must be in peril.' Under such changed circumstances the English statesman would be forced to give way over Ireland. Yet, during that same summer, a general strike was underway in Britain. It was the first such strike in any country, and a later writer judged it as 'more serious than the Chartist disturbances of 1839'. In the event, the government was forced to take decisive action to put it down. Davis seemed to take no notice of the strike, which indicates that he only saw England threatened by foreign powers, probably France or America.[31] Any possible threat to English social and economic stability from within did not occur to Davis because he could see the consequences of the industrial revolution only on a semi-spiritual level. Accordingly, his principal conclusion was that 'Modern Anglicanism', which could be called 'Englishism' or even 'Yankeeism', was simply a variety of Utilitarianism. This 'damned thing' was preached from the pulpits, practised by the professions and believed in by the politicians and hence threatened 'to corrupt the lower classes, who are still faithful and romantic'. Brought into Ireland under the Whigs and now the favourite creed of the Tories, it had become a religion which 'measures prosperity by exchangeable value, measures duty by gain, and limits desires to clothes, food and respectability'. As their foremost duty, Irish patriots had to fight it by 'every literary and political engine'. Indeed, it was a greater danger than papal supremacy, which he would rather submit to than to see such a form of 'Anglicanism' succeed. He was confident that papal supremacy would not last longer than twenty years because a few laymen like himself could conquer it, whereas 'Anglicanism' and its pernicious effects would endure.[32]

Furthermore, Davis said he would prefer to take 'the hazard of open war' rather than lie down before the inroads of Anglicanism, sure in the knowledge that, with success, the military leaders would put the bigots down and 'establish a thoroughly national government'. Failure would at least mean that, before death, they could 'throw up huge barriers against English vices, and, dying, to leave example and a religion to the next age'. He concluded by again saying that he was getting involved in the press, but asked Madden not to tell anyone. He was certain that he needed to get more deeply involved in active pursuits, otherwise 'my mind would fall into the old melancholy or the older love which wasted most of my life.' Given that no other candidate can be offered for 'the older love', Davis surely meant a purely scholarly involvement in literature and history for their own sake. The use of the expression 'melancholy', coupled with the admission that it was a constant factor in his life and that Madden knew of it, suggests that Davis was afflicted with an illness that later became known in its various forms as depression. Whether he suffered from a mild form of recurring depression, or from a graver form, is unclear but it is a matter that warrants serious consideration as an explanation for his mood swings from elation to 'melancholy'.[33]

What the convert Madden thought of this diatribe against his newly-chosen Anglicanism is not known, but he had probably long since become inoculated against attacks of such a kind by Davis. In any event, Davis's words reveal that he had lost all hope for, and probably even belief in, Anglicanism as he now understood it to have become. He was not speaking of the Church of England, nor of its expression as the Church of Ireland, based on the Thirty-Nine articles, but of a system which he now saw as a religious, social and political expression of English capitalism and imperialism. He was convinced that its effects in Ireland would change the very nature and characteristics of the Irish people, as well as inhibit the development of any vital concept of nationality. Davis did not believe that such effects would flow from Catholicism, even were it to become supreme. However, were Catholicism to do so, the worst effect would be to temporarily 'leave the people mad ... but not sensual and mean'. That he even contemplated the need for revolution in the event of being forced to suffer 'the iron gates of that filthy dungeon [Utilitarian Anglicanism] to close on us' is indicative of how great a danger he perceived it to be.[34] Small wonder that, for the rest of his life, he showed no close connection with the faith and the Church in which he had been reared. On the other hand, he wanted to leave a religion to the Irish people, by which he meant Catholicism, even though he feared the possibility of it having stupefying effects on them.

At the end of their trip around the north Davis left Webb, who joined his wife and family, and went to Belfast. The city held a strong fascination for him and he wanted to visit Duffy and talk over the prospectus. While there he was given at first hand some idea of the obstacles to be met in the form of committed Protestant support for the Union, whereas previously he had hoped for a union of Protestant and Catholics in 'the Athens of the North'. To Duffy, Belfast was 'as ugly and sordid as Manchester' and was thronging with 'noisy fanatics', congregated in their 'hideous little Bethels' where they fanned the flames of their bigotry. Davis himself seemed an odd fish to Duffy's Catholic friends who had been reared in a city from which the spirit of Wolfe Tone and Emmett was long gone, to be replaced by that of Cooke who had converted the Ulster democrats to Unionism. The Ulster Catholics had no, or very little, experience of an educated Protestant who was also a nationalist but his meeting with the local Catholic bishop and clergy, to whom Duffy introduced him, was fruitful. They had never met an Irish Protestant who was prepared to assert that he and his co-religionists were as much part of Ireland as those Catholics with whom he now stood in defending and propagating Irish nationality.[35]

The concept of nationality which Davis had developed grew from his inner being rather than as a result of what others had taught him. Even Wallis was unable to make the same claim for Davis as he did for Dillon whom he stated had become a nationalist under his tutelage. With Davis, who never used the word nationalism which had not yet come into use, nationality was not merely a sentiment but a conviction shaped by his own experience as an Irishman exposed to the conditions of his country and her people since the Union. It was fed on the long traditions of Ireland which he discovered in his reading and by his exposure to Ireland of the past, with her physical characteristics and her monuments. More especially, it arose in an innate way from the depths of his own character which instinctively forged in him a deep bond with the people of Ireland and, more particularly, the Catholic majority. That his concept of nation and of nationality was unstructured and that it never evolved into a clear formulation of the shape of the Irish state in an independent Ireland of the future, is evident from his writings. Freedom to choose and decide that future was enough, while theoretical formulations could wait their turn. That, when the time came, no clear concept of the state emerged in an independent Ireland says much for the power of Davis's initial, but innocent, dream as well as for the strength of the state that the English evolved and imposed on Ireland over centuries.

It is unlikely that Duffy and Dillon, much less those others of the Trinity College world, who had been influenced in varying degrees by Davis would have been drawn to follow him had they detected in his ideas on Irish nationality the atheistic and anticlerical bent which was clear in Mazzini and most of the continental thinkers. The same holds true for German romanticism which had little, if anything, to teach the Irish. On the other hand, the idea of uniting Catholics, Protestants and Dissenters was fundamental in Davis. Such an aspiration resembled that of Tone and the United Irishmen, although it had become much more difficult to achieve since O'Connell started his ultimately successful agitation for Emancipation and, since 1841, for Repeal of the Union in a much more determined way than had previously been the case.

Duffy was the foremost to admit the spell that Davis held over them. It was a spell which grew from his person, his gifts, his character and his learning. Duffy had been chosen as the logical editor of their proposed publication because of his experience in the newspaper world and recognised as its owner, given that he was prepared to fund it. Nonetheless, he was already convinced that Davis's contribution was absolutely fundamental to the success of the venture and he was prepared to pay him as a full-time fellow editor and writer. Dillon was understandably concerned about his legal career and was convinced that he had to devote almost all his time to it, so that he told Duffy not to depend too much on him and, in early 1843, Thomas MacNevin took his place as a regular writer. Duffy, admittedly years later when the magnetism of O'Connell had grown dim, generously accepted that 'Davis was our true leader. Not only had nature endowed him more liberally, but he loved labour better, and his mind had traversed regions of thought and wrestled with problems still unfamiliar to his confederates. His comrades had the same careless confidence in him men have in the operations of nature, where irregularity and aberration do not exist.'[36] It was a vast trust to place in a young man with such limited experience and one, moreover, who had shown himself so hot-headed in his brief editorship of Staunton's *Morning Register*. Furthermore, despite his 'habitual temperance' were he asked the day of the month he was unlikely to be able to state it, and he still 'dressed and walked as carelessly as a student'. Nevertheless, they had no one else to whom they could turn. Isaac Butt had temporarily taken the path of Torydom, while O'Connell had grown old with the years of combat and seemed to have nothing new to say about Ireland and her future, although he was still the acknowledged leader of the Irish masses and could be crossed only at peril. In short, were there to be a leader of the young men it had to be Davis.

The first and most important suggestion made by Davis, and accepted by Duffy, was to call the new weekly the *Nation*, rather than the *National* as Duffy had suggested. There has been an attempt to see in such a name a relationship or an apeing of the Paris journal of the same name, but there is no evidence that such a thought ever crossed Davis's mind or that the ideas of Mazzini and other continental nationalists were part of his thinking as has been suggested.[37] Davis had never been exposed to revolutionary thought at first hand, especially that of the Italians, nor is it clear that he even read their ideas on nationality, at least before the foundation of the *Nation*. It seems to be more the case that Davis had imbibed a great deal of material from continental historians and social theorists, such as De Beaumont, Sismondi and Thierry, and he was prepared to apply them to Ireland to the degree that they fitted the case.

When Duffy and Davis considered the prospectus, they only had Davis's draft to work on as neither of the others had managed to get anything down on paper. They were fully aware of the importance of a clearly-stated objective in their future writing and it had to be one upon which their readers could judge them. It was essential that it define Irish nationality in a way that would be immediately intelligible, even to those who rejected it, and at the same time be couched in terms that would also appeal to the virtue of patriotism. Davis's draft promised that they would conduct the new paper 'ably and carefully ... boldly, zealously, independently, and without personal offence'. He was convinced that 'the New Mind which has grown up' went far beyond the mere winning of battles against the 'sectarian ascendancy'. The result was that a new spirit was abroad that wanted to redress a wider range of wrongs than those that flowed from the Ascendancy and achieve higher victories in the form of education, pride in the past and independence. The press, and especially the liberal press which had a greater responsibility to the public, had proved inadequate so far in promoting those objectives.

While the journal was an absolute necessity to help the new movements growing up in Ireland and to make their fruits 'more racy of the soil', above all it had 'to direct the popular mind and sympathies of all educated men of all parties to the great end of Nationality'. To do that, the journal had to be 'free from the quarrels, the interest, the wrongs, and even the gratitude of the past.' With a single amendment and a small insertion, suggested by Duffy, the prospectus was completed by giving the names of the intending contributors as a warrant of good faith, together with the signatures of a group of supporters, including O'Connell's son John. The major part ran,

> Nationality is their first great object – a Nationality which will not only raise our people from their poverty, by securing to them the blessings of a *Domestic Legislature*, but inflame them and purify them with a lofty and heroic love of country – a Nationality of the spirit as well as of the letter – a Nationality which may come to be stamped upon our manners, and literature, and our deeds – a Nationality which may embrace Protestant, Catholic and Dissenter – Milesian and Cromwellian – the Irishman of a hundred generations and the stranger who is within our gates; – not a Nationality which would prelude civil war, but which would establish internal union and external independence; – a Nationality which would be recognised by the world, and sanctified by wisdom, virtue and prudence.[38]

The prospectus was printed and given wide circulation. It was decided that the first number would be on the streets on Saturday 8 October but Duffy had a great deal to do winding up his affairs in Belfast and disposing of the *Vindicator* to James M. Conway.[39] On the other hand, Davis was determined to continue with his holiday and, as further proof of his indecision about the long-term viability of the *Nation* and his own role in it, he had promised to contribute only the one article per week. Before leaving Belfast he did manage to put together an editorial for Duffy's *Vindicator* which was entitled 'A plea for Repeal' but it was much more a direct appeal to the Presbyterians of the north to join the rest of Ireland in striving for nationality. ''Tis a sad thing to find the Ulster Protestants ill-affected to Irish freedom', and 'the Irishmen who resist the restoration of Ireland's nationality, and look to English principles and English arms, will be bitterly remembered.' He reminded the Presbyterians that 'they are Irishmen, not English' and that it was absurd to fear a Catholic ascendancy. He asserted that the Catholics had not persecuted when they had power and, in their hearts, the right to differ, the right to go wrong and the right to the completest religious equality were all enshrined. He called on the Presbyterians to 'disencumber themselves of the calumnious traditions of Musgrave, and Archbishops King and Temple, and to remember that 'Ireland is young, uncorrupted, unAnglicised'. Why then attempt 'to chain her to decaying England?' There is no recorded reaction among Presbyterians to Davis's plea, but it is unlikely that many of them read it.[40]

Duffy had moved to Dublin by mid-September to attend to the practical aspects of launching the paper. Together with orders from country outlets, a healthy list of subscribers had been obtained and Duffy was heartened by the fact that the two earliest, Eugene O'Curry and John O'Donovan, were men with a love for genuine Irish literature and widely respected as eminent scholars of the Irish past. At the same time there were pessimists, especially among the Dublin journalists, who warned Duffy that the new paper would not be sustainable. Alone in Dublin, with both Davis and Dillon out of town, Duffy's increasing anxiety was understandable. On 23 September, he wrote to Davis to say that he had been expecting his return, that publication of the first number was only two weeks away and that 'there are a vast number of questions to be considered in respect of it, which will require time and you. Pray come home'.[41] Whether this plea had its effect or not, Davis did arrive back in Dublin on 7 October to find, understandably, given his absence, that there was no possibility of meeting the deadline set for the next day and that several well-meaning prophets of doom were saying that the delay would cause the death of the new-born paper as public expectation would dwindle when its appetite was left unsatisfied. Perhaps the feeling that he was in some measure responsible for what had occurred caused him to get immediately into the turmoil of that last week and he managed to get four pieces together over the next few days. In any case he had quickly learnt that, were the *Nation* to succeed, his wholehearted involvement was fundamental.

One week in arrears, the first edition of the *Nation* came out on 15 October 1842, the day after Davis's twenty-eighth birthday, with a print-run of 12,000 copies. The 16-page paper sold out on the first day, despite the high cost of sixpence per copy. The format, based on the *Vindicator*, was set from the start and Duffy's hand was clearly discernible. The new paper contained no illustrations and was replete with advertisements, including one from a dentist who assured 'the Nobility and Gentry' that he would deal with their teeth on 'the best principles'. The front page was taken up with the O'Connell Tribute and the need for subscriptions so as to keep the Liberator free to devote all his time to 'the restoration of our National Independence'. Two full pages were given to a report on the Repeal Association, there were law reports, and a large section devoted to communications from correspondents, with replies to them. A racing column was included, but not persevered with later. The readers of the new paper had been drawn to it because they wanted to know what it had to tell them on the matter of Irish nationality. They found their answer in the editorials and verse, in the section given to literature and in the articles on local and foreign affairs, all of which were mixed together in an attempt to make the whole an appealing fare.[42]

The first thing to strike a reader was the motto. 'To create and foster public opinion, and make it racy of the soil.' Despite his pro-Union convictions and his reluctance to support the paper, Madden had suggested the motto which came from a speech by Stephen Woulfe, although Davis had used it previously in the *Citizen*. Woulfe was speaking at Westminster during a debate upon municipal reform in Ireland when Peel asked what good corporations would do for such a 'pauper' country as Ireland. Woulfe replied, 'They will go far to create and foster public opinion and to make it racy of the soul.' It was a most felicitous motto indeed in that it struck the right note immediately, both to heart and to intellect.[43]

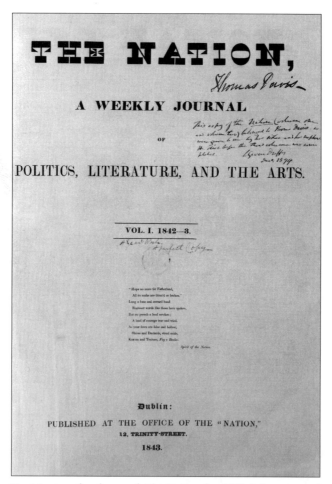

Davis's signed volume of *The Nation* for 1842-3 (courtesy of Royal Irish Academy).

Duffy's unsigned editorial hit at Ireland's 'mendicant spirit' which he said must be replaced by a true concept of nationality which rejected rubbish 'nicknames' such as Orangemen and Ribbonmen, Whigmen and Torymen. He only recognised two parties in Ireland, 'those who suffer from her National degradation and those who profit by it'. In his article on 'Aristocratic Institutions', landlords and land reform, Dillon quoted Mirabeau, 'Society is composed of three classes – those who work, those who beg and those who rob.' He thought that 'The existence of a landed aristocracy is incompatible with public institutions' and that the landlords were 'the real cause of this unnatural, monstrous combination of poverty and profusion' which would soon cause the poor to eat grass instead of potatoes. He thus drew on his first-hand experience of rural conditions in Ireland, especially of the kind he had witnessed since his youth in Roscommon.

To celebrate 'The Nation's First Number', Mangan put his conviction on the need to emancipate the tenantry into ringing verse, but, for him, of dubious quality,

> We announce a New Era – be this our first news-
> When the serf-grinding landlords shall shake in their shoes,
> While the ark of a bloodless yet mighty Reform
> Shall emerge from the flood of the popular storm!

Mangan's words asserted that the work of 1829 was unfinished but that it would continue along the pacifist path traced by O'Connell and use the power of a united people rather than the sword. T. M. Hughes reinforced the same message with verses entitled 'We Want No Swords', in which he said that freedom would be won by something the Irish could gain, namely 'the conquering Mind', rather than by the spilling of blood, whether 'barbarian blood or Roman'. Davis made a quiet start with a review of the October *Citizen* but he also brought in a few of his own themes. He gave his hearty approval to temperance, provided it did not turn an Irishman into a 'phlegmatic, monotonous glutton' like John Bull and he wanted the Irish to have their own music back so that they could 'mourn in frantic strains the baffled hopes of '98'. Given that O'Connell and his followers never mentioned the rising of '98, his words indicated that Davis would continue to be his own man. He submitted his own poem, 'The Geraldine's Daughter', to Duffy without claiming authorship and it was run in full. Finally, he wrote a 'mock proclamation to the Irish soldiers', which was ground he had covered before, as well as an article on 'The English army in Afghanistan', drawing on the research he had already done on that topic. These first pieces perhaps indicated the rush to get the first edition together but they did, however, give him the opportunity to proclaim to a wider audience than that enjoyed by the *Citizen*, that the action of the English in invading Afghanistan had 'no pretext save a lie, and no design save aggrandisement'.[44]

On the day of publication of the first edition Davis wrote to tell Madden that it had been sold out before noon and that impatient newsmen had broken the office window in their rush to get more copies. He outlined the contents and encouraged Madden, who had been strongly opposed to the whole project, to contribute something himself, which he began to do later on a regular basis. On 17 October, Wallis wrote to Davis and let forth some of his spleen. He was concerned that Davis seemed backward in keeping up his contributions to the *Citizen* and he again expressed his worry that the *Nation* would quickly become an O'Connellite organ and that Protestants would reject it for that reason. He had felt it better for them to eschew politics completely and rely on history and literature to build a new and united concept of nationality. But it was now too late and all Wallis could do was bewail the name of the paper, which he regarded as too 'holy' to permit a mere journal to claim it for itself, and to make fun of the founders because they had not printed ten times the number of the first copy, which would have sold, but 'you had not the spunk to venture.' However, Wallis was graciously lighthearted and threatened to pun Davis to shivers for his 'hebdomadal blasphemy' which was a cause of intense 'indig *"nation"*' and deserved 'all sorts of damn *"nation"*'.[45]

Whatever about the jealousies, unease or outright rejection of the paper by some among the newspaper world and the Dublin intelligentsia, success was instantaneous. Some added spice to the interest was perhaps given when it was known that Davis and Dillon, after their notoriety during the *Morning Register* debacle, were major contributors. Within a short time Duffy was able to claim that the *Nation's* circulation soon surpassed that of any other Irish paper and that it had a readership of 250,000, partly attributable to its availability in Repeal reading rooms throughout the country. The fact that the poor, or the illiterate, to whom it otherwise would not have been available, had it read to them as it was passed from hand to hand, also spread its message into quarters where others had not been heard. Henry MacManus painted a delightful scene entitled, 'Reading the *Nation'* of a group of people listening to an old man as he read them a copy of the paper, thereby expressing vividly the eagerness with which its arrival was awaited each week throughout Ireland and the attentive way in which its contents were received. The main reason for its success was that it had something much more positive to say than any other public organ, including the other Repeal journals, in response to the widespread thirst amongst large sections of the people for an understanding of nationality. That the new weekly said it with such vigour and clarity made its message so much more effective.

There can be no doubt but that the policy put forward so early in the *Nation* of achieving Repeal by peaceful means was deliberate and that Duffy, Davis and Dillon embraced it as a method of action. Even had they thought that moral means, as distinct from physical ones, would prove inadequate they were in no position to oppose them. Thus they had to go along with O'Connell because the Irish people were neither sufficiently united on the question of Repeal, nor sufficiently educated on the long list of grievances put forward as arguments for Repeal. They ranged from the state of the economy since the Union to the much more complex matter of land reform and a great deal of work would have to be done to make the people aware of such matters, and feel aggrieved to the degree that they would in any number take the means necessary to achieve their goals. Mere talk of independence and freedom was not enough to cause a mass movement of passive resistance and, so far, O'Connell had not spelt out in any practical way the steps he would take to motivate the Irish people in such a way that England would have no option but to listen and to act.

As a result, the young men were in a dilemma which the very act of throwing in their lot with the Repeal Association made inevitable. From the first issue of the *Nation* onwards the only path they could follow was to respond to the demands of the moment because they could not change the overall strategy imposed by O'Connell. It was idle, and destructive of morale, to look forward and ask what attitude they would adopt if and when the day came that the people were united and wanted a form of independence that England would not grant. From the beginning, therefore, the contradiction caused by spelling out consistently, logically and emotionally the need for independence, while proposing means for its achievement that had scarcely any hope whatever of success, meant that the problem lay hidden but never ceased to be relevant.

The other problem that was not addressed was the existence of the nation within the framework of a state that had been shaped by the British. To Davis, the fundamental striving had to be one of the spirit so that the concept of what it was to be Irish would revive in her people after the long centuries during which it had been virtually expunged in any practical sense. Yet, he and others knew that Ireland had long lived under British structures of civil government, including that of education in the past decade, which had shaped the mentality and responses of the Irish people at all levels. The old laws, the old structures of authority, even the relationship between Church and State that had evolved in Ireland since the conversion of her people to Christianity had largely passed away, to be replaced by other and alien forms. In effect, the civil state in Ireland had been shaped by foreigners for centuries and to a marked degree it was alien to Irish concepts of the organisation of the state. It was a frail vessel into which Davis and his friends wanted to pour the new wine of nationality, which thus ran the risk of remaining a literary, artistic and emotional ideal, an abstraction to be sung and spoken of and written about. It would be a thing of the spirit to which no flesh could be given until it was also outwardly expressed through the shape of the state. To disregard or to be unaware of that problem was to sow the seeds of another contradiction that would, eventually, prove more fatal than the choice between physical or moral force. In the end, to gain independence and not to possess the instruments to express it in a profoundly national .sense would perforce result in a nation truncated at its core. Meanwhile, the euphoria of success was there to be enjoyed and, as young men, Duffy, Dillon and Davis deserved to the full whatever happiness or sense of achievement came their way, for the moment at least.

References

1. See Duffy, *Young Ireland*, part 1, pp 24-9.
2. O'Connell to John O'Connell, 29 May, 1841 in O'Connell (ed.) *Correspondence*, vol. vi, p. 78.
3. Duffy, *Young Ireland*, pp 10-16; *Dublin Evening Post*, 1, 8, June 1841. The editor even spoke of Duffy's Belfast *Vindicator* as 'our excellent and indefatigable contemporary' which further proved its intention to seek any port in a storm because the *Vindicator* was emphatically a Repeal paper. Ibid., 27 May 1841.
4. See Davis to James Finn, 27 October 1841 asking for the return of £18, 'advanced by me for the use of the Committee'. F. S. Bourke collection, Ms 10,731 (6), NLI.
5. For the correspondence between Davis and Webb see Duffy, *Davis*, p. 735. The letter quoted on walking and Dublin is to Webb, from 61 Baggot Street and dated 4 August, 1841. Ibid., p. 74.
6. John Foster, *Essays in a series of letters to a friend*, 2 vols., third ed. (London, 1806). The copy of the work held in the RIA was owned by Davis and has his signature on the inside cover of volume one. The text is heavily scored with his customary markings.
7. Ibid., pp 94, 134, 162, 215.
8. *Dublin Evening Post*, 13 March, 20 May, 19 June, 3, 10, 20 July 1841; Oliver MacDonagh, *O'Connell*, pp 479-80.
9. Davis to Thomas Wyse, 10 July, 1841 in Wyse papers, Ms 15026, NLI.
10. Davis to Webb, 15 August, 1841 in Duffy, *Davis*, pp 75-77.
11. John Dillon, *An address to the College Historical Society* (Dublin, 1842), Tracts 1841-48, vol. xvii, Tract 27, Box 484. RIA. The address was given on 8 November 1841, but not within Trinity itself.

12. Ibid., passim.
13. See Duffy, *Davis*, pp 64-5.
14. Hone, *Davis*, p. 64.
15. See Jeanne Sheehy, *The rediscovery of Ireland's past: the Celtic revival 1830-1930* (London, 1980), p. 36 on MacManus. Sheehy also treats of Petrie, Burton, Ferguson, William Wilde and others, all of whom were contemporaries of, and many of whom were close to Davis.
16. For the foregoing on Duffy see Leon O'Broin, *Charles Gavan Duffy: patriot and statesman. The story of Charles Gavan Duffy (1816-1903)* (Dublin, 1967); Cyril Pearl, *The three lives of Gavan Duffy* (Sydney, 1979). Pearl, p. 9 says that Duffy met Davis and Dillon while they were working on the *Register* in 1839 which was impossible because they did not start with the paper until after Duffy left Dublin for Belfast. James Clarence Mangan (1803-49) was judged by some as the greatest Irish poet of his time. He was one of the writers whom Duffy approached to contribute to the *Vindicator*. Mangan replied that he was incapable of writing political material, but that he could contribute 'verses', some of which he sent. J. C. Mangan to Duffy, 4 May, 1840, Ms 12 P 19, RIA.
17. See Jonathon Bardon, *A history of Ulster* (Belfast, 1992), pp 255-6.
18. See Duffy, *Young Ireland*, part 1, p. 17; Duffy, *Davis*, p. 71. In both accounts Duffy says he first met Dillon and Davis in the autumn of 1841. The meeting had to have taken place between mid-April and the end of June and therefore in the spring. Prior to that time they had not joined the Repeal Association. After the end of June they were no longer connected with the *Morning Register*. Duffy can be forgiven for this and other minor lapses. He was writing over forty years after the events he describes.
19. See O'Sullivan, *Young Irelanders*, p. 25. Emily died in 1845. Their only child, John Gavan Duffy, became a cabinet minister in Australia. In 1846, Duffy married his cousin, Susan Hughes, who died in 1878. In 1881, he married Louise Hall of Cheshire, who died in 1890. Four daughters and six sons survived Duffy, who died in 1903.
20. See Joseph Hone (ed. with intro.), *The love story of Thomas Davis told in the letters of Annie Hutton* (Dublin, 1945), p. 5.
21. See manuscript of an article by Davis, May, 1842 in Ms 12 P 19, RIA, and MacDonagh, *O'Connell*, pp 175-77.
22. *Vindicator*, 11, 21 May; 22, 25, 26 June 1842. The circulation of Duffy's paper in June was 1,231 compared to 1,308 for the *Northern Whig*. Ibid., 25 June 1841.
23. John Cornelius O'Callaghan, *The Green Book or gleanings from the writing-desk of a literary agitator* (Dublin, 1841). O'Callaghan was admitted to the Bar in 1829. He was always loyal to O'Connell. See Anne M. Brady and Brian Cleeve, *A biographical dictionary of Irish writers* (Mullingar, 1985).
24. See Duffy, *Davis*, pp 71-72. and Moody, *Davis*, p. 27. Hughes was editor of the London *Charivari* which preceded the *Punch*. O'Neill Daunt remained a close associate and staunch supporter of O'Connell, so it was a wise strategy to include him. See W. J. O'Neill Daunt, *Ireland and her agitators* (Dublin, 1867), passim.
25. See Duffy, *Young Ireland*, pt. 1, p. 145. At the time, every copy of a paper bore a penny stamp allowing it free through the post. The Custom House issued quarterly returns of stamps, thus giving the number of papers printed. See also Jacob Venedey, *Ireland and the Irish during the Repeal year, 1843*, trans. from the German with notes by William Bernard MacCabe (Dublin, 1844), p. 155.
26. See O'Broin, *Duffy*, pp 7-8; Duffy, *Davis*, pp 78-81; Richard Davis, *The Young Ireland movement* (Dublin, 1987), pp 23-4.

27.	See Duffy, *Davis*, pp 78-9. Duffy was the only one of the original trio to leave any account of these matters. Given that he was constantly so careful to put the best gloss on anything to do with Davis, the mild note of criticism in this account makes it ring true.

28.	Dillon to Davis, no date but late June 1842 in Duffy, *Davis*, pp 79-81. Many of the letters by and to Davis in this period, which Duffy used for his biography of Davis, cannot now be located in the Duffy or Davis papers in the NLI or RIA, or elsewhere.

29.	Davis to Waddy, 6 July 1842. Ms 432, NLI. This letter is also printed in Duffy, *Davis*, p. 81 but with omissions and changes. The Shan Van Vogt, the 'poor old woman' was used to refer to Ireland in verse form.

30.	Madden to Davis, mid July, 1842 and Davis to Madden, 24 July, 1842 in Duffy, *Davis*, pp 81-2.

31.	Ibid. and F. C. Malher, 'The general strike of 1842' in R. Quinault and J. Stevenson (eds.), *Popular protest and public order, 1790-1920* (London, 1972), pp 115-40.

32.	Davis to Madden, 24 July 1842 in Duffy, *Davis*, p. 83.

33.	Ibid., pp 83-4.

34.	Ibid.

35.	Ibid., pp 84-5.

36.	See Duffy, *Young Ireland*, pp 32, 49, 50, 52 and Duffy, *Davis*, p. 369; Ó Cathaoir, *Dillon*, p. 26.

37.	For the suggestion re the Paris journal and Mazzini see Ó Broin, *Duffy*, p. 7.

38.	See the original prospectus pasted on the fly leaf of Davis's own volume of the first year of the *Nation* held in RIA. The inclusion of John O'Connell was a clever ploy by Duffy. John was his father's right hand man in all political matters and he would never have lent his name to the new journal without his father's acquiescence. John deserted before the first number but returned for a while when the paper became a success.

39.	*Vindicator*, 14 September, 1842.

40.	Ibid., 17 August, 1842.

41.	Duffy to Davis, 23 September 1842 in Ms 2644, NLI and in Duffy, *Davis*, p. 87 but edited slightly by him.

42.	For the first edition of the *Nation* and the background to its publication see the *Nation*, 15 October 1842. Davis's own run of the paper in its first three years is held in the Royal Irish Academy which I was kindly given permission to read. Davis signed the frontispiece of the bound volume, 1842-43 and wrote 'A Year's Work. A Perfect Copy'. Davis's copy was given to Duffy by Charlotte Davis. See also Duffy, *Davis*, pp 78-90; Moody, *Davis*, pp 27, 32-33; Hone, *Davis*, pp 69-72; Ó Cathoir, *Dillon*, pp 11-12; Richard Davis, *The Young Ireland movement*, pp 23-29.

43.	See A. Locker Lampson, *A consideration of the state of Ireland in the nineteenth century* (London, 1907), p. 210.

44.	*Nation*, 15 October 1842. For over a year, Davis identified most of the authors of the material it ran in each copy of the paper.

45.	See Davis to Madden, 15 October 1842 in Duffy, *Davis*, pp 89-90 and Wallis to Davis, 17 October, 1842 in Ms 2644, NLI.

Chapter 6

From past to present

Despite his hectic, but brief, involvement with the *Morning Register*, his more serious work on the *Citizen*, the euphoria of the election period, his momentous decision to join the Repeal Association and the heartsearching connected with the founding of the *Nation*, Davis had continued work on an academic project of considerable importance to him. He was an indefatigable worker whose singleness of purpose was plain to all about him, and the spiritual, intellectual and physical regime under which he had lived from his youth had brought him to a maturity of mind, expression and behaviour beyond his years. He kept his word once given, never lost his temper, refused to descend to petty criticism of individuals and had a capacity for deep and lasting friendships. His humble involvement with his work made him self-effacing and he often wanted to give credit to others for what he did himself. He lived a rigidly disciplined life both at home and at work and his main failing, a large one perhaps in a man so proud of his Gaelic spirit, was a lack of humour unless in the company of those few whom he called close friends. Nevertheless, there was nothing forbidding in his manner and those he trusted felt free to make fun of even the things he held to most dearly. Madden, to highlight Davis's pride in his ancestry, sometimes addressed him as 'Thomas O'Sullivan Davis', and Davis himself, perhaps to soften the formality of his name, no longer used Osborne after his early days at Trinity, but contented himself with either 'Thomas Davis' or, more simply, 'T.D.' as his signature.[1]

Davis had long been convinced that a huge step would be taken for the overall development of the Irish nation through an independent Parliament which would exclusively frame and implement laws for all the Irish people. An independent Parliament did not necessarily imply that all ties with the British Empire needed to be broken. The first step was the Parliament. With that in mind, he looked back to the Irish past to examine the nature of just such a Parliament and he chose that of James II, called in 1689 by a Catholic king and made up largely of Catholic members. It was the last independent Irish body that formulated legislation for the whole of the island, even if briefly. Davis studied its proceedings closely in order to judge whether the laws made by it were just and beneficial. He also wanted to establish whether an Irish parliament was capable of undertaking its own responsibilities without interference from abroad. He was aware that many of his co-religionists were convinced that, were Repeal successful and Ireland granted its own Parliament, they would suffer discrimination. Some of them harkened back to James's Parliament to prove their case and Davis wanted to see for himself whether their fears were historically justified.

His work appeared initially in the *Citizen* in early 1843 as a series of articles, but it does not appear to have caused any marked reaction perhaps because the *Citizen* was then in its death throes with its readership dropping to a devoted few. Although the first article had been praised in the *Freeman's Journal*, the fruits of Davis's extensive labours were then lost sight of until the 1870s when Duffy drew the articles to the attention of the foremost Irish historian of his age, William Lecky. Lecky thought that it was unfortunate that the articles had never been reprinted because he judged Davis's work as 'the best and fullest account of this Parliament with which I am acquainted' and said that the evidence had been 'collected and sifted with an industry and a skill that leave little to be desired'. He also thanked Duffy for making him aware of these 'most valuable but now almost forgotten papers'. Lecky clearly relied heavily on Davis's account of James's Parliament and it was probably his high estimate of the work that prompted Duffy, in his retirement at Nice, to edit the articles in book form in 1893.[2]

Principally, Davis's work on the Irish Parliament helps to establish his credentials as a serious scholar because it was the most important piece of research he ever undertook. As well as explaining the concerted thrust for Repeal he had thrown himself into with such vigour, he also helped to clarify the role of the 'Irish Parliamentary tradition as the central core of Irish political development'.[3] Furthermore, his work throws light on how his mind was developing before he started to write for the *Nation*. His ideas on nationality, to be expressed later, as he hoped, by the Irish people in a Parliament of their own, he saw enshrined in embryonic form in that under James. That judgement makes Davis's work even further worthy of study.[4]

James II succeeded to the throne in 1685. He was a Catholic who made it plain that 'though he would have the Irish see that they had a king of their own religion, and that they should enjoy all the freedom thereof, yet he would have them see, too, that he looked upon them as a conquered people'.[5] Nonetheless, he suspended the penal laws and tried to bring about religious equality and toleration in his realm. He began to redress the balance of power away from the Protestant minority in Ireland by giving the Catholics a considerable role in its government but even some Protestants admitted that, under James, they enjoyed greater privileges in Ireland than they had ever conceded to Catholics when themselves in the ascendancy. However, James's Catholicity was not acceptable in England to the aristocratic and wealthy elite whose power was considerable. As a result, secret negotiations took place to secure the succession of William of Orange, who landed at Torbay in England on 4 November 1688. In December, James fled to France to enlist the support of Louis XIV who gave him a little of everything, but none of what he most needed, soldiers. The throne was pronounced vacant on 6 February 1689, the crown offered to William and Mary on 13 February and, poorly equipped to wage war, James landed near Cork at Kinsale on 12 March. He proceeded to Dublin where he was accepted with genuine acclaim by the Irish. Among his first acts was a proclamation calling a sitting of the Irish Parliament for 7 May 1689 and it is possible that he was urged to do so by Catholic landed interests whose ambition to procure more land overshadowed any concern they may have felt for their disadvantaged co-religionists.[6]

Parliament sat in the King's Inns and was mainly Catholic in composition with a handful of Protestant members, but there were scarcely any Catholic members with experience of a legislative body and, in that light, their actions must partially be judged. Despite the inexperience of the new members and the fall in representation on the part of the, until now, ruling minority, Davis was convinced that 'Knowledge, Charity and Patriotism are the only powers which can loose this Prometheus-land' and that those virtues were present to some marked degree in the Parliament of James II.[7] As a consequence, he was outraged at the way that Irish history had been perverted by an 'alien Government' who, as soon as 'any great deed had been done here', did their best to 'blacken the honour of the statesmen, the wisdom of the legislators, or the valour of the soldiers who achieved it'. To this end, it was customary in a later age to use the Irish Government in the time of James as a specimen 'of what an Irish Government would be – unruly, rash, rapacious and bloody'. To Davis, however, the King, Lords and Commons of 1689 were 'a sight to make us proud and hopeful for Ireland, when they were judged honestly and justly'.[8]

James opened the proceedings of his Parliament by proclaiming his determination to stand by 'Liberty of Conscience', despite the fact that his prior adherence to such a principle in the neighbouring island had turned so many of the powerful and wealthy among his English subjects against him. Liberty of conscience to them meant their freedom to remain Protestants, with all that such a freedom meant materially, but to grant a similar freedom to Catholics, even if only on the spiritual plane, was an anathema. James, who clearly regarded the whole Irish people, Catholic and Protestant, as the Irish nation, went on to say that he wanted laws made for the general good of the nation and the happiness of all its people.[9] Thus his Parliament enacted a whole series of laws that, had they come to fruition, might have been of immense benefit to Ireland and its people. The first Act of the Parliament was to proclaim the independence of Ireland as a separate kingdom from that of England; Acts passed in England purporting to be binding in Ireland were repudiated and appeals to the Lords declared void. 'The full and free exercise of their respective religions to all that profess Christianity' was guaranteed and provision made that tithes be paid to the Protestant Church by Protestants and by Catholics only to the Catholic Church. The importation of coal by foreign colliers was forbidden, immigrants, especially 'Merchants, Traders, and Artificers' were welcome to come and settle in Ireland, ship-building was encouraged, foreign trade freed-up and embargoes stopped, free schools of mathematics and navigation provided for in Dublin, Belfast, Cork, Waterford, Limerick and Galway and there is some evidence that an Act had been passed to establish 'a school for general (national) education in every parish in Ireland'. All of this Davis warmly praised.[10]

However, the main problem for the Parliament was how to confront the matter of an equitable division of land. Land had been the key to power in Ireland and its possession by erstwhile foreigners meant that the country was largely ruled and governed by masters, very few of whom had a relationship of trust with the majority of the people. The power that they wielded was difficult to wrest from its holders and, since the days of Elizabeth, religion had been added to race as another means to dispossess the Irish. The fact that such dispossession was often clothed in zeal for the self-proclaimed reforming religion only served to make the subjection of the native Irish even more abject. That they would look to James for redress is understandable, even if the futility of their reliance on English monarchs had hitherto been proven. The thing, above all, that Catholics whose families had been land-owners looked to was the restoration of the lands they had lost since 1641. That no compensation would be offered to the many who had improved land, or to those who had bought it in good faith was clearly unjust, but such a fine point may have seemed of little moment to James's legislators in the light of the injustice of the past.

In effect, from the mid-1650s, 800,000 Catholics, the 'Irishry', owned, between them, a fifth of the whole of Ireland and much of the land they held was inferior or situated in the less accessible regions of the island. The rest was held by 300,000 Protestants, the 'Englishry', who were in the main of the Established Church. Thus, those who had rebelled and then decapitated their King, Charles I, were rewarded, while those who had remained faithful were despoiled with the approval of the same king's son.[11] It is unsurprising that the Parliament decided that the old Irish had a right to reclaim their properties and that those who had rebelled against James had forfeited their land. Davis accepted the justice of this step, fully aware that his own family was among those that had been put in jeopardy. That it all came to nothing with the final fall of James throws into greater relief the futility of claim and counter-claim based on justice. Then, as always, the spoils went to the victors.

Davis recognised that the Parliament was unable to act freely and proclaim the complete liberty of Ireland as an independent nation with no connection to England. To have done so would seem to be ungenerous to James who had tried to do his best for Ireland and was at the same time a 'refugee' in what he claimed to be part of his own realm. Thus, his parliamentarians could not take that ultimate step of breaking with the crown because they did not want to oppose James and further alienate his English subjects from him. By supporting the retention of the crown, Davis revealed that, like the Irish Parliament, he had not read the lesson of history. For centuries it had been plain that the English monarchs, no matter how benevolent, were never able to do justice to their Irish subjects in situations in which large numbers of landholders relied on their support to keep them on land which they had either taken or been granted, to the injury of the former occupiers. They were also unable to see that the House of Stuart was a weak mast on which to pin their flag, or that its hopes would wither into nothingness on the dreary fields of Culloden and in the effete salons of Rome.

Looking rapidly over the whole proceedings of Parliament, Davis was in warm agreement with the major part. In the attempt to make the only laws binding on the Irish those that had been passed in Ireland by an Irish parliament, he saw a forerunner of the argument of Molyneux, of the aspirations of Swift and Lucas, of the work of Flood and of the temporary achievement of Grattan and the Volunteers. To him, 1689 was 'an epitome of the Protestant patriot attempts, from the Revolution to the Dungannon Convention', so that Nagle and Rice of James's Parliament stood with Flood and Grattan in a rightful claim for gratitude. Nonetheless, he deplored the fact that the king had rejected the Bill creating Irish Inns of Court so that, to his day, the future advocates and judges of Ireland were 'hauled off to a foreign and dissolute capital to go through an idle and expensive ceremony, term after term, as an essential to being allowed to practice in the courts of their native kingdom'.[12] The Acts of the Parliament that attainted absentees' goods in the king and attainted some of the insurgents themselves, earned his hearty disapproval. In a typically forthright and honest way, he regarded their passing as 'the mistake of the Irish Parliament' and rightly saw that the action of the Irish Parliament was politically disastrous in that 'It bound up the hearts and the interests of those who were named in it, and of their children, in William's success.'[13] The fact that the Act was never enforced, indeed could not be enforced, did nothing to lessen its psychological impact. Its passing proved conclusively that land and the possession of Irish estates were at the heart of the whole struggle, although it was scarcely necessary for a later scholar to remark that the efforts of the Parliament were those 'of a selfish, though ill-treated, majority to regain their rights'.[14]

To the degree that religion entered the question, it was mostly a pretext to cover greed on the part of some, and the desire for repossession of land on that of others. The reaction to the Act showed that large sections of the English aristocracy placed possessions far higher than loyalty, so that the switching of their allegiance from their former monarch, James, to William the 'Usurper', was little more than an expression of their desire to hold or obtain land. Davis made this point with cruel precision. Among the grants which William made to his followers were King James's estates in Ireland which, to James's honour, he had passed over to the general fund for the use of his wronged Irish subjects. William gave those same estates of over 95,000 acres, worth £25,995 annually, to Mrs Elizabeth Villiers, Countess of Orkney. The lady happened to be 'William's favourite mistress', a fact which Davis noted to sum up cryptically the whole sordid affair of the succession of the House of Orange to the English throne.[15]

Since the early 1790s, and therefore only fifty years before Davis was researching and writing on James's parliament, the vast majority of the Irish people had been relieved of their status as second-rate citizens and most of the disabilities imposed on them by virtue of their religion had also been lifted. He did not live to see the loss of its standing by the Church of Ireland in 1869 when it was disestablished, but all that he ever wrote on religious matters indicates that, despite his membership of that Church, he would have been in favour of such a course of action. Yet, almost eighty years were to pass from the time of his death to the day when another Irish Parliament enjoyed the right to exercise a form of independence in one part of the island and to make laws for the benefit of its own people in the economic and social sectors. That such a step was not achieved by moral force alone would not have surprised him.[16]

He was also not to know that, in a largely peaceful manner, the lands of Ireland would revert to the Irish and that the power of the old Protestant Ascendancy would be broken to the degree that they would become as shadows in the land. Even further in the future, he could not foresee the day when the words of the United Irishmen became a dawning reality, 'Our Union (between England and Ireland) rests on our mutual independence. We shall love each other if we are left to ourselves.' Davis perhaps did not need to live to see these things because he had studied the Acts of a Parliament which had enacted all but the last, yet its spirit was such that, in time, it too would have been given shape with the breaking of ties with the crown. It is not difficult to understand why some historians have concluded that Davis's judgement of James's Parliament was 'tendentious', but it is less easy to accept that it was 'a distortion of historical reality' because the judgement of an 'historical reality' is more capable of distortion when one is writing in an Ireland that has gained independence.[17]

That the Acts of the Parliament of 1689 were soon thwarted in their application takes nothing from their validity in their enactment. In 1843, Davis felt compelled to reject the use made of James's Parliament to frighten the people of Ulster against Repeal, saying that, 'It is a gross lie to say that James II's Parliament persecuted men for their creed, or established a Catholic ascendancy, or tried to establish it.'[18] Yet he could lay down his pen on the matter in the hope that, in the future, a few persons at least 'will not allow the calumnies against our noble old parliament of 1689 to pass uncontradicted'. While the calumnies have not been repeated by serious scholars there is one instance at least of modern Irish scholarship where the Parliament of James II rates no mention except as part and parcel of 'the hasty and ill-considered actions' of that 'impetuous arriviste', Richard Talbot, who went under 'the grandiose title of duke of Tyrconnell'. As if that were not a sufficient putdown, in the Chronology the entry for 1689 reads 'Catholic "parliament" underway in Dublin.' Davis acknowledged that James's Parliament had its faults, but he concluded, 'It might have been better, but this is well.'[19]

From the rarified atmosphere of the pages of the *Citizen*, in which he had written with such enthusiasm of an Irish Parliament of the past, it was necessary for Davis to turn to the weekly task of getting out the *Nation*, where, from the very first edition, it was clear that the main, practical message was Repeal. Nonetheless, what Repeal meant, apart from the desire to have an Irish Parliament set up once again in Dublin, was unclear. Was Ireland to remain subordinate to the British crown? Was there to be a viceroy in Dublin exercising the prerogatives of that crown? Indeed, what were the prerogatives of the crown? Was the Irish Parliament to have full control of all Irish public matters, finance, trade, foreign affairs and whatever else that touched Ireland's interests? Would the system of national schooling in Ireland be controlled by Dublin? Would the Church of Ireland remain the state church with the Catholic, Presbyterian and dissenting bodies standing to the side in a position of legal inferiority? Finally, where and by whom would the land question be decided? That problem may not have been as vital as it was in the seventeenth century, but there were thousands of landlords, absentee and resident, to whom it was paramount. At the same time the Catholic Irish who were landless may not have felt dispossession as keenly as their ancestors who had been removed from their lands, but they knew they were landless and why it was so. In short, Repeal as an idea without clear definitions lacked substance because no one knew what it entailed. It was a fine and hearty cry to rally the masses, but little else.

Despite the unease on tactics that may have already touched the minds of its editor and his closest collaborators, the *Nation* manifestly stood four square with O'Connell. It could not have afforded to do otherwise, because not to do so was to risk losing its readership and hence lead to its closure. Furthermore, the Repeal Association was the vehicle accepted and fostered as the major means by which Repeal was to be achieved. The hub of the Association's activities was the Corn Exchange on Burgh Quay. It was situated only a few hundred yards from the offices of the *Nation* in D'Olier Street, and there were constant comings and goings between the two. Throwing in his lot with the *Nation* and the Repeal Association meant for Davis that his world had scarcely moved from its axis based on Trinity. It was within that small but vibrant geographical space that he spent the rest of his days of labour.

They were days filled with activity for Davis, the core of which was writing. Based on his published material and his correspondence, even if the latter is only judged on those remnants which remain extant, his output was prodigious. He was prompt to answer his correspondence and normally he did so in a firm, clear hand. He rarely found room or time for idle comments or mere gossip, but came directly to the point with precision and spirit. The postal service was sufficiently efficient for him to be able to write before noon to a friend or acquaintance with a residence in Dublin, and make an appointment to meet later that day in full confidence that his letter would have been delivered within hours of its being posted. It was a kind of efficiency that frequently worked to the disadvantage of later historians because correspondents often saw no need to date their letters. Davis did almost all of his writing in his study at home on Baggot Street where his material needs were attended to by his manservant, Neville, and where he had the comfort of the presence of his mother and sister. Trinity, with its already magnificent library, was now open to him as a graduate, and his own personal library grew steadily in volumes and range as his interests diversified into such areas as economics and political theory.

In 1913, an article in *The Irish Book Lover* by John D. Noonan, an Irish-born civil servant and book collector based in London, stated that he had recently bought some remnants of Davis's personal library. They were on sale at Westell's second-hand bookshop in Charing Cross Road and had been acquired from the Reverend John Davis, son of Davis's eldest brother, John Atkins Davis. The collection was mainly of magazines and pamphlets, but there were also some books. J. D. O'Donoghue, librarian of the National University, had unsuccessfully attempted to buy the collection, but Noonan acquired it 'at a very reasonable price'. In a brief note in the same journal in 1947, P. S. O'Hegarty says that 'after he retired from the civil service Noonan sold his collection to Hodges Figgis and Co. I don't know if these [Davis's collection] were amongst them.' In 1925, Marsh's Library acquired the pamphlet collection from Hodges Figgis. In the collection there was a volume of the *Irish Penny Journal* which was presented to John Atkins Davis by 'his attached brother Thomas Osborne Davis' with the date 21 March 1845. Atkins Davis later wrote on it, 'This was the last day I saw my darling Tom.'[20]

As was his custom, Davis frequently annotated, or marked with personal notes and remarks, whatever he read in his own collection and they are all entirely consistent with his public writings. *Bolster's Quarterly Magazine* of 1827 was heavily scored by him and an article 'Reading made easy' had the note, 'This paper is, I should think, by Prout', while several passages in an essay on 'Irish Art and Artists' were underlined. He showed his disapproval of an article 'Notes on Ireland' with the remark, 'A very ignorant writer only could have written this,' and went on, 'The most flourishing time of Ireland was when she was Pagan, the next was from the 7th to the 10th centuries, when her monks and religious schools were the best in Europe, and this latter civilisation was destroyed long before the Norman invasion in the 12th century. It was destroyed by the Danish and Civil wars.' He thought that it was 'utterly wrong' to state in an article on Thomas Moore that 'song poetry' in Ireland was 'very inconsiderable and scanty' and 'of an inferior quality' before Moore. On an article prophesying the rapid decay of the Irish language, manners and habits, Davis simply wrote, 'God forbid!' An article laudatory of Wellington for 'staying that mighty power' of Napoleon, elicited the response, 'His staying. He had as soon have stayed Lucifer. Moscow and Leipsic [sic] stayed Napoleon.'[21]

Apart from an extremely rare copy of the Acts of James's Parliament of 1689, which Davis had used for his work on that Parliament, the most interesting part of the collection were the sixteen volumes, each containing fourteen or fifteen pamphlets relating to Ireland, that were bound at Davis's direction. The earliest dated from 1786 and the latest 1844. Some of the titles that Davis gave to individual volumes were Irish Trade, Statistics, Irish Agriculture, Irish Education and the Poor Laws, which further prove the point that Davis was no idle romantic, uninterested in the practical concerns of his country. Others were, Roman Catholic Questions, United Irishmen and Defenders, Union and Anti-Union, a large collection of Repeal pamphlets and a volume entitled Miscellaneous. One pamphlet entitled 'A fair representation of the present political state of Ireland' roused his ire because it tried to justify the Penal Laws and condemn the Volunteers. Davis saw it as 'An attack on the Irish Roman Catholics in all times and places' in that it calumniated 'every man' and was 'intolerant of toleration'. He did, however, concede that the pamphlet was not 'weak or unfounded in its reasoning against Papacy'. Finally, on a pamphlet containing O'Connell's letter to Lord Shrewsbury, who had accused him of being 'greedy in accepting the public's financial support', at that part of the letter where the Liberator strongly criticised the continental Liberals, Davis wrote in the margin, 'hypocrisy and falsehood'. True however to his loyalty, where O'Connell replied to Shrewsbury by spelling out the sacrifices he had made for Ireland, Davis wrote, 'Just and worthy'.[22]

The successful birth of the *Nation* had convinced Davis that, henceforth, he ought to give the major part of his energies to it. He was the only paid member working on the staff of the paper. Understandably, given his position, he was its major contributor with articles, verse, and reviews flowing from his pen weekly. At the same time he still had to attend the meetings of the Association's sub-committees, which often sat three or four times a week.[23] The demands of a weekly publication did not differ greatly from those of a daily one in that most of its contents had to be a response to the immediate. Thus, Davis no longer enjoyed periods of long reflection, of protracted and concentrated study, and he had to draw on the store of knowledge he had amassed in previous years and often merely repeat in various modes the things he had already written about elsewhere. Throughout all that he wrote, one major strand remained intact to the end. Davis was utterly and sincerely convinced that the disabilities and limitations of Ireland, whether material or spiritual, had their roots in the bonds of domination that the English had forged between the two countries and their peoples, both before and after the Union. His single purpose became the breaking of the Union, although he was never so naïve as to imagine that all would be well for Ireland once that step had been taken. Concomitant, therefore, with the struggle for independence had to stand the struggle for the development of the character of the Irish people. Their education in both the realm of the spirit and that of the material had to be fostered, and they had to be taught, based on their pride in the culture of their past, that they were a people worthy to stand with the nations of the world as both an equal and as an inspiration to others in their struggles.

In the first few months after the founding of the *Nation*, Davis continued to go to the regular Monday meetings of the Association, although he rarely spoke and never at any length. The Corn Exchange was a busy place with the number of clerks rising from nine in 1841 to forty-eight in 1843 and the great room held 500, which was often over-flowing once Repeal took off in earnest. Visitors, including priests, lawyers, labourers, and beggars stood, if male, while the women sat in a section reserved for them around the main hall. The debating chamber was eight yards wide by sixteen long, with a raised chair for the president and a table in the middle where the press sat. There was only one emblem in the room, consisting of a green flag with the word Repeal on it in golden letters. The whole place was laden with memories of the past because there the victory of Emancipation was planned and won and many of those who surrounded O'Connell were veterans of that battle. Those who worked at the Corn Exchange, including the voluntary members like Davis, resembled the staff of a government minister, indeed, in the case of O'Connell, a prime minister. There were two permanent auditors of the account book of the Association, both of them well respected in the community, and the general committee was made up of about eighty members.[24]

O'Connell, with his remarkable stamina, was normally present at every meeting of the Association and always spoke, usually for well over an hour. At the meetings in Dublin, and those that were beginning in late 1842 to attract large crowds elsewhere, O'Connell followed well-worn themes and did not hesitate to repeat them in the manner of a schoolmaster who knows from experience that repetition is the proven way to ensure that others learn the lesson. He was then followed by lengthy reports given by lieutenants in the organisation, such as his son John or O'Neill Daunt. This would be capped off by long-winded praises of O'Connell by Thomas Steele, whom O'Connell had made 'Head Pacificator of Ireland with a hope of taming Steele's too fervent zeal in his cause'. The meetings frequently went on for over six hours, but O'Connell's energy never seemed to flag, despite his normally being in the chair throughout.[25] One result of all this oratory was that there was little room for interventions by others.

The Leader regularly rejected violence as a means to achieve his objectives and he was sincere in so doing, although he accepted 'the morality of a just war and the necessity for professional armies'. He remained horrified at the uprising of 1798 and Emmett's revolt in 1803, and, on both occasions, he had played a minor role on the side of law and order. Nonetheless, he sometimes played with his words in a way that puzzled his hearers. 'It was never safe to use physical force until it became absolutely necessary', scarcely sat well with 'Let there be no assault – no tumult – let physical force be banished from the land', which he said in the same speech at Limerick. In like manner, he often coupled his protests against the Union and demands for its abolition with extreme expressions of loyalty. 'The Irish were more loyal than the people of England – they were attached with a purer, because a higher, feeling of allegiance to the throne and constitution. They were attached by the ties of personal affection to the excellent and amiable being [Victoria] that now filled the throne. They loved and respected her.' This fulsome adulation, probably sincere on O'Connell's part, was met with cheers and 'continued cheers'. Yet, he could go further along the path of creating confusion with 'The Repeal Association did not want to separate from England ... whilst he lived no such attempt would ever be made', and he called upon the members of the Association 'to maintain and preserve at the utmost peril of life, if necessary, the connexion [sic] by the golden link of the crown between the two countries'.[26]

Apart from the curtailment of Irish liberties by the lack of its own Parliament, there were few aspects of the connection with England, however, that galled O'Connell deeply. He was aware that, in some areas of administration and innovation, the rule of England had been beneficial to Ireland and in this Davis did not disagree with him. The experiment in national education had already begun to show its fruits in literacy and in greater opportunities for employment among Irish youth. The general health services in Ireland were probably in advance of those in England and certainly so in Dublin, but O'Connell rejected the introduction of the Poor Law into Ireland and he wanted it totally abolished. He considered that it encouraged pauperism, inhibited endeavour and initiative and destroyed charity. As far as his political allegiances of the past were concerned, he was now able to throw them off with little discomfort now that the Whigs had lost government. He said that 'He had supported the Whigs, but support them again he never would', but those who knew him well realised that, were the Whigs to return to power, he would follow the course he had taken through the years and support them as a lesser evil than the Tories.[27]

As a native Irish speaker, O'Connell did not deplore the concomitant loss of the Irish language which meant little to him except for its sentimental value and he accepted its passing as inevitable, and even necessary, were Ireland to take its place on the stage of Empire. Thus, in their attitudes to the language, indeed in much that concerned the preservation of the Irish past, there was a wide gulf between O'Connell and Davis. Davis assuredly envied O'Connell's ability to speak Irish as a native speaker, while he himself had to struggle to pick up even a few words. He must have been surprised when he realised that O'Connell meant it when he said, 'The superior utility of the English tongue, as a medium of all modern communication, is so great that I can witness without a sigh the gradual disuse of Irish', and 'I am sufficiently utilitarian not to regret its abandonment.' It may be going too far to assert that 'there is little doubt but that Ireland might be still Gaelic speaking and in possession of its native culture' had O'Connell not entirely lacked 'understanding or sympathy for the Gaelic past'. As a result, O'Connell, the acknowledged leader of his people for at least forty years, did not realise he was condemning them to 'the awful emptiness of a nation without a history'.[28] However, the point at issue for an understanding of the true relationship between O'Connell and Davis is what united them. Two things certainly did so, their love for Ireland and its people and their desire for Repeal, whatever their respective perceptions of it. Time would reveal the differences between them.

By 1842 O'Connell had given almost the whole of his life to Ireland and to the Irish people and now his years of service were ebbing away. That life had neither been shaped nor influenced by the young men who now followed him. Yet the influence, both positive and negative, on them, of his personality, his fame and his purpose, was decisive. As a result, the Davis known to history in the active and public part of his career, can scarcely be understood apart from O'Connell. The great difficulty for Davis and those around him was that they did not know their leader; perhaps they did not want to know him too closely. It was not simply a gap between them based on age, but more a matter of the spirit. In his long years as a campaigner O'Connell had gained experience and he had profited by reflecting on his experience. Almost as a latter-day Moses, compared by Irish ballad writers and in the aisling poetry to Napoleon, it was not the final outcome of Repeal that mattered to him but the struggle for delivery itself.[29] His biographer, Oliver MacDonagh, hints at this interpretation of O'Connell's attitude to the Repeal struggle. 'Thirty years of mass politics had taught him that a great deal of dreary labour had to precede the blaze of a crusade – and indeed that it was often more profitable to preach and prepare for one than to set out, in true earnest, for a Holy Land.'[30] To Davis and his friends Repeal was not even the end of the struggle. It was to be the beginning of real independence for Ireland.

Again, like Davis, O'Connell wanted unity among all those who lived in Ireland and he did not want Protestants to harbour any fears of a Catholic ascendancy in the event that justice was done to his own co-religionists.[31] They were noble sentiments, but there was little evidence that many of the Protestant leaders wanted to forget the past, or that they looked to Repeal of the Union as other than a complete disaster for their churches. Indeed a ballad of the period, entitled 'Protestants, Awake!' expressed their sentiments, although in terminology they would have hesitated to use. It began by pointing out that Catholics already had their freedom and continued,

> What want they more? The road to power! Oh, be their wishes vain!
> Wake, Protestants, I cry – Awake! Let not the Papists reign.
> Wake! for the foe is at your gates, he thunders at your door,
> With the traitorous voice, and the threatening hand,
>   that he ever had of yore.

> Speak for your *God*, your Church and King,
> Shout thousands – let them hear –
> That ye know their strength, that ye
>   know their *hate*, but that ye do not *fear*![32]

The intellectual voice of the Irish Protestant Ascendancy was heard in the pages of the *Dublin University Magazine*. In it, the fears of the Protestant minority were articulated and O'Connell, as well as Davis, had to take them seriously because they 'attributed most of Ireland's problems, political, social and economic, to the failings of the Roman Catholic majority'. Since 1793, when the franchise was extended to permit Catholics of a requisite economic status to vote, the Protestant minority had seen the growing threat posed to its power in Parliament, which threat had been further strengthened by the partial reform of the corporations. Protestants generally felt that 'The blame for Ireland's ills, and for the admitted faults of the Irish poor, was not to be attributed to defective genes or inherent cultural blight, and still less to any Protestant sin of omission or commission, but to the Roman Catholic Church, its hierarchy and its teachings.' As well, many of them still felt, in the words of Lord Clare whose support for the Union with England had been decisive, that their security depended upon 'the powerful and commanding protection of Great Britain. If, by any fatality, it fails, you are at the mercy of the old inhabitants of the island.'[33] Amidst all this, here was O'Connell, regarded by most Catholics as a kind of lay bishop, if not pope, trumpeting the need for the Repeal of the Union. Perhaps even more depressing to them was the evidence that some of their own, including Davis, stood by his side.

Davis, Duffy, Dillon and those close to them had to accept O'Connell's pre-eminence and they did so graciously even if on some measures, in some areas of his thought, and in some aspects of his behaviour and character, they were at odds with him. Thus Davis quickly made it clear that he would not tolerate cant and self-deception, nor would he forget the past simply because it was unpalatable to bring it up for judgement. Richard Robert Madden, a regular correspondent with Davis but no relative to Daniel Owen Madden, had recently written a book on the United Irishmen and, in the second number of the *Nation* Davis flayed a reviewer of the book for saying that the Penal Laws 'had to be adopted in self-defence'. In the context of elucidating Davis's thoughts and judgements, no purpose is served by entering into the argument as to whether the Penal Laws were less severe in their application or endurance than they have been frequently painted in the past. The relevant point at issue is to record, and try to understand, what Davis and his associates thought. Oral history aside, any distortion of Irish history in its written form had not been the work of those who were subjected to the Penal Laws, but of those who belonged to the class who had constructed and imposed them. Accordingly, to Davis, the Laws 'were enacted by intolerance to facilitate plunder. Religion was their pretence, robbery their purpose. They crushed the Catholic with a code borrowed from Hell, and corrupted the Protestant by making him the minister of it ... our Protestant fathers were tyrants and our Catholic fathers were slaves' [34] They were sentiments that O'Connell certainly shared although, at the time, he was more circumspect in his utterance of them.

Politically, Davis was most removed from O'Connell in that he had neither respect for the past dealings of the Whigs with Ireland, nor did he place any hope in them for the future, whereas O'Connell would assuredly have returned to the Whig camp had they won the elections. Davis's lack of faith in the Whigs was plain when he beseeched the Canadians, who had been successful in their 'Revolution', not 'to fall for the credulous and confiding policy whereby *Grattan* lost for us in twelve years what we took fifty to gain, and have not yet retrieved,' and, in comparison, he praised Tone as one of the greatest leaders that Ireland ever produced, exactly because Tone knew nothing of the meaning of compromise. At the same time he despised the Irish-born generals who fought against the Afghans and deplored Dublin Corporation's moving a vote of thanks to them for their 'foul sin against

View from Carlisle Bridge, Dublin, 1820.

God and man'. His idea of the kind of allegiance the Irish owed to Victoria, queen of England, was much narrower than that of O'Connell but, whatever about allegiance to the queen, no allegiance was owed 'in *law* or *conscience* to the prosperity of English crime'.[35]

On his side, Dillon engaged in scathing attacks on the Irish land-lords, despite his certain knowledge of the extent of land held by O'Connell himself, but, hopefully, also his awareness that O'Connell was a landlord whose care for his tenants was generally constant. He also went directly contrary to O'Connell in an editorial entitled 'The Poor Law' on the same day that the leader was reported as having called for the 'total repeal' of the Law. Dillon, with whom Davis and Duffy both agreed, wanted reform rather than abolition of the Law and a recognition that it was merely an alleviation, albeit faulty, rather than a remedy for poverty.[36] Thus, even in those early days, the young men served notice that they were not going to be complacent toadies, merely parroting the judgements of O'Connell. At the same time, they were careful to give him every possible support towards the main objective, as stated by himself, of achieving the Repeal of the Union. Nonetheless, they found it hard to bear with some of those who surrounded the leader. Many of them, such as O'Neill Daunt and Tom Steele, had stood beside him for years. They were still involved and, justifiably, they could and would not forget the glory of victory. Others, such as Thomas Ray, had come to him in more recent years, but they relied upon him even for their livelihood, while he looked to them for unconditional support and almost always received it. No one ever dreamt of imputing the 'misappropriation of a shilling of public funds' to O'Connell, but there were many 'scamps' on the General Committee who used the Association to their own ends.[37] At times, some of their behaviour cast O'Connell, who was always loyal to old comrades, in a poor light, and it was always difficult for the ardent young men in Davis's circle to see that human frailty had sometimes to be borne with, rather than scorned as incurable.

To Davis and his friends the recent past held no allies and, in the struggle for Repeal, only the present counted. They knew the importance, but did not stand in awe, of the victory of 1829 and they had little sense of the mythical proportions it had assumed. More importantly, they had either no time to devote to understanding the man they had to work with and, in many senses, work under, or they did not appreciate the importance of doing so. They were young men in a hurry and, as they often said, those 600 years that they saw as centuries of foreign bondage were that much too long and they wanted to get it all over with. Finally, it is not too harsh to sense in some of them a tinge of what a later age would call intellectual snobbery. The accents and the grammar of the Corn Exchange were not those of Trinity, but it would have been a great mistake to have judged intellectual strength or fixity of purpose, masked by speech, as deficient in those whom they encountered in the building on Burgh Quay by the Liffey. Jacob Venedey, an intelligent German journalist, was present at Conciliation Hall in 1843 at a meeting addressed by John O'Connell. He judged his speech as good as the one he had recently heard given by the young Gladstone in London. He also praised Tom Steele's 'nobility of soul' and 'disinterestness of purpose'.[38]

An especially important lesson learnt by O'Connell in his Emancipation campaign, not shared in by Davis and his friends, was that the success or failure of any Irish cause was heavily dependent on the position taken up by the Catholic hierarchy and clergy. By 1841 he had made some headway in winning the bishops over by presenting the Catholic cause and the Repeal cause as one, but he regretted to Bishop Higgins that they were not all Repealers and, indeed, one bishop was '*actively* opposed', while others were not with the people and some were mixed up with the 'congenial spirit of Orangeism'. He was thoroughly convinced that 'we Catholics cannot hold what we have got without the Repeal and *a fortiori* that we cannot get anything that Ireland wants without an Irish parliament ... I could weep tears of blood at seeing that the opportunity of now making a great and powerful rally for Catholic Ireland is lost'.[39] Thus, as the leader of Catholic opinion in Ireland, as well as of the Repeal movement, it was necessary for him to argue that the benefits flowing to the Church in Ireland from Repeal would be so great that they would counterbalance any negative side effects that may ensue elsewhere. The person he chose to act through was Paul Cullen, rector of the Irish College in Rome.[40]

He began his argument to Cullen with the hope that the pope would never interfere with the work of the Irish clergy for Repeal. To that end he wanted him to be made aware that 'the Repeal of the Union would be an event of the most magnificent importance to Catholicity, of an importance so great and so valuable that I am prevented from presenting it in its true colours to the British people lest it should have its effect in increasing their hostility to that measure.' He then listed sixteen reasons why Repeal would be beneficial to the Catholic Church in Ireland, but only a few of them were vital to his case. The Protestants of Ireland were politicians first and only 'religionists' in a secondary capacity. Their 'participation in political power' made them 'political Protestants' and, were that power taken from them by Repeal, they would 'with little delay melt into the overwhelming majority of the Irish nation'. Thus, 'Protestantism would not survive the Repeal ten years.' The only thing that could possibly ensure its survival would be persecution and 'the Irish Catholics are too wise and too good to persecute'.[41] These arguments were not ones which Davis and other Protestants would have cheerfully heard or agreed with in the Ireland of the 1840s. Davis would have been even more astonished had he read the words in which O'Connell pictured an almost theocratic Ireland of the future, which he imagined would surely meet the approval of the pope and the Vatican,

> So rich, so prosperous a country with a legislature devoted to religion, to Catholic truth in doctrine, discipline and submission to authority, with an undeviating attachment to the authority of the Holy See, a legislature devoted to civil liberty, to peaceful arts, to science, to the promotion of every virtue – abhorrent of crime – giving a glorious example to the nations.[42]

It is reasonable to ask how O'Connell could be sincere in wanting an Irish state that would pledge itself 'to Catholic truth in doctrine, discipline and submission to authority, with an undeviating attachment to the authority of the Holy See'. There can be no doubt whatever that, although he wavered in his youth, at this stage of his life and for the remaining years of it, O'Connell was a thoroughly devout Catholic with absolute loyalty to the Church and its authority in religious matters.[43] To some extent, therefore, it cannot be argued that he was insincere in the hope he had of an independent Ireland which would accord in its outlines with the picture he painted in his letter to Cullen, even though the future Ireland he praised so fulsomely seemed to resemble a theocracy. Nonetheless, in 1842, O'Connell's words revealed there was a vast gap between the Ireland of his dreams and that of Davis, who was repelled at the thought of the very thing O'Connell seemed to hope for.

Another area that the young men approached with diffidence was that of financial support for the Association. They gave publicity in *The Nation* to the effort made to collect money, but it seemed remote from their principal interests. O'Connell knew that no movement could succeed without a ready supply of finance, and to that end the support of the Church was vital. Through the Catholic parishes he was again able to organise the 'Rent' system, by which the members of his chameleon-like organisations were kept solvent by the penny payments of the members and he maintained the system despite the fact that he wanted to embrace Protestants in the wider movement. That the 'Rents' were often collected at the church gates did not bother O'Connell, nor did it seem to unduly alarm the bishops.[44] He encouraged the secretary of the Association, Ray, whose idea it was, to set up parish Reading

Rooms in 1842 as a venue where some form of rudimentary educative process could be undertaken and where local tactics on the day-to-day level could be worked out. Thus the lessons learnt for the mobilisation of the masses in pre-Emancipation days were applied again in the 1840s.[45] All this activity went on apace, organised on Burgh Quay and directed from there, which explains the growth in the number of clerks. Across the way in *The Nation* office, the small staff worked on and did their best to support the wider work, but in some measure they had other priorities. To Davis the principal question in 1843 was whether O'Connell would be able to win over significant elements of Protestant support in the Repeal struggle. Without that support the campaign was doomed to ultimate failure, although the leader never indicated that he knew that to be the case. On the other hand, Davis could not even conceive of a struggle for Repeal without Protestant support because its goal, in his eyes, was the unity of all the Irish people. Winning that support became one of his highest priorities.

It is worth asking what concept O'Connell had of the Irish people because so much of his relationship with the young men who joined his Repeal movement revolved around that very matter. To O'Connell there was no sense in thinking of recreating the Irish nation because it already existed. The people to whom he belonged, and whose leader he was, were that nation. They were the Irish Catholics. Davis did not deny that in the Irish past the Catholic people had been the nation. What he insisted on was the right of all the inhabitants of Ireland in the present to become part of the new flowering of the old nation. Indeed, to him, that unity was an absolute necessity were Ireland ever to be independent and free. However, there were manifestly two peoples in Ireland, divided on the extent of their material possessions, the power they wielded and their religious loyalties as Catholic and Protestant. Those two peoples suffered their own divisions, but in respect of the Protestants there was always the certainty of their cohesion because an upheaval of the *status quo* in Ireland threatened their well-being. On the other hand, in at least one respect, the Catholics as a body did not need to be shaped and formed because the Church had already done that. As Catholics they were generally in agreement on basic matters, and, to O'Connell, what had to be done was to organise the Catholics as an effective force. Thus his work was essentially directed at the politicisation of the Catholic people and the clergy, which in itself made Davis's longing for unity even more difficult to achieve because it painted independence and freedom as strictly Catholic objectives. In effect, one ally in the shape of the Catholic hierarchy merely tended to alienate the other, hoped-for, ally of liberal Protestants. The words of the Irish novelist, Maria Edgeworth, even though exaggerated, were to find an echo in many a Protestant home. She wrote, 'We poor Protestants ... did not like, only one million as we are, to be trampled on by seven and to have our Church pulled down about our ears and to have our clergy buried under the rubbish and their church lands and our estates taken from us. She was sure that history had confirmed 'the encroaching and predominantly predatory nature and art of Catholics'.[46] It was a judgement with which Davis had no patience whatever, but he had to be mindful of it and he had to try to understand the reasons that gave it such strength.

The problem remains that O'Connell assuredly knew the English statesmen were not willing to pay the price of Repeal. Why then did he go back into the ring? Why did Davis and his friends follow him in the struggle? On one level, the answer is as simple as it was for Catholic Emancipation. What was at stake was again a matter of elemental justice, which involved the rights of the Irish people. O'Connell and his immediate followers knew that the Union had dealt an almost fatal blow to the concept of Ireland being an independent entity. The loss of the right to work the land as owners rather than as modern serfs, which they saw as a right to be regained later, was a corollary to the loss of the right to make their own laws for the good governance of the people who made up the Irish nation. As a beginning, the rights of tenants, fixity of tenure, compensation for improvements and twenty-one year leases were fundamental, especially in a country in which ejectment procedures were being taken against persons at such an alarming rate.[47] They were convinced that those rights would never be achieved without a home Parliament, so that the claim to them became part and parcel of the movement for Repeal. Thus O'Connell was intent on moulding the political consciousness of his people, and the crusade for Repeal was his chosen vehicle. It is understandable that the young men could see no other vehicle as the first step on the road to freedom.[48]

Davis and the others were aware that, before their joining the Association and before *The Nation* was founded, there had been little response in Ireland to what appeared an ambiguous objective. There was also reluctance by the prudent to involve themselves in a movement which appeared to have no chance of success, but a real possibility of bloodshed, as they judged it impossible that Westminster would concede Repeal in the normal legislative sense. The fact remains that Emancipation had meant no loss to England except perhaps some degree of face, while Repeal would mean the loss of part of her Empire. Repeal was thus an international question and O'Connell gave up his only strong card of the threat of force by substituting for it the abstract proposition that force is never valid unless one is attacked first.

That left O'Connell's card in England's hands. Because they followed him, it was a card the young men could not even pretend to hold.

With its roots in a turbulent Catholic past, rent by the struggles of warring chieftains, and its actuality splintered in a present divided by traditions, both religious and civic, the task of nation-building was a daunting prospect. Thus, to the new men, Repeal was the external symbol of independence, while unity within the one nation was the essential ingredient that would make Ireland free and allow her to stand proud amongst the nations of the world in the possession of her own integrity. Perhaps in a clearer way than anyone else in Ireland, the young Thomas Davis saw the need to achieve unity by healing the divisions based on ancient and diverse traditions. Although he knew that there was a pressing need to give the workers in urban Ireland and the population of rural Ireland a role in the nation based on economic stability, Davis was not troubled by the thought that class division might transcend other traditions. Dublin artisans had shown little interest in Catholic Emancipation because it achieved nothing for their economic and social betterment. On the other hand, they stood with O'Connell on Repeal for the reason that they looked back to pre-1801 as a kind of workers' paradise which the Union had ruined.[49] As one Repeal publication put it in stark simplicity, 'Before the disastrous union, we had prosperity, wealth and happiness. Since the union, we have decay, poverty and wretchedness.'[50] It was one way of seeing Samuel Johnson's words to an Irish friend fulfilled, 'Sir, do not rush a union with us. We would unite with you only to rob you. We would have robbed the Scotch had they anything worth robbing.'

To his close associates and to the many thousands who heard and followed him, O'Connell's vision, which he espoused with increasing devotion and from which he would accept no diversion, was simple, clearly understood while it remained confined to one word, and as a signpost it seemed to indicate a pathway to a prosperous Ireland. To Davis, the road to freedom was unity based on the sense of being Irish and unity in the struggle for Repeal was a step to the final goal. There need not have been divisions based on those simple visions. That divisions arose stemmed more from the complexity of the religious, political, sociological and strategic factors than from a lack of unity among those working for Repeal. Yet the young men, especially Davis, seemed to labour under the curious conviction that an effective number of Irish Protestants would eventually see the wisdom of standing alongside the Catholic Irish in a situation in which their own dominant role in society seemed threatened. There was no sense in harking back to the days of the Volunteers as an example of unity. The struggle in those years before the Union was for an Ireland that would have a measure of independence, but in which the balance of power would not shift one whit from the Protestant ascendancy. Indeed, it was exactly because that struggle met with some degree of success, both political, and economic, followed by the ill-cloaked fomenting through repression and worse in the 1790s, which led inexorably to 1798, that resulted in the hasty imposition of the Union. To use Protestant support for, or acquiescence in, Catholic Emancipation as another example of unity was meaningless because most liberal Protestants who stood for Emancipation had acted in the hope that, while Ireland was ruled from England, their interests would be preserved, even if concessions were made to Catholics.

It was a greater and more dangerous illusion to imagine that the Protestant Irish of the 1840s would stand with the Catholics in demanding, or even supporting Repeal, than it was to imagine that the English would grant it without bloodshed. The danger lay in the fact that relying on Protestant support, and seeing hope in any small indication that it may be forthcoming, was to create a false reality out of the paper tiger called Repeal. Thus, were the struggle for Repeal to have any meaning, it could only lie in the impetus it gave towards the concept of nationality, in the educating of the people to understand their past, their culture and their language and to prepare them for a distant day when Ireland could stand with other free nations. They are the only grounds upon which to judge the contribution of O'Connell, and those who became known as Young Ireland and their descendants, to the building of the Irish nation from the 1840s onwards. In that light one judgement made of the effects of the campaign run in the *Nation* that went wider than the demand for Repeal must be considered, even though it only applied to one county. 'The programme of national regeneration, self-reliance, cultural revival, the hopes of reconciliation between Protestants and Catholics and the call for national leadership from the landed gentry ... had little or no impact in county Longford where the leadership, both lay and clerical, were out and out O'Connellites.'[51] It was a difficult task which Davis and his young friends had undertaken.

References
1. Irrespective of whom he was writing to, he never signed with only 'Thomas' and Denny Lane seems to have been the only one of his friends who wrote to him as 'Tom.' For Madden see Duffy, *Davis*, p. 92.
2. *Citizen*, January to April 1843, pp 25-42, 75-90, 105-34, 182-201 and Davis 'Proceedings of the Parliament of 1869' in *The Dublin Magazine*, April 1843, pp 170-82; *Freeman's Journal*, 29 January 1843; William E. H. Lecky, *A history of England in the eighteenth century*, 8 vols (London, 1878), vol. 2, pp 133-203 and

fn. 2, p. 184; Thomas Davis, *The patriot parliament of 1689 with its statutes votes and proceedings*, edited with an introduction by Charles Gavan Duffy (London, 1893). I have used Duffy's edition, while paying attention to the fuller version in the *Citizen*.

3. Brian Farrell (ed.), *The Irish parliamentary tradition* (Dublin, 1973), p. 272. See also Davis to Ferguson, 26 February 1843 in Ms 12 N 20, RIA.

4. R. F. Foster in 'History and the Irish Question' in *Transactions of the Royal Historical Society*, fifth series, vol. 33, 1983, p. 174 speaks of Davis's 'vigorous but tendentious rehabilitation of the "Patriot Parliament" of James II'.

5. Clarendon to Rochester, 12 October 1686, in Philip Wilson, 'Ireland under James II' in R. Barry O'Brien (ed.), *Studies in Irish history 1649-1774* (London, 1903), p. 186.

6. See ibid., pp 127-158.

7. See Davis, *The patriot parliament*, pp xcii, 39.

8. Ibid., p. xcii.

9. A decade later, in his famous plea for the independence of Ireland, William Molyneux made it plain that he regarded only the Irish Protestants as the nation. See his *The case of Ireland being bound by Acts of Parliament in England stated* (Dublin, 1698).

10. Davis, *The patriot parliament*, pp 48-62, 149-50; R. Barry O'Brien (ed.), *Studies*, p. 167. In his *The case*, pp 48-50, Molyneux made exactly the same case for Irish independence as James's parliament had done.

11. Philip Wilson in 'Ireland under Charles II' in R. Barry O'Brien (ed.), *Studies*, p. 80.

12. Davis, *The patriot parliament*, pp 64-7.

13. Ibid., pp 141-148.

14. Buckley, 'Thomas Davis', p. 260.

15. Davis, *The patriot parliament*, p. 148.

16. In his 'The paradox of Irish politics' in Brian Farrell (ed.), *The Irish parliamentary tradition*, Farrell argues strongly that Davis rejected violence as a means to attain independence, pp 19-20.

17. Brian Farrell (ed.), *The Irish parliamentary tradition*, in the bibliographical notes at p. 272. He also refers to James's parliament as 'an illegal body', p. 23.

18. *Nation*, 29 July 1843.

19. See Nicholas Canny, 'Early Modern Ireland' in R. F. Foster (ed.), *The Oxford illustrated history of Ireland* (Oxford, 1989), p. 150 and p. 362 for the Chronology; Davis, *The patriot parliament*, p. 153.

20. John D. Noonan, 'The Library of Thomas Davis' in *The Irish book lover,* vol. v (London, October 1913), pp 37-41; ibid., p. 37. Note by P. S. O'Hegarty in Ibid., vol. xxx, February 1947, pp 40-41 and further note p. 66, February 1949, from Newport B. White, then Marsh's librarian.

21. Noonan, 'The Library', p. 38.

22. Ibid., pp 40-41. For O'Connell to Shrewsbury, see MacDonagh, *O'Connell*, pp 108-9.

23. See William J. O'Neill Daunt, *Personal recollections of the late Daniel O'Connell, M.P.*, 2 vols (London, 1858), vol. 1, p. 64.

24. See Seán Ó Faoláin, *King of the beggars* (Dublin, 1970), p. 294; Duffy, *Young Ireland,* part l, p. 80; Venedy, *Ireland and the Irish*, pp 110-11.

25. Steele has been made the butt of much sarcasm, in his lifetime and since. O'Neill Daunt, who knew him well, wrote that, although he was a queer personage, he was a Clareman with a Cambridge degree who became an engineer and published several scientific papers. He had 'high and noble qualities' and an

'intense fidelity to Ireland'. See William Joseph O'Neill Daunt, *Eighty five years of Irish history, 1800-1885*, 2 vols (London, 1886), vol. 2, pp 118, 123; Alice O'Neill Daunt (ed.), *A life spent for Ireland: being selections from the journals of the late W. J. O'Neill, Daunt* (London, 1896), p. 24. After O'Connell's death, Steele attempted suicide in the Thames, but was rescued to die peacefully and be buried in Glasnevin. See also Venedy, *Ireland and the Irish*, p. 116 for O'Connell's stamina and p. 137 on Steele.

26.   See Maurice R. O'Connell, 'O'Connell, Young Ireland, and Violence, in *Thought*, vol. 52 (New York, 1977), pp 381-406; G. Shaw Leferre, *Peel and O'Connell*, London, 1887 pp 296, 300; MacDonagh, *O'Connell*, p. 26; *Nation*, 22 October, 5, 12 November, 1842; Daunt, *Personal recollections*, p. 195.

27.   *Nation*, 31 December 1842; W. E. H. Lecky, *Leaders of public opinion in Ireland*, 2 vols (London, 1903), vol. 2, pp 203-4, recalls how O'Connell was a foremost supporter of his 'darling Queen'.

28.   Michael Tierney, 'Politics and culture: Daniel O'Connell and the Gaelic past', in *Studies* (Dublin, September 1938), vol. xxvii, pp 367-8.

29.   See Rionach uí Ógáin, unpublished manuscript, 'Folklore on Daniel O'Connell', Department of Irish Folklore, University College Dublin. 'They (the old Irish speakers) had such respect for Daniel that he was like a small God to them.' p. 54; on aisling poetry, pp 83-4; as 'Saviour of Ireland', p. 101; on Napoleon and Moses, p. 104. An amusing example of the stature of O'Connell is that of the 'rustic' who once started a letter to him with 'Awful sir'. See G. Locker Lampson, *A consideration*, p. 212, fn.

30.   MacDonagh, *O'Connell*, p. 473.

31.   *Nation*, 5 November, 1842.

32.   See autographed manuscript by Davis of a collection, mostly made by him, of Irish street ballads, as well as 'some broad sheet songs in Gaelic'. '45 Irish Street Songs', p. 55 in NLI. On p. 27 there are several lines of an Irish ballad with an English translation in Davis's hand, which strongly indicates that he was studying the language with some considerable application.

33.   See Douglas Simes, 'A voice for Irish conservatism: the *Dublin University Magazine* 1833-41' in papers of The Australasian Victorian Studies Association (Auckland, 1993), pp 40, 44; Moody, *Davis*, p. 13.

34.   *Nation*, 22 October, 10 December 1842.

35.   Ibid., 10 December 1842.

36.   Ibid., 22 October, 31 December 1842.

37.   Patrick James Smyth, *Thomas Francis Meagher*, ed. J. C. Waters (Dublin, 1867), p. 11.

38.   Venedy, *Ireland and the Irish*, pp 93, 113.

39.   O'Connell to Higgins, 10 April 1841 in O'Connell, *Correspondence*, vol. 7, pp 35-6. For two excellent studies on the role of the Church in the period see S. J. Connolly, *Priests and people in pre-famine Ireland 1780-1845* (New York, 1982) and Donal A. Kerr, *Peel, priests and politics* (Oxford, 1982).

40.   O'Connell to Cullen, Liverpool, 9 May 1842, in O'Connell, *Correspondence*, pp 155-60.

41.   Ibid., p. 159.

42.   Ibid., p. 160.

43.   See MacDonagh, *O'Connell*, pp 492-6.

44.   One Irish ballad spoke of O'Connell misusing the parochial apparatus to collect money for his cause from the poor. In folklore, the struggle for Emancipation had little meaning, while that for the abolition of tithes was regarded as

important because the people were directly affected. See Rionach uí Ógáin, 'Folklore', pp 36, 99.

45. See O'Connell to Fitzpatrick in David Steele, 'Daniel O'Connell', p. 88.
46. See Edgeworth in R. F. B. O'Ferrall, 'The growth of political consciousness in Ireland: 1823-47. A study of O'Connellite politics and political education.' Ph.D. thesis, University of Dublin, 1978,' p. 698.
47. See O'Ferrall, p. 701 and O'Neill Daunt, *Eighty-five years*, p. 104.
48. See Donal McCartney (ed.), 'The world of Daniel O'Connell' in *The world of Daniel O'Connell* (Dublin, 1980), p. 5.
49. See Fergus D'Arcy, 'The artisans of Dublin and Daniel O'Connell, 1830-47: an unquiet liaison.' *Irish Historical Studies*, vol. xvii, no. 65 (Dublin, March 1970), pp 221-43.
50. P. O'Donohue, *Irish wrongs and English misrule: the Repealers' epitome of grievances* (Dublin, 1845), p. 46. To back up the assertion, the numbers of tradesmen in Dublin were said to be 61,000. In 1845 they were about 12,000, of whom 2,000 were unemployed.
51. O'Ferrall, 'The growth', p. 706.

Chapter 7

Teacher of nationality

While editor of the *Vindicator*, Gavan Duffy had realised that poetry, ballads and songs were a valuable addition to editorials, news and advertisements. When the contents of the *Nation* were discussed, Duffy convinced Davis and Dillon that the same flavour should be added to its pages. With some reluctance they agreed to Duffy's suggestion that they should begin to contribute verse to the paper. Dillon gave up after his first effort, but with Davis it was otherwise. Long after she had become 'Speranza' of the *Nation*, Lady Jane Wilde, seated in a darkened room, 'where no ray of light was admitted to show where time had withered', told a story to W. B. Yeats that he repeated in 1914 at a meeting held in Dublin to honour the centenary of Davis's birth. The same story, with expected variations, was also told by Jane's son Oscar. As a young woman of eighteen, she was in a Dublin street on the day of Davis's funeral. Jane saw the huge crowd that accompanied the cortege as it wound through the city and she asked a shopkeeper whom they were taking out for burial. To his reply, she asked again, 'Who is Thomas Davis? I have never heard of him.' The man replied simply and correctly, 'He was the poet.' At the time, Jane was twenty-three rather than eighteen, if one accepts 27 December 1821 as her birthdate. Although, the record was 'always obscure where Speranza is concerned', like Oscar, she could tell a good story and there is no reason to doubt that her discovery of nationality came through reading the *Nation*, and especially Davis's contributions. To assert, however, that she had never heard of Davis was pure fiction. His name was known throughout Dublin society well before 1845, and Davis's friend and contemporary at Trinity, Cadwallader Waddy, himself a potential contributor to the *Nation*, was her cousin. Whatever else, Jane was right in what she heard in the Dublin street because, for a brief time, Davis was the poet and balladist of the Irish people.[1]

Of Davis, Yeats said, 'He was not, indeed, a great poet but his power of expression was a finer thing than I thought.' Expert opinion, to the extent that it exists, agrees that most of Davis's poetry lacked quality when judged in the light of technical perfection. His gifts were lucidity, rhythm and a certain pleasing swiftness that made him more a balladist than a poet. The balladist has been said to possess a greater power to shape and sway the minds of the generality of the people than the law maker. In his own land, Davis was a perfect example of that power, cherished by the Scottish patriot, Alexander Fletcher of Saltoun, in his saying, 'If a man were permitted to make all the ballads, he need not care who should make the laws of a nation.'[2] As a balladist, Davis's convictions flowed forth in verse in a way that directly spoke to his readers. It was therefore fitting that the Dublin shopkeeper should sum him up simply as a poet because, in the minds and hearts of many thousands of his Irish contemporaries, he was first and foremost their poet. His poetry has been discarded as of little merit by the academic critics of a later age and it must be recognised that, because of the immediacy and pragmatism of its purpose, of which Davis never lost sight, there is, in his poetry, a lack of that quality of timelessness and universalism that are the elements of great and lasting poetry. He was also constrained by the need to almost dash off his verses late at night, given the ever-present pressure of the needs of each Saturday when the pages of the *Nation* had to be filled. Nevertheless, the content and style of Davis's poetry remains as a testimony to his character, his passion and his beliefs.

The verses Davis wrote ought to be judged on his own concept of their purpose and he was explicit in his explanation of it. His main medium of expression was the ballad which he constantly and consciously adopted to teach history to the people. He admitted that even poorly-written narrative history was better than the ballad as historical writing, but that most written history largely went unread. The ballad was not concerned with 'exact dates, subtle plots, minute connections and motives' but, nonetheless, the highest ends of history were achieved by it. The ballad perfectly fitted the moods of child-hood, youth and old age in every generation when the words and tune passed from mouth to mouth. Thus, he regarded the ballad as an immensely valuable weapon of instruction, provided it was based on historical truth, which he held firmly must never be perverted to make the data fit with the theme.

> To hallow or accurse the scenes of glory and honour, or of shame and sorrow-to give to the imagination the arms, and homes, and senates, and battles of other days – to rouse and soften and strengthen and enlarge us with the passions of great periods – to lead us into love of self-denial, of justice, of beauty, of valour, of generous life and proud death – and to set up in our souls the memory of great men, who shall then be as models and judges of

our actions – these are the highest duties of history, and these are best taught by a ballad history.[3]

Davis made his first, acknowledged contribution in verse to the third number of the *Nation*. The old melancholy was in his spirit and the poem was entitled 'My grave'. He began to sign himself as 'A True Celt', perhaps to assert both the lineage he was proud of, as well as to claim a rank with the bards of the past. He wondered where he would be buried, at sea, in Italy or in Greece, and said,

> No! on an Irish green hill-side,
> On an opening lawn – but not too wide;
> For I love the drip of the wetted trees –
> I love not the gales, but a gentle breeze
> To freshen the turf – put no tombstone there,
> But green sods decked with daisies fair;
> Nor sods too deep, but so that the dew,
> The matted grass-roots may trickle through.
> Be my epitaph writ on my country's mind,
> *'He served his country, and loved his kind.'*[4]

The only poem in the next edition, 'The men of Tipperary', was also by Davis and clearly stemmed from his experiences at Templederry as a child on holidays. It was much praised in the correspondence section of 12 November with some variations suggested. They were all rejected, several because they were regarded as too extreme to print. Clearly, the experiment with Davis as a poet was meeting Duffy's approval. Duffy's judgement was confirmed when, on the evening before the publication of the sixth number, Davis brought him some new verses. They proved his innate mastery of the ballad form and vividly illustrated his power to hold the attention of a reader with the first stanza and wrest a response from the heart as well as from the head. The ballad bore the title, 'Lament for the death of Owen Roe O'Neill'. A contemporary lamentation was written soon after O'Neill's death, but there is no indication that Davis read it. However, there may be a casual connection between Davis writing the ballad and a letter he received from a friend of Trinity days, Nick Kearney, containing a translation Kearney had made of an Irish ballad he found in 'an old worn-out paper' entitled 'Gathering chant for Sir Pheilim O'Neill'. Davis was pleased with it but he did not like some parts of the translation, which he considered were 'awkward'.[5]

In the ballad on O'Neill, and in much else that he wrote, Davis called on the years when he had steeped himself in the annals of Irish history, and especially her military history, with its recurrent theme of defeat on the battlefield. On this occasion the leader was struck down before battle was joined so that hope itself dried up in the loss of what might have been. The ballad was a cry of anguish for O'Neill, who allegedly died of poison on 6 November 1649 at the hands of the 'Sassenach' while on his way to do battle with the Cromwellian forces. On his death-bed the Ulster leader said that the purpose of his life had been 'the preservation of my religion, the advancement of his Majesty's service, and the just liberties of this nation'. It has been conceded that, 'Without Roe O'Neill, native and Catholic Ireland was defenceless against Cromwell and his New Model Army.'[6]

Strengthened by the use of repetition, Davis expressed the poignancy of the pent-up longing for a leader who,

> Had he lived – had he lived – our dear country had been free;
> But he's dead, but he's dead, and 'tis slaves we'll ever be,

and the sense of loss is powerfully brought out in the plaintive lamentation of the seventh stanza, where the same terminology Davis used in 'The Geraldine's Daughter' is repeated.

> We thought you would not die – we were sure you would not go,
> And leave us in our utmost need to Cromwell's cruel blow –
> Sheep without a shepherd, when the snow shuts out the sky –
> Oh! why did you leave us, Eoghan? Why did you die?

The more probable explanation for O'Neill's death was tetanus, but the story of the poison was widely believed at the time, and later. It moved Davis to engage in a form of malediction that was frequently used as part of traditional Irish ballads. In so doing he revealed his deep knowledge of the ballad form that was still much in evidence in Ireland. In Dublin, Cork, Belfast and Drogheda several publishers lived by exclusively printing political ballads and rebel songs and indeed it was a widespread phenomenon. Davis wrote in his first verse,

> 'Did they dare, did they dare, to slay Eoghan Ruadh O'Neill?'
> 'Yes, they slew with poison him they feared to meet with steel.'
> 'May God wither up their hearts! May their blood cease to flow!'
> 'May they walk in living death, who poisoned Eoghan Ruadh!'[7]

The ballad was immediately accepted as of first-rate quality and ranks with 'The West's Asleep', 'A Nation Once Again', 'The Geraldines', 'The Sack of Baltimore' and 'Fontenoy' as among the best that Davis wrote.

W. B. Yeats said that in the 'Lament', Davis was 'mourning, not as poet, but as man, over the sorrows of Ireland.' To Yeats, 'It has the intensity of the old ballads, and to read it is to remember Parnell and Wolfe Tone, to mourn for every leader who has died among the ruins of the cause he had all but established, and to hear the lamentations of his people.' Perhaps because many of his ballads were put to an already familiar air, thus enhancing the rhythm but tending to lessen the poetic structure, it was easy to be critical of them later. Malcolm Brown regarded the ballads of the *Nation* not as poetry but as song, but said that about twenty of them, almost all by Davis, are 'a permanent fixture among Ireland's great cultural possessions'. On Davis, Brown also made the pertinent remark that 'about the most important single figure in the history of Irish cultural nationalism, Thomas Davis, the postwar historians seem almost bound by a conspiracy of silence' and that it is supposed to be 'inelegant' to cite Duffy on him as 'his treatment is said to be unhistorical, but who would know?'[8]

Thoroughly imbued as he was with a quickness of spirit that responded to human emotions and their entwining with nature, Davis was also able to sustain the essential elements of poetry when he was writing prose. Sometimes he used the prose-poem form to describe Irish scenes in an attempt to entrance the reader with their wildness. Without giving any hint that it was his own poem, he commented on 'The Geraldine's Daughter', in language that is almost gothic in the way it plays on the senses,

> To us it calls up a lone lough, and the wild lament sweeping on the autumn wind along the hill sides, till the twilight had gone and the wilder wind was left to cry alone. This may be mere association; but let the reader picture the scenes in the verses twice to his imagination, and listen thrice for the Banshee's shriek, and the mourner's ululu, and the wind's sad howl, ere he says that we, not the poet, were dreaming.[9]

The use of such language in verse or in prose, combined with his desire to develop the concept of nationality and by that make the people thoroughly Irish, has frequently caused critics to dismiss Davis with thinly-veiled contempt as a mere romantic. The fact that his followers were mostly young like himself, that they espoused a cause that went beyond the allegedly pragmatic goal of Repeal and that, in the end, they departed, willingly or unwillingly, from the path marked out by the Liberator, made them easy targets for dismissal as idle dreamers. Moreover, the later adherence to the cause by John Mitchel and Fintan Lalor and the admiration and gratitude shown by Patrick

Pearse, Arthur Griffith and others of 1916 towards Davis in particular, helped to seal his historical fate, as well as that of his companions. Thus they became seen as minor actors on the stage of Irish historical and political drama, whose contribution at best was negative and at worst pernicious. The charge brought against them was of being idle, romantic dreamers, whose lack of a grasp of reality was profound. Some of the modern reaction to Davis is summed up by Tom Dunne who argues that, 'there was no "Romantic era" in early nineteenth-century Ireland, only romantic impulses' which Davis shared and that 'The attempted colonisation of Gaelic culture by Davis, in the interests of his hybrid brand of nationality, was as crude, as calculated and as pejorative as anything in [Lady] Morgan.'[10] Such accusations have clearly been lasting in their effect and deserve serious consideration which can best be done, as a first step, through an examination of Davis's published verse.

Davis spelt out his understanding of the nature and role of national poetry in his essay on *The Ballad Poetry of Ireland*. Such a form of poetry essentially grew from the idea of Irish nationality that Davis was bent on creating. Poetry of that kind 'must contain and represent the races of Ireland'. Consequently, 'It must not be Celtic, it must not be Saxon – it must be Irish', thereby bringing enrichment and vitality through blending the gifts of each of the races. Any country without its national poetry 'proves its hopeless dullness or its utter provincialism', because 'National poetry is the very flowering of the soul – the greatest evidence of its health, the greatest excellence of its beauty'. To Davis, national poetry had to become a treasure to all those for whom it was written and achieve a high role as 'the recognised envoy of our minds among all mankind and to all time'. He was affronted by much of the content of contemporary street ballads, in which there was 'some humour, some tenderness, and some sweetness of sound'. Overall, however, they were marred by 'bombast, or slander, or coarseness, united in all cases with false rhyme, conceited imagery, black paper and blotted printing'. As a result, they 'demean and mislead the people'.

As for the Anglo-Irish songs, mostly of the last century, he judged them as being 'generally indecent or factious'. Perhaps out of reverence for his birthplace, he granted that 'The Rakes of Mallow' was vigorous, musical and Irish, but scarcely 'fit for this generation'. He was particularly anxious that balladists weave their thoughts and words on to the rich background of Irish airs, and he insisted that the tune should always suggest to the writer 'the sentiment of the words'. Were all this done it would not be long before 'Fair and Theatre, Concert and Drawing-room, Road and Shop' would echo with songs evoking 'Love,

Courage, and Patriotism to every heart'.[11]

In his preface to *The voice of the Nation*, which was published as a companion volume to the *The spirit of the Nation* by James Duffy in 1844, Davis further elaborated his thoughts. He said that nationality wanted a literature written by the Irish that would be 'coloured by our scenery, manners and character' while art would be 'applied to express Irish thoughts and belief'. In that way nationality

> would create a race of men full of more intensely Irish character and knowledge, and to that race it would give Ireland. It would give them the seas of Ireland to sweep with their nets and launch on with their navy; the harbours of Ireland to receive a greater commerce than any island in the world; the soil of Ireland to live on by more millions than starve here now; the fame of Irishmen to enhance by their genius and valour; the independence of Ireland to guard by laws and arms.[12]

In all this Davis was no mere theorist. He steeped himself in music as well as history and he paid serious attention to street ballads. Furthermore, he attempted to understand their significant role in a contemporary society that often lacked any other means of communication except the spoken or sung word. In his travels through the countryside, he was constantly on the lookout for little-known ballads and their airs and he immediately committed them to paper, as well as being grateful for any sent to him by his friends. One person on whom he relied was John Edward Pigot who had been his contemporary and close friend at Trinity. Pigot became a barrister, but was 'a musician by nature and training' with 'a perfect passion for Irish music'. Many of the old airs, to which the ballads in *The Nation* were put, were contributed by Pigot and by William Elliot Hudson, also a friend of Davis who was an Irish scholar and a patron of all Irish literary enterprises.[13] Facets of Irish history, the understanding of their past by the people, their facility in the creation of music and Davis's own knowledge of the language were all enhanced in this way. He did not hesitate to be critical, when appropriate, of the contents and style of some ballads and the shoddy methods used by the publishers appalled him. It is possible that someone else was responsible for adding later a bawdy ballad, 'The Humour of Donnybrook', to Davis's collection of street ballads. In any case, it well illustrates the truth of his remark on coarseness.

Davis had an extensive collection of Carolan's airs, with the musical notation all done by hand, and he tried to ensure that his own work lived up to the tradition set by former masters, and especially Carolan.

To some degree he took Moore, 'Glorious Moore', as a model, although he thought that, apart from his love songs and a few of his political lyrics, the rest of Moore's work lacked 'the idiom and colour of the country'. They were also 'too subtle in thought', with the result that they remained confined to the drawing-room. Davis, therefore, tried to bring his songs to the people in a form that was neither Moore's nor that of the street ballad. With their vivid imagery, immediate sense and their basis in airs known to the people, Davis was able to surpass the effect of Moore with his own ballads, but the old tradition of the street ballad lived on throughout Ireland, alongside the songs from *The Nation*.[14]

Long dead before the charge of romanticism was laid against him, Davis, nonetheless, had his own reply. He had become increasingly conscious and proud of the Irish past and he wanted all his countrymen to share its richness with him. Yet that richness did not flow from nature alone, or even from that special blending of nature with human involvement which was unique to the Irish people. To Davis there was a greater and far more embracing civilisation with its heartland in Europe and in the past that had given birth to Europe which he knew of through his classical education. Ireland belonged to that civilisation and had contributed to its development, while becoming an integral part of it. Recognising that Ireland had also drawn from the well springs of Europe did not make him a mere provincial who looked to the metropolis for inspiration. Nor did he harbour the seeds of an aberrant nationalism that set his own concept of the Irish above the level of other people. He wrote,

> This country of ours is no sand-bank, thrown up by some recent caprice of earth. It is an ancient land, honoured in the archives of civilisation, traceable into antiquity by its piety, its valour and its sufferings. Every great European race has sent its stream to the river of Irish minds. Long wars, vast organisations, subtle codes, beacon crimes, leading virtues, and self-mighty men were here. If we live influenced by wind, and sun, and tree, and not by the passions and deeds of the past, we are a thriftless and hopeless people.[15]

Apart from the fact that he had grown up in a home in which the army was woven into the very atmosphere through his father and his brother, John, who also became deputy inspector of Army Hospitals, Davis realised that violent conflict and military exploits were deeply etched into Irish history. A military theme was strong in the ballads he wrote, because he looked back to the past to evoke the figures of the heroes he felt he had to highlight, if not glorify. A deep loathing of violence as the means by which Ireland was made subject had produced its own reaction in that many saw violence in equal or greater measure as the only path to liberty. The recurring invasions of Ireland, the historical remnants of the course of battles across the landscape and the memory of the flight of the 'Wild Geese' to Europe, where they spilt their blood under foreign banners, all coalesced to make it almost impossible to write of the past, and especially in patriotic verse, without the military theme. In Western Christianity, since the days of Tertullian before the conversion of Constantine, pacifism as such was practically unknown. Moral force, as preached by O'Connell, was a remarkable departure from the norm for a leader of Catholic forces, which those of the Repeal movement undoubtedly were. As part of that movement, Davis was prepared to accept moral force because Ireland in its state of unpreparedness had no other option. Some of his ballads suggested that he thought that, given time and thorough preparation, another means could be chosen to achieve independence if moral force were to fail. The men of 1916 had very sound reasons to look back to Davis for inspiration.

After a hesitant start, Davis began to contribute prose and verse each week to *The Nation*. He soon became its most prolific author and his whole life began to revolve around the paper and those who wrote for it. Its urgency and immediate appeal admirably suited his style of journalism and its contents differed from his more academic work in that the paper responded to the problems of the day and was directed at a far wider audience. With the enthusiastic support of a wide range of writers the paper prospered remarkably. Wallis, Pigot, O'Neill Daunt, T. M. Hughes, Madden, Mangan, John Cornelius O'Callaghan and John O'Hagan were among the most frequent contributors. Davis led them all in the first twelve numbers, from 15 October until 31 December 1842, with sixty-six pieces of either verse or prose, followed by Dillon with thirty-one and Duffy with eighteen. An inner circle met for supper each week, at which they discussed future policy. There is no indication that Duffy, either as proprietor or editor, played any role except as a team man although he had to be responsible for the day-to-day management of affairs, including their financial aspects.

Nonetheless, public success had to be won in a way that did not cross the leader whose approval, if not patronage, was vital. The Repeal Association almost immediately signified its support by taking the paper and distributing it to the Repeal Wardens. O'Connell himself began to contribute a piece entitled 'The Repeal Catechism', while his son John wrote one article and two sets of verse in the early numbers. John admitted that his verse was poor and showed his instinctive caution by entitling his article 'Repeal or Degradation', which he insisted was a better heading than 'Repeal or Death'. He thought that the latter smacked 'too much of idle vapour', although the consequences of the Famine perhaps gave him pause for thought after 1845. His father had just retired as lord mayor of Dublin in late 1842, which gave the leader more time to attend to Repeal, and probably greater leisure to read the papers. Whether he intended any snub was unclear, but perhaps as a slight warning to the young men O'Connell took occasion to mention the papers in his speech at the meeting of the Association on 7 November. Despite the fact that the *Nation* had so rapidly become the most potent ally he could possibly have wished for in his struggle to rejuvenate the Repeal movement, he warmly praised the *Weekly Register* and the *Freeman's Journal* as 'excellent' papers, but merely said that he approved of the *Nation*. After his two articles in November 1842, Daniel O'Connell did not contribute further to the paper. John only wrote the one article in November and contributed two minor pieces of verse in December 1842, although he seems to have continued on with his father's 'The Repeal Catechism' which was still being published in some editions in early 1843. In effect, the O'Connells had little direct relationship with the *Nation* after the end of 1842.[16]

Davis had been apprehensive at letting O'Connell's first contribution on 'The Repeal Catechism' be published, especially because it did not arrive at the office until ten o'clock on the Friday night before publication, which meant that they had to drop several leading articles. However, he came to 'like it greatly' and, realising that O'Connell's name would help sell the paper, he 'resolved to be practical, and therefore sacrifice some of my projects, otherwise his alliance with its natural results would have driven me from the journal.' In other words, he had set aside his innate dislike of being allied to a project that inevitably would draw him further into the old Catholic world of O'Connell, which equally would lessen his ability to speak for, and to, the world from which he came. Understandably, given his own background, there is no indication that Duffy had any misgivings about associating his paper with the O'Connell name.[17]

In an attempt to make Repeal more attractive to Protestants, Davis began to run a series of 'Letters from a Protestant on Repeal' which started in the *Nation* on 17 December 1842. Quoting Burke's 'a nation is a spiritual essence', Davis insisted that an educated public was necessary to make that essence a reality, 'for knowledge is power, the power to be free'. He stressed that 'all the races and creeds in the country have at different times acted nobly for Ireland, and generously towards each other', and, for the occasions when that was not so,

Royal Exchange.

repentance and forgiveness were needed. The obstacle to freedom, however, was that many Protestants feared a Catholic ascendancy with, as they thought, the outcome being eventual civil war. Davis claimed that such thinking was wrong because the real interest of Protestants coincided with those of Catholics, both of whom wanted Ireland 'governed *by* and *for* its inhabitants, and by and for them alone'. Speaking to both sides of the religious division he said, 'If you would liberate Ireland, and keep it free, you must have Protestant help.' In his next article he admitted that hitherto, except for 1779-95, there had been little evidence of a desire for unity, but all public relationships had been based on the personal interests of clan and sect. Nonetheless, no independence was possible without unity and, given there were one and a half million Protestants among eight million inhabitants in Ireland their strength was such that no Catholic ascendancy was possible even were it the case that the Catholics wanted it.[18]

After arguing strongly that the Irish had all the necessary qualities to be able to govern themselves, Davis upbraided his Protestant readers because 'they learnt their own history in the literature of their tyrants'. They had only to walk the streets and see how their very names and statuary boasted with 'monuments to oppression', while the great heroes such as Brian Boru, Sarsfield, O'Neill and Tone were all missing. When one looked at the inhabitants of the towns, 'the artisan scares us with his gaunt vision and tottering limbs'. In Dublin, the Custom House had become 'a museum for miscellaneous trifles', the Exchange was 'a lonely vault', the Castle was 'the eyrie of the invader' and the old Parliament was 'a den of money-changers'. Had they read it, that latter remark would scarcely have endeared him to the directors of the Bank of Ireland who had set up their headquarters in the noble building. He longed for a voice to proclaim, 'Let there be a nation', especially given that Ireland compared so well in comparison to other nations. He instanced Belgium with 3,850,000 inhabitants, a revenue of £3,800,000 and a surface area of 11,000 square miles, compared to Ireland with 8,750,000 inhabitants, £4,4000,000 in revenue and 42,000 square miles in area. Despite all it potential richness, Davis said, 'Ireland has a body but no soul.'[19]

The primitive concept of the nation as a quasi-person had taken some shape in Davis's thinking. 'For great is the strength of a young nation when it becomes an organised and completed being, and God has breathed into its nostrils the breath of life, and given it a reasonable and passionate soul,' he wrote in November 1842. He had not experienced the excesses to which such thinking so easily led, with the nation becoming an entity unfettered by any laws other than those it saw fit to make for itself. Similarly, nature took on aspects of the transcendental, as in the poem he based on the German of Stolberg entitled 'Mother Earth', where Davis spoke of 'Sweet holy Nature'. He saw in the change from the religion of the Druids to that of Christianity an instance of how 'rites may change and creeds may fail'. He also had an article on Jean Paul Richter who never indulged in 'debasing (people) or driving them high flying mad about creeds and liturgies', but saw heaven and earth in the land. Richter was said to play 'at ducks and drakes with children on the shores of infinity which surrounds the world island . . . The surface of his deep soul ever leaps and sparkles in the sunshine'.[20] What his readers, or those who had his words read to them in rural Ireland, or those others who pondered over them in the Catholic presbyteries of the land, made of such material, to the extent that it was not mere nonsense used to pad out the paper, is unclear. The fact remains that a kind of a belief in a mystical Ireland had begun to grow in Davis, which only his exposure to the complex economic and social problems of a real Ireland could displace or round out. The wonder is that Duffy ever permitted the publication of such material. It was likely, if persisted in and taken at all seriously, to do as much harm to the cause among Catholics as the writings of O'Connell would do among Protestants. In the event, commonsense gained sway and Davis rarely ever wrote in that vein again.

Davis read and could translate with ease Latin, French, Italian and German. Without depending on them, he had exposed his mind to the writings of the Europeans and he drew something that appealed to his own spirit from the prevailing intellectual climate that had swept through Europe under the title of romanticism. That is not to say that he swallowed its ideas *bolus bolus*, that he did not adapt them to the Irish scene, or that his own thoughts did not predate his reading of the Europeans. He was conscious that an alternative was needed to the two prevailing ideological categories that pertained throughout Ireland, so he sought one that would unite them. The category used by O'Connell was of old Ireland, Catholic, loyal to the crown, steeped in the centuries of wrongs and now ready to assume its role as the true expression of Ireland. The other was that of the Protestant ascendancy. For them the Irish nation for so long had been the Protestant nation and through the maintenance of the union with England they were determined to hang on grimly to their position of supremacy, although they were a minority. Davis wanted to cut through both categories with a new vision of a united Ireland, based on a semi-spiritual idea. Through language, art, history, geography and an identification with the land, the true nation would express itself once it had grasped and acted upon the ideal of nationality. He would have accepted wholeheartedly the statement of Turgenev who claimed that without nationality there is 'no art, nor truth, nor life, nor anything'. Above all, Davis understood that nationality could not be organised, paraded, or lightly won. Education was the means to achieve it and the *Nation* was seen by him as a singularly effective vehicle to diffuse education among the Irish people. The problem he seems to have underestimated was that his chosen vehicle of instruction was not much in circulation among the Protestant Irish. Without them, his dream nation would never be born.[21]

In an attempt to set his agenda he began, in the very early editions of the *Nation,* to write about the Irish language, at the sound of which Ireland 'would grow bright and eloquent'. He wanted religious harmony and he tried to gather in the Protestants by praising the late Protestant bishop of Cashel, Dr Stephen Sandes, who, despite his Protestantism, went to his grave at Trinity College 'with the blessing of all sects, parties and classes'. He longed to see an Irish merchant navy, built and financed in Ireland, which would form the basis of a 'National Navy'. Davis was not defending peasant outrages when he granted that the crimes of both landlords and peasants arose from 'the system', but he was quick to assert that the landlords were able to act with impunity because they were 'backed by English force'. Thus, 'God gave the land to the People, Conquest took it from them. Let justice restore it.' Scotland should become Ireland's ally, but she too had to struggle for self-government if she wanted to be truly Scotland. Furthermore, a Scotland won to the cause of freedom would 'conciliate the feelings of our Presbyterian countrymen' and by increasing the confidence of Irish Protestants would help to relieve them of their 'unreasonable fear of Catholic ascendancy'. While he accepted that the Westminster Confession 'may be most objectionable' to Catholics, he tried to draw a lesson in freedom of conscience because the Scottish Presbyterian had 'the right to judge and act on [his] own conviction, though others think the conviction erroneous. For this we contend; let us, if we are real advocates of religious liberty, concede it to others.' In that and other ways, he tried to share his conviction on the need for perfect religious freedom even though he was aware that most of his readers were Catholics.[22]

Davis was also insistent that Ireland should never turn her back on any assistance she might receive in her struggle for independence, whether from Paris or Washington, and laughed at the way in which critics tried to belittle the *Nation* by saying it was a French organ and her writers a French party. This latter sally towards France and America brought a response from the *Standard* which accused him of 'high treason'. Davis asked, 'Traitors against what? Against debasing and villainous tyranny! Traitors against English supremacy and Irish slavery.' When the *Monitor* joined the *Standard* in criticism, Davis proved he could give back what he got with interest by saying that the paper was a whining, 'sour old maid' and that it had 'no principles and represents no party'. He went on, 'We said and we repeat it, that no man who is not profoundly ignorant can doubt that England has ruined and re-ruined us by every species of oppression, military and civil, commercial and agricultural – that she has lavished every species of fraud and cruelty, and insult on us, in war and peace, from Strongbow's time to Elizabeth's ... and from thence to this day.' He insisted that he would do all possible to continue to make friends with France, 'the enemy of our enemy'. Surprisingly, given the suspicion of, if not latent hostility towards the *Nation*, that had already begun to manifest itself in the circle around O'Connell, John O'Connell also asked for a foreign policy for Ireland that would include attempting to attract the sympathy of the French. His father, who wanted no truck with England's enemies, including France, was being given every cause to become disturbed at the trends evident in every edition of the new paper.[23]

At this time, at any rate, Davis was not going to permit himself to lose sight of his objectives by any manner of reproof from elsewhere, no matter how authoritative. Thus, he meant no offence to the Chinese as a race when he spoke of 'Poor China', as 'a big, feeble, bed-ridden old woman' who was despicable because she would not resist the English 'barbarians'. His terminology in that passage was neither racist nor sexist when seen in its contemporary setting, but it was assuredly excessive. He had been charged with religious sectarianism because of his articles on the behaviour of the English towards China and Afghanistan, which he refuted by saying he was not a Catholic although his articles, as all the rest of the paper, remained anonymous. He went on to detail the 'ferocity and deceit' of England in China, the Cape, India, Canada, West Africa, Argentina and in North America against the indigenous and white populations. 'She has rotted away by her avarice and vices, half the population of Australia and Polynesia; and cleared out, with bullet and bayonet, the "last man" from the great island of Van Dieman (sic) – thus accomplishing at the Antipodes that extermination so often and vainly tried in Ireland.' When the queen's speech to Parliament was reported in February 1843, Davis wrote that it was of no concern to him that she did not mention Ireland because, while it would be well and good were England to liberate Ireland, if England refused to do so then 'we shall liberate ourselves'. In any event, he thought there was nothing worth noticing in the speech which he called 'this vapid and faithless document'. O'Connell could not continue to let all this pass without notice, but he was conciliatory and spoke in a mild tone at the Association saying that, 'He had never through life been anxious for French or foreign alliances' but that he always relied on Irishmen. He concluded that statement of gentle reproof with a further and fulsome proclamation of loyalty to the queen on behalf of the Irish people.[24]

By early February 1843, Davis had already seen twelve of his poems or ballads published in the *Nation*. Some of them were merely ephemeral, such as 'Sir Robert Peel' and 'Lord Eliot a repealer', but they all contained the same message of nationality.[25] His fifth poem was 'Lines in imitation of Burns' which speaks of Ireland as a 'rich and rare land'. The manuscript survives and proves that he wrote on the run in that, with a few swift corrections, the first version became the final one.[26] His weekly output was such that he normally contributed 15,000 words or more to each edition in the form of articles, reviews, poems and ballads, though some misinformed public opinion held that William Carleton was the sole writer. Carleton asked Duffy to assert publicly that he had never written a single line in the paper. Duffy complied, while making it clear to the readers of the *Nation* that Carleton would be a welcome contributor 'even though he has wronged and misrepresented the people of Ireland'. Carleton was already a friend of Duffy and later contributed 'Valentine McCarthy' as a serial in the paper, but he never became a Repealer or associated himself on any basis other than friendship with the young men.[27]

Davis's ability to attract to himself so many like Carleton, whom J. M. Synge said was the father of modern Irish literature, and that they felt the power of his personality reveals something of the magnetism of his character. They could disagree with him on a fundamental point, but they could not turn away from him. Carleton said, 'That he was my friend is at once my pride and sorrow.' The sorrow blended with the pride because Carleton differed from Davis in that he was against the Repeal of the Union. To Carleton, Davis had 'a character so full and complete, a mind so large and comprehensive', that he was a man of genius 'without the shadow of those errors which almost always accompany [genius]'. In him, Carleton treasured the one quality that surpassed all others because Davis 'added the spell of a child-like and loving heart' to them. Thus Davis, although he had not grown from birth with the old language as Carleton had, was still one worthy to say to others whom he loved, 'my soul within you'. Characteristically, Carleton wrote of Davis, 'As a poet he could have sung a people into freedom; as a statesman he had the capacity to deal with empires; in the field he would have led armies; in the council he would have balanced and guided the destiny of nations.' Carleton also said that Davis had an indelible influence on him and that principally it was

Davis who moved him to do all he could in his writings for the peasantry from which he was born.[28]

It would probably be too much to read into the immediate success of the *Nation* and the enthusiasm of his new group of supporters any direct connection with the fact that, from a sense of despondency regarding Repeal, O'Connell shifted into a higher gear. There had been successful meetings with large crowds at Rathkeale (20,000), and Roscommon (25,000), in October 1842 and O'Neill Daunt reported from Kilbeggan that all the priests and prelates he had met were pro-Repeal. There was an increasingly clear connection between the seriousness of much of the Catholic population on political matters and the development of the temperance movement. Davis railed against drunkenness as 'the luxury of despair and the saturnalia of slaves', while admitting that its source lay in the great suffering of so many of the people. He linked temperance to industry, education and material well-being and he praised Father Mathew's Temperance Movement which was flourishing. In Cork, 60,000 people took the pledge, 14,000 of whom did so in the one day and many of the same people began to attend Repeal meetings. The large gathering of Repeal faithful allegedly put it into the heads of Davis, Dillon and their friend and fellow member of the Association, Michael Doheny, to suggest that they be further developed. According to Doheny, they had 'one great object with them [which] was to train the country people to military movements and a martial tread. This object it would be unsafe to announce, and it was to be effected through other agencies.'[29]

The Association's meetings in Dublin rapidly took on a new urgency and O'Connell saw the good sense of linking Repeal with other questions more likely to have an immediate appeal to the people, such as the Poor Law and land tenure. Furthermore, there was a growing insistence on the link between the Union with England and the allegedly deplorable state of the economy in Ireland as a kind of cause and effect. A great deal has been written in recent times on the state of the Irish economy in the period after the Union that tends to argue against contemporary judgements made by the Repealers. The Repealers, however, could only observe and react to what they saw about them. They lacked the 'scientific' methods of later economists and economic historians, but many of them had experienced the miserable conditions they described. In that manner, Ray reported to the Association that in Millstreet the poor were now forced to save manure to pay their rents of 15s to £1.5.0 for mere 'huts'. In 1800, there had been 2,000 looms in Bandon and 300 in Dunmanway, all of which were now closed and falling into ruins. In his judgement, the only remedy for the state of the economy was employment, but the continuation of the Union made it impossible to carry out policies designed to increase employment. The Association then set up a useful body with the title 'The Repeal Board of Trade', which took responsibility for examining the Irish economy. In one report it asserted that, in 1800, there had been 1,100 workers engaged in the hosiery industry at an average wage of £1.5.0 per week. By 1842 that workforce had been reduced to a mere seventy-nine on a wage of 6s. per week, only half of whom were in constant employment. Through such bodies as the Repeal Board of Trade and in other ways, but notably through the rapid spread of the Reading Rooms, the movement was taking flesh.[30]

Thus by 1843 O'Connell sensed his moment had come and in any event he had nothing to lose. His enemies were in power in Westminster and the tedium of arduous journeys across the Irish sea, to engage in futile debates as a member of a hostile Parliament, had begun to weary him. He was no longer engaged in his duties as lord mayor and the contributions to the fund raised through the parishes for his own support had risen appreciably, so it seemed an appropriate time to strike. He began with a long letter on New Year's Day 1843 to the people of Ireland from his home at Derrynane Abbey. He wanted the abolition of tithes, fixity of tenure for tenants, the development and protection of goods manufactured locally, the extension of the franchise, a vote by ballot and the abolition of the present Poor Law. Thus, 1843 would become 'glorious in the history of Ireland' with the breaking of the Union, but three million Repealers would be needed and their recruitment would depend on the Repeal wardens. In another letter of 12 January he said, *Let this be the Repeal Year. The Union will be repealed and Ireland will be free.*'[31]

There could be no turning back once all this had been said, but the question remains just how the leader thought he would achieve his objective. What he had done was to let forth a rallying cry that rested on the assumption that England would be moved to grant Ireland her freedom merely by the pressure exerted through the force of logical argument and the spell of enthusiastic crowds. Macauley summed up succinctly the attitude of those who held power in England, 'The Repeal of the Union we regard as fatal to the Empire and we will never consent to it . . . till the four quarters of the world had been convulsed by the last struggle of the great English people for their place among the nations.' The Irish could scarcely have been said to be English, but their role, like that of India or any other subject people, was clear. They served the interests of Empire and through their land and economy they fostered the aggrandisement of 'the great English people'.[32]

The *Nation*, now with a direct readership said to be 60,000, did not waver in its adhesion to Repeal despite the continuation of the, as yet, small rifts that were opening between it and the Repeal leadership. The latter spoke with a single voice and that voice was O'Connell's, while the contributors to the paper were allowed a wide rein in the opinions they expressed. The question of the Poor Law simmered on as a bone of contention with the *Nation* insisting on reform, while O'Connell still wanted abolition. Duffy entered the lists against O'Connell who, at a meeting of the Association, had sharply criticised Dr Maginn of Cork and Father Prout as pseudo-liberals because they directed their great powers of ridicule 'against their country'. To Duffy, every Irishman should be proud to acclaim the fame of those who shared their blood or name, because their achievements provided a strong argument why Ireland should not remain a province. O'Connell retorted sharply at an Association meeting saying that the Irish people would never agree with any writer who defended Maginn and Prout. Perhaps in reference to the successful and growing numbers that had begun to attend Repeal meetings, Davis sounded a slightly sour note with an article on 'Self Education', which even large-minded O'Connell must have taken as unnecessary criticism of the tried and trusty weapon of mass organisation that he had used with such effect before 1829. Davis said that 'assemblies' were not the best places for education and that home or solitude were better. In the home the 'greatest things', such as 'reverence for the old, affection without passion, truth, piety and justice' were all learnt, as well as mechanical skills, labour, decorum, cleanliness and order. More significantly, and provocatively, he wrote, 'Thinking cannot be done by deputy – they (the people) must think for themselves.' He seemed to overlook the fact that the *Nation* itself was engaged in doing a great deal of thinking for the same people whom O'Connell was attempting to instruct and awaken by his oratory.[33]

Some of this unpleasantness had undoubtedly been called forth in response to an article by Richard Barrett, editor of the *Pilot*. Nonetheless, none of it served a useful purpose when such matters more usefully could have been dealt with privately or at the meetings of the Association. From the beginning Barrett had left no doubt about where his sympathies lay. When the *Nation* was first published it had not rated a mention by him, but by January 1843 he had clearly become uncomfortable with its marked success. He decided to use Davis's recent attack on the *Monitor* as his target. 'The last *Nation* contained a raving article,' wrote Barrett, because it had denied that it had any connection with the *Monitor*. The fact was that the *Nation* was printed by the press owned by the *Monitor*, which proved to Barrett that both papers were mere 'sham-antagonists' and 'masked professors of patriotism'. Thus, 'true to the hatreds and virulence of its *Monitor* paternity, the *Nation* promises another stereotyped edition of *Monitor* rascality'. Furthermore, Barrett claimed that the writers in the *Nation* were the same writers who had published so much 'objectionable' material in the *Citizen*.[34]

Although Duffy effectively repudiated the 'lies and innuendoes' of the *Pilot*, with this volley the young men were given a clear warning that they were in Barrett's sights. It is safe to assume that Barrett did not act without the knowledge and approval of John O'Connell, if not the leader himself, even though the *Nation* gave a favourable notice to O'Connell's recently-published book on Irish history entitled *An historical memoir of Ireland and the Irish Native and Saxon addressed to Her Majesty, Queen Victoria* and Davis defended the work from an attack in the *Spectator*, 'a London hybrid which barks like a Radical and bites like a Tory'. In any case Duffy was able to put the unpleasantness straight back to O'Connell who had once told him, 'Never vex yourself that your opinions are misconceived or disputed. When you have to complain of an attack, refute it, as I do by doubling your exertions for your country.' Duffy then wrote, 'to which philosophy we say, Amen'.[35]

On 28 February 1843, O'Connell well and truly launched the Repeal Year with a motion he put before the Dublin Corporation in favour of Repeal. O'Connell, as was agreed between the Catholics and Protestants on the Corporation, had been succeeded by a Protestant lord mayor, Alderman Roe, who tried to stifle the debate from the chair, but he was outnumbered by O'Connell's supporters. The debate went ahead and O'Connell spoke for four hours and ten minutes in measured tones and with reasoned argument which reiterated all that he had said elsewhere. Duffy was so pleased that he called the speech 'a wonderful one, even for him'. Isaac Butt, who had been appointed to the chair of Political Economy at Trinity at the age of twenty-three and who continued his remarkable career at the Bar, unsuccessfully opposed the motion with an amendment to adjourn discussion *sine die*. Butt then spoke for two hours and gave Ireland a foretaste of his future high competence and integrity when, having seen in another light where things lay between England and Ireland, he would defend the Young Irelanders in 1848, the Fenians in the 1860s and be the leader of the Home Rule party in the 1870s.[36]

Butt pointed out that, unless they went for outright separation, 'they could be nothing but a paltry, pitiful province of England – a mere provincial and colonial parliament'. In short, he argued that, without separation, there could be no nation, as Tone had made plain, but O'Connell was refusing to clarify what he wanted by not spelling out what kind of national independence he sought. He confronted O'Connell and asked him to recognise that separation would mean taking the well nigh impossible step of having to create a new and untried state. Finally, Butt asked, 'How were they to get the British parliament to agree with a Repeal unless by physical force?' and he argued, probably unwisely as very few agreed with him, that Ireland had become better off economically since the Union. By bringing in physical force he effectively undercut the reiterated statement by O'Connell in his speech that he would not consent to spill blood, except his own, 'for all the universe contains'. In his conclusion Butt pleaded with the Catholics to 'abandon all schemes of wild ambition of ascendancy which was the real object of Repeal'. It was an unfair accusation and could only be based on speculation. Furthermore, it begged the question because, if a Protestant ascendancy was acceptable to him, what could be so damaging about a Catholic one unless it was intended as a means to reduce the Protestants to the general level of material misery endured by so many of the Catholics? The debate languished on tediously for three days and was widely reported in the press, locally and in England. When the vote was taken the motion was upheld by 41 votes to 15 and the Liberator was again Ireland's hero. Davis praised him and rejoiced that Protestants and Catholics were uniting 'for the glory and independence of Old Ireland', but, like O'Connell, he was careful not to spell out what kind of independence he wanted.[37]

To the extent that Davis and O'Connell agreed on Repeal it was because they both wanted an Irish nation. For Davis that nation was to be essentially an amalgam of all its parts and thus a new thing. He felt it was his special mission to help create it by diffusing in song and story and article the deepest meaning of nationality. The Irish past was ever present in his idea of nationality and from that flowed his intense interest in archaeology, the preservation of the ruins of the past, the folklore and, above all, the language and the literature. The present too had to express itself as Irish in education, commerce, foreign relations, institutions, navy, army, flag and whatever else gave outer and physical shape to nationality.[38] To Davis, nationality was truly the soul of the people and he asked, 'What shall it profit a man or a nation, if they gain the whole world and lose their soul.'[39] To O'Connell, the nation was already a reality and he did not feel the need to concern himself with such matters in the same way as Davis, nor did he need to dwell on the meaning of nationality. Others could live in harmony within his Gaelic Catholic nation, but they could only contribute to it fully by becoming part of it.

Neither Davis nor O'Connell were willing to face the question of the shape of the state on the political and legal level. Butt was sufficiently acute to point out in the great debate that, by asking for Repeal, all that

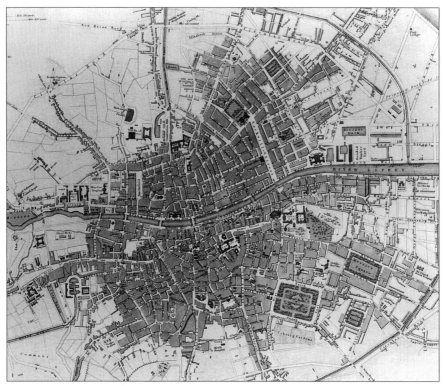

Map of Dublin in 1836 by the Society for the Promotion of Useful Knowledge (Map courtesy of Joe Brady, University College Dublin, photograph by Sarah Cully).

was sought was of British origin in that the parliament with its two houses, which they hoped to restore to College Green, was a mere replica of that which existed across the Irish Sea. He asked whether, as an alternative, they wanted to go back to the past, adopt the old Brehon legal system and organise social life based on the hierarchical system of chieftains. By such an argument, he cleverly made his point, even though it was in a facile way.[40] The refusal by O'Connell to confront that problem was of little moment, especially given that he wanted no separation and that he accepted the monarchy whole-heartedly, together with the institutions of British origin that flowed from it. This, in effect, meant that he accepted that his Gaelic Catholic nation could clothe itself in the shape of the British state and suffer no loss. In his favour, the probability is that he thought that, while a form of independence which meant Ireland's total separation from Britain and its Empire would never be granted, the possibility was there that conditional independence within the Empire would be acceptable. To him that would be enough in that it would at least return to the status quo that obtained before 1801.

For Davis, any such form of vacillation was fatal. Unless his idea of nationality could be expressed in the form of a state that gave it visible vitality, the soul would be stifled in an alien body. Separation based on the threat, at least, of the use of force was the only way ultimately to achieve, even minimally, the Ireland of Davis's dreams. To remain aligned to O'Connell and his Repeal movement, as O'Connell spelt it out, would seem to spell the end of Davis's hopes. At the time, to leave either the leader or his cause was unthinkable because there was nowhere else to go. He could only fight for Repeal provided he could continue to think of it as a first step towards complete independence.

Davis was always seeking examples of other nations in a similar situation to Ireland and he found one in Italy. He quoted from Rome's *Notizie del Giorno* of 9 February, in which the *Nation* was commented on favourably and he claimed that Ireland's cause was the same as Italy's because 'we are provinces resolved to be nations.' Disunity had been the downfall of both peoples but, united internally, they would both throw off the yoke of the 'barbarians' who kept them subject. His knowledge of Italian history, as well as the language, was clearly sufficient for him to repeat the ancient cry of the Italians as they tried to rise against their invaders, 'fuori i barbari', 'out with the barbarians'. He read with interest the fulsome praise heaped upon the *Nation* by the newly-founded *La Nation* of Paris and then went on to lecture his readers on the development of democracy, which he said had only 'kept half the promises given by its apostles'. The greatest danger of democracy was its tendency to centralisation, which he termed 'an official form of despotism'. Such an aberration was 'at least as great a foe to freedom, to spirit, and to prosperity, as aristocracy'. The upheaval caused by the swallowing of smaller states in the Napoleonic era moved him to say that, just as Ireland had to repeal the Union, Europe had to repeal centralisation and 'to create as many separate nations, with separate governments, laws, manners, characters, and languages' as the respective peoples deemed desirable and possible. 'Local governments, national institutions, round which national gems of literature can grow, which national recollections can adorn – this is, this ought to be the policy of the patriot and the philanthropist, this should be the propagandism of our age.'[41] For Ireland, and for some other nations groaning to be born or reborn, the problem was that the state was already shaped by their 'barbarian' invaders. Such a state could be reformed. It could not be reshaped without the possibility of shattering the whole fabric.

In 1843, Thomas Davis turned twenty-eight, but no hint of romance had entered his life. The prevailing tendency to marry within one's own class and religion made his choice narrow. Despite his closeness to many young men who were Catholics, to contemplate marriage with a Catholic woman was bordering on the unthinkable. Even the old penal law forbidding Catholic priests, under pain of death, to officiate at the marriage of a Catholic with a Protestant had not been repealed until 1833 and a mixed marriage for a Protestant was generally as unacceptable as such a marriage was for a Catholic. Although not unique, the way in which Davis had gathered about him such a number of Catholic friends was in itself both remarkable and a possible source of estrangement from his own co-religionists. There seemed to be in Ireland 'a mutually agreed upon decision to keep apart' and in 1835 a Protestant lawyer told Alexis de Tocqueville that there existed 'between the members of the two religions a distance that you cannot conceive.' He had only once in his life dined in a Catholic house and then 'quite by accident' and he said that in Dublin there were about as many Catholic barristers as Protestants, but despite the links that bound them professionally, they 'see each other, but do not associate with one another'.[42]

In his own Protestant circle Davis could scarcely be regarded as a suitable candidate by the parents of any young woman with whom he came into contact. He had no profession except that of journalism, slender means to support himself, much less a family, and no apparent prospect of a successful career. Above all, his public life had put him well beyond the pale in the eyes of most Dublin Protestants, among many of whom he stood almost as an exile. Publicly, he was known as a versifier of ballads and writer of articles that bordered on the treasonable, an associate of O'Connell and, as its enemies regarded it, the Catholic rabble of the Corn Exchange. Finally, he was a determined advocate of Repeal and perhaps even of separation from the crown and Empire, with all its dire implications for the future of Protestant power. More importantly to some observers, he was a young man whose very demeanour of absentmindedness and untidiness made him appear an oddity in any drawing-room.

Only a rash or a brave woman would dare cross all those barriers to enter into a romantic attachment with Davis. Possibly, some such thoughts were in his mind when he wrote a poem he called 'The Exile'. Its apparent purpose was to describe the loneliness of those young exiles who had been forced to flee Ireland for religion and politics in the past and who had pined away their days in a distant land. One verse came close to his own situation,

> When soft on their chosen the young maidens smile
> Like the dawn of the morn on Erin's dear isle,
> With no love – smile to cheer me, I look on the while,
> For, ah! the poor exile is ever alone.[43]

References

1. See W. B. Yeats, *Tribute to Thomas Davis,* with a foreword by Denis Gwynn (Cork, 1947), p. 17; Richard Ellman, *Oscar Wilde* (London, 1988), pp 6-7; Terence de Vere White, *The parents of Oscar Wilde* (London, 1967), p. 17; Hone, *Davis,* pp 118-9.

2. See Yeats, *Tribute,* p. 12; *The poems of Thomas Davis: now first collected with notes and historical illustrations* (Dublin, 1853), p. xiii. The editor of the poems, and author of the introduction, notes and historical illustrations, signed himself as T. W. on 20 April, 1846. The T. W. was Thomas Wallis. On Andrew Fletcher, see the introduction by Leonard R. N. Ashley to Gavan Duffy (ed.), *The ballad poetry of Ireland,* New York, 1973, p. vii. The book was first published in Dublin in 1845, by James Duffy (1809-71), no relation to Charles Gavan Duffy, who became the unofficial publisher for the *Nation* writers. The inscription on his tomb at Glasnevin bore the words 'the historical works he published have exalted the character of his native land, and saved its saints and heroes from oblivion.' See O'Sullivan, *Young Irelanders,* p. 421.

3. See Rolleston (ed.), *Prose writings of Thomas Davis* (London, 1899), p. 201.

4. *Nation,* 29 October 1842.

5. Ibid., 29 Oct; 5, 12, 19 November 1842; Duffy, *Davis,* pp 93-4. See Kearney to Davis, n.d. but after October 1842. Ms 230.47, RIA.

6. See Jerrold I. Casway, *Owen Roe O'Neill and the struggle for Catholic Ireland* (Philadelphia, 1984), pp 252, 261. In the original 'Lament' printed in the *Nation,* 19 November 1842, Davis used Owen Roe. He changed to a variant of the Irish Oeghan and Ruadh when the poem was printed in later collections.

7. See George-Denis Zimmerman, *Irish political street ballads and rebel songs* (Geneva, 1966), pp 22, 28. The Irish Ruadh is pronounced as Roe, See Rolleston (intro.) *Thomas Davis, selections from his prose and poetry,* London, 1914.

8. See Yeats, *Tribute,* pp 13-14.; Malcolm Brown, *The politics of Irish literature from Thomas Davis to W. B. Yeats* (London, 1972), pp ii, 64-5.

9. *Nation,* 15 October 1842.

10. Tom Dunne, 'Haunted by history: Irish romantic writing 1800-1850', in Roy Porter and Mikulas Teich (eds.), *Romanticism in national context* (Cambridge, 1988), pp 69-9, 79, 88.

11. *Nation,* 2 August 1845 where Davis reviews Gavan Duffy's, *The ballad poetry of Ireland* (Dublin, 1845), which contained many of Davis's ballads. It was a huge success and, by the time of its 39th edition in 1866, it had sold 76,000 copies around the world. Instead of working from the *Nation,* I generally used the collection of Davis's essays in Rolleston (ed.), *Prose writings.* This essay is found at pp 193-4.

12. See O'Sullivan, *The Young Irelanders,* pp 73-4.

13. See 'Letters of Thomas Davis' in *The Irish Monthly: a magazine of general literature,* vol. 16 (Dublin, 1888), p. 261.

14. Thomas Davis, '45 Irish song sheets', NLI (no call number); Carolan's airs, Davis's copy, Ms 14099, NLI; George-Denis Zimmerman, *Irish ... ballads,* pp 77, 81.

15. Wallis (ed.), *The poems,* p. 72.

16. See the *Nation,* 5, 12, 19 November, 5, 10, 17 December, 1842; Duffy, *Davis,* p. 95; Kevin McGrath, 'Writers in the "Nation", 1842-5', in *Irish Historical Studies,* vi (Dublin, 1949), pp 189-223. McGrath's is an exhaustive study of the contributors but after 1843, when Davis no longer specified contributors in his copy of the *Nation,* it is less useful.

17. Davis to Madden, 6 November 1842 in Duffy, *Davis,* pp 94-5.

18. *Nation*, 17, 31 December 1842. The letters were later reprinted in an edition by Thomas Meagher. See Thomas Davis, *Letter of a protestant on repeal* (Dublin, 1847).

19. *Nation*, 25 February, 24 June 1843.

20. Ibid., 26 November, 31 December 1842; 7 January 1843.

21. See Turgenev in Malcolm Brown, *The politics*, p. 14.

22. *Nation*, 12, 26 November 1842.

23. Ibid., 3, 10, 17, 31 December 1842; 4 February 1843.

24. Ibid., 18 February 1843.

25. Ibid., 29 Oct, 5, 12, 19 November, 3, 17, 24, 31 December 1842; 7,14, 21 January, 4 February 1843.

26. Ms 12, p. 19 (12b) in RIA; *Nation*, 3 December, 1842.

27. Ibid., 26 November, 1842.

28. See Benedict Kiely, *Poor scholar. A study of the works and days of William Carleton (1794-1869)* (Dublin, 1947), pp 91, 92, 107-10; Ibid., p. 110. See also Foster (ed.), *The Oxford illustrated history of Ireland*, pp 307-8.

29. Michael Doheny, *The felon's track* (New York, 1849), 3rd ed. with a preface by Arthur Griffith (Dublin, 1918), p. 20.

30. *Nation*, 9, 22 October, 5, 12 November, 10 December 1842; 28 January, 11 February 1843.

31. Ibid., 5 November 1842; 7, 21 January 1843.

32. See Malcolm Brown, *The politics*, p. 5.

33. *Nation*, 25 February, 4 March 1843.

34. Ibid., 4 March 1843; *Pilot*, 30 January 1843.

35. *Nation*, 28 January, 18, 25 February, 4 March 1843; Daniel O'Connell, *An historical memoir of Ireland and the Irish Native and Saxon addressed to Her Majesty, Queen Victoria,* vol. 1, 1172-1660 (Dublin, 1843). No more volumes appeared.

36. *Nation*, 4 March 1843.

37. Ibid., 4, 11 March 1843.

38. R. F. Foster in his *Modern Ireland* said, 'In many ways the spirit of the *Nation* was as modernist and utilitarian as O'Connell,' p. 311.

39. Ibid., 18 March 1843.

40. Ibid., 4 March 1843.

41. Ibid., 25 February, 18 March 1843. The copy of *La Nation* from which Davis quoted on 18 March was dated 17 March, which reinforces the judgement of the efficiency of the British postal services.

42. See Denys Scully, *A statement of the penal laws, which aggrieve the Catholics of Ireland* (Dublin, 1812) pp 16-17; Donald Harman Akenson, *Irish Catholics and Irish Protestants, 1815-1922: an international perspective* (Toronto, 1981), p. 111; Larkin (trans. and ed.), *Alexis de Tocqueville's journey*, p. 73.

43. Ibid., 4 March 1843.

Chapter 8

Play and counter play

The English statesmen initially took little notice of O'Connell's new movement, even when it began to assume faintly alarming proportions in early 1843. They had become accustomed to his tactical manoeuvres and they hoped that, whatever he was up to now, would lead to nothing other than repeated bombast. Pondering on the new agitation, some of them thought that it was a mistake to have given in back in 1829. Only fourteen years had passed and here O'Connell was at it again, but this time he was asking for something that made Emancipation seem like a matter of little moment. At least, they could console themselves with the fact that the concessions made in 1829 had resulted in only marginal progress for the Catholic majority in Ireland. The right to vote by those who held a freehold worth forty shillings was abolished and that right was granted only to those whose freehold was worth at least £10. The result was that the electoral rolls were slashed and landlords no longer felt constrained to cajole or favour their tenants in return for votes. The Municipal Reform Act of 1840 seemed to be a liberal measure, except that it contained a clause giving the lord lieutenant the right to nominate the sheriffs of the counties, thereby ensuring the control of juries by the Crown.

Tenants still paid their rents to landlords, many of whom spent the proceeds in Britain, or elsewhere abroad, to the amount of about £5,000,000 in 1843. An alleged surplus of about £1,000,000 from the Irish exchequer went annually to British coffers. In 1843, nearly 100,000 people migrated from Ireland, much manufacturing industry had stagnated or disappeared entirely and most primary products were still exported annually to Britain to the level of about £15,000,000. Despite the long and bitter protests of the Catholic majority who, in the main, could scarcely support themselves, they were still forced to pay tithes to a minority, and largely alien, Church, even if the reformed method of payment was through an addition to rent. Meanwhile, the new system of national education, with all its considerable merits, was run in great measure by Protestant commissioners on a small budget of £50,000. They did not seek directly to subvert the Catholic children from their faith, but merely from adhesion to the nation into which they were born. As a first step, that meant they learnt nothing of the past of their people. On school walls a verse was put up for the edification and instruction of the pupils. It said,

> I thank the goodness and the grace
> That on my birth have smiled,
> And made me in these Christian days,
> A happy English child.[1]

In the legal arena, Coercion Act had followed Coercion Act with powers to proclaim districts, disperse meetings, declare a curfew, introduce martial law in proclaimed districts, search houses at will and suspend *Habeas Corpus* for three months. In normal years over 20,000 regular troops were stationed in Ireland. They were constantly on the move so as to make the population aware of them, while the main towns were dominated by the presence of military barracks which made them in effect garrison towns in the same manner as in convict Australia. Correspondence from selected leading figures in Ireland, including O'Connell, was subject to inspection, detectives abounded, 13,000 policemen were heavily armed and, by mid-1843, 35,000 troops were scattered throughout the land. The Savings Banks were government institutions which ensured that would-be agitators had to contend with the fact that insurrection was unlikely among people whose meagre savings depended upon the maintenance of peace. On the other hand, among the unemployed, the landless and the indigent, it was always possible that resentment would express itself in forceful means. The so-called Poor Houses, which had sprung up throughout the land since 1838, ensured that such potential malcontents remained tranquil as an alternative to starvation. Evictions went on with dreadful regularity but government charity through the Poor Houses ensured that some of the more fortunate of the evacuees did not remain roofless. Nonetheless, the Poor Law and its application was everywhere a cause for concern. Yet, when Smith O'Brien moved in the House of Commons in late March 1843 for a Select Committee to probe the manner of its being carried out in Ireland, he spoke to an almost empty house and the vote was lost by 108 to 23.[2]

'Monster meetings', a name given to large meetings in English-speaking countries in the nineteenth century, was quickly used by the *Times* to describe the occasions organised by the Association to hear O'Connell set forth the case for Repeal. The Association, and the press that favoured Repeal, took up the term with enthusiasm because it seemed to give the meetings greater power to persuade the government to listen to numbers, if not to reason. That rapidly became true and greater notice was taken of Irish affairs by English statesmen than had been the case for some years, while ever-larger numbers of people in Ireland began to realise that something serious was afoot. The *Times* became alarmed at the possibility that the authorities would act hastily. It asked for moderation, saw Repeal as a national instead of a sectarian movement, and warned the government against coercion. Davis reacted with cynicism to this new attitude of the *Times* and judged it as recognition by 'the cold sensualists of "the City"' of the loss to commerce were a civil war to follow, rather than as an acceptance of Repeal as a just objective for the Irish to pursue. For his part, Prime Minister Peel, on 9 May 1843, was quick to assure the Irish agitators that all possible English 'power, influence and authority' would be used to prevent Repeal. He had used almost the same words in March 1827 on Catholic Emancipation and resigned from cabinet because of his opposition to the measure. By 1828 he had changed his mind and prepared the bills relating to Emancipation. However, there was no reason to hope that he would shift his ground again because this time, the cause of Empire, as the English saw it, was at stake.

Davis had his own way of summarising the contempt he held for the Empire and English attitudes to it. 'Her [England's] motley and tyrannous flag she proclaims the first that floats, and her tottering and cruel empire the needful and sufficient guardian of our liberties.' He never hesitated to flay the English press that 'has defamed all other countries in order to make us and her other slaves content in our fetters' and English law that 'has hung like a bloodhound upon the heel of Patriotism'. He rejected English justice in which he held no confidence and said that it was an 'idle boast' for the English to call themselves just, but admitted that in their private dealings the English had 'some claim to the title'. For the policy of England towards Ireland he reserved his greatest ire, essentially because he saw it as 'true to no party' but simply one of expediency, and he said that even were England to give to Ireland every possible gift on the condition that Ireland remain a province, 'We tell you, and all whom it may concern, come what may – bribery or deceit, justice, policy, or war – we tell you, in the name of Ireland, that Ireland shall be a Nation.' Between England and the English he often strove to make a distinction, but one with its own barb,

> We repeat, again and again, we have no malice against – no hatred of – the English. For much that England did in literature, politics and war we are as men, grateful. Her oppressions we would not even avenge. We would, were she eternally dethroned

from over us, rejoice in her prosperity; but we cannot and will not try to forget her long, cursing, merciless tyranny to Ireland; and we don't desire to share her gains, her responsibility or her glory.[3]

O'Connell seemed to remain confident of, and grateful for, the support of the small group that revolved around Davis. Despite the rifts on matters peripheral to Repeal, nothing they wrote in the *Nation* gave him cause to question their loyalty to the main cause, although Davis's intemperate attack on the *Dublin Review*, published in London and initially funded by O'Connell, must have pained the older man. Davis called it a 'costly aggregation of fanaticism and servility', the purpose of which was to 'forward theology, not freedom', which meant that only rarely did it not speak 'in politics like an oligarch and in religion like a bigot'.[4] Nonetheless, the contribution of the *Nation* was the single, most powerful means of propagating the message of Repeal. The young writers appealed to an audience among the more vital, better-educated members of Irish society who were, in the main, young themselves and inclined towards a form of nationality that could fit in with O'Connell's aspirations. They wrote powerful prose and poetry in a way never before attempted in Ireland and the fact that some of them saw Repeal as a mere step towards the goal of Irish nationality, instead of an end, did not matter to O'Connell. The unease with which Davis and his friends often regarded their leader's tactics was no cause for any grave rift between him and them. In effect, it was more difficult for the group of young men to disown O'Connell than it was for him to turn from them, but the dependence of each on the other was vital to their mutual cause.

Davis's attitude to the monster meetings was evident in a leader he wrote for the *Nation* in April. Entitled 'Nationality', it rejoiced, optimistically, that 'Ireland is already a nation', told its readers that 'those on whose fiat their hopes were based [were] remorseless, truthless, cold, selfish, and bloody, in every age and every clime', showed them that 'to lean there was to lean on death ...' and asked them whether 'with our conscience as our guide, and the world to cheer us, is it not marvellous that we could have stooped so long to a beggarly servility?' He acknowledged that 'Our enemy may be aroused, and so must Ireland', and then trod in even more dangerous waters. With a thinly-veiled, almost contemptuous reference to the 'monster meetings', at which the people did little but 'gaze and shout' and then returned 'to a listless indifference to our country's fate' he referred to two meetings shortly to take place in Tipperary where he seemed to see signs that mass meetings may begin to fulfil a military purpose. Those who attended them in Tipperary would pledge to purchase their country's redemption 'at whatever cost'. He summed up by saying that, at the meetings, there would be 'twenty thousand Tipperary men, who would as soon, if called upon, pay their blood as their subscriptions'. Collectively, such men 'would not form a bad National Guard for Ireland'. They were dangerous words in the prevailing climate with their memories of the French Revolution and they did not go unnoticed. They were read out later by the chief justice in his charge to the jury at the trial of O'Connell and others.[5]

Given his attitude it is not surprising that, except on one occasion at the Curragh in May 1843, at which he sat with O'Connell on the stage set up for the occasion, where according to Venedey, 'every third man was a priest', Davis remained physically aloof from the meetings. He was inclined to think that the 'popular organisation', or Repeal movement, was tending to become 'too exclusively political'. He carefully avoided public appearances and even at the Association's weekly meetings, at which he must have felt more at home given his involvement at committee level, a year passed before he spoke and then only to ask membership for an acquaintance.[6] Davis was certainly aware of the progress of the 'monster' meetings and their effects on the cause. Throughout 1843, some forty meetings attracted crowds, if the analysis of attendance at the time is trustworthy, of between 100,000 and 800,000 on each occasion, but the latter figure is probably an exaggeration. O'Connell addressed thirty-one such gatherings and aroused his followers to fervent pitches of enthusiasm, even if most of those present were unable to hear what he said.[7] The fact that he continued his insistence on non-violent protest, and that the level of organisation was extremely effective, ensured the peaceful nature of the proceedings, which was aided by the prevailing, high degree of sobriety caused by the successful temperance campaign of Father Mathew throughout the preceding years. By March the Repeal 'rent' in the preceding two weeks had reached the unheard of level of £7,171-1-4. With great exuberance and confidence a stone was laid on 31 March in the foundations of the 'Conciliation Hall of Ireland' as an adjunct to the Corn Exchange and designed to hold an audience of 4,000.[8]

None of these exciting events shifted Davis from his main purpose of the building of nationality. The attempts to revive the Irish language overjoyed him because, 'A people without a language of its own is only half a nation,' and 'To lose your native language, and learn that of an alien, is the worst badge of conquest – it is the chain on the soul.' 'A nation should guard its language more than its territories, it being a surer barrier. Should they abandon this for the mongrel of a hundred breeds called English?' He admitted that it was likely that

Parliament Square, Trinity College Dublin.

English would continue to be spoken by many Irish for generations and that it had its own great literature, but he was certain that, even if the effort at the revival of Irish proved futile, it would at least rescue the literature, of which history, fiction and lyric poetry were the three great branches. In that way he hoped that his generation would 'hand down to our descendants proofs that we had a language as fit for love, and war, and business, and pleasure as the world ever knew'. With scarcely-veiled contempt he added that the attempt to record the language would prove 'that we had not the spirit and nationality to preserve it'.[9]

Davis began to show increasing interest in practical matters, yet he still kept up his largely vain attempt to woo Protestant readers with his 'Letters by a Protestant on Repeal' where he proclaimed again that 'Ireland has a body but no soul.' He objected strongly to the switching of the Temperance procession from St Patrick's day to Easter Monday, although he was sure Patrick's origins were French. He wrote, 'Do everything, in God's name, to remove sectarian feeling, except sacrifice great popular rights', which proved that he thought even the evil of sectarianism had to be endured at the stake of principle and that 'any sacrifice' had to be made for liberty. The uses to which the reading rooms of the Association were put interested him keenly and he wanted graphic art and music, as well as printed material, to be available in them. In the midst of these exhortations to nationality the old melancholy came back in 'The Grave' in which he wrote of death as if it were something for which he longed because, if it were possible to see her face, 'Who would shun her mild embrace?'[10]

The renewed speculation about a visit from Queen Victoria brought a reaffirmation of his judgement that the English were simply using Irish loyalty to wean them from independence. He warned that, just as with the visit in 1821 of 'that unhappy creature of the cook and the hair-dresser, George the Fourth', this time around the Irish must not allow themselves to be humbugged by another royal visit. This kind of reaction to royalty could scarcely have gone down well with the leaders of the Association. After the 'monster meetings' there was always a dinner, at the end of which O'Connell presided over toasts to the Queen, Prince Albert, the Prince of Wales and the Princess Royal, all of which were received 'with great enthusiasm'. Nevertheless, O'Connell approved of Davis's thought that 'Ireland must be a nation' and could not continue as a province. He also took occasion to accept and admire, 'to a certain extent', the principles of democracy, but he made it plain that he and his followers 'were not the less attached to the hereditary monarchy under which they lived, conscious that it was the best mode of government to be obtained'.[11]

A bill that aroused Davis to a new level of literary fury was introduced into the English parliament in May. Occasioned, probably, by the unease felt at the success of the 'monster' meetings, and perhaps by Davis writing in April that 'Arms, not complaints, repel the pirate' and that petitions and memorials are 'poor, hopeless expedients', the bill was designed to forbid the possession of arms in Ireland. It was a draconian measure in both intent and penalty. To possess a pike or a spear, or an instrument serving as either, was to earn transportation for seven years, presumably to Van Diemen's Land, the last colony in eastern Australia to which convicts could still be sent. Davis called it 'The Slaves Disarming Bill', because the English had always tried to disarm the Irish to enslave them, and argued that 'to carry arms is the ultimate guarantee of life, property and freedom', which was probably based on his reading of Blackstone. By the provisions of the bill, private houses could be entered and searched at any time under the pretext of looking for arms, which Davis thought would result in 'insult, cruelty, lust or rapacity'. He urged that the bill be resisted with every possible means and, if they failed, 'the course will be simple – time, prudence, energy!' The bill was duly passed in June by 270 votes to 105 and Davis immediately made fun of it. He said that a cook had written to ask him whether she was obliged to register her tongs, spits and poker as arms? He replied that he would refer the question to *Punch*.[12]

Local reaction to Repeal set in and a large meeting attended by about 1,000 people was held in the Rotonda in Dublin on 14 June. A fiery parson named Gregg, Isaac Butt and several other speakers aroused the crowd to varying stages of frenzy as they proclaimed 'No popery', 'No peace with Rome' and 'No surrender'. Davis went along, either as a reporter or merely as an interested citizen, and rose to new heights of sarcasm and incisive criticism with his report of the meeting. A new, more mature Davis was also revealed in that he began to see more clearly the corrosive nature of the long-harboured hatred of Protestantism for Catholicism, as well as the incapacity of its leaders to present a positive way forward to their followers. Thus, to him, the whole affair was an anti-Catholic demonstration, which both opposed Repeal and also wanted to repeal Emancipation. He described his heartfelt pity for the 'poor, honest, misled bigots' as they responded to the speakers with louder and louder shouts of enthusiasm. They were mostly working men 'whom the hard hand of national decay has struck down' so that they now sought relief 'from the pangs of hunger in the luxuries of bigotry'. He especially despised Isaac Butt, whom he accused of using the occasion to stimulate bigotry rather than nationality, and he flayed the other speakers who could only harangue their hearers into frenzy, but were incapable of uttering a word on such practical and relevant matters as 'improved trade, new markets, and national rank'.

Seated on the platform in the Rotonda were two noblemen, 'so imbecile in intellect that, if born of low estate, they would probably have been the inmates of some charitable asylum' and several country squires 'full of ignorance and punch'. For them 'we have an easy remedy, though we are loath to use it'. The people would only have to refuse to pay their rents for three months and their landlords would rapidly petition *'for entry into the workhouses of which they are now ex-officio guardians. Let them take timely warning. We are slow to strike, but if we do, we'll hit hard'*. Two weeks later the Protestant Operatives Society, which had organised the meeting, replied to Davis by saying that all the suffering in Ireland resulted from God's abhorrence of the false religion [Catholicism] practised there. Davis came back with statistics on the Dublin workforce immediately before the Union and those prevailing in 1843. The cloth and carpet making trades alone had employed about 30,000 tradesmen before the Union. By 1843 there were 1,587 jobs in those trades and the flannel trade had disappeared entirely. The Irish now paid £5,000,000 in taxes to England while nothing was being done 'to support, instruct or encourage the Irish operatives, be they Protestants or Catholics'. He said that he wanted to see Dublin changed 'from the sepulchre of industry to its home', and concluded that the Dublin tradesman 'who is not a Repealer is half-mad'.[13]

Meanwhile, O'Connell kept up his anti-violence theme at the meetings, both public and at the Corn Exchange. Nonetheless, on any occasion, such as that at Mullingar in May, when the leader seemed to favour resistance, or to waver on non-violence, his hearers cheered enthusiastically, frequently for several minutes. They had reason to do so because his ambivalence was evident in such remarks as, 'The Irish people would attack no one, but he would not say that, if attacked, they would not defend themselves,' and that, if even more troops were sent from England, the Irish would not resist but, 'should they persevere too far, our patience would become exhausted and human nature would call for a more steady resistance.' He promised that 'If any magistrate or person in authority commanded them [the crowds at his meetings] to disperse, they should do so at once', which was sound advice given that the appropriate Act allowed only three minutes before the troops could fire at the people. Wellington publicly said that he would put down the Irish by arms, which caused O'Connell to call him the 'stumbling, stuttering Duke', but Davis found uncouth and unworthy some of the expressions that O'Connell used, and especially his repeated jibes at Wellington whom Davis considered a 'gallant soldier and most able general', while O'Connell was given to calling him that 'stunted corporal'. With even greater bombast, Lord Edward Stanley, secretary of state for the colonies, talked about 'striking off the heads of the tallest poppies', which surely meant O'Connell as the first objective. Nonetheless, O'Connell remained composed and, although he condemned the arms bill as 'diabolical' because it was directed specifically at the Catholic masses, he said he would help the government to disarm the Irish, provided that all the Irish were included in its provisions.[14]

In keeping with his heightened military mood, or to weaken O'Connell's argument for non-violence, Davis produced a steady output of ballads extolling the means of resistance taken by the Irish in the past. The seeming disinterest in Repeal in Connaught roused him to stinging reproval and impassioned exhortation with one of his finest ballads, 'The West's Asleep.'

> And if, when all a vigil keep
> The West's asleep, the West's asleep –
> Alas! and well may Erin weep,
> That Connaught lies in slumber deep.
> But, hark! some voice like thunder spake:
> *'The West's awake! the West's awake!'*
> 'Sing oh! hurra! let England quake,
> We'll watch till death for Erin's sake!'[15]

With some justification the *Warder*, a Protestant paper edited by the gifted author Joseph Le Fanu, said the *Nation* was *'the most ominous and formidable phenomenon* of these strange and menacing times'. With a print run of 10,730 by December 1843, the paper achieved a publication almost equalling the combined rate of the daily *Saunders* (2,461) the *Evening Post* (2,932) and the *Warder* (weekly, 7,230), its most widely-sold rivals on the conservative side. Furthermore, its circulation was greater than that of the Catholic, pro-Repeal *Freeman's* in its three editions (10,150).[16] Articles and poems were regularly reproduced in American papers, as were articles in French and Italian ones. In Ireland itself the *Nation* was widely read among the educated classes, but the most remarkable thing was its circulation among the poor. Dillon wrote to tell Duffy that in his home village, one 'poorer in itself or surrounded by a poorer population' than any in Ireland, twenty-three copies were sold on the previous Sunday and 'there are scarcely so many houses in the town, and such houses!' That is even more remarkable given the price of 6d per copy – a small fortune to millions of Irishmen. Duffy gave the price of 'an ass-load of turf (meaning two panniers full) as one penny if the vendor did well;

otherwise he might get only a half penny. His usual purchase with the penny was a candle and a salted herring. The *Nation* cost him the price of six candles and six herrings.' Duffy gave excerpts from the letters of some of his readers at the time which all convey the excitement and genuine happiness that each edition of the paper aroused. 'My calender for the week dates from the time the *Nation* arrives till the day I may hope for another *Nation*. I often walk three miles to the post-office to bring it home a few hours earlier than it could otherwise reach us.' A Dublin tradesman wrote, 'I work hard all the week and on Sunday I am repaid by lying in bed an additional hour or two to read the *Nation*.'[17]

The way in which the paper was distributed increased its readership enormously, or at least those who listened while others read it. Duffy calculated that 300 copies went to newsrooms and Teetotal Societies, where each copy was read by 'at least fifty persons'. A further 1,100 copies went to the Repeal Wardens, who read the paper aloud at weekly meetings to from 50 to 100 persons. The remaining 9,000 were sold by agents or sent directly to subscribers and, 'as the *Nation* was handed about like a magazine, and preserved for binding, it is certain that each of these copies reached more than a dozen readers, probably more than a score.' Even the 'official class', through whom the paper was distributed in its various ways, could not resist its attraction and complaints were constantly heard that copies were missing or that the agents did not receive their proper numbers. 'To remedy this inconvenience it was suggested, by some person wanting in reverence for constituted authority, that an additional paper should be attached to each parcel with the inscription, "Please to steal this copy."'[18]

Davis read the correspondence that came to the office and his confidence and sense of purpose were strengthened by the response to the paper. His spirits, and those of thousands of others, were lifted by the memorable ballad on the 1798 rising, 'The memory of the dead', run in the *Nation*. It was written by a young Trinity scholar of Ulster origins, John Kells Ingram, who, temporarily, had begun to share Davis's attitude to nationality. Davis had wanted to add 1689 'to our memory', but its revolutionary significance paled in comparison to Ingram's 1798. At a 'symposiac' held on St Patrick's Day, 1843, the young men of the *Nation* gathered and sang their ballads. Among the company was Davis, 'the silver-tongued "Celt"', as Duffy called him, and they were all stirred when they sang Ingram's lines,

> Who fears to speak of Ninety-Eight
> Who blushes at the name?
> He's all a knave, and half a slave,
> Who slights his country thus.[19]

O'Connell surely read Ingram's ballad, although he would not have known who was its author. He was impatient with the awakening of memories he hoped had been put to rest, including his own minor role in helping to put down the rising. When Isaac Butt used the ballads at the Rotonda meeting to prove the untrustworthiness of the Repealers, if not their treason, O'Connell was quick to reply. He said that Butt was only able to produce as proof 'the poor rhyming dullness of the *Nation*', although Butt, thinking the ballads were produced by one writer, said he 'deserved the name and had the inspiration of a poet', and Le Fanu wrote that the *Nation* was 'a genuine and gigantic' illustration of 'the opinions and feelings of some millions of men' and was written with 'vigour', 'singleness of purpose' and 'vivid precision'. O'Connell, admitted, ironically, that the 'songs' in the *Nation* were very good but they lacked a great deal when they were recited rather than sung, and, then rejected the main point of Butt's speech. He said that Butt had brought an accusation, not only against the paper, but also 'against the people'. Simply because of its name Butt wanted to make the Irish nation answerable for the opinions contained in the paper. O'Connell sternly affirmed that the Irish people were 'not responsible for the *Nation*'. Two weeks later he said that he regarded the 1798 rising as having no national character and that those who took part in it were the 'unfortunate dupes of British policy'.[20]

This kind of forthright criticism by the leader proved too much for Davis. In early June he had tried to state clearly where he stood on the morality of war and rejected the suggestion that the 'glorious names' of the battles of Irish history should not be set out on the member's card of the Repeal Association. He said that 'a just war is as noble to him who has justice on his side as any other just act'. Indeed, he thought that there was more nobility and heroism in the act of war 'than in almost any other human occupation' and that it is 'as much our duty in a just cause as any other mode of sustaining justice'. Therefore, if a man fights for 'truth, country and freedom, may glory sit upon his tomb', but if he does so 'to rob or oppress' or 'in the ranks of an invader or a tyrant, may his name rot in eternal infamy'. He denied that he wanted to encourage war, 'but whenever the occasion comes, here or elsewhere, may sagacious and informed souls, bold hearts and strong arms be found to plan, lead and fight.' In the wake of O'Connell's words on the *Nation*, he did not hesitate to refute him by using his own review of Richard Robert Madden's volume on the United Irishmen. The review appeared, perhaps coincidentally, in the same issue of the paper in which O'Connell was reported. Taking his cue from what had happened to the memory of the United Irishmen in that their 'name has been made a name of reproach', he compared the

Irish to slaves who echo their 'master's calumny' when they acted in that way towards those to whom they owed so much They were harsh words, but Davis was in no mood to quibble and he went on to plead eloquently that the past heroes of Ireland should not be forgotten but, instead, remembered with gratitude and love.[21]

Whether O'Connell read and thought about Davis's article on the morality of war, a week later he spoke at Mallow, the birthplace of Davis, and used words that were dramatically called the 'Mallow Defiance'. At the meeting itself, attended by about 200,000 people, he praised the Irish as 'the most moral, the most temperate, the most religious people in the world', who excelled all others in 'the virtue of politeness and deference to the female sex'. At the subsequent banquet he seemed full of melancholy, grieved the loss of his wife, 'my heart is widowed,' and said that he didn't feel like speaking. His speech lacked consistency, but he seemed to imply that, were the rumours proved correct of the government using force to suppress the Repeal movement, the Irish would use force to resist. Of himself he said, 'I say they may trample me, but it will be my dead body they will trample on, not the living man.' He probably meant that, while he could understand why his followers would use force to resist when he said, 'Gentlemen, you may learn the alternative to live as slaves or die as freemen' and when he asked them 'Do you think I suppose you to be cowards or fools?', he indicated that, upon force being used, he personally would die, but he would not resist.[22]

Nonetheless, his words were sufficiently enigmatic as to leave large doubts in the minds of his readers, as well as in those of his aroused hearers, about what he would do in a violent conflict. Furthermore, the words he uttered on the same occasion about the queen possibly caused some of the more serious-minded who pondered on them to wonder whether he was engaged in hypocritical hyperbole or deliberately fooling himself and his followers. He said that they were all loyal to, and full of affection for Victoria, 'who has ever shown us favour, and whose conduct has ever been full of sympathy and emotion for our sufferings'. In the same week, however, at Ennis, he was much more forthright, so that any direct defiance he expressed can be claimed by Clare rather than Cork. Claiming that he felt at home in Clare because the blood of his family was there, he admitted that Emancipation had been useful 'principally to the rich and wealthier classes', but Repeal 'would be useful to the poor and humble – the working classes and the industrious classes' for whom, 'blessed be Heaven, I am working now'. He went on to promise that the law would not be violated, but warned that no one ought to imagine they could attack the Irish people with impunity and asked was there anyone present who 'would join me in such a day?' The response was several minutes of tremendous cheering, after which he continued, 'were [the English] to assail us against the constitution and the law, they know little of me who think I would be amongst the last who would stand up for Ireland.'[23]

Perhaps as a result of O'Connell's apparently heightened degree of belligerence, Davis seemed to find more to approve of in his general leadership at this time. Two peaceful, but potentially inflammatory, ideas put forward were for the appointment of arbitrators in every barony to adjudicate disputes between the people and that 300 trustworthy men should come together 'to consider and prepare a Bill for the Repeal of the Union'. Davis was certain the decisions of the adjudicators would be 'obeyed more exactly than any judges in the land' and that the basis of a native judiciary would be laid. He pledged his support for the 300 to 'the last man and the last shilling', especially because he saw in it the nucleus of a future Irish parliament. The reaction to the 300 proposal in Westminster was immediate. Lord John Russell asked Parliament 'Will you allow this Convention to go on? Will you allow the powers and functions of the government to be wrested from the lord lieutenant, and him to remain sitting helpless in the Castle of Dublin?' The *Warder* was more to the point. 'This is the legislature in whose womb lies, even now, fixity of tenure, abolition of tithe-rent charge, [and] universal suffrage.' It is scarcely believable that either O'Connell or the *Nation* writers imagined that England would allow either measure to proceed to fruition.[24]

In his first substantial speech, at the Repeal Association meeting in mid-May, Davis again agreed with O'Connell who had said that he would welcome into the Association those who stood for a federal parliament in Ireland subordinate to Westminster. In June Davis said that 'no man pushed his nationality further than he did' and insisted that a federal parliament could only be seen as a first step on the road to freedom, but that it would help to entice Protestants to join in the national cause. He looked upon their assistance as 'invaluable' and if they joined in working for the country it would not be long before the Irish people 'would be qualified for total independence'. He expressed his confidence in the leader, asked the people to stand behind him and uphold the Constitution, be patient and prudent even in enduring persecution but 'if they will hereafter hesitate to face suffering, danger, and death itself, for liberty, let them at once abandon a contest for which nature never fitted them'. As an example to them he held up Oliver Plunket, the Presbyterian William Orr and other 'great martyrs' of the Irish Church, who he said 'died nominally for creed, but really for country'. O'Connell's reaction to this later statement went unrecorded.[25]

It may seem strange that, between winning Repeal by force or being defeated by the refusal of Westminster to accede to the popular will, there was a third way that appealed to Davis. He realised intuitively that it was one thing to separate from England and another to develop the institutions of a viable and independent state. Thus, he momentarily wavered between outright repeal of the Union and some form of federal government that would retain the links between the two countries and the rest of the Empire. Federalism would give a degree of necessary autonomy to Ireland in matters directly connected with its own well-being, while leaving larger concerns, such as defence, to the deliberations of Westminster. Moreover, as the first step towards complete autonomy, federalism would give Ireland time to mature its spirit and clothe that spirit with appropriate institutions, rather than merely to retain the shape of the state which England had imposed over the preceding centuries. If Davis thought that such was possible, he did not realise that, once established, institutions tend to take on their own life and that it is far easier to retain them than to abolish or change them radically.

It was not the time for Davis to write openly on federalism, given the prevailing, massive wind of Repeal, but he did so privately to Daniel Madden saying that he would agree with and support a federal government because it was better than the one they lived under at the time. Furthermore, it seemed the only way to win substantial Protestant support for at least a measure of relaxation of English control. He wanted Madden to return from England to Ireland and to become editor of 'a Quarterly Review advocating federalist principles'. Perhaps mindful of the fate of the *Citizen*, he was prepared to give '*exact* calculations and *practical* suggestions' about how to accomplish the plan. His main hope was that the new review would help to win the adhesion of high-minded people who could not then swallow the pill of Repeal, but through federalism, they might eventually be brought a step closer to his own ideas of nationality. He was convinced that his own 'principles' would succeed, even if he and those who stood with him were hanged for standing by them.

Dillon had told Davis to treat with civility all who held out the hand of friendship and especially to those whom Dillon called 'the Saxon sympathisers'. Dillon's friendly words may have helped Davis to see the federalists as potential allies, even given their sympathies, but he still deplored the disunity of the country and wrote, 'Feud! Feud! Feud! that is our history. From the hill-side to the library, before assembled men and at the altar of God, Irishmen keep trampling on each other.' At the time he was writing nearly all the *Nation* and, perhaps in explanation of his own total dedication or exhaustion, he wrote of those 'who leave the gentle ways of love and literature because they detest injustice, because they long to rectify the disordered and feeble condition of society and are moved to realise some great idea of national life'. In the end the plan for a review under Madden's editorship came to nothing and the federal idea was left in abeyance for a time.[26]

In London there was little doubt about what the Tory government intended to do about Repeal and, if the queen put value to her own words, she fully agreed with them. At the closure of Parliament in August she said that 'it is my determination, with your support, and under the blessing of Divine Providence, to maintain inviolate that great bond of connexion between the two countries.' Her prime minister, Sir Robert Peel, was more forthright. He was determined to maintain the Empire and said that 'deprecating as I do all war, but above all civil war, yet there is no alternative which I do not think preferable to the dismemberment of this empire.' English reactions became more and more heightened and the *Times* descended to a new level of invective by calling the people who attended the monster meetings 'a filthy and felonious rabble', the bishops 'surpliced ruffians' and the priests 'a demon priesthood'.[27] To such people the concessions of the 1780s and 1790s were not going to be repeated. O'Connell would not be permitted to rouse up an armed rabble, similar to the Volunteers and the United Irishmen. It was one thing to allow him to use rhetoric, which was merely telling the truth in a way unpalatable to Dublin Castle and to Westminster. He could even be given some latitude to engage in inflamed rhetoric, which told the truth about how most of the Irish experienced their oppression. That, however, was where it would cease and, if O'Connell and the Repeal Association stepped even gently across the bounds of legality as imposed and interpreted by the Imperial Parliament and the judiciary, they would be in trouble. If they showed the slightest inclination towards, or preparation for, armed resistance they and their deluded followers would be dealt with decisively.

In short, the Union would be retained by whatever means seemed appropriate to secure its retention and Davis seemed to accept that England would never relent. The fields of Ireland 'shall be manured with the shattered limbs of her sons, and her hearths quenched in their blood, but never, while England has a ship or a soldier, shall Ireland be free.' But 'come what may, bribery or deceit, justice, policy or war – we tell you, in the name of Ireland, that Ireland shall be a nation.' Intimidation by legislation or the dubious application of legislation was another way to keep Ireland subject, but it had begun to wear thin in the face of the passionate mobs gathering week by week at the monster meetings. The fact that 20,000 gathered in the United States to listen to powerful politicians and other luminaries proclaim that they stood with the Irish in their bid for self-determination, and that a motion was passed to take Canada if England acted against Repeal by force was of some concern in London. To the Americans, Davis said, 'God bless you', surely knowing that O'Connell would not have echoed the sentiment. He said, however, that Ireland's friends mistook her position, 'We are *not* on the verge of war.' Yet if England tried to rule by military government, 'Then we will take care of ourselves.' Much closer to home, in Paris, there was considerable agitation with the usual fulsome, but forlorn, promises by sundry sympathisers to raise arms and men to help the Irish cause. What is more important, O'Connell's speeches and the stream of articles on Repeal in the *Nation* were translated into French and gained a wide readership with the possibility that genuine support might be eventually forthcoming; although the futility of previous French efforts to assist the Irish ought to have comforted the English statesmen.[28]

Despite the enormous support for Repeal, few inroads had been made into the upper classes who remained generally impervious to either the reasons behind it or to the emotions that fuelled it. Under those circumstances it was injudicious of the government to give a hostage to fortune by creating a substantial group of political martyrs, which partially improved the standing of the popular movement. Peel had trumpeted his determination to retain the Union, even at the cost of civil war, but O'Connell was careful to give no pretext for starting such a war as the meetings remained peaceful with no show or even hint of violence. It was one thing to remain cool in Westminster, but the authorities in Dublin Castle saw matters in another light and wanted action. When it came it was in the form of withdrawing the commission of the peace from thirty-four members of the Repeal Association, including Lord Ffrench and two others of his family, O'Connell and his son John. One of the thirty-four, Daniel Clanchy of Cork, had merely attended a Repeal dinner at which he had refused to drink a toast to Repeal because he was undecided on the matter, while another had simply promised to attend a Repeal meeting. The response was immediate when William Smith O'Brien, Whig MP for Limerick, handed in his commission because he was 'unwilling to act under a despotic government'. He was followed by others, including some Irish Whigs such as Lord Cloncurry and Henry Grattan. Twenty Irish barristers joined the Association en masse, among whom were Thomas MacNevin and Michael Barry who soon began to contribute to the *Nation*.[29]

Davis was delighted with this turn of events and wrote to Madden in a jubilant frame of mind about future prospects, although he sounded a realistic note when he said that most educated Protestants would become Repealers if they could be given an assurance that Repeal would not mean a Catholic ascendancy replacing the old one. He seemed not to be aware of the fact, or to give weight to it, that many English Catholics and the educated Catholic Irish upperclass, such as Father O'Mahony, the celebrated critic and wit who wrote under the name 'Father Prout', shared similar views. Prout even refused to write for the *Nation* because he loathed O'Connell and rejected any concept of Irish nationality, although he admired Davis greatly and said that he 'first turned the youthful intelligence of Ireland into pathways of manly independence and self-respect'. When Dr Edward Kenealy attacked Davis in 1847 as a 'dog-faced demagogue', Prout sprang to his defence calling him 'the late, pure-souled and gifted Tom Davis'.[30]

The unease of the times was such that Davis was worried about the possibility that his correspondence might be subject to official scrutiny and told Madden to destroy his letters 'for your own sake and mine'. He went on, 'We are threatened here with a search for papers and it might be extended to England. Any rash phrase could be used to persuade the Parliament that there was some plot here. There is not; we are too wise to conspire.' Whether Davis was suffering from a persecution complex or Dublin was rife with rumours is unclear, but he wrote an article in the *Nation* entitled 'Search for Papers', saying that the word was out that the houses of those connected with Repeal would be searched. Madden wrote back to Davis saying, 'Don't tell me any secrets or to anyone who is not in your political confidence. Recollect that [word unclear] honourable men might injure you by thoughtlessness or imprudence.'[31]

In order to illustrate the strength of the cause, Davis told Madden that the Irish Catholics were 'more united, bold and orderly than they ever were' and thus provided the means of 'defence or attack, civil or military', while the 'hearty junction of the Catholic bishops is of the greatest value'.[32] He was mistaken in his estimate of both the laity and clergy because there were elements of division among them that made the ultimate goal more difficult to achieve. Archbishop John McHale of Tuam was the strongest and most influential of the seventeen pro-Repeal bishops and he joined the Association, together with many of his priests, on 29 April 1843. But it was not true, as one bishop asserted in May, that all the hierarchy was in favour of the movement. Archbishop Murray of Dublin took occasion to deny that he agreed with Repeal and wrote to his priests to tell them that he would never take part in a strictly political movement while five other bishops were privately opposed, confused or hostile to Repeal.[33] In this, and in other ways such as their seriously mistaken underestimate of the strength of will in England to deny Repeal, whether by legislation or force, Davis and many of his followers lived in a land of make-believe. O'Connell, as their senior and more experienced leader, ought to have pointed that out to them and that he did not do so perhaps shows how far his own rhetoric and the enthusiasm of his mass following had started to deceive him.

The population of the country according to the 1841 census was 8,175,278 and, given that the English authorities had made it plain that Repeal would never happen while they controlled Ireland, it was deemed necessary to take steps to ensure their control.[34] That they did so even to the extent of having armed vessels patrol the coast and to the refurbishment of the Martello Towers that had been erected by the English to repel a possible invasion by Napoleonic forces, was a sure guarantee that violence would be used at the appropriate moment. It is not too far-fetched to say that some of those in authority, whether in Dublin Castle or in the military stationed in Ireland, wanted to use violence. On the other hand, there is an indication of what Davis was thinking at the time when he wrote to William Tait, proprietor of one voice of British radicalism, *Tait's Magazine*, asking his opinion on the Irish using violence to resist. The whole tone of Tait's reply, dated from Edinburgh on 30 May 1843, bears clear testimony to the fact that Davis had been contemplating the possibility of some eventual form of violence, perhaps even war itself, and there is no indication that he was opposed to it. Tait replied, 'War would be perfect madness. Ireland would be crushed in an instant and the justice or injustice of her cause be utterly disregarded ... While nothing but ruin be looked for from armed resistance to Britain, everything is to be hoped for from peaceful agitation.' Tait almost virtually begged him to imitate the tactics of the Anti-Corn Law League and to try to achieve progress by completely peaceful means.[35] The way Davis was thinking clearly indicates he harboured an element of wishful thinking in his mind. He knew, more than most, the long litany of Irish failures to throw off their yoke in the past, as well as the history of the behaviour of the English to suppressed people elsewhere. It is difficult to imagine what factors he saw operating in 1843 that would change the situation in favour of the Irish.

Meanwhile, from London, Madden was attempting to dampen Davis's ardour. O'Connell's proposal to bring together 300 men to deliberate on Ireland's future had now firmed up into a body that was to be called the 'Council of Three Hundred' which the *Times* was inclined to scorn as 'a convention of 300 bogtrotters'. Each of the 'districts' in Ireland would send a non-elected representative to a meeting of the Council in Dublin in August. The first 'Bills' which it would debate would be the repeal of the Union and the re-institution of the Irish House of Commons. Such a proposal set many alarm bells ringing, but Davis saw nothing unusual in it and told Madden that he wanted to be part of the Three Hundred. Madden replied that, under whatever form of duress, were Ireland given a Parliament, 'England will at once cease to be a substantive power'. Such a step would destroy her glory and her 'character throughout the globe for sagacity, ability, and capacity for ruling' would be ruined. He implored Davis 'not to entangle yourself in what is *now* a hopeless and vain endeavour', because 'This country will fight to the last against you, and the present and the late governments have wary sentinels that watch your movements.' Finally, he warned Davis that 'Lord John (Russell) would go on to the last in a war for the integrity of the Empire. Therefore keep out of mischief.' Davis's reply was direct. 'I shall go into the Three Hundred. Would that you were with us there! It will be a post of danger, and of power for good or ill.' They were scarcely the words of one committed to accepting the inevitably of violence without resistance and they make it plain that he was convinced it was up to the Irish to make the running and let the English respond as they saw fit, whatever the consequences.[36]

References

1. See Davis, 'No Redress – No Enquiry', *Nation*, 15 July 1843. See also R.B. McDowell, *Social life in Ireland, 1800-1845* (Dublin, 1947), p. 69.
2. *Nation,* 1 April 1843; McDowell, *Social life*, passim.
3. Davis in Arthur Griffith (ed.), *Thomas Davis: the thinker and teacher. The essence of his writings in prose and poetry* (Dublin, 1914), pp 16-20.
4. *Nation*, 25 March 1843.
5. Ibid., 29 April 1843, 17 February 1844.
6. Ibid., 13 May, 5 June 1843. Denny Lane and Thomas MacNevin joined the Association on the latter occasion and O'Connell referred to Davis as 'my friend, Mr Davis'. For the remark by Davis on the Repeal movement see Duffy, *Davis*, p. 100. See also Venedey, *Ireland and the Irish*, p. 27.
7. Oliver MacDonagh has an excellent map indicating where the meetings took place. The meeting at Dungannon was the only one of significance in what is today northern Ireland. O'Connell did not attend it and went no further north than Carrickmacross. See MacDonagh, *O'Connell*, p. 507.
8. *Nation*, 1 April 1843; 15 July 1843.
9. Ibid.
10. Ibid., 18 April, 24 June 1843.
11. Ibid., 1, 8, 22 April, 6 May, 24 June, 8 July 1843.
12. Ibid., 8 April, 6 May, 3 June 1843, 10 June 1843. At the trial of Duffy for seditious libel in 1846 his defence counsel used Blackstone's words on the bearing of arms. See *Mr Holmes' defence of the Nation* (Dublin, 1846), p. 12.
13. *Nation*, 17 June, 1 July 1843. The spelling Rotondo for the Dublin building was consistently used by the *Nation*. It would be difficult to place Davis among those

whom Mary Daly accused of neglecting Dublin for the sake of sustaining the Irish rural myth. See her 'An alien institution? Attitudes towards the city in nineteenth and twentieth century Irish society', *Etudes Irlandaises*, no. 10 (Lille, December, 1985), pp 181-194.

14. Ibid., 20 May, 15 July 1843. Duffy, *Davis*, p. 118.

15. *Nation*, 22 July 1843.

16. Ibid. and Duffy, *Young Ireland*, pt. 1, p. 145.

17. Ibid., vol. 1, p. 70; Patsy Adam-Smith, *Heart of exile* (Melbourne, 1986), pp 27-30.

18. Duffy, *Young Ireland*, pt. 1, p. 145.

19. *Nation*, 1 April 1843. Ingram (1823-1907) made only one foray into nationality. He never repudiated his authorship of the ballad even though he became a committed Unionist. He became Regius Professor of Greek at Trinity in 1866 and vice-provost in 1898. See George D. Burtchaell and Thomas U. Sadlier, *Alumni Dublinensis*, pp 426-7 and O'Sullivan, *The Young Irelanders*, pp 296-300. Other ballads written at this time by Davis were 'The death of Sarsfield', 'Song of the volunteers of 1782', 'The march to Cashel' and, on another form of resistance, 'William Tell.' *Nation*, 22, 29 April; 13, 20 May 1843.

20. Ibid., 24 June, 8, 15 July 1843. A collection of ballads that had been published in the *Nation*, under the title *The Spirit of the Nation*, came out in June 1843 with a preface by Davis. It was printed at the office of the paper and sold by its agents for 6d. It was an immediate and huge success and the ballads were even sung in the military barracks in Ireland. See *Nation*, 24 June 1843 and Duffy, *Davis*, pp 141-2.

21. Ibid., 10, 24 June 1843.

22. Ibid., 17 June 1843. Mary O'Connell died in 1836. Daniel never ceased to grieve her loss.

23. Ibid., 17 June 1843. See also Duffy, Davis, p. 154 and John Mitchel, *The history of Ireland*, 2 vols, 2nd. ed. (London, 1869), vol. 2, p. 356.

24. *Nation*, 29 April, 12 August 1843.

25. Ibid., 13, 20, 27 May 1843; 10 June 1843.

26. See Ms 1791, NLI, for jottings by Davis as well as a scrap of a letter to Madden, n.d. but mid-1843. MS 3199 contains Davis's assertion that, by the spring of 1843, he was writing nearly all of the *Nation*. The manuscript passed through Duffy's hands and he did not deny the assertion. For Davis to Madden see Duffy, *Davis*, pp 111, 114. Dillon to Davis, 21 March 1843, Davis papers, Ms 2644, NLI.

27. Duffy, *Young Ireland*, pt. 1, p. 82; *Nation*, 26 August 1843. A new writer, M. J. Conway, had begun to contribute to the *Nation*. His prose was more inflammatory than that of Davis. His first article, in which he called the Union an 'iniquitous but an illegal and invalid act', Davis judged as the 'most imprudent article in the *Nation*'. See article 'The crisis is upon us', and Davis's handwritten note on it, in ibid.

28. Ibid., 1, 15 July 1843.

29. *Nation*, 10 June 1843 gives the names of thirty-three suspended magistrates. Duffy, *Davis*, p. 112, speaks of twenty-five, but MacDonagh, *O'Connell*, p. 515, has thirty-four.

30. See Ethel Mannin, *Two studies in integrity: Gerald Griffin and the Rev. Francis Mahony (Father Prout)* (London, 1954), pp 228-31, 252.

31. *Nation*, 6, 20 May, 6 June 1843; Davis to Madden, n.d. but June 1843 Ms 5758, NLI; *Nation*, 10 June 1843; Madden to Davis, 13 July 1843, Ms 5756, NLI.

32. Davis to Madden, June 1843, MS 5758.

33. *Nation*, 27 May 1843.

34. The population rose by 965,574 in the years 1821 to 1831, but only by 407,827 in the next decade to 1841. See *Nation*, 29 April 1843.

35. Davis's questions, or suggestions to Tait cannot be ascertained from the surviving manuscript as knowledge of the letter only comes from Tait's reply. Duffy was clearly puzzled by Tait's letter and tried to make the unsustainable case that Tait was not responding to anything that Davis had asked him about the outcome of a war but rather to 'the apprehension in his own mind'. See Duffy, *Davis*, p. 159.

36. See Oliver MacDonagh, *O'Connell*, p. 503 and Duffy, *Davis*, pp 156-8. Davis to Madden is found in Duffy papers, Ms 5758, NLI; The *Times* was reported in the *Nation*, 30 September 1843.

Chapter 9

Traveller

The most striking thing about Davis's behaviour in 1843 was that, when the monster meetings reached their peak during the autumn and when the Three Hundred was allegedly about to sit in Dublin, he decided to accept an invitation to travel to Cork to attend a meeting of the British Association. It was a body devoted to the development of the sciences and was supported by businessmen in Cork. Local members of the Repeal movement also gave it much support, with the result that conservative elements refused to join it, which possibly accounts for the invitation to Davis in the hope, in the event fruitless, that his presence might induce some of his fellow-religionists to change their mind.[1] Davis had also decided to take a tour of the South, and the West, including Connemara, for two months. He wanted to take a holiday and travel around the country, making contact with people involved in the nationalist movement, as well as to have time to reflect on the situation and generally restoke his fires. The success of the *Nation* had brought him to the attention of thousands who had never heard of him a year before and some well-wishers had decided to try to help him financially by getting up a subscription list in his favour. A friend urged him to agree to the proposal, while fully accepting 'the delicacy of your feelings on the subject', but it seems to have come to nothing.[2] Perhaps he felt the need to retire from the public gaze for a time and a prolonged absence from Dublin seemed the best way to do so. In any event, he clearly needed a break from the constant grind of journalism, although his spirits were not low except that the old melancholy hung over him occasionally still. Tom MacNevin described a supper in Dublin shortly before Davis departed on his tour. Davis, Barry, Dillon and a few others were present, but MacNevin and Davis were the only 'choice spirits' of the night, although Davis became 'sentimental, and talked – yes, seriously – of having speculated on death in infancy and having concluded it to be a very comfortable sort of phantasy and sweet dream'.[3]

Davis left Dublin on 3 August. He had written to various people for introductions, including James Hardiman, 'The Historian of Galway' whom he had been encouraging to publish poems in Irish. Davis urged him to do so with music because a song with music 'is a better apostle of Irish than 20 without'. Before leaving he wanted advice on how to get permission to read Lord Ormonde's papers in Kilkenny and to receive help from Hardiman while in Galway. 'From what you know of me you will probably and rightly judge I don't care for what are commonly called hospitalities but for information, facilities to see places worth seeing and to know men worth knowing.'[4] The journey to Cork took him via Kilkenny, Waterford and Cashel, taking notes of monuments, making maps of towns and battlefields, assembling the words of Irish phrases and of local songs, such as a version of the old Gaelic ballad 'Shule Aroon' and of another ballad portraying the peaceful acceptance of their lot by the peasantry under the rule of their overlords. When he read the ballad Duffy said that 'like the French chansons under the First Empire, it is the whine of contented slavery'. Davis also drew up lists of men whom he judged would be useful to the cause and jotted down notes for future articles to be written by himself or others. In Tipperary, and elsewhere, he found evidence of oppression that had almost maddened the people. A priest told him that he remembered 'Sir John Fitz-Gerald bidding all the people in Cashel fair kneel, and they knelt, and he waved his sword over them, walking through them.' Another instance he recorded of 'Beecher's great grandfather [who] came here possessing nothing. Young O'Driscoll got him to take care of his house while he was abroad with his sister. When he came back Beecher prosecuted him under the Penal Laws (as a Papist) and got his property.' Another referred to the Penal Law that obliged a Catholic to sell his horse if it was worth five pounds or more. 'O'Leary shot for outlawry for refusing horse for £5 at Mallow, and Matthew of Thn. on being asked for his 2 fiery chariot horses drove to the Archbishop's and read his recantation.'[5]

Thus he was kept as busy as he had ever been in Dublin. He was in a cavalier mood and he refused to take any notice of Madden who had told him that Cork was 'a very dressy place' and therefore he ought never take off his gloves while there and that he should 'affect for a time a pretty strut, and you will be sure to fascinate'. Davis replied, 'I'll do as I like and dress as I like, and let it like me or not as it likes, and be damned to it. I fear no one, and I hope I shall court no one for vanity, applause, or anything but a great end.' He also told Madden that he need fear no rebellion by the people who, at the worst, would refuse to pay their rents and stop consuming excisable articles. He summarised his own stand and future intentions with the words, 'My projects begin where they end,' by which he meant that Repeal, and nothing short of Repeal, remained his objective and, having achieved it, he would begin again and go on from there. For his part Madden was equally forthright on the prospect of an Irish rising. 'If there be a rebellion I hope that it will be vigorously put down.'[6]

The Cork meeting of the British Association went off well, although the number present was only 600 instead of the 1,500 who had attended in the past. However, the Ball held by the Association attracted a thousand revellers, which cheered Davis, although there is no proof that he was other than a bystander when the dancing commenced. Davis had made a report to the meeting but refused to speak to it perhaps because, as he wrote to Duffy, 'Here the people are British Associationized and cold, but Lane and many others have begun to work.' Duffy had always shown an interest in genealogy and Davis said to him, 'I wish you knew my eldest brother, who has the most extraordinary gifts in that way I ever met. There is no family in Munster but he knows the pedigree of; but, alas, he is an English-minded man.' Mindful of practicalities he asked Duffy to print the census sheets of the population of the cities and major towns of Ireland he had left with him at the office, and to do so 'at once', correcting them by reference to the 1841 census volume which he ought to buy. If Duffy was unable to get the work done, Davis wanted him to send down the material so that he could do it himself. Duffy had already printed the list in the *Nation* of 26 August, but Davis had not seen it in time.[7]

Denny Lane, like Madden and Barry, was a Corkman, and he was amused that Davis should be thought to be so retiring. A letter he wrote to Davis reveals how his closest friends could banter with, and about him, without occurring his resentment. It also indicates that Davis was perfectly composed and steady in the quiet possession of his own intellectual and moral qualities, and in the vast store of learning that he had amassed since his childhood. It also seems to show that he feared no rival. Lane wrote,

> Oh, Thomas! Thomas! ... I was obliged to wait until I got to secret places to guffaw at the credulity of the people of Cork who thought Thomas Davis a modest man, – the man who sets to at every art and science with a perfect certainty of beating anyone – ... who makes bold attempts to surpass Grattan, Courier, and Carlyle in their respective styles, – who's as ready to deliver his opinions on a theory of refraction or the metaphysics of Fichte, as on a sonata, a painting, or a lobster salad, – and who utters all his judgements with an *ex cathedra* air that tempts his best friends to throw him out of the window. Talk of Tom MacNevin, why he is no more able to hold a candle to Tom Davis, than Davis himself is to – draw a declaration on a bill of exchange.'[8]

In Cork, Davis met the Catholic Bishop, Murphy, 'a glorious hearty Johnsonian bookworm' and a 'courtier' with his magnificent library of 100,000 volumes. Although Murphy made him very welcome and would scarcely permit him to leave his house, 'I am not quite sure of him,' said Davis, presumably because Murphy showed little interest in Repeal. Through the bishop he got to know the work of John Hogan who had begun life as a carpenter and became the most eminent Irish sculptor of his day. One piece, now beneath the altar of St Theresa's Church off Grafton Street, Dublin, had been done by Hogan in Rome for Bishop Murphy, who was Hogan's principal patron. Davis described it, 'Dead Christ, large noble man in full health; drapery round, fine and true, but at side too heavy stone lying; head on right shoulder, right foot over left, elbows on ground, hands on sides, wedged-up head, neck, flesh. A cemetery angel by him, deep, gentle, reflective, wing exquisite.'[9]

He spent a few days in and about Cork and went along the coastline making notes,

> All these Southern heads have castles and as many are peninsulas; these castles are on the necks – thus securing some 20, or 30, or 50 acres for tillage, cattle, plunder and stores. There the galleys were beached, doubtless in winter, [when they were not] plundering in more gentle seas. All these O'Heas, O'Donovans, O'Sullivans, Burkes, O'Malleys, O'Loghlens, O'Driscolls, O'Mahoneys, etc, were doubtless pirates or sea-kings.[10]

A letter to Duffy on 29 August expressed his horror at the witness system in a capital trial he had been present at in Kilkenny. It was further proof to him that 'The government of this country is damnable.' In Cork, he sat down and wrote an article against capital punishment which he enclosed and asked that, under no circumstances, should it be omitted from the next edition of the *Nation* because he was 'seriously anxious on the subject'.[11] The article was a calm but damning condemnation of capital punishment and ranks among his finest pieces of prose. In Ireland, the manifest injustice of the laws, the neglect of education, the forced hunger and the loss of land all contributed to criminality. What right then did the authorities possess to have people 'scientifically slaughtered' and to engage in the cold-blooded killing of 'powerless children of the human family'? He was sure also that, in Ireland, where bribery abounded, to assume guilt from conviction was 'ever fallible'. Yet, even if the persons in jeopardy were guilty and had acted from malice, he would spare them all,

Sackville Street, Post Office & Nelson's Column, *c.* 1821.

Punish them, and severely too, we would; but not with death. We would punish them in such a way as to prevent the repetition of the offence, and to serve as a sharp but not corrupting example upon other ill-inclined men. We would not suddenly and violently send their souls to eternity. We would not inflict what we cannot modify or compensate for. If transportation or imprisonment were the utmost punishment justice would be more sure ... All the political literature in the world is against public manslaughter, and nothing but the negligence of the public allows the continuation of it ... Must it continue? We pray to God that it may not be so. Civilisation, Christianity, and policy, unite to reject it.[12]

Despite his seriousness, he was sufficiently relaxed in a letter to Pigot to compare the girls of Cork with others he had seen on his trip. 'In Tipperary and Kilkenny, grey eyes, black lashes, rich brown hair, middle or small size, oval-faced arch girls; now dark hair, flashing black eyes, brunette, sunny cheeks, bearing graceful.'[13] He also wished that Pigot could be with him 'to take down word and music from every second person I meet', and he asked for an introduction to Hogan, of whom he had heard so much from Bishop Murphy as to take 'a strong liking to him'. He also wanted to know whether Wallis's 'heart [was] so hard, or his joints so rusty, as to look on idly now?' After Cork, he 'tracked the Nore and Sure [sic], roused the echoes of Comushenam [sic]', and was fortified by an occasional draught of poteen as he travelled through Tipperary. He was taken in Sir Richard Musgrave's steamer to Cappoquin and then went on to the Cistercian abbey at Mount Melleray in the company of a Signor Mayer from Florence, Dr Olave, vicar-general of Bengal, and a priest who had been elected bishop of Clogher who was to make a retreat at the abbey. He asked Pigot to picture the abbey 'with its tall white spire and thriving ascetic unnatural community staring in heaven's face from the side of the great free lordly wild mountain'. He described the abbey and its monks, with their brown and white habits, who were under the charge of 'a *mitred* abbot, the only one in Ireland'. It seemed to have amazed him that only those few members of the community who had public duties spoke while 'the rest are eternally silent day and night, in and out'. The monks made him welcome and showed him their fine manuscript of the Psalms with music they said was in the writing of St Bernard, their founder. He was taken with the industry of the monks who were self-supporting, examined everything, including their school which was 'new but not bad' and in his turn impressed them so that they were insistent he return for a protracted stay whenever he felt inclined. He also told Pigot that the monks had said that O'Connell, a few years previously, had withdrawn for some time from his many pursuits to make a spiritual retreat in the monastery which was of such severity that even the monks, well-known for their own austerity, were impressed. With his letter, Davis sent a geranium blossom from the abbey garden.[14]

A letter from Pigot, who was in Dublin, crossed with that from Davis. It began on a whimsical note that gives an insight into some of the more normal fantasies of the minds of the young friends, whose lives were not all bustle and crusading for nationality. Pigot said that Davis was such 'a whimsical celt' that he, Pigot, could not guess how he was occupying his time. Perhaps he was consulting another 'aspirant to Irish liberty over potions of potheen or lying on your back in the grass looking up to some of those dear wild mountains and hating to be disturbed with politics'. More appropriately, perhaps he was 'talking, or maybe sitting in the corn or the hay with some pretty peasant girl leaning on your shoulder, learning Irish better than we could have ever learned it in Dublin! – turning yourself to the poetry and melody of real Irish occupations'. There is no indication that Davis was engaged in any of the latter activities, but Pigot surely thought that the ability to behave like any young male was not beyond him. The fact that Duffy, while printing in full the rest of this letter, omits the above lines, lends some weight to the argument that his biography was, in part at least, hagiography.[15]

Coming to the matters of the hour, Pigot gave an account of the 'monster meeting' of 15 August at Tara, which had attracted an enormous crowd of probably more than 500,000. With a touch of the supercilious attitude towards the political wing of the movement that had become customary among some of the young men, Pigot himself, 'needless to say', was not present at Tara. He had been given an eyewitness account by John O'Hagan of the way in which O'Connell had been received with huge acclaim. 'Surely it is impossible for a man to fill such a position, even for an hour, without an ambition beyond the petty trammels of "constitutional" hypocrisy,' wrote Pigot. He also said that nothing was happening of any consequence in Dublin to foster the cause, that the Congress of Three Hundred would not now meet until November and that 'the Association is next to useless.' He seemed preoccupied with the way O'Connell would be sculpted for history and he was concerned that none of the Corn Exchange personalities, and especially that Tom Steele the Head Pacificator, should be prevented from interfering with the sculptor, John Hogan, in creating a work, 'fit as the statue of the President, some years hence, as well as the leader of now'. Pigot was certain that, 'if you or some one of sense and taste does not interfere, I predict there will be some infernal blunder.' Hogan had spent a day with Pigot in Dublin and he wanted to do 'a figure for Ireland, no more of weeping and weakness but of pride and command'. Pigot's main preoccupation, however, was with the impending absence of O'Connell from Dublin. As 'the fine season' was coming to its close, O'Connell was about to depart for his home at Derrynane for a well-deserved holiday. The Repeal Association would thus be left in the hands of incompetents and, in particular, those of John O'Connell. Pigot wanted Davis or someone with standing to propose that activities at all levels be adjourned until the Leader was back in command. It is an indication of how far removed some of the 'young men' were from reality. There is no likelihood that Davis, or anyone else, would be listened to on such a matter, as Duffy later admitted. The juggernaut of Repeal was destined to roll on, leaderless if necessary, provided it rolled on.[16]

By 8 September Davis was at Bantry, having been along the south-west of Cork through Kinsale, Bandon, and Cloughnakilty [sic]. He was enchanted with the Old Head which he thought the 'best bit of coast in this country' and 'felt as a pirate as I stood on its green top, cut off by a castled ravine from the rest of the promontory, so "handy" for supporting a garrison and guarding plunder', but Kinsale, with every second house in ruins, dispirited him, as did the departed beauty of its abbey. He took a local vessel, called a hooker, from Baltimore, which inspired his last, splendid ballad, 'The Sack of Baltimore', sailed to Cape Clear, which was 'crawling with people, and is not savage nor sweet enough for me', and thence on to Skull. Lough Hyne caused him to go into a long description to Robert Webb which is lyrical in its composition and conveys the intensity of his love for the natural beauty of Ireland,

> The glory of the coast I have hitherto passed is Lough Hyne; it is a lagoon surrounded by the craggiest hills. On its longest bank is a pretty, small cottage and demesne; on the west corner, close to the shore, is a smaller cottage guarded and caressed by trees. In the centre is a straggling rocky isle with a ruined tower; on the north is a ravine overhung by one of the steepest mountains I know. The mountain is a heap of checquered terraces of rocks and trees, with a white cabin strung on it, like a baby at the breast. The lagoon joins the sea through a narrow, twisted, rocky gap, through which the stream actually leaps. Place yourself on the east side of this gap, with the demesne on your right, the small cottage at the opposite side of the lake, the mountain and ravine mouth north of it, the crag stretching south, and the isle before you.[17]

His diary, written as he went along, is filled with many scraps of descriptions of the scenery, of 'broad dashing wild craggy hills' and the like. Denny Lane had accompanied him part of the way after Cork and they had been through 'the whole course of the Blackwater', the river of his native place, Mallow. As he went he eagerly sought material for the *Nation* so that Davis sat and listened while Lane took down 'an English and an Irish version of a glorious song on the fight of Ceim agan Feigh [sic], a Whiteboy battle in 1822'. Thinking of those people whom it was important that he visit on his journey, he asked Webb for an introduction to William Smith O'Brien at Limerick. 'I want not his hospitality, but to know his character.' Webb replied on 15 September from Dundrum enclosing a note to O'Brien in which he spoke of Davis as 'my most intimate friend' whose 'own earnest and disinterested enthusiasm for the welfare and nationality of Ireland, his talents and information once known, will better recommend him than anything in my power to add.'[18]

He next visited the remains of the O'Sullivan seat near Kenmare and, as he was close to Derrynane, a visit to O'Connell was in order. He found most of the household absent at a meeting, which gave him time to explore the surrounding countryside and on his walk around O'Connell's estate he took notes for a sketch he made later. He also visited the kennels where he found a few old beagles and went to the chapel which struck him as 'coarse'. He sat on rocks near the beach and was enraptured by the wild beauty of his surroundings. His unpunctuated diary entry gives an impression that his mind was in a ferment. He wrote, 'the glossy water with the dark rocks covered with grey white and yellow lichens on weed in the water the edges browner and richer than ringlets and so sharp in the water ...'; 'finest I ever saw the rocks pure and pillowed'. He spent the night with the family, including the leader, but made no remark on the company except that the chaplain, Father O'Sullivan, suffered from rheumatics. The next day he went around the Ring of Kerry, visiting the birthplace of O'Connell near Cahirciveen on his way to Tralee where he arrived on 17 September.

As he journeyed he was all the while reading and taking notes. He read Colonel Shaw's *Portugal* and made the observation that it 'contains valuable hints on working drill, military economy, outpost duty , and rationale of discipline, etc'. As an indication of the ingenuity of the Irish, the gullibility of the upperclass English or the general attitude to historical monuments, he struck a lighter note with a story about a castle. It seems that the owner decided to have what remained of his castle preserved by the erection of a wall around it. Being absent, he contracted with a local mason to undertake the work. The mason did so, building the wall out of 'the stones of the castle itself!' At Limerick he met the brother, and biographer, of the novelist Gerald Griffin who told him something of Gerald's life. Griffin had been 'sensitive, not strong' and went to London 'plump and fresh', but in six weeks he was 'starved and sallow'. He refused to accept help from friends and, although there was 'no love disappointment', he suffered because 'his passions were deadened with grief'. Davis was convinced that Griffin was the greatest Irish novelist of his time, an opinion confirmed by many later critics, and he especially praised Griffin's novel *The Collegians*. Davis then stopped to do a sketch of the Treaty Stone which was being used as pillion-stone outside a hotel on the Dublin road into Limerick. By 30 September, after five days in Tralee, and with short stops along the way, he was in Galway and went on to visit Dillon at Castlebar. It was perhaps on that visit that he tried to improve the little Irish he had mastered by taking lessons from Dillon's aunt, a native speaker. Bad weather detained him and he feared he would not be able to return to Dublin until mid-October. He had been absent for a critical two months.[19]

Clearly, the holiday had only been one in geographical location, in a release from work around the office and generally a change of air from the bustle of Dublin. Throughout the trip, his restless mind was never idle as the stream of articles he wrote for the *Nation* and the correspondence he kept up with Duffy and others illustrate. He drew up a list of eighty subjects fit to be embodied in a gallery of Irish historical paintings, ranging from the landing of the Milesians to O'Connell at Mallow and concluding with the 'very revolutionary' suggestion of one depicting 'The Lifting of the Irish Flags of a National Fleet and Army'. Probably unaware that Gabriel Beranger had already done a series of magnificent views of Ireland, he wanted two artists to travel the country 'accurately painting its ruins and natural scenery', and a report written by him was read and adopted in his absence at the Association suggesting that prizes be given for designs of churches, libraries and halls.[20] His interest in military matters was never more evident than in one letter he wrote to the *Nation* which he signed 'An Old File'. Prior to his departure on his trip south, thousands of pro-Repeal tradesmen of Dublin had marched to Donnybrook for a meeting. Davis had observed that many marched out of step and he felt obliged to give exact details as to how they ought to have comported themselves. 'An armed footman in rank occupies 20 inches – in file, in close order, 14 inches. 'He had the grace to sign this harmless trivia with 'Pray, sir, excuse the garrulity, and accept the good wishes of An Old File.'[21]

Nonetheless, he had other concerns on his mind and especially his intended membership of the Council of Three Hundred, as was the nature of the Council itself. He was no longer sure whether he should represent Down or Dublin, or even whether he, with two or three others, should remain clear of it entirely in order to be 'out of the power of our foes'. He feared that postponing its formation for a year would make the people 'grow lawless and sceptical', but to set it up now could be premature. Nonetheless, if O'Connell, or others to whom he entrusted the task, could set out clear policies for it, some success might follow. His main worry was that reaction to it by Westminster and the Castle might be decisive because he was certain that sufficient preparation had not been made to resist in an emergency. To him, the time to fight had not yet come because the Irish forces had not been marshalled. Thus he felt, 'Ours is a tremendous responsibility, politically and personally, and we must see where we are going.'[22]

The cost of nomination to the Council was £100, which Duffy secured for Davis together with the services of a Down priest, John Doran, to manage affairs. Davis was anxious to have a sense of security about O'Connell's approval, so he took the unusual step of asking John O'Connell, whom most of the young men regarded with thinly-veiled contempt, to ascertain his father's opinion of Davis's nomination. The reply was that the leader 'would not wish to have it [the Council] without you'. John also thought that it would be good politics for Davis to represent a northern district, where there would be a lack of men but not of financial backing, and that 'To have a non-Catholic there would also be a good thing.' Davis wrote back to Duffy to say that he had decided upon Down and he asked Duffy to tell the interested people in Down that, 'I am one not likely to shrink should the duty imposed upon me be dangerous, so I should look for confidence and manly backing whatever turn affairs take. I shall not work for praise or popularity. I want our cause to succeed, and shall in pursuit of success shrink from nothing but dishonour. I am not, nor shall I try to be, an orator. I would, if possible to my limited powers, be a politician.' He wanted his prospective constituents to understand him thoroughly and concluded, 'In such a struggle as ours, mistakes in character are terrible things. We can succeed if we earn success.'[23]

It was not so much about Davis's steadiness of purpose, but that of his leader's, that concern needed to be felt. They stood in differing situations. Davis spoke to millions through his ballads and articles in the *Nation*, but he was as one removed. O'Connell stood before them as their representative and embodiment. In a very real sense he was responsible for their safety, indeed for their lives, if matters came to the bloody pass desired by Wellington and other military hotheads. In the very same week that Davis was stating his determination to pursue his course with courage and tenacity, O'Connell was writing to his English Whig acquaintance, Lord John Campbell, for a brief period successor to Plunket as lord chancellor. In effect, his letter was a plea to Campbell to use his good offices with Lord John Russell to persuade him to promise publicly the implementation of a series of initiatives for Ireland, once the Whigs were in power again, which would conciliate the Irish people and strengthen 'the British empire'. In other words, he was back to his old tactic of trying to win favours by promising to behave which, at the very least, would involve releasing the Repeal screw several turns. The imminent threat of the use of British military power, now evident everywhere throughout Ireland with the pouring in of more reinforcements, must have been sufficient to make O'Connell rethink the possibility of gaining Repeal by moral force. He had done nothing to get the Council of Three Hundred off the ground, although he had promised that it would sit before Christmas, but at a monster meeting at Clifden in Connemara on 17 September he went as far as making public his intention of not going ahead with the Council at that time. Two weeks later, at Mullaghmast, he again rejected French or American help, repeated the, by-now, ritual of promising to stand with his people in the field if they were unjustly or illegally attacked and then wooed them with visionary hopes of a land where they and he would see 'the evening sun set down amongst the uplifted hands of a religious and free population'. He begged his hearers to stand by him, to join with him, to obey him 'and Ireland shall be free.'[24]

Gone was his dream of an Irish Parliament and with it the hope that mere numbers, even though in hundreds of thousands at tumultuous meetings, would persuade the British Lion to retreat. Huge mobs of 'bogtrotters' shouting themselves hoarse at meetings, provided they behaved themselves and remained under O'Connell's control, were of little moment in the scheme of imperial affairs. There were far more tangible and serious matters for English statesmen and their servants in Ireland to concern themselves with, and the hour for action was fast approaching. Repeal had taken other and more practical faces. The formation of the arbitration courts, suggested by Gray of the *Freeman's Journal*, was based on what had happened in Canada in the agitation under Papineau when dismissed magistrates had begun to act as arbitrators. The example was not lost in Westminster, especially as the Irish courts were working successfully. Indeed, Davis was expressing English fears when he asserted that the people had won another victory with the setting up of the courts and exhorted them to 'establish Law Courts, Judges, and Justice, for yourselves!' In the minds of those at Dublin Castle, there was still the threat that O'Connell could be persuaded or forced to call together the Council of Three Hundred, with its reminder of the French Revolution, despite the fact that the government had decided to suppress it should it meet. Some knew of the events of two generations earlier when the Volunteer army sent 300 delegates to meet at Dungannon, resulting in some measure of legislative independence for Ireland, and later when another 300 met in Dublin to ask for reform of the Irish parliament. O'Connell had been careful to base membership of his Three Hundred on popular acclaim by districts which set aside £100 out of the Repeal rent on a person in whom they had confidence. Elections were proscribed by law, but O'Connell's attempt to evade the law was of little use.[25]

Even more ominously, there was a groundswell of support for Repeal within the army itself which was made up of at least 50 per cent Irish troops. Some of them had added cheering O'Connell and his cause from Mallow to Galway to singing the ballads of the *Nation*. Perhaps most importantly, there were stirrings in Carlow and Tipperary of a movement to refuse to pay rents to landlords, which was surely a final straw in the bundle of discontent. The *Warder* was warning that a refusal to pay rents was not much of a step away from a refusal to pay tithes, and Davis was insisting that no concessions should be made to landlords, but that they be reined in by 'popular restraint'. One decisive way to restrain them was clearly by a refusal to pay rents, although Davis did not suggest it be adopted. In the end, even O'Connell had been unwise enough to give a hostage to fortune by criticising the queen's speech, but not in the vulgar tones of M. J. Conway. O'Connell merely said that the queen had no right to stop Repeal and that the Irish would 'never give up their country and their constitutional rights and privileges to any queen or king'. Conway wrote, 'Are they cowards, sots, idiots, to be affrighted by the fishwoman jargon that a criminal faction have not scrupled to put into the mouth of the queen?' Conway, who was at Trinity in Davis's time, wrote only three articles for the paper, all in Davis's absence. One was on 'The movement in the university'. The Trinity authorities had dissolved the Historical Society but would permit it to be revived provided no politics were discussed and a fellow or a master held the chair. As further evidence of Trinity's determination to suppress free discussion and thought within its walls, a resident student had been fined ten shillings for having a copy of 'the *Nation* exposed in his window'.[26]

Despite the repeated bombast, it seemed to some in London that a mere growl would be enough to bring O'Connell to heel, and Sir Charles Trevelyan, who had been sent to Ireland in the autumn to look at the situation, was convinced that the leader was insincere and was merely leading the people on, but would never stand beside them if they resisted. Were it the case that Trevelyan was correct in his judgement, it was not because O'Connell was a craven who did not love the people he led. Had he refused to stand with them, it would have been because he judged resistance would have caused more bloodshed. On the other hand, Trevelyan thought differently of 'the young men of the capital', meaning Davis and his friends. To him they were radicals who 'supplied all the good writing, the history, the poetry, and the political philosophy, such as it was, of the party'. If anything was to be feared, it was from them but, without O'Connell, they also were powerless.[27]

To Davis, Madden again put the case plainly from London on 27 September. He was certain that the Council of Three Hundred would never be allowed to assemble and that, in any case, it was a useless forum for Davis to place himself in as it would achieve nothing, and he would be circumscribed from action by his membership of it. Madden knew his Davis well and thus could write, 'It is pretty plain that you must have either a pen or a pike in your hand, and is the council the place for you to work with such implements?' He warned again that there was a determination to use force by Britain and that O'Connell would lose his glorious reputation were he to confound 'the enthusiasm of applauding multitudes with the steadiness of an army'. There is no record of Davis replying to Madden, but he must have thought that a reasonable case could be put to the Duke of Wellington dissuading him from the use of arms to render the Irish submissive. He wrote in the *Nation* reminding him that the use of coercion is double-edged in that, 'If the sword of the despot strike a coward, he falls or flies. But beware, my lord – beware of striking some hard and devoted man with your battle-axe over such a combustible as Ireland. You remember your brother's saying, "Ireland is quiet – quiet as gunpowder".' They were sentiments the duke could afford to ignore while O'Connell stood firm against the use of violence, and he could also ignore the other letter Davis publicly addressed to him containing the plea that, if Prussia could be an independent and powerful state, so also could Ireland. He reminded Wellington that Ireland had a greater population and higher revenue than those of 'any of the twenty-one independent States on the Continent'. The duke was certainly mindful of the revenues of Ireland, as he was of its being part of the British Empire. Prussia, unlike Ireland, was afar-off. Ireland was dependent because it was deemed good by the English that it be so, and dependent it would remain while the duke and his fellows had control.[28]

There were strong rumours in Dublin that the privy council had already decided to proclaim the Repeal meetings because they were 'calculated to excite alarm and lead to a breach of the peace'. Yet some

Reproduction of J.P. Haverty's painting, 'Daniel O'Connell and his followers'. Davis is fifth from left in second row.

more concrete pretext was needed to act given that the peace had not been breached anywhere in Ireland, whether during the meetings or arising from them. Mere excitement, even if stemming from the alarm of the timid, was difficult to prove. The pretext for action was at last offered when the final monster meeting for 1843 was announced to take place at Clontarf on 8 October. Hundreds of thousands of Repealers from Dublin county, the nearby counties, as well as Irish on Merseyside and Clydeside were expected to be present on the ancient battlefield. The platform was to be erected on the mound where the bodies of the Danes were said to have been buried and the occasion was to be the culmination of all previous efforts. Davis wrote a strange and perturbed article that appeared in the same issue of the *Nation* as the announcement of the meeting. He reviewed a book on the defence of Ireland that showed how a landing by foreign troops could be prevented by patient defence, which must have given pause for thought to his readers, whether in the Castle or in the comfort of their homes around Dublin bay. On the other hand, he was able to keep a sense of balance on other matters and, on the day before Clontarf, ran his own letter in the 'Answers to Correspondents' section of the *Nation*, signing himself 'A Dalcassian'. As one who wanted 'to efface the very footsteps of the foreign spoliator from our soil', he suggested 'that the old names of places shall be restored in the mouths of the people, wherever it is possible to do so.' He was particularly displeased with the name of Lake Belvedere in county Westmeath. 'Away with it! We want neither Italian nor Saxon. Call it Loch Annin once more, and we will feel that it is Irish. It was in an island of that lake that our last King Roderic died.'[29]

On previous occasions, many men had come to the meetings mounted on horseback. It had happened as recently as 16 September at Clifden in county Galway, where O'Connell publicly referred to them as 'mountaineer cavalry' and showed his delight in them. Unarmed and with no intent other than to be present, they posed no threat to good order. When the public programme for Clontarf was drawn up, a position was given to the 'Repeal Cavalry' who would fall in behind the leader's carriage. They were to muster in troops of twenty-five with their officers who would have 'wands and cockades'. The language was indiscreet, but the intention was not warlike, no arms were mentioned and the programme ended with 'God save the Queen'. Yet it alerted the authorities to their chance, despite the fact that O'Connell, when he became aware of the indiscretion, repudiated it publicly. His repudiation served no purpose. The decision to proclaim the Clontarf meeting had already been taken.[30]

It is stretching charity to its limits to ascribe to pusillanimity the fact that the Castle authorities waited until 3.30 p.m. on 7 October, the day before the meeting, to issue the proclamation forbidding it. Such a judgement takes no account of the reaction of Wellington when he saw the proclamation. He expressed misgivings that strong action had not been taken earlier and then said, 'Ten years of misrule in Ireland have rendered our task more difficult, but we must now bring the rascals on their knees; they give us now a fair pretext to put them down.' The Duke recognised that an 'eager zealot', rather than O'Connell himself, was probably responsible for the document that spoke of cavalry, but nonetheless he rejoiced at 'the unguarded opening which O'Connell has given us to set him at defiance' and he repeated the words allegedly used by the papal nuncio in Lisbon when insurrection took place there, 'Pour la canaille, Faut la mitraille' which meant that the only way to put down an unruly mob was by the force of arms.[31] The long history of English suppression of popular protest, before and after Clontarf, in Ireland and elsewhere, suggests that some irresponsible authorities hoped that preventive action would prove impossible, that with or without their leader, the Irish mob would assemble, unarmed and unprepared and that, with guns trained on Clontarf from the defences in the bay, as well as military ready on the spot, they would be dealt with as persons acting against the law. Even Peel was aghast at the lateness of the proclamation. 'It is very fortunate that there was no collision at Clontarf,' he wrote later. 'The shortness of the notice would have imposed a heavy responsibility.' He did not specify upon whom that responsibility would have fallen.[32]

There was no bloodshed at Clontarf because of the prompt action of O'Connell and the efficiency of his organisation. He was having a meeting with his executive committee on Saturday afternoon when a copy of the proclamation arrived from the Castle. He submitted instantly and no one present objected, except that Thomas Reynolds whispered, as the committee dispersed, 'Ireland was won at Clontarf, and she is going to be lost at Clontarf.' Messengers met the crowds already coming in from the country and turned them back. 'Nearly the whole of the garrison of Dublin – horse, foot, and artillery' was assembled at Clontarf, according to W. R. Le Fanu who was an eye-witness, and there can be no doubt that bloodshed would have followed rapidly had the anticipated crowd assembled. When no one turned up, the huge stage was dismantled and the custodians of the law held the field in peace. O'Connell was content to continue calling for peaceful submission, while condemning the proclamation as 'the grossest violation of the law'. The 'monster meetings' were over and Repeal had not been achieved.[33] As for Thomas Davis, on 8 October 1843, he was still in the west.

References

1. See Duffy, *Davis*, p. 160 and Davis to Pigot, 26 August 1843 in ibid., p. 164 where he said that he had 'stomached science in Cork'.
2. R. Cranfield to Davis, Enniscorthy, 6 August 1843 in Ms 2644, NLI.
3. MacNevin to Duffy, n.d. but August 1843 in Ms 5756, NLI.
4. Davis to Hardiman, n.d. and I August 1843 in 12 N 20, RIA. Hardiman must have obliged because Davis wrote back to him from the Victoria Hotel, Cork, on 2 September saying, 'If the rest of the people of Galway have a tithe of your good nature I shall lament the necessary shortness of my stay there.' Ibid.
5. Duffy, *Davis*, pp 165-7.
6. Madden to Davis, 1 August, in Davis papers, Ms 2644, NLI. The correspondence of Davis on his journey is mainly published in Duffy. For this letter see Davis to Madden, n.d. Duffy, *Davis*, pp 162-77. Remnants are scattered through Letters of Davis and others to Duffy, Ms 5756, NLI and Davis papers, Ms 2644. NLI.
7. Davis to Duffy, 29 August 1843 in Duffy, *Davis*, pp 173-4.
8. See Lane to Davis, n.d. September 1843 in Denis Gwynn, 'Denny Lane and Thomas Davis', *Studies*, vol. 38 (Dublin, 1949), pp 18-19 and in Duffy, *Davis*, p. 177. The reference to MacNevin stemmed from the fact that some of Davis's friends were beginning to say, probably in jest, that MacNevin's contributions to the *Nation* were as good as Davis's.
9. Duffy, *Davis*, pp 162-64. Davis said that Hogan did not finish the head of the Christ in Italy. 'I wished to prevent jealous people saying I got Italian help. I shall do this here under their eyes,' p. 164.
10. Ibid, p. 165. Davis referred to 'Thorpe's pamphlets and coast traditions.' and Duffy said they were 'a valuable collection in the Royal Irish Academy.'
11. Davis to Duffy, 29 August 1843, Ms 5756, NLI. He told Duffy that he felt 'scribbleways' and that more articles would be forthcoming. In all, eleven articles were written during the trip.
12. The article was run in the *Nation* on 2 September 1843.
13. Duffy, *Davis*, p. 165.
14. Davis to Webb, n.d. August 1843. Davis to Pigot, 26 August 1843, Duffy, *Davis*, pp 162-66. Some of the letters to Pigot are also found in *The Irish Monthly. A magazine of general literature*, vol. 2 (Dublin, 1883), pp 263-5. For the trip see also Davis's diaries, August 1843, Ms 12 P 19, RIA.
15. See Duffy, *Davis*, pp 168-9 and original letter Pigot to Davis, 23 August 1843 in Davis papers, Ms 2644, NLI.
16. Ibid. Pigot need not have worried about the O'Connell statue. Hogan was a master sculptor. He did a splendid, but formally stylized, statue of O'Connell for Dublin's City Hall.
17. Davis to Webb from Bantry, 8 September, 1843 in Duffy, *Davis*, pp 169-70.
18. Webb to Davis, in O'Brien papers, Ms 432, NLI.
19. Davis's diaries, September-October, 1843, Mss 12 P 19, RIA and 12 P 114. Duffy, *Davis*, pp 170-74. For a judgement on Griffin's (1803-40) work, see A. W. Ward and A. R. Waller, *The Cambridge history of English literature*, vol. xiv, p. 354. Griffin became a Christian brother but died soon afterwards. For Davis learning Irish, see Daniel Corkery, 'Davis and the national language' in M. J. MacManus, (ed.), *Thomas Davis and Young Ireland* (Dublin, 1945), p. 22 and Ó Cathaoir, *Dillon*, p. 26.
20. See the splendid edition by the Royal Irish Academy with text by Peter Harbison of *Beranger's views of Ireland* (Dublin, 1991). See also Jeanne Sheehy, *The rediscovery*, p. 31 for the flags. See Appendix I for a list of subjects suggested by Davis.

21. *Nation*, 12 August 1843.
22. Ibid., 5, 12, 19 August, 23 September 1843. Davis to Duffy, n.d. September 1843 in Duffy, *Davis*, p. 173.
23. Davis to Duffy, 8 September 1843; John O'Connell to Davis, 20 September 1843, Ms 2644, NLI. Duffy to Davis, n.d. September 1843 in Duffy, *Davis*, p. 174.
24. See O'Connell to Campbell, 8 September 1843 in O'Connell (ed.), *Correspondence*, vol. vii, p. 224; *Nation*, 23 September, 7 October 1843; Duffy, *Davis*, p. 178; MacDonagh, *O'Connell*, pp 519-20.
25. See Duffy, *Young Ireland*, part 1, pp 112-113.
26. *Nation*, 2, 16, 30 September, 7 October 1843.
27. See Duffy, *Davis*, p. 177.
28. Ibid., pp 178-81.
29. Ibid., 9 September, 7 October 1843.
30. *Nation*, 23, 30 September, 7 October 1843. The order for the cavalry was printed on the front page of the paper on 30 September.
31. See Duffy, *Davis*, p. 182 and *Young Ireland*, p. 140.
32. For Peel see Oliver MacDonagh, *O'Connell*, p. 521. For an occasion, at Ballarat, Australia in 1854, when normally law-abiding and peaceful citizens, drawn from many nations including Ireland, were deliberately pushed into protest and then massacred see John Molony, *Eureka* (Melbourne, 1984).
33. See Oliver MacDonagh, *O'Connell*, pp 521-2; Duffy, *Davis*, pp 182-3; *Young Ireland*, part 1, p. 136; W. R. Le Fanu, *Seventy years of Irish life*, 3rd ed. (London, 1894), p. 296.

LAMENT FOR THE DEATH OF EOGAN RUAḊ O'NEIL.

(COMMONLY CALLED OWEN ROE O'NEIL.)

BY THOMAS DAVIS.

Time—10th Nov. 1649. Scene—Ormond's Camp, County Waterford. Speakers—A Veteran of Owen
O'Neil's clan, and one of the horsemen, just arrived with an account of his death.

I.

"Did they dare, did they dare, to slay Owen Roe O'Neil?"
'Yes, they slew with poison him, they feared to meet with steel.'
"May God wither up their hearts! May their blood cease to flow !
May they walk in living death, who poisoned Owen Roe ! "

II.

'Yes ! from Derry we were marching, false Cromwell to o'erthrow,
And who can doubt the tyrant's fate, had he met Owen Roe ?
But the weapon of the Saxon met him on his way,
And he died at Cloċ Uaċtair, upon Saint Leonard's Day.'

III.

"Wail, wail ye for The Mighty One! Wail, wail ye for the Dead ;
Quench the hearth, and hold the breath—with ashes strew the head.
How tenderly we loved him ! How deeply we deplore !
Oh ! it breaks my heart to think we shall never see him more.

IV.

Sagest in the council was he, kindest in the hall,
Sure we never won a battle—'twas Owen won them all.
Had he lived—had he lived—our dear country had been free ;
But he's dead, but he 's dead, and 'tis slaves we 'll ever be.

V.

O'Farrell and Clanrickarde, Preston and Red Hugh,
Audley and MacMahon—ye are valiant, wise, and true ;
But—what, what are ye all to our darling who is gone ?
The Rudder of our Ship was he, our Castle's corner stone !

VI.

Wail, wail him through the Island ! Weep, weep for our pride !
Would that on the battle-field our gallant chief had died !
Weep the Victor of Beinn Burb—weep him, young man and old ;
Weep for him, ye women—your Beautiful lies cold !

VII.

We thought you would not die—we were sure you would not go,
And leave us in our utmost need to Cromwell's cruel blow—
Sheep without a shepherd, when the snow shuts out the sky—
Oh ! why did you leave us, Owen ? Why did you die ?

VIII.

Soft as woman's was your voice, O'Neil ! bright was your eye,
Oh ! why did you leave us, Owen ? why did you die ?
Your troubles are all over, you're at rest with God on high ;
But we're slaves, and we're orphans, Owen !—why did you die ? "

Chapter 10

Twilight of Repeal

Taken at its most elementary level, the conscious act of claiming nationality includes the desire of a people to be governed by those who are drawn from among themselves, and whom they accept as their own representatives. For centuries, many of the Irish had made it plain that the continued rule of the English over Ireland was not acceptable to them. A disorganised, largely provoked attempt to throw off the yoke had ended in disaster in 1798. The struggle of 1843 differed because it was undertaken without violence and with considerable skill. It ended in high farce with the dismantling of a platform and the despatching of trustees to intercept the crowds converging on Dublin in hope.

The events of 8 October 1843 wrought a profound change in the nature of the Repeal Association and in those who supported its aims, whether in that small group bound up with the *Nation* or in that multitude who followed O'Connell. The whole year had passed in high emotion, engendered both by the purpose proclaimed so forthrightly by the Leader of achieving Repeal within the year and by the means taken towards that end. Conservative estimates of those who attended the monster meetings would suggest that no less than two to three million Irish, men, women and children had been moved and motivated either by hearing the leader's words, or by the enthusiasm of those vast crowds.[1] Why, then, did O'Connell bow before the threat of British intimidation with scarcely a murmur? At its highest level his motive must arise from his constant refusal to countenance bloodshed. Nonetheless, he had continued to promise what he could not deliver, given the means he used of mass agitation that fell short even of passive resistance. There was neither a call nor a need to bear or use an Irish pike or a firearm at Clontarf on 8 October. It would have been enough for the Irish multitude to be there and refuse to move. Their Leader did not want them at Clontarf because he was rightly afraid that some of them might die and he had set his face against having their blood on his hands. His principal mistake was to make them think that he meant what he said when he spoke of resisting an unconstitutional invasion of their rights. The great problem was that no one, not the least his closest followers, knew what he meant.

For months before the day of Clontarf, Davis had been preparing himself mentally for the eventuality of action by the authorities. He was convinced that the time had not yet come for defiance because the Irish were not ready to begin any realistic form of insurgency, and he thought that, unless their leaders properly calculated the price of violence, and prepared for it, the Irish cause would be imperilled by another bloody defeat. In ways that, perhaps, were imperfectly understood, Davis tried to make his mind clear to his readers. Blind loyalty to the crown could never be used as a pretext not to resist. He wrote, 'Loyalty is a conditional virtue,' and 'Technical loyalty becomes a crime when resistance becomes a duty. Let us not deny the creed of liberty in order to gain the toleration, or help, of any man, woman, or party.' However, to underestimate, much more to scoff at, the might of English power was ridiculous and it was folly to believe anyone who told them that an unarmed multitude gathered at a meeting 'could conquer a great army'. England was 'formidable still' and her troops would do their duty as 'hangmen and slaughter-slaves', when ordered into action. In the person of Wellington, England had 'one great captain', although, by serving Ireland's oppressor, he was 'unmindful of his duty to his native land'. Despite Ireland's military impotence there was, nonetheless, much to be done because freedom would be useless unless the people were prepared for its use. A national history and literature must be written, men needed to be trained to be politicians and economists, and the people had to be educated to be virtuous, otherwise it was idle to dream of 'wealth or independence'. He concluded with a prayer,

> That it may please Almighty *God* to confirm the virtue and wisdom of our Chief, and increase the energy and truth of all other leaders, and give the People honour, patience, faith, and valour, is our humble and anxious prayer.[2]

On the role of the Chieftain, Davis had already made his attitude clear in a poem that dealt with Hogan's proposed statue of O'Connell. It was written at Cork in late August and spoke of O'Connell as 'Pious, generous, deep and warm' and of the Union with its 'fetter vile'. He begged,

> Let trampled altar, rifled urn,
> Knit his look to purpose stern.

Most of all, he wanted the statue to engrave the defiance at Mallow, and elsewhere, when O'Connell was 'content to die but never yield'.

Thus he spoke, and thus he stood,
Proffering in our cause his blood,
Thus his country loves him best –
To image this is your behest.
Chisel thus, and thus alone,
If to man you'd change the stone.[3]

A week after Clontarf, the anniversary number of the *Nation* was published. Davis's copy in the Royal Irish Academy has in his writing on the frontispiece of the bound set for 1843-44 'a perfect copy T.D' and the words, taken from the *Spirit of the Nation*, 'Firm, unshrinking, Bide your time'. From that number onwards, he never ascribed any of the contents of the paper to an author so that, except for his poetry, which has been largely acknowledged by Duffy and others, it is on mainly internal evidence that Davis's authorship of articles and reviews has to be established.[4]

On the previous Monday, the day after the abortive Clontarf episode, O'Connell had addressed a large crowd at the meeting of the Association. He said that Sunday had been a miserable day for him because he feared the bloodshed that would have occurred had he not interposed and stopped proceedings. Asking the people to obey the law and promising them that all would be well, he said that he would go ahead with the Council of the Three Hundred. Given that the word had got around that arrests were to be made of the ringleaders, it was unwise to threaten a revival of the idea of the Council but O'Connell possibly thought that the authorities would rest on their laurels. He was mistaken, even if his language was conciliatory rather than defiant. On the motion of Father Tyrell, who had done a great deal to warn the people not to go to Clontarf when the meeting was proscribed, the resolutions that had been drawn up for that occasion were adopted by the Association. Two days later a warrant for the arrest of nine 'traversers', as they became known, was issued and on Saturday 14 October, Daniel O'Connell, his son John, Thomas Ray, secretary of the Association, Thomas Steele, three journalists in the persons of Duffy, John Gray of the *Freeman's* and Richard Barrett of the *Pilot*, together with Father Tyrell and Father Tierney, a priest from the north who had only attended one meeting of the Association, were arrested and given bail pending trial.

The charge against the 'traversers' was that of conspiring to 'unlawful and seditious opposition to ... [the] government and constitution'. The indictment for the prosecutions was nearly 100 yards long. Several of Davis's articles, including 'Something is coming' [on the Council of 300], 'The Morality of War' and an article suggesting that the modern names of places in Ireland should be abandoned and the old Celtic names revived, were included in the charge against Duffy, as also were 'The Memory of the Dead' by Ingram and 'The Crisis is Upon Us' by Conway. It was also alleged that 3,610,000 persons had attended the 'monster meetings' from 19 March to 1 October, not including the 800,000 said to have been at Tara. This time the lion apparently decided to roar again by threatening Ireland with the strictest application of the law, but only time and events would reveal whether threats of that kind were effective in the longer run.[5]

Davis had heard the news of the proclamation against Clontarf while he was still at Galway. He went immediately to Castlebar to talk about the future with John Dillon who was staying in the countryside near there. He also sent word to his mother at Baggot Street to destroy papers he had left there which could have been dangerous to others, as well as to himself. With little left but the pen, Davis took it up again to express his sense of anger, shame and contempt for what had happened, in a ballad entitled, 'We must not fail.' It was one thing for O'Connell to surrender with dignity and to protest long and loudly against the nature of the acts that had brought Repeal to such a pass. It was another to speak meekly of obedience to the law when it was plain that Repeal led by him contained no elements of violence or subversion, so that its whole course had been conducted within the law. Davis knew what would be thought in Ireland and elsewhere because,

> We must not fail; we must not fail; however force or fraud assail;
> By honour, pride and policy, by heaven itself we must be free.
> We promised loud, and boasted high, 'To break our country's chains or die';
> And should we quail, that country's name will be the synonym of shame.

His next lines were harsh and uncompromising,

> Earth is not deep enough to hide the coward slave who shrinks aside;
> Hell is not hot enough to scathe the ruffian wretch who breaks his faith.

As an exhortation to his readers, and to himself, the last lines ran,

> But – calm, my soul! – we promised true, her destined work our land shall do;
> Thought, courage, patience, will prevail – we shall not fail – we shall not fail.

The original in Davis's copy of the *Nation* has an added, pencilled verse in his hand. Its bitterness is such that it was better omitted.

> Better that Ireland now should yield
> A bloody corse in every field
> An honoured waste for future men
> Were nobler than a helot's den.[6]

At Castlebar, he heard of the arrests and expected that there would be an insurrection. Dillon shared in that expectation and wrote in 1848, 'I fully participated in his anticipations or his *hopes*, ... If those hopes had been realised – if the people of Ireland had risen as one man at that moment, and in the blood of their tyrants had washed out the shame of 600 years, Mr O'Connell or any other man would not now dare to say they had done wrong.'[7] While in Castlebar, Davis made no attempt to conceal his presence from the local authorities and, when nothing happened, he started for Dublin within two days, 'alleging as a reason for his departure the necessity of being at headquarters in such a crisis'.[8] He was certainly puzzled that he had not been among those arrested, but Dublin Castle must have decided that, in arresting the editors of the papers deemed to be preaching sedition, honour was preserved intact and, if necessary, others could be dealt with when appropriate. Nevertheless, in March 1848, John O'Connell publicly repeated in the *Freeman's Journal* the 'calumny' of 'vile or malignant slanderers who originated it', accusing Davis of '*hiding* in the country' at the time of danger for prominent Repeal supporters in Dublin. John Dillon probably expected some such attack because he had attended an election meeting in Waterford a few weeks previously at which a friar, Reverend Father Cuddihy, called Davis a 'coward who ran away from the Monster meetings'. Dillon firmly defended his late friend against John O'Connell's accusations, but considerable damage had already been done to Davis's memory. As well as cowardice, Davis, and other writers of the *Nation*, were also accused of hiding behind their anonymity in that, at the trials of the 'traversers', their articles and ballads in the paper were used as evidence and they had not come forward to claim them as their own. Apart from the fact that it would have been useless to do so, given that the three editors were charged because they were responsible for what was run in their papers, the important point was that had all, or many, of the *Nation* writers been arrested and perhaps imprisoned, the paper would have been struck a blow from which it might have never recovered. For the present, Davis had his own way of resisting and a constituency to follow him in the quarter million readers of the *Nation* who could not be scattered by edicts from the Castle. The paper had to survive and, with the arrest of Duffy, Davis knew that he was essential to its survival. In his own lifetime, and later, it was acknowledged by thousands that his manner of resistance bore no shred of cowardice. As far as Dillon was concerned, he thought that Davis's behaviour, instead of convincing him that Davis was a coward, tended in his mind 'to exhibit his heroism and his devotion to the Irish people ...'[9]

The account given by Duffy of the reaction of Davis, and those who collaborated in producing the *Nation*, reveals their pain and shock at the turn of events. Duffy said that, when Davis met his Dublin friends on his return from the West, 'we found him painfully discomposed by the retreat before the proclamation.' To Duffy, the work Davis had done by his writing and persuasion had been of profound benefit to the whole Repeal movement in that he had moved the people to a determination that 'their acts might adequately correspond with their words'. O'Connell's submission had seemingly thoroughly dissipated that determination. Thus the hopes of the young men were dashed because they knew immediately that the advantage had been taken by the English and that, during O'Connell's lifetime, it would be idle to expect the Irish to rally to the cause of Repeal again in the way they had done in 1843. Understandably, 'It was a time of despondency and misery, of rage and despair.'[10]

Duffy also leaves no doubt where Davis had stood regarding resistance. 'He desired that the passion and purpose of the people should be raised to the scale of 1782, when England would again yield to the will of a united nation, or, if she would not yield that the Repealers should do what the Volunteers would assuredly have done, fight for the liberty denied to them.'[11] There were, however, aspects of 1782 and of 1843 that differed markedly. In 1782 there was no Union between England and Ireland and the struggle, in some serious measure uniting all religious traditions in Ireland, was one for the granting of appropriate powers to an Irish Parliament. In 1843 there were no Volunteers and those who rallied around O'Connell stood unarmed because their Leader would not permit his followers to prepare for battle or fight for their freedom. In the event, he would not so much as permit them to die for it. Finally, O'Connell was old and exhausted in 1843 with the battles of over thirty years behind him. Thus, between O'Connell and Davis there was a vast gulf and Davis had done nothing to bridge it in the practical sense. To do so would have entailed promoting the concept of armed struggle by means that went well beyond the pen. It was an action that O'Connell would not have tolerated, and Davis surely knew it.

According to Duffy, Davis was so downcast by the turn of events that he resolved to leave the Association and devote himself to Ireland in another way. His friends were able to persuade him to accept the situation, bad and all as it was, and to plan for victory by continuing to build up the idea of nationality in ways that were longer-term but more lasting, such as education. The confidence of the people in their Leader must not be destroyed by their attacking him, because without him, no national movement was possible. Moreover, they had their own responsibilities to the future and the generation that was growing up around them. They had set themselves up as the standard-bearers of nationality, of Irish culture and of education for the people and now was not the time to withdraw. As a result, they decided to hold back from causing any split in the ranks, while making it plain that they deplored the apparent weakness of capitulation. Furthermore, the widespread sense of helpless outrage caused by the arrests temporarily helped swell recruitment to the Association and there was a subsequent rise in Repeal rent to the sum of £2,287.19.6 in the week to 23 October.[12]

Amid all the excitement, the new Conciliation Hall was opened with great fanfare on 23 October. It held 3,000 people with 1,500 in the ladies gallery and no one seemed disconcerted that it bore on its stone an inscription that proclaimed 'The Repeal Year 1843'. In the same week, the decision by Smith O'Brien, after 'a painful struggle' which caused him to hesitate 'too long', to join the Association and to take a prominent role in its proceedings, heartened many. In the event of O'Connell being rendered ineffective as leader during the process of the trial, or by his consequent imprisonment, someone with authority and standing was needed, otherwise the leadership mantle might pass into unacceptable hands. Smith O'Brien seemed to be the ideal solution. He came of an ancient family, he was a Protestant, and, at forty, he was of more mature years than the Duffy-Davis group. He was a public figure in that he had represented Ennis at Westminster as a Tory, but also as an Emancipationist from 1828 to 1831, and Limerick as a Repealer in recent years. Above all, he was modest, moderate and possessed a conciliatory nature. It was easy and natural for him to assume the mantle as second-in-command to O'Connell.[13]

In the *Nation*, Davis immediately continued to build on the basis he had laid down before Clontarf, but he was aware that the situation was totally changed. Exhortations to stand resolutely behind the Leader were useless now that O'Connell seemed to have no idea where he was heading. Instead, the best possible light had to be put on what had happened, while insisting that the work of inculcating nationality had to be persisted in continuously. To him, the absence of '*A self-respecting spirit of nationality*' was the great defect in the national

211

Lying-In-Hospital and Rotonda, Dublin.

character, especially among the upper and middle classes. When he wrote, 'Nationality was our first great object. *All* social and political movements we valued only as they promoted it', it was clear where the Repeal Association stood in his priorities. Tenure, just rents and compensation for improvements made by tenants and, in the future, the reduction of the great estates and the creation of small proprietors, were vital, but he 'was not ready to jump into a servile war for this'. Above all, there must be no retreat from persevering in upholding principles. To do so would be to invite the enemies of Ireland to press on and reduce the country even further. Sections of the English press held that 'Ireland needs Repose', but Davis replied, 'Let no man bid the Irish peasantry repose when their houses are mud kennels without furniture, and their food, roots ... The repose which Ireland wants, and can alone obtain, is that which health, strength and liberty bring.' Finally, he attempted to put paid to the adulation of empire that O'Connell clung to so grimly and which he had repeated on 19 November at the Association meeting. Davis replied, 'We, we and the people of Ireland, do not love the Empire. Its foundations were piled in the blood and property of our fathers. Its unholy shadow dwarfs the mind and spirit of every land on which it falls ... Empire is a word of reproach to its achievers, of terror to its subjects, of abhorrence to the profound and good.'[14]

The main thing that preoccupied the minds of most loyal Repealers was the forthcoming trials of the 'traversers'. Even in this, Davis was not prepared to allow himself to be sidetracked. He took some satisfaction in seeing the bungling that so blatantly perverted the legal system as it attempted to secure a particular form of English justice against the accused. At the same time, Davis did not want the whole Repeal movement to dissipate itself by uselessly following the sideshow taking place at the Four Courts in Dublin. 'We trust the people spend, and will spend their time, not in idle curiosity about trials, but in improving their minds, increasing their union and qualifying themselves for nationality.' He was evidently not worried about the outcome of the trials, indeed he seemed to welcome the sobering effect they were having on the movement, but he insisted that agitation had to be persevered with and enthusiasm maintained. If the Repeal rent could be taken as a barometer of the general adhesion to the cause, there were good grounds for concern because, within three months, it had dropped from a high of over £2,000 to less than £300 a week. Even more ominously, there were signs that O'Connell was losing his grasp on the reality of the situation. If ever the occasion warranted clear and resolute leadership it was now and it had to be based on a continuation of the campaign for Repeal or admit that the English had won at Clontarf and that Repeal was finished. Instead, O'Connell said on 13 November that he would now accept an Irish Parliament with control over local affairs, while the rest would be left to Westminster. It was a form of mitigated federalism that satisfied neither the genuine Repealers, nor those federalists with some slight notion of what they were aiming for, although the *Nation* tried to put a brave interpretation to the proposal by describing it as holding out for Ireland all the powers she possessed in 1783. O'Connell quickly backpedalled, but the signs were there that Clontarf had diminished his stature and unless he were to give decisive leadership again, a dubious outcome given his passing years and wearied spirit, it was unlikely that he would retain the wholehearted following of his young lieutenants. Indeed, even the *Freeman's Journal* warned O'Connell to stick to Repeal, saying that the people had never warmed to federalism. One reason may have been that the people never understood what it meant, which is not much more than saying that its proposers were unsure themselves.[15]

If Davis and his friends needed any proof of deliberate mis-government it came in the trial of the 'traversers'. After the crown successfully challenged eleven Catholics drawn by lot, the jury was packed with twelve Protestants picked from rigged lists and the three judges were of the same religion. In the upshot, two Protestants and six Catholics, including the leader of the Irish, Catholic people stood trial in their own country before a travesty called a Court of Justice. One of the priests charged, Father Tyrell, parish priest of Lusk, county Dublin, and a most unlikely conspirator, had died in December, and the trial of the other priest was not proceeded with. To Davis, any evidence the crown saw fit to bring forward would suffice to secure convictions, because the whole affair had been so organised as to achieve that end. Davis wrote that, to obtain convictions, 'Protestantism may be disgraced. Justice may be trampled on. Our nationality and prosperity may be sacrificed.' However, the essential question that had to be confronted and decided, was whether the accused had conspired to achieve a legal object by illegal means, which made hard going for the crown given that it was legal to agitate.[16]

O'Connell spoke in his own defence with his usual mastery and Davis called his speech 'a perfect argument for Repeal ... with passages of great beauty'. The Leader could claim, truthfully, that the monster meetings had all been conducted without injury to person or property, which the judge conceded when passing sentence. O'Connell, however, missed the point as he was on trial for seditious conspiracy, although no one seemed quite able to say what he had conspired to do. He pointed out that others had contemplated physical force to achieve freedom if other means failed, but 'I have again and again declared my intention to abandon the cause of repeal if a single drop of human blood were shed by those who advocated the measure.' He was careful to avoid any reference to the determination of those in authority to shed blood if necessary to achieve their objective. In the event, the trial lasted three weeks with much high oratory by defence counsel. The chief justice laid great emphasis on the Council of Three Hundred and the arbitration courts in summing up for the jury and used the very sentence about the Union being iniquitous, illegal and invalid that Davis had struck out too late from Conway's article in August. The foregone conclusion of guilty was reached on 10 February 1844 and sentencing was postponed. In his own summing up in the *Nation*, Davis said 'Ireland must attempt *nothing* which can *fail*. She must *never again* be dishonoured by defeat. Listen to us. You want to make Ireland a nation. So did your fathers. They failed. And why? Because they were impatient. Because they yielded to passion'. Favours from England, as Russell seemed to promise in a speech he made in Parliament, were to be treated with indifference because 'We have done with trusting strangers.' Solemnly he said that, henceforth, 'Ourselves alone' had to be their motto.[17]

Already O'Connell was contemplating a new, tactical manoeuvre to confound his enemies. At a meeting of the General Committee he proposed that the Repeal Association be dissolved, the arbitration courts be abandoned and a new body be formed that would exclude newspaper proprietors. The young men strongly rejected the proposal and made it clear to their Leader that they would not follow him into another association. Sean O'Faolain later wrote, 'The behaviour of the young men in that extremity makes one of the really inspiring chapters in Irish history. They sustained, with a real magnificence, the continuity of the Irish struggle.'[18] O'Connell quickly withdrew his proposals and a compromise was reached by which any official connection with the arbitration courts was given up and the four editors, Gray, Barrett, Staunton and Duffy resigned from the Association. The incident served to make the Leader aware that the old days, when his *fiat* sufficed to cause immediate obedience by his followers, were over.

O'Connell was clearly seriously shaken by the verdict of guilty and much concern was expressed about his intention to accept an invitation by his Whig allies to visit England before sentence was handed down. The young men feared that he would capitulate on Repeal and accept a series of reforms for Ireland that would virtually be a desertion of the 'national cause'. They realised that only O'Connell could lead the people in such a direction and his weakening in resolve would mean the end of the movement for Repeal while he lived. Davis, however, thought that O'Connell would be better out of the country than in it in his present frame of mind. 'If O'C were firmer I would say he ought not to go to England; but fancy his speeches at ten meetings here with the State Trial terror on him. I fear we must keep him out of that danger by an English trip ....' he wrote to Smith O'Brien.[19] In the event, O'Connell went to England where, by making it appear that he would accept the promise of some reform in Ireland in case of a return to power by the Whigs, at the price of the death of Repeal, he did more harm than he could ever have done by remaining at home. On 8 March 1844 Davis wrote to John O'Connell and told him that he had recommended the visit to England after being assured that O'Connell would remain firm and recant nothing. The very opposite had happened. The Leader of the Irish people 'now prizes the cheers, the rights and the feelings of the British, as much and more than the Irish'. As far as Davis could judge, by his present behaviour O'Connell had not gained one sympathiser in England more than he already had, but if he hoped he would escape prison as a result of his speeches and his association with the Whigs, he was mistaken because nothing but the dissolution of the Repeal Association would achieve that end. 'To dissolve the association would be to abdicate his power, and ruin his country. He is incapable of it ... and so I gladly pass from this insulting suggestion of the Whigs.' In the certain knowledge that John would pass the letter to his father, he warned, 'Ireland is not what she was a month ago. If this continues we shall have neither a Repeal Association nor a Liberal Government [in Westminster], whereas a vigorous pursuit of Repeal now would retain the one and give the only chance of the other.' His strongest words were addressed both to father and son. He wrote, 'believe me, John O'Connell, every single inconsistency injures the character and weakens the power of a statesman.'[20]

Through every line of Davis's letter there is a singular blending of naïvety, clear-mindedness and trust. Davis knew that the Leader had already moved sufficiently far from the retention of the Association as to make all his behaviour in England plausible, irrespective of whether he expected a reprieve from prison for it. He must surely have wondered also whether O'Connell had ever seriously contemplated the possibility of achieving Repeal, as distinct from a series of further concessions for Ireland. Nonetheless, he still hoped O'Connell would remain loyal and strong and lead them all along the hard road of Repeal while knowing that, without resistance and the consequent certainty of bloodshed, Repeal would never be granted. It had become increasingly clear to Davis that he only had O'Connell and Repeal to work with to free Ireland. Neither was adequate. Nor, indeed, were his own words at the time. 'We have always glorified, and shall ever worship, the brave, profuse of their blood in a good cause.' Moral force was always admirable, but when it fails, 'God and your conscience command you to do or to die.'[21]

At the time, the collection of material from the paper entitled *The Spirit of the Nation* was being reviewed extensively and, in the main, favourably. The London *Tablet* said that, of the fifty-nine articles, twenty-six were contributed by 'a certain Thomas Davis', that they contained 'more matter' than was found in the eighteen by Duffy and were interwoven with 'very extensive thoughts indeed' which were 'apt, pointed, sharp and decisive'. Moreover, the 'very considerable vein of warlike images and thoughts [that] seem to be embedded in the writer's cranium', made the reviewer 'blue with apprehension of another 98'. As a result, he was certain that the imprisonment of Duffy would not 'chain the war spirit of the *Nation*'. Throughout all this period of turmoil, with articles and editorials, Davis had concentrated on his main purpose in every way that seemed appropriate, but it is a mistake to imagine that Davis wrote the *Nation* virtually alone. On 23 February 1849 Duffy, then in Newgate prison, wrote to Thomas D'Arcy McGee, 'When Thomas Davis was performing miracles of industry, McNevin, Dillon, Barry, McCarthy, Doheny, Daunt, etc, were playing at least a very effective chorus.'[22]

O'Connell returned from England while still awaiting sentence and further illustrated his loss of reality, while practically inviting imprisonment, by stating, 'Give me but six months of peace, and I will give you my head on a block if we have not a parliament in College Green.' He went to an Association meeting where he refused, with great resoluteness, the sum of £178-14-9 from New Orleans because it came from potential slavers, rejoiced that the flag of Ireland and Great Britain flew over lands inhabited only by freemen and lamented that the pre-Union workforce of 160,000 in Dublin was now reduced to less than 14,000. On 30 May, instead of his head on a block, he was sentenced to twelve months imprisonment and the others received nine months. O'Connell called for peace, order, quiet and tranquillity throughout Ireland and, with much emotion among the public, the prisoners were accompanied to Dublin's most comfortable prison, Richmond Brideswell, by Davis, Smith O'Brien and many others, where the governor welcomed them warmly. As at Clontarf, so also in Her Majesty's prison, it was again time for high farce. Davis, however, stood his ground. 'We are past the Rubicon – to recross it involves eternal shame. He is worse than a traitor who would turn his step, or blot out from his heart the word "Nationality". The *Newry Examiner* followed events in Dublin closely and read Davis assiduously. It had decided that he was a very doubtful proponent of moral force and that 'had he lived in '98 he would have been shot, or hanged, or exiled.'[23]

Richmond Bridewell, late prison of O'Connell and the Repeal Martyrs.

Davis, in his 'Letters of a Protestant on Repeal' kept up the flow of reasoning and cajoling to Irish Protestants and reached number 14 by June 1843.[24] More striking was the stream of ballads and poems that he poured forth in this period. It was almost as if he felt a greater need to uplift the spirits of the people and keep alive the idea of nationality in proportion to the waning of the Repeal movement and the lessening of the hold of the Leader on his followers. The momentum created in 1843 prior to Clontarf could be partially sustained by prose, but it was much more effectively done by the ballad with its appeal, through words and music, to both head and heart. His sense of urgency was apparent in a letter he wrote to John Pigot in April, 1844. He said that John O'Hagan, the last of whose six poems had appeared in the previous August, and John Kells Ingram, whose 'The memory of the dead' was published over a year previously, were 'inexcusable' for their inactivity. Davis said, 'One poem now is worth twenty to be brought out in five years time' and he tried to prove his point by his own output.[25] Thomas Wallis later undertook, as his special task the preservation of Davis's written material and brought out an edition of his poetry in 1846 with a lengthy introduction. Most of the poems and ballads had already appeared in the *Nation* and then in the collections based on the paper entitled *Spirit of the Nation* and *Ballad poetry of Ireland*. Wallis, however, asserted that his, *The poems of Thomas Davis*, contained thirty additional poems that were not included in the anthologies.[26]

Whatever about Davis's public allegiance to pacifism as preached by O'Connell, militarism looms large in his ballads, as does the fact that he saw virtue in bearing, and using, arms which alone could ensure final victory. This idea he retained throughout his adult life. The ballad 'Nationality' proclaimed,

A nation's right, a nation's right –
   God gave it, and gave, too
A nation's sword, a nation's might
   Danger to guard it through.

In 'A Song for the Irish Militia', which was published in February 1845, the theme is set in the first verse and repeated in the last,

The tribune's tongue and poet's pen
May sow the seed in prostrate men:
But 'tis the soldier's sword alone
Can reap the crop so bravely sown!
No more I'll sing nor idly pine,

But train my soul to lead a line –
A soldier's life the life for me –
A soldier's death, so Ireland's free!

However, a line in verse three, 'That blood-bought freedom's cheaply bought', shows that he was uneasy with such a forthright enunciation of naked militarism and his fifth verse combines the higher virtues of wisdom and patience with strength and steel as the true means to 'make the English reel.'[27] In another thirty poems, or ballads, militarism is either explicit throughout, or sufficiently present as to heighten the theme. That element is more strikingly apparent when Davis deals with an historical battle, thus leaving him free to highlight war and its violence without running the risk of being accused of inciting his readers to either war or violence in the present. The line, however, between the two was thin. The events of May 1689 were very familiar to Davis through his own study of the Parliament of that period and he used his gifts to make the military aspects of the Revolution familiar to his wider audience in the *Nation* with a ballad entitled 'A Rally for Ireland'. The refrain and last verse of the ballad encapsulate his message, or what he at least seemed to want to say,

Rally, then rally!
Irishmen, rally –
Fight now or never,
Now and for ever!
Laws are in vain without swords to maintain;
So, muster as fast as the fall of the rain:
Serried and rough as a field of ripe grain,
Stand by your flag upon mountain and plain:
Charge till yourselves or your foemen are slain!
Fight till yourselves or your foemen are slain![28]

Irish history was not the only source from which Davis drew examples to extol resistance with the sword to the incursion of a foreign tyrant. In a long poem entitled 'A Ballad of Freedom' he sang his praise to the 'freeman's heart' of Abdel-Kader who fought against the French invasion of Algeria; to the lion of Pakistan, Akhbar Kan, who slew the British sepoys until they fled from his land and to the warriors of the Caucasus in 'The fountain head, Whence Europe spread' who drove out the Russians. In Poland, Italy, Bohemia, Serbia and Hungary he saw free peoples bowed under subjugation, and to them he joined Ireland 'who struggles gallantly in England's loosening grasp'. Preferably united but, if necessary, alone he wanted all subject peoples to resist so that from the Indus to the Shannon, 'Shall gleam a line of freemen's flags begirt by freemen's cannon!' In such manner they would herald, 'The coming day of Freedom – the flashing flags of Freedom![29]

To the air of 'The gentle Maiden' Davis wrote a ballad on the flight of the Wild Geese entitled 'When South Winds Blow'. He centred it around an Irish maiden who was 'as noble as the hill' but, compared to her, 'battle-flags are nobler still'. Though she was as 'graceful as the wave', her beloved refused to 'live a tranquil slave' under the control of Ireland's conquerers. Instead, he was in France fighting with 'the foe of Ireland's foe' while she pined away in sorrow. The same theme, that it is better to go abroad to fight against England by joining the forces of her enemies, than to bow under the yolk at home, is also found in other ballads and especially in one dealing with the Battle of Fontenoy. Davis recalled with bitterness the breaking of the treaty of Limerick 'ere the ink wherewith t'was writ could dry'. He went on,

> Their plundered homes, their ruined shrines, their women's parting cry,
> Their priesthood hunted down like wolves, their country overthrown,
> Each looks, as if revenge for all were staked on him alone.

It is a ballad shot through with animosity towards the invader and in his commentary on it, Wallis, to indicate what a loss the fighting manpower of Ireland was to the English once the Irish had been alienated from any association with them on the battlefield, recalled the words of George II. The king, when he was told of the defeat of his forces, 'uttered that memorable imprecation on the Penal Laws', saying 'Cursed be the laws which deprive me of such subjects.'[30]

It is surprising that such sentiments should appear in a paper directed at people of differing religious traditions, given the proclaimed intention of the *Nation* to unite all shades of opinion and traditions in Ireland. The only explanation is that so much of the history of Ireland was intertwined with oppression, coupled with the sporadic and fruitless attempts by some Irish leaders and their followers to overcome it. Any attempt to teach that history, in ballad form at least, would have to draw upon the bloody past to evoke a positive response in the present. It is hard to imagine, however, that history learnt in such a way would achieve the lofty educational and spiritual objectives that Davis saw as the essential basis of Ireland's regeneration.

The Saxon as the foe of the Irish is another thread throughout Davis's verses, although the *Nation* assured its readers that 'We sup not on pickled Saxons.' He tried to make it clear that the Irish Saxons were not in his mind when he cursed the Saxons, but, even so, the Irish Saxon had to be true to Ireland to merit 'Friendship's ready grasp'. However, the Saxon who proved he was an enemy merited execration even when Ireland was not his object of domination. In a bitter ballad, 'Cymric Rule and Cymric Rulers', Davis used an air much loved by him, 'The March of the Men of Harlech', as the melody. Wallis excused himself for putting it in his section of 'National Ballads and Songs', but Davis had written that the Welsh 'are of our blood, nearly of our old and un-English language'. As a result, any Saxon aggression against the Welsh was, by extension, aggression against the Celt in Ireland or, at the very least, a lesson could be learnt from Saxon behaviour in Wales. An excerpt is sufficient to give some idea of the tone of the ballad,

> Ours the toil, but his the spoil, and his the laws we writhe in;
> Worked like beasts, that Saxon priests may riot in our tithing;
> Saxon speech and Saxon teachers
> Crush our Cymric tongue!
> Tolls our traffic binding,
> Rents our vitals grinding –
> Bleating sheep, we cower and weep, when, by one bold endeavour,
> We could drive from out our hive these Saxon drones for ever.[31]

The unworthiness of the Saxon, not simply as an enemy, but as a race whose agents were a worse pestilence than typhus as they tried to impose their 'yoke' on the shoulders of the native Irish, is sometimes stressed as, for example, when Davis insists that no loyalty is true unless it is proffered with the consent of the people and an unbent knee is better than one that is forced to bend. The conclusion is that,

> The Sassenach serfs no such homage can bring
> As the Irishmen's choice of a True Irish King!

and the Sassenach is sometimes called plainly the English as in,

> Sad, wounded, and wan was the face of our isle,
> By English oppression, and falsehood, and guile.[32]

Davis used the history of Ireland under the Penal Laws to recall to his readers the manner in which the English, for centuries, had tried to extirpate the Catholic religion from among the people. In his poem, 'The Penal Days', while he hoped that time would heal or, at least, 'veil in twilight haze', their memory, he was not prepared to let them be forgotten. He recalled the fact that, in those days, the Catholic 'lords' of

Ireland had no power and the peasant, who starved in his 'ruined shed' on land over which he had no tenure, bowed down before the law and lacked education. Consequently, the peasant became a 'disarmed, disenfranchised, imbecile'. To Davis, it was no wonder that still, in post-penal Ireland, 'our step betrays, The freeman, born in penal days'. In one verse, which throbs with anger, he summed it all up,

> They bribed the flock, they bribed the son.
> To sell the priest and rob the sire;
> Their dogs were taught alike to run
> Upon the scent of wolf and friar.
> Among the poor,
> Or on the moor,
> Were hid the pious and the true –
> While traitor knave,
> And recreant slave,
> Had riches, rank and retinue;
> And, exiled in those penal days,
> Our banners over Europe blaze.[33]

Except to those who hold that the presence and behaviour of the English in Ireland had been dictated solely, or even mainly, by the need for England to pacify the turbulent Irish, it can be argued that Davis had adequate reasons drawn from the historical sources available to him to condemn much of that past. In his prose and poetry he used terminology and images of a kind that were at times inflammatory, and they were even more so when put in a form that allowed them to be passed so readily among the people in song. Additionally, his message was of such a kind that its purpose would be defeated were it not to give issue to the determination to reject the English presence, which had become even more markedly evident since the Act of Union. Yet Davis, had it ever happened that anyone pointed out to him that his ballads ran the risk of inciting his readers to violence, would have replied that his direct purpose was to awaken the Irish to the ongoing reality of their situation. If that awareness of reality resulted in violence, Davis would only have blamed himself for taking part in inciting it for one reason. He would have felt guilty if he had not also taken the necessary steps to prepare the Irish participants in such a way as to ensure that they stood some chance of victory.

He would also have been taken-back had he been warned that his ballads tended to incite hatred against the English as a race and that, were such a hatred to be further embedded in the Irish national consciousness, it could prove difficult to erase in the future. A plea that racial hatred too readily reveals itself in hatred against the individual, no matter how innocent he or she may be of the transgressions perpetrated by some members of his or her race in the past, would not have awakened a response in Davis. His own nature and refinement, as well as his education, were such that he could readily make the distinction between the mass and the individual, which he constantly did in his relationship with the English. Nevertheless, it is not surprising that his ballads were sometimes read, sung and interpreted as a justification for violence and for racial intolerance. Read in their entirety, however, the ballads and poems of Davis help to redress the balance away from violence and revolution as a primary means to secure independence. Davis was fully aware that freedom was essentially a thing of the spirit, which he expressed well with 'Freedom is the soul's creation – Not the work of hands', and he knew that, without a development and understanding of its spiritual aspect, the mere physical presence of so-called freedom, won by repelling the occupying power, could become a mockery. In 'Our Own Again' Ireland would win freedom 'By honour, pride and policy' and

> Bravely hope, and wisely wait,
> Toil, join and educate;
> Man is master of his fate;
> We'll enjoy our own again.[34]

Davis's ideal nationality was no mere form of independence from foreign rule but one which,

> would thus create a race of men full of a more intensely Irish character and knowledge, and to that race it would give Ireland. It would give them the seas of Ireland to sweep with their nets and launch on with their navy; the harbours of Ireland, to receive a greater commerce than any island in the world; the soil of Ireland to live on, by more millions than starve here now; the fame of Ireland to enhance by their genius and valour; the Independence of Ireland to guard by laws and arms.

Thus he saw the value of 'Self-reliance' and affirmed that it, rather than reliance on America or France for liberation, was the true path to follow,

> A Nation freed by foreign aid
> Is but a corpse by wanton science
> Convulsed like life, then flung to fade –
> The life itself is Self-reliance!

Likewise no nation of integrity would ever go to war except 'in an honest cause' and he hoped that defeat would follow the wickedness of unjustly waging war. A nation with just and equal laws for all, 'fixed in right and truth', would win God's favour, while the voice of such a nation would be noble and godly, 'When righteous triumph swells its tone.' He asked his own nation to,

> Still hold to Truth, abound in Love,
> Refusing every base compliance –[35]

His finest paean to nationhood also achieved a kind of immortality and became for a time an unofficial national anthem. Entitled 'A Nation Once Again', it was first printed in the *Nation* on 13 July 1844, set to original music in *The Spirit of the Nation* and circulated among the Irish in all countries to which they had migrated, as well as in Ireland itself. To Davis, the nation meant a people free from subjection and guided by righteous and dispassionate leaders who would use their gifts and powers to mould its consciousness. He confessed that the rebirth of the Irish people as a nation had been the overwhelming passion of his life and it had burnt from him all personal ambitions. In fact, his passionate attachment to Ireland was such that it had surpassed any love for a woman he may have felt in the past,

> When boyhood's fire was in my blood,
> I read of ancient freemen.
> For Greece and Rome who bravely stood,
> Three hundred men and three men.
> And then I prayed I yet might see
> Our fetters rent in twain,
> And Ireland, long a province, be
> A Nation Once Again
>
> And from that time, through wildest woe,
> That hope has shone, a far light;
> Nor could love's brightest summer glow
> Outshine that solemn starlight.
> It seemed to watch above my head
> In forum, field, and fane;
> Its angel voice sang round my bed,
> 'A Nation Once Again'
>
> It whispered, too, that freedom's ark
> And service high and holy,

Would be profaned by feelings dark
And passions vain or lowly:
For freedom comes from God's right hand,
And needs a godly train;
And righteous men must make our land
A Nation Once Again

So, as I grew from boy to man,
I bent me to that bidding –
My spirit of each selfish plan
And cruel passion ridding;
Oh! can such hope be vain? –
When my dear country shall be made
A Nation Once Again.[36]

The ideal set out in his ballad of the love of nation outshining that of human love between man and woman had become easier for Davis to aspire to in July 1844 when he wrote the ballad. Some time before one of his friends had asked him whether he had ever been in love and he replied, laughingly, 'I have never been out of it.'[37] Were that the case, the fleeting loves of his past had made no lasting impression on him. However, when he wrote 'A Nation Once Again', Davis was in the throes of a love that seemed destined to be thwarted. That such was the way of things, despite the fact that his love was reciprocated by the young woman upon whom he had set his heart, made his pain even greater.

Anna Maria Hutton was the youngest of the three daughters of Thomas and Margaret Hutton of Elm Park, Drumcondra. Thomas had inherited a substantial coachbuilding business from his father that survived the depressed times after the Union and the family lived in relative wealth with a parkland of fifty acres surrounding their home. Annie, as she was always known, was reared in an atmosphere of restrained gentility with music, reading and languages, especially Italian, as a staple cultural diet. The painter Frederic Burton and other members of Dublin intellectual circles often visited the home, and the essayist and novelist Mary Russell Mitford called Mrs Hutton her friend. Robert Hutton, Annie's uncle, was an MP for Dublin at the same time as O'Connell, of whom he was a political ally except on the question of Repeal. The Hutton home, at least in respect of the females, was deeply religious, of the Presbyterian faith, committed to the Union and, in all ways, highly respectable. Nonetheless, as they were not of the Anglican ascendancy, Annie's mother never presumed to visit Dublin Castle socially.[38]

Christopher Moore's marble bust of Annie Hutton (courtesy National Gallery of Ireland).

Despite the strong unionist convictions of the Huttons, Davis's friends John Pigot and John O'Hagan were also friends of the Hutton family, in which there were also six sons. They probably introduced Annie to his and Dillon's writings in the days of their early, but failed venture with Staunton's paper, and she would have again read Davis in the early numbers of the *Nation*. On 23 December 1842, Thomas Hutton brought Davis home to Elm Park to dine. Annie was eighteen and Thomas twenty-eight. An acquaintance said later that Annie, with her 'pale, chiselled features' was a woman of 'remarkable beauty, intellectual gifts, and noble character'. Although Davis's name was already well known in Dublin and increasingly throughout Ireland, he came from an obscure family, his prospects were slender and, even worse, his politics were deplorable given his association with O'Connell and the Repeal movement. In any event, Annie is alleged to have fallen in love from that first meeting and Davis soon had other things to think about besides the *Nation* and Repeal.[39]

Within weeks, Davis had become a regular visitor at Elm Park. He felt sufficiently at ease with Mrs Hutton as to be able to make light of her 'chance patriotism'. She wrote to him, 'Oh that such spirits as yours would see that no good can come through bad means! and then you would mourn as I do, heart and soul, that the character of our brave, noble, generous countrymen is debased and deteriorated, not by their oppressors, but by their friends.'[40] The 'mass meetings' were then in full swing so, to make her meaning even plainer, she concluded, 'Don't believe I love my country less because, with all true and deep acknowledgment of Mr O'Connell's early services, I abhor his late and present courses, and fervently wish such minds and souls as yours and a few others were exorcised of this evil spirit and its influences.' It was scarcely conceivable that Davis would change his convictions on nationality and the need for them to be expressed by Repeal because of a desire to placate the mother, or perhaps the whole family, of the woman for whom he had begun to feel a deep love. Not to do so might have stood in the way of the fulfilment of that love, but Mrs Hutton did not know the man she was dealing with. Nonetheless, her graciousness towards Davis remained intact despite her misgivings, and she urged him to walk out to Drumcondra when he felt so inclined as a restorative for his depressed spirits.[41]

By September 1843, while Davis was away on his journey through Ireland, there is a hint that some progress was being made in his relationship with Annie. Davis wrote to Pigot from the south, 'You have Hibernicized the Huttons so much that they have borrowed a lot of my collection of Irish airs, and the lady whose name you write so flippantly sings the Bonny Cuckoo. Are you very vain for all this?' Pigot replied from Kilkee, 'You are amusing about the Huttons – but your coquetry is all fair when you can get that graceful wild girl to sing Bonny Cuckoo and Annie Dear for you. 'Tis very pleasant too to have collections of music books for such disinterested proselytisms.' Perhaps surprisingly, given the tensions that existed between them on political matters, Davis must have told John O'Connell something of his love for Annie and of his intentions in her regard that had firmed to the extent that marriage was on his mind. His letter has not been preserved but, in his reply, on 20 September 1843, O'Connell said, 'I am glad to find that there is a chance of an admixture of Milesian blood, with that of the sturdy Presbyterian! A union of good augury for "Young Ireland".' Annie returned both his affection and intention, but Mrs Hutton, a woman of great strength and purpose, had other ideas, and in respect of any proposed marriage, she was prepared to act on them.[42]

References

1. Venedey said that 1,400 vehicles left Dublin alone for the monster meeting on Tara Hill in August 1843. There were 42 teetotal bands playing, among other pieces, 'God save the Queen' and 'Saint Patrick's Day'. Venedey, *Ireland and the Irish*, p. 130.
2. *Nation*, 30 September 1843. Wellington is alleged to have thought lightly of his native land. On one occasion he was asked whether his Irish birth did not make him feel Irish. He is said to have responded by asking whether, had he been born in a stable, he ought to have felt like a horse. In fact, he was born in a mansion on Merrion Square, Dublin.
3. Ibid., 14 October 1843.
4. Ibid.
5. See *Freeman's Journal*, 16 October, 1843; *Nation*, 14, 21 October, 11 November 1843; Duffy, *Davis*, p. 183; *Young Ireland*, part 1, pp 136-140, 148; MacDonagh, *O'Connell*, pp 522-3.
6. *Nation*, 14 October 1843.
7. Ó Cathaoir, *Dillon*, p. 26.
8. Dillon to Duffy, 17 March 1848 in Duffy, *Davis*, p. 380.
9. See Dillon to his wife, Waterford, Sunday, n.d. but February 1848 in Dillon papers, Mss 6455/34, 645/7E, Trinity College; *Nation*, 25 March 1848; Duffy, *Young Ireland*, part 1, p. 137.
10. Duffy, *Davis*, pp 183-5.
11. Ibid.
12. *Nation*, 28 October 1843.
13. See letter from Smith O'Brien, 20 October 1843 to the Association in ibid.; Duffy, *Davis*, p. 186.
14. *Nation*, 14 October, 4, 25 November, 9 December 1843.
15. Ibid., 18, 25 November, 9 December 1843, 6 January 1844; MacDonagh, *O'Connell*, pp 522-3; *Freeman's Journal*, 28 December 1843.
16. *Nation*, 9 December 1843; 6, 9 January, 10 February 1844.
17. Ibid., 10, 17 February 1843; 4 May, 1 June 1844. The *Freeman's Journal*, reporting the sentencing on 31 May, black-bordered all its pages. The proceedings of the 'State Trials' were written up at great length in all major

papers. The *Nation*, 6 January-17 February 1844 and *Freeman's Journal*, 6 January-15 February 1844 are examples. See also John Simpson Armstrong, *A report of the proceedings on an indictment for a conspiracy in the case of the Queen v Daniel O'Connell* (Dublin, 1844).

18.   O'Faolain, *King of the beggars*, p. 309.
19.   Duffy, *Davis*, pp 188-9, *Young Ireland*, part 1, pp 164-5. The letter to Smith O'Brien is undated but February, 1844. See p. 166 in ibid.
20.   Davis to John O'Connell, 8 March 1844 in Duffy, *Davis*, pp 190-1. For comment on Daniel O'Connell's visit to England see *Nation*, 2 March 1844.
21.   Ibid., 2 March 1844.
22.   Ibid., 2 March 1844; Duffy to McGee, in *Irish Monthly*, vol. 2 (Dublin, 1883), p. 337.
23.   Duffy, *Young Ireland*, part 1, pp 174-5; *Nation*, 1 June 1844. It ran a black border around the editorial page.
24.   Ibid., 24 June 1843.
25.   Davis to Pigot, 17 April 1844 in Duffy, *Davis*, pp 200-1.
26.   Wallis (ed.), *The poems of Thomas Davis*. Wallis also repeated the commonly-held belief that Davis never wrote a line of poetry until three years before his death. He said that he had been 'assured' of this, probably by Duffy, p. xi.
27.   Ibid., 'Nationality', p. 166 and *Nation*, 2 March 1844; 'Song for the Irish Militia', pp 21-3. *Nation*, 1 February 1845.
28.   Wallis, *The poems*, 'A Rally for Ireland' pp 122-4. The poem was written at the peak of the monster meeting period in June 1843. See *Nation*, 17 June 1843.
29.   Wallis, *The poems*, 'A Ballad of Freedom', pp 16-19. O'Connell himself was not loathe to draw from ballads with warlike tones and Moore, who later became a darling of the Whigs, was no pacifist as some of his work proves. See, for example, his 'Remember the glories of Brian the brave' in William Michael Rossetti (ed.), *The poetical works of Thomas Moore* (London, 1870), p. 335. See also Richard Davis, 'The violence of poetry: O'Connell, Davis and Moore', in *Threshold*, no. 37 (Dublin, 1986-7), pp 48-56.
30.   Ibid., 'When South Winds Blow', pp 145-6; 'Fontenoy', pp 149-53 and Wallis at p. 232. George II was the last English monarch to lead his troops to battle.
31.   Ibid., 'Celts and Saxons', pp 27-9; 'Cymric Rule and Cymric Rulers', pp 215-6 and Wallis, pp 14-15; *Nation*, 9 September 1843.
32.   Ibid., 'A Scene in the South', pp 191-3; 'The True Irish King', pp 85-8; 'The Dungannon Convention', pp 153-5.
33.   Ibid., 'The Penal Days', pp 131-33.
34.   Ibid., 'We Must Not Fail', pp 178-9; 'Our Own Again', pp 24-6.
35.   Ibid., p. 166. 'Self-Reliance' pp 169-71; 'Nationality', pp 167-9.
36.   Ibid., 'A Nation Once Again', pp 73-4. The three hundred men and three men referred to in the first verse are the 300 Greeks who fell at Thermopylae and the three Romans who stood against the tide of invaders on the Sublician Bridge. The copy of *The poems* from which I worked is held in the library of University College Dublin. On 20 December 1854, it was given as a present by Daniel Mahony to a recipient whose name is obscure. There is only one personal note throughout the book and it occurs in reference to this poem. The third last line of 'A Nation Once Again', 'Oh! can such hope be vain?' is underlined and below are found the words in faded pencil 'Alas! it can.'
37.   See Duffy, *Davis*, p. 355.
38.   See Hone (ed. with intro.), *The love story*, pp i-vii. Duffy, who did not know the family, later confused Thomas and Robert Hutton when he said that Annie's

father, 'an opulent and honourable citizen', was MP for Dublin. See Duffy, *Davis*, p. 356. The only remains of the Elm Park property visible today is a capstone on a pillar with the one word 'Lodge' on it outside a house on Whitworth Road.

39. *Irish Monthly*, vol. 18, part ii (Dublin, 1890) p. 335; Hone, *The love story*, pp vi-vii. Hone dates the dinner to 23 December 1843 which is incorrect.

40. Margaret Hutton to Thomas Davis, from Elm Park, Friday morning but n.d. Clearly spring 1843. In Duffy, *Davis*, p. 361.

41. Ibid.

42. Davis to Pigot, September 1843 in ibid., p. 356. Pigot's reply, 16 September 1843, is also in Duffy, same page, but the original is in Ms 2644, NLI. John O'Connell to Davis, 20 September 1843, ibid.

MY GRAVE.

BY THOMAS DAVIS.

SHALL they bury me in the deep
Where wind-forgetting waters sleep ?
Shall they dig a grave for me,
Under the green-wood tree ?
Or on the wild heath,
Where the wilder breath
Of the storm doth blow ?
Oh, no ! oh, no !

Shall they bury me in the Palace Tombs,
Or under the shade of Cathedral domes ?
Sweet 'twere to lie on Italy's shore ;
Yet not there—nor in Greece, though I love it more.
In the wolf or the vulture my grave shall I find ?
Shall my ashes career on the world-seeing wind ?
Shall they fling my corpse in the battle mound,
Where coffinless thousands lie under the ground ?
Just as they fall they are buried so—
Oh, no ! oh, no !

No ! on an Irish green hill-side,
On an opening lawn—but not too wide;
For I love the drip of the wetted trees—
On me blow no gales, but a gentle breeze,
To freshen the turf : put no tombstone there,
But green sods deck'd with daisies fair.

The matted grass-roots may trickle through—
Be my epitaph writ on my country's mind,
" He serv'd his country, and lov'd his kind "—
Oh ! 'twere merry unto the grave to go,
If one were sure to be buried so.

Chapter 11

A forsaken Mí-na-Meala

Once Annie Hutton began to take a place in his heart, Davis seemed to double his workload. It was as if he felt that he had to compensate for the new emotional involvement that revolved around her person. He tried to do so by throwing himself with even greater vigour into the pursuit of nationality and Repeal of the Union. In the practical sphere, the loss of O'Connell as commander of the campaign, Ray as his chief and most effective lieutenant and Duffy in the day-to-day running of the *Nation,* left a large gap in the few reliable individuals upon whom so much depended. The conditions under which the state prisoners lived were extremely free and comfortable. Duffy described the 'luxurious' table enjoyed by the prisoners, made possible by gifts from wellwishers. They had separate quarters with their own servants and visitors were unrestricted. Nonetheless, their confinement meant that their contact with the realities of the business of the Repeal Association was perforce perfunctory. For a short period Davis became dispirited and suggested to Duffy that he retire from active involvement, but his discouragement was merely temporary and perhaps stemmed from a bout of depression, rather than from disillusionment with the cause.[1]

It is also possible that Davis felt he could do more good by devoting himself to a quieter and more intellectual pursuit of nationality by promoting literature, art, archeology and other areas of culture and science. There were already bodies devoted to those tasks, such as the Royal Irish Academy, the Royal Hibernian Academy, the Irish Library Association, the Irish Celtic Society and the Royal Dublin Society and Davis gave all the support he could to them. He also felt the need to bring the great Irish orators of the past to the attention of the general public. Duffy made the point that their speeches were unavailable to the public as there were only six public libraries in Ireland. A calculation was made by an anonymous writer in 1840 that there were only 220,000 volumes in all the public libraries in Ireland. In Dublin there were 148,000 volumes, of which 100,000 were held at Trinity and another 13,000 volumes were in Belfast.[2] This may have inspired Davis to turn to Curran for the last of his substantial publications, *The speeches of the Right Honourable John Philpot Curran,* which came out at the end of 1843. Davis had undertaken the laborious task of collecting Curran's speeches but he was hesitant about writing the accompanying memoir. He asked Wallis to do it and, upon his refusal, he turned to Madden, pleading that he would be the most appropriate writer to do justice to 'the honest valorous patriot, the wit never excelled, the most poetical of all secular orators, the unrivalled advocate, the thorough Irishman'. Madden, like Wallis, perhaps felt unequal to the task of comprehending the mind of one whose patriotism and love of Ireland were as strong as Curran's, so that Davis was forced to do the memoir. The result was the finest piece of prose writing he ever penned.[3]

The high note on which Davis began is reminiscent of the opening paragraph of that masterpiece of Italian literature, *I Promessi Sposi,* by Alessandro Manzoni which, in the allegorical form of a love story, dealt with the longing of Italy to be freed of its invaders. As with Manzoni, so too with Davis, the evocation of place was all important in striking the right note for a beginning.

> In the north-west corner of the county of Cork stands the little town of Newmarket. It is in a land of moors and streams. Just north of it slope the Ure hills, part of the upland which sweeps forty miles across from Liscarroll to Tralee, and far south of it, over the valley of the Blackwater, frown the mountains of Muskerry, changing, as they approach Killarney, into precipitous peaks. A brook tumbles on each side of it to the Avendala river, and, a few miles off, the Avendala and Allo, and a dozen other tributaries, swell the tide of the Blackwater.[4]

Davis regarded Tone as 'the greatest of all great men' of Curran's era, but Curran's greatness lay in other ways. He spoke both Irish and English, 'before he could read either' and he was reared on Irish traditions and music. His speeches owed more 'to the wakes and his mother's stories about ghosts and heroes, and to the Bible and Sterne than all the classics' which 'he read a little at Trinity (unlike most young men about him)'. Later, Curran (born 1750), 'learned to labour, because he longed to enjoy. He continued to labour for labour's own great sake – for labour is practical power.'[5] As a lawyer, Curran defended the Volunteers at their trials in 1794, William Orr at his in 1797 and some of the older leaders in July 1798. His involvement in '98 gave Davis the chance to write of the rising. Mindful of Fitzgerald and priests such as Father John Murphy, he said, 'The leaders were brave, especially the few priests who fought. But all were ignorant to the last degree. No organisation – no commissariat – no unity of action – no foreign aid.' When the hangings and reprisals began during the rising there was no retaliation by the insurgents who, 'if they had a right to rise, they were entitled to the rights of war, and were weak, wicked, and impolitic in neglecting to enforce them.' He said that the insurgent chiefs should have shot those peasants 'who lifted their hands against property or person without orders', but that the leaders were equally bound to defend the rest and to retaliate for 'every execution, coolly, judicially, and uniformly'. His last words were on the outcome of the '98 rising. 'The government, with arms victorious over the insurgents, advanced against the liberties of the people; a vanguard of villains, armed with gold and titles preceded them, terror was in their march, and falsehood pioneered their way. The Union was carried.'[6]

For some time Davis had been collecting materials for a life of Tone. He made little headway with the actual writing in that last hectic year of his life, although he did get ten pages done in manuscript and managed to bring in a favourite in the person of George the Third, 'that pestilent maniac'. He also planned the whole volume with an outline of twelve chapters, giving it the title 'A life of Wolfe Tone', and roughing out a cover for the book.[7] To the end he worked on the book and showed the determination of a good historian wanting to track down all possible sources and he was intent on interviewing any remaining oral sources on Tone. A week before he died, he received a letter from Robert Cane telling him that there were two ladies still resident in Dublin who knew the Tone family very intimately.[8] Nonetheless, he was able to render a service to Tone's widow, as well as to the memory of Tone himself. In late 1843, from Georgetown in America, Mrs Tone wrote to Dr Gray, editor of the *Freeman's Journal*. She said that she could not come back to Ireland to be buried with her husband as she wished, because she was then seventy-five. Tone, 'the husband of my youth and of my love', and 'a self-devoted martyr for his country', had been dead for forty-five years. His family had been destroyed and his race was all but extinct, except for a female grandchild, and 'yet that generous heart moulders in an obscure grave, and *no stone tells where he lies.*' She begged Gray to undertake a 'holy office 'for her and to do it quickly so as to give her the consolation of knowing that it had been done. She wanted the place where Tone lay marked in some appropriate way and his virtues commemorated.[9] Gray enlisted Davis's help in the matter which, typically, he began with a poem entitled 'Tone's Grave' suggested by Mrs Tone's letter, a visit to the cemetery with Gray where they met an old man who told them that 'no one walks on that grave' and Tone's last words from the dock.

In Bodenstown Churchyard there is a green grave,
And wildly along it the winter winds rave;
Small shelter, I ween, are the ruined walls there,
When the storm sweeps down on the plain of Kildare.

******

Once I lay on that sod – it lies over Wolfe Tone –
And thought how he perished in prison alone,
His friends unavenged, and his country unfreed –
'Oh, bitter', I said, 'is the patriot's meed;
'For in him the heart of a woman combined
With a heroic life and a governing mind –
A martyr for Ireland – his grave has no stone –
His name seidom named, and his virtues unknown.'

******

In Bodenstown Churchyard there is a green grave,
And freely around it let winter winds rave –
Far better they suit him – the ruin and gloom –
Till Ireland, a nation, can build him a tomb.[10]

Together with Gray, Davis was able to get together enough funds from their friends for a monument made from a large, black, marble slab which was to be set down on 21 April 1844. The words on it were to be,

THEOBALD WOLFE TONE,
Born 20th June, 1763;
Died 19th November, 1798,
for
IRELAND

Davis told Pigot that he liked the inscription, 'though 'tis mine. It says enough for this and perchance for all time.' Although there was a delay in the ceremony due to unease at coinciding it with the period when sentence was still be considered for O'Connell and the others, it duly took place later in 1844. To this day, Davis's simple words remain on Tone's grave. However, some recent writing on Tone departs markedly from Davis's estimate of him. One author states that Tone held 'the liberty and independence of my country' as his first priority, but then claims that his main driving force was 'the ambition to win fame and fortune' and that his disappointed expectations 'more than any other factor ... shaped the ideas and course of his life', while another asserts that Tone was not a genuine democrat and that he placed his reliance

Inside the illustration:

```
...s Burial Place Belong...
...m Tone & his Family He...
...eth the Body of the abo...
...ho Departed this Life y'24...
f. April 1766 aged 60 year...
also 3 of his Children

The original Slab
been accidentally broken
the Members of the Dublin
Wolfe Tone Band
in respect to the memory of their
Noble Patron
erected this Slab 14 Sept. 1873
GOD SAVE IRELAND
```

Wolfe Tone's grave.

only on those in Ireland who had property. Despite these recent interpretations, the memory of Tone, as well as a pilgrimage to his grave, have lived on.[11]

Despite the workload involved in trying to maintain the high standards of the *Nation*, Davis continued to be restless and he put it to Duffy in early 1844 that he would be better occupied engaged in a history of Ireland, which he had been thinking about for a considerable time. Duffy had set aside some additional funds to be paid to Davis during the period when he would have to be virtual editor, as well as the main contributor, to the paper. Davis suggested that Duffy should use the money to commission others whose writings would 'compensate for the absence of my harum-scarum articles'. Part at least of his reason for such a suggestion was that he had already done a great deal of preparation for the history. He had completed an outline of contents with chapter headings and lists of sources, some drawn from the Trinity College Library which he now used regularly. He had sought manuscript material from John O'Connell, and corresponded with a leading scholar of Irish antiquities, John O'Donovan, with Madden and others. Davis could not have been pleased with the observation of

O'Donovan that 'we have but few national glories to boast of in our history, which only proves that, though we were vigorous and partially civilised, we never had any national wisdom.' He was probably better satisfied with O'Donovan's judgement that the *Nation* had done more 'to liberalise the Irish and implant in the minds of the Anglo-Irish and Iberno-Irish the seedlings of national union, than all the histories of Ireland ever written' and that, were it to continue to prosper and remain true to its principles, 'its effects on the national mind will not be easily removed.'[12] In the end, Davis despaired of being ever able to do the history alone so he drew up plans for it based on historical divisions. Duffy would work on Ireland in the early period after the Anglo-Norman invasion, he would do the middle section up to 1800 himself and Madden would take the story on to 1844. Even that plan had to be relinquished as an impossible task given the demands on his and the others' time so that, in the end, he settled for persuading the Committee of the Association to offer a prize for a history of Ireland to be used in the schools that, to avoid controversy and unpleasantness over the O'Connell period, would end at the Union. So it came to be that the two major publications Davis dreamt of, and prepared for in his final years, the history of Ireland and a biography of Tone, remained among the unfinished tasks of his life.[13]

Perhaps Davis was unable to accept that, from the day in late 1842 when he finally committed himself to the *Nation,* the course of his life was already determined, despite the strength of his own inclinations towards a scholarly life of study and writing. His involvement with a weekly that had become the largest of Dublin's papers, and the best known and read Irish paper, meant that he had little time for other pursuits.[14] Whether he was overwhelmed, or merely tired, he jotted into his diary a sketched itinerary for a tour around Europe. With the hiatus in the operations of the Association while O'Connell was off the stage and O'Brien in charge, he perhaps thought that his absence would not have serious effects. As for the *Nation,* there were others he felt sure could responsibly rise to the occasion and keep the paper viable, which was surely an optimistic hope when he could not get Dillon to do anything useful.[15] He would leave in August 1844, visiting Scotland, Norway, France, Germany, Switzerland, Italy and Spain or, alternatively, take a full six months and leave in June with a return to Dublin for Christmas.[16] That plan, also, came to nothing because the demands made on his time while the 'traversers' were in prison became too great. He could not refuse the pleadings of his friends, the problems of the Association and the paper, the circumstances of the age, and the plight of the Irish people so that he was obligated to remain their activist, journalist and poet.

In February 1844, Charlotte Ridley, widowed sister of Mrs Davis, died at the Baggot Street home and Thomas told Pigot, who was engaged in legal studies at Boulogne, that it was 'a severe blow to my family'. Charlotte's late husband John was also an army surgeon which strengthened the military connection in the Davis household. She had been ill for some time and Davis's sister, Charlotte, had helped to nurse her with adverse effects on her own health so that she became 'dangerously ill'. In early May, Davis himself became ill.[17] 'I have had a dash of scarlatina, but am convalescent and I hope to be out in a day or two.' His greatest annoyance was that he could not shake hands with his friends 'for fear of infecting them', but he was unaware of the insidious nature of the disease that can live in the body and occur again unless treated with the drugs that only became available a century later. At the end of the month he told Pigot that his sister was recovering, 'poor soul', and that, although he had not been idle, he was taking things easy because 'a man must rest sometime.' The reason for resting was that 'I had a relaxed throat and some debility after my illness.' Clearly, the disease was still present and, without prolonged rest and warmth, the likelihood was that it would recur. His own attitude to rest, or even to a holiday, seems to have become extreme by this time, as if he had a presentiment that his sands were running out. Apart from his other correspondence, and his continued output of articles and ballads, Davis wrote four letters to Pigot in May which illustrates that he had a wide view of relaxation. In one he wrote, 'I believe I shall go to London in the summer, but am not sure. I fear you and I would idle each other cruelly there.' In typical fashion he was more concerned with his friend's health than with his own. He was insistent with Pigot, 'Do, dear John, take care of yourself.' 'Believe me, who have tried it, that 'tis flat folly to be reckless about your health, as you are prone to be.' Duffy's young wife, Emily, suffered from consumption and Davis hoped that she would not continue to suffer long in a lingering illness from which there could be no recovery. In September 1844 Duffy told Pigot that her life was 'near its close' and that 'She has no chance of seeing the May flowers again ...'[18]

Apart from his ill-health, there was a more powerful reason why Davis was intermittently in low spirits in 1844. A curious account of a 'Meeting of the "Green Brotherhood"' at Inch-Liffey castle near Dublin on St Patrick's Day 1844 appeared in the *Nation* on 30 March. De Courcey O'Brazil was host, there was much fine eating, music by pipers and singing, including 'Bells of Shandon' by Roche Fermoy 'till our eyes watered'. There were also rousing stories. The one about Owen Roe O'Neill, on the way to help in the relief of Kinsale in 1690 showed that the 'Brotherhood' was able to laugh at itself. The company passed a castle and O'Neill asked whose it was. On being told that it belonged to a Barrett, whose family had been in Ireland for four hundred years, he said, 'I hate the Norman churl as if he came but yesterday.' However, one of the company did not join in the general merriment. 'The Celt [Davis], who was observed to be unusually absent and dispirited during the evening ... sang a sweet, melancholy little song, more in accordance with his own feelings than his company's.' Entitled 'The Lost Path', the song was set to the air of Molly Astore. The subject of the song had only 'sweet thoughts' left as his consolation because 'every hope was lost to me.' He begged his thoughts,

> Oh! throng around, and be to me
> Power, country, fame and bride.[19]

If Duffy, or another of the 'Brotherhood', a body that had no existence and its name only adopted for the purposes of the article, wrote the piece it could only have been published with Davis's approval because he was known in a wide circle as 'The Celt'. If Davis wrote it, he did so in the hope that another would read it because, before the end of 1843, he and Annie Hutton were not able, and for her part, not permitted, to meet. The story of their love must need be told because it was central both to their young lives and to their deaths.

It is unclear when, and by whom, the decision was taken to bring the romance to a close, except that neither Davis nor Annie was responsible. Hone suggests that her mother, Margaret Hutton, with her loathing of O'Connell, forced the separation. He says also that it could have been because of the precarious health Annie suffered and perhaps even because of Davis's own health. There is some probability that Annie's health, possibly an incipient form of consumption, was central to the decision, but it is unlikely that much concern would have been expressed about Davis's general health at the time, despite the bout of scarlatina. It is equally unsafe to suggest, as Hone does, that Mrs Davis 'would have disapproved of a person in trade and never encouraged marriage even if it meant marrying "a small heiress".' To sum up the highly respectable and honoured Hutton family as being 'in trade' seems an exaggeration. In any event, it is difficult to maintain the proposition that Davis would have accepted any prohibition on their meeting by his mother, and especially so given that he continued to write to Annie after she had been forbidden to have contact with him. The only certain thing is that Mrs Hutton intervened at the moment when Davis felt sufficiently sure of himself as to write his first letter to Annie in which there was no need for Davis to profess his love for her because she already knew it to be the case, but it is possible that he told her he intended to broach the subject of their marriage with her parents. The reaction to his letter in the Hutton household was immediate, which is clear from a later letter Annie wrote to him in which she told him of her mother's abrupt and decisive intervention. There was to be no more contact between Thomas and Annie and she was commanded to surrender into the hands of her mother the poetry and whatever else that Davis had given or sent her. 'I gave her all you had ever given me, and in the bitterness of my grief, wondered if ever I should be happy again as I was before,' wrote Annie later.[20]

It is impossible to do other than surmise what a blow to Davis the separation was, but it is likely that he was deeply stricken by it. It had given him both the love and security that he needed as an individual who had trod a lonely path in life. Furthermore, he surely felt that his acceptance into the Hutton home gave him a sense of respectability in Irish Protestant circles that his association with the people who surrounded O'Connell had tended to put in question. Finally, he was among a group of young men, many of whom were either married or about to marry, his own years were adding up and he had looked to marriage as a fulfilment of his personality. The silence from Elm Park was unbearable and there is no likelihood that he had been given a reason for it. However, there was one way in which Davis could communicate with Annie with some reasonable hope that she would thereby be given his assurance that he still loved her. Acting on the assumption that she would have, or obtain, access to the *Nation*, perhaps through one or other of her brothers, he started to contribute love songs to the paper. None of them reached the measure of his ballads, but in their own genre they serve a purpose in that they encompass the strength of his love for his Annie. The songs also help to put in perspective the emotional ordeal through which Davis was passing, even if they can say nothing of how the enforced break caused her to suffer.

His first poem, in November 1843, in which he assured her that his heart had not 'grown cold' helps to date the time of the break.[21] 'Love Chaunt', which followed in May 1844, was in essence a praise of Annie's beauty, although no name is mentioned while 'Love's Longings' points to the possibility that pressure may have been exerted to convince Annie of the preferability of a rival for her hand who held out both rank and wealth as contributing attractions. Were that the case, Davis was not prepared to let his suit go by default, even if he could not plead it directly. After saying that he knew he was not worthy 'Of one so young and bright' he was nonetheless sure that she would 'wed whom you love best' and that she would be prouder 'as the struggling patriot's bride' than she would be if

241

surrounded by rank and riches.[22] Perhaps defiant and anxious with the passing of time and no word from Elm Park, he refused to believe that she had ceased to love him and remained certain, 'You'll wed me Annie dear.'[23] Finally, after a gentle sound of happiness mixed with plaintive hope in a poem entitled 'The Mí-na-Meala' (honeymoon) in July 1844, Davis seemed to have given up hope by August. Annie had taken a holiday in Munster and Davis longed to be her guide as she visited the places of its quiet loveliness. He admitted, 'Ah! 'tis a wild romance! Annie dear.'[24]

Given the cessation of the romance, Davis's proposed tour of Europe fitted into a period when he was at his lowest ebb emotionally. Annie's health was still precarious and Mrs Hutton intended to take her to Italy over the winter of 1844-45 and to remain there together until March 1845. In that event, Annie would be in Italy at the time of his own visit, although it is improbable that he would have had any chance of meeting her. Under the circumstances, the only escape from his turmoil was to immerse himself in work, of which there was a great deal at hand. The time, even though it had been brief, for the relaxation of love poetry, was over.

It is not surprising that, in his solitude and longing for reassurance, Davis quickly became close to Smith O'Brien, even though he found him 'cold in manner' but 'true, friendly and laborious', while MacNevin said there was too much Smith and too little O'Brien in him.[25] They shared some element of a common tradition in their background, as well as their religion, and Davis soon looked to the older and more experienced man for leadership in the enforced absence of O'Connell. For his part, O'Brien had absolute trust in the integrity of Davis even if, at times, he thought his judgements were hasty or imprudent. O'Brien visited O'Connell and the other prisoners twice weekly to discuss the business of the Association and he tried to follow the policies the Leader still attempted to lay down. Davis, too, visited regularly and described how, 'The prisoners have two large gardens, a sitting-room and bed-room each, constant visitors and good spirits.' Duffy later called his time in Richmond a 'mock martyrdom' but according to Davis, Duffy suffered with 'a cold from dining in a large tent which they set up in one of the gardens. Just think of their audacity, they had a tricolour flag at the head of the tent, till the governor of the jail struck it!' The tricolour with its orange for Protestants, green for Catholics and white for unity had been used in Ireland in various forms since the 1830s. It was not, therefore, specifically a product of 'Young Ireland', as was sometimes thought, but by 1845 they had made it their own flag. To Pigot, Davis insisted that he not go about telling people 'how well our friends are', lest their liberties be curtailed. However, he clearly felt comfortable with the situation because 'All anxiety for them is over, so we can move on with light hearts.'[26]

Understandably, much of the work of continuing to agitate for Repeal fell to Smith O'Brien and Davis so that, publicly at least, the Association was led by two Protestants. The government still felt uneasy about the possibility of further unrest in Ireland, despite the fact that the Association was empty of promise and Conciliation Hall seemed to have become no more than a sounding board for ineffectual speeches that Davis refused to participate in. 'I am busy at everything but speech-making which I resolutely avoid and so shall continue.' Stubbornly, and probably mistakenly, his resolution about public speaking remained firm, but the constant sore throat from which he suffered after his first bout of scarlatina possibly helped to strengthen his resolve. Nonetheless, he remained confident because 'We have played our game well and out-manoeuvred the government, and, as far as I can judge, we are an over-match for them', although he admitted that there was '"a long cry to Loch Awe" as the Scotch say and I'm in no hurry.'[27] When a rumour went about that the Association was to be suppressed and the Hall closed, O'Brien dared the government to take the step. Wiser counsel prevailed in Dublin Castle, possibly on the grounds that the better course was to placate the Irish with scraps of reform than antagonise them further, so that nothing happened. O'Brien, Davis and their handful of committed associates were thus able to get on with their work.

At the time, the most important task they engaged in was setting up a 'Parliamentary Committee' to which Davis, O'Hagan, Dillon, Doheny and Duffy were all appointed. It began to issue reports on matters of national importance, as if the Association were the official arm of a legislature. As they came out the *Freeman's Journal* was delighted with the reports and especially with the intelligent way they were put together, as well as their 'business-like nature'. The specific brief of the Committee was to examine and report on bills with relevance to Ireland that were coming forward in Parliament. In the event, it served as a springboard for a whole range of diverse publications. Matters such as the land question, the franchise, the police department, postal services, jury laws, the estimates, the Poor Law Commission and the education system all had to be looked into and reported on. It was the kind of work Davis could throw himself into and he did so willingly to the degree that he suggested most of the topics, wrote sixteen of the reports himself and either helped with or revised the remaining seventeen. The fact that the Committee entrusted him with the major part of the work shows how much they trusted him and turned to him for intellectual leadership. His output was prodigious and his energy unconquerable and the contribution he made puts paid fully to the canard that Davis was a mere romanticist with his head shrouded in Irish mists. On the contrary, he was a diligent scholar of the practical matters that then affected the Irish people and he strove constantly to express his judgement on such matters based on wide reading and prolonged thought. All this fitted his ideal of nationality and he told Pigot that he, O'Brien and a few others were 'working up all manner of political information for Association Reports, and we hope to make every Repeal Warden know the statistics of Government and the structures of all public departments, etc., etc. These are preparations for self-rule.'[28]

His interest in the Irish past led him to do a report on 'The Ordnance Memoir of Ireland' which he regarded as an excellent means to foster the knowledge of Irish topography, history, antiquities and natural history. He praised the survey of 1825 and the work of Griffith which was done 'with consummate skill and care' and he thought that the plan for the forthcoming survey was, in the main, 'mature, sagacious, practical' and that it would be 'serviceable to Ireland in a high degree'. He proved that, when appropriate, he could rise above being merely critical of all things English and said that the survey should be 'urged and aided by the Repeal Association, and by all Irishmen, no matter what their party or religion'.[29] Clearly, he had begun to realise that no purpose would be served by merely declaiming wildly on the injustices done to Ireland and the publication of Robert Kane's *Industrial resources of Ireland* in mid-1844 filled him with delight. He told Pigot to get a copy quickly as "'tis *almost* all it should be.' His slight reticence can possibly be explained by Kane's shortness on nationality. The book was based on a series of lectures to the Royal Dublin Society and it was eminently practical. It recognised that timber could no longer be used as fuel in Ireland because it was almost all gone. With an abundance of water, it was to her river system that Ireland would have to look for power in the future. A seventh of the 20,000,000 acres of land were bog, but 4,600,000 acres still lay uncultivated. The transport system was grossly underdeveloped with 1,742 miles of rail in England compared to 64 in Ireland while passenger traffic on the Grand and Royal Canals had increased very little in the previous decade. There were 36,000 farms of less than fifty acres with 720,000 people dependent on them. Another 4,500,000, or 850,000 families, had to try to survive on a breadwinner's wage of less than 5s a week. As the lowest in Europe and less than half the English wage, it was not possible to subsist on this. Kane concluded that 'a wretched man' trying to support a family and pay rent for a dwelling with such a wage 'must be so ill-fed and depressed in mind, that to work, as a man should work, is beyond his power.'[30]

The most important report drawn up by Davis was on the estimates for 1844-45. The document was over forty pages in length and bore the mark of much and intensive labour. It was full of data, comparisons between expenditure in Ireland and in other countries like Canada and comment on matters such as England's alleged national debt of over £800,000,000, to which Ireland was pledged to contribute a share. True to his determination on public speaking, or because of his 'sore throat', Davis's report was presented at the Association by MacNevin, as were almost all his reports. The *Freeman's Journal* was full of praise for the report and said that it proved Irish 'capacity and sufficiency for the business of legislation'. Smith O'Brien also said before the Association how decisively it proved the ability of its author. He went on, 'I am extremely sorry he cannot be prevailed upon to comply with the wishes of his friends to address this Association, and make himself personally known to you, but you have already had abundant evidence of his anxiety to forward the national cause by devoting the labours of one of the most powerful minds in literary composition to its advancement.' There were loud and prolonged hear-hears but they did not serve to fill the gap left by Davis's absence at a time when he could have been most effectively heard, given that both the O'Connells were in prison.[31]

A particular source of irritation to Davis was the way in which bills on Irish affairs were invariably listed last at Westminster, behind bills on India, Canada, Jamaica and elsewhere and then rushed through Parliament so that, in one instance, only eight days passed from the introduction of the bill to its final stages. He considered the practice 'unjust' and demanded time for the Irish public to examine all the appropriate bills 'leisurely'. Recognising that there was little hope of improvement in the situation, he returned to the need for Ireland's laws to be made by Irishmen sitting in their own Parliament in Ireland.[32] He also objected strongly to the requirement that all letters passing through the Post Office were potentially subject to inspection by the chief secretary's office and that, in the Mazzini case in England and in Ireland itself, such a practice was regular for correspondence by persons whom the government suspected of subversive activity. Davis thought it was a 'direct breach of common honesty and common honour' and called upon the Association 'to denounce this infamous practice' and expose it.[33] His report on the attendance of Irish members in Parliament caused Lord Wicklow, and others, some misgivings, as well it might have. Davis argued that, in general, elected members were bound in conscience to attend Parliament. This was a sufficiently unusual statement in itself, especially when he more than hinted that attendance figures for Irish Members, which he listed, should be an important yardstick for their future chance of election. With misplaced zeal Davis then argued that Parliament was a useless forum for members who wanted Repeal and that all experience had proved it to be so. His conclusion was that a Repeal MP had 'an imperative duty before God and his country' to stay at home in Ireland and work for Repeal through the Association, which entirely overlooked the fact that such a person had been elected to Parliament, and not to the Association. Lord Wicklow corresponded with the *Nation* on his disagreement with Davis's argument, but Davis replied that Wicklow should be very happy that the Association engaged in 'the cheering and noble occupation of educating, nationalising, and binding in closer union the whole people of Ireland, Protestant, Roman Catholic, Whig and Tory'.[34]

His knowledge of the history of Ireland flowed naturally into his prose and poetry, and especially into his ballads. Throughout all he wrote, Davis took every opportunity to draw upon his immense competence in military history, whether Irish, European or international. His wide reading meant that he had become an expert, rather than a mere dilettante, and his knowledge was technical as well as historical. On the Parliamentary Committee, Davis was acknowledged as the expert on military matters but his interests ranged much wider than an examination of the sums of money expended on the army in Ireland. He concluded, with Charles Dupin, that the differing regulations applying to the army in England and Ireland meant that Ireland was looked upon as a province, rather than part of the United Kingdom itself and he agreed with Dupin's judgement that England's military province of Ireland was comparable to 'a Roman pro-consulate'. This intense interest by Davis in military matters primarily stemmed from Davis's upbringing in a family circle in which at least four of the males were connected with the army and from his conviction expressed in his own words that 'No nation, whether enslaved or free, has a right to abjure the principle of defending its existence by arms if need be', which was a direct contradiction of the principle upon which O'Connell based his campaign for Irish freedom. Through his ballads and his articles in the *Nation* he was able to communicate to the public a pride in the Irish military campaigns of the past, within and without Ireland, and a century later an officer of the general staff of the Irish Army said, 'Thomas Davis had, has, and will continue to have, a considerable influence on Irish military affairs.'[35]

Davis wanted education to issue forth in the fruit of public involvement by competent and trustworthy people on corporations, school boards and, above all, as candidates for election to Parliament.

For the latter he was clear what qualities they should not have. 'We want legislators; we do not want mere farmers, mere fops, mere scamps, or mere fools.' On the contrary, 'We want, in London or Dublin, men trained in the whole circle of knowledge – familiar with the country's agriculture, and trade and resources.' It troubled him that 'industrial ignorance is a prime obstacle to our wealth', that Ireland had no 'national theatre' and that ignorance of history prevailed everywhere. The stage, on which the Irish were represented as buffoons, enraged him, especially in its ultimate insult of the audience seeming to enjoy their own degradation. How could these defects be remedied? Libraries were one way but, while he could praise the richness of Trinity's library he had to admit that it was useless to the public. Marsh's Library, at St Patrick's Cathedral, while public enough was 'very precious to the curious in school divinity (happily a small but perishing class)', which indicated his bent to practicality in thought and his fear of religious sectarianism based on the study of possibly biased ecclesiastical sources. The Dublin Library was the only hope, but it was small and badly run down. He pushed successfully for a committee devoted to its reform with the respective Dublin archbishops, Whately and Murray, as well as John O'Connell, Duffy, Smith O'Brien, himself and several others from the *Nation* group on it.

Finally, Davis wanted a return to the artistic values of the medieval past when the land was clothed with abbeys and churches of grace, gentility and beauty. So many of them now lay in ruins, but would it not be possible to restore some, build others like them, treasure the relics that remained, such as the Round Towers and, in this way, give back to the Irish their joy and pride in native workmanship, taste and cultural values? He lamented that he had seen 'pigs housed in the piled friezes of a broken church, cows stabled in the palaces of the Desmonds, and corn threshed on the floor of abbeys, and the tearing wind tenant the corridors of Aileach.' Davis deplored the use of whitewash on the exterior of houses and the interior of churches, forgetting that, in many instances, the people had no other material or no incentive to beautify their dwellings as they did not own them. His instinct on the Round Towers was surer and he was aghast when he heard that a group of antiquarians had dug into the foundations of one on Devenish Island in Lough Erne so that it was about to fall. He insisted that it be saved.[36]

To further the purpose of education among the rural masses, a drive was undertaken by the Association to set up more Repeal reading rooms, indeed the unrealistic number of three thousand, instead of three hundred, was mentioned. The organ of Dublin Castle, the *Packet*, was alarmed and said that 'these establishments will afford opportunities for the concoction of treason, and facilities for the diffusion of the intolerant and dominating spirit of repeal', but it had shown no such anxiety about intolerance a month earlier when thirty boys were expelled from a national school for 'wearing an emblem of their national feeling' in the form of a Repeal button.[37] Davis looked to the day when there would be a reading room in every parish, holding newspapers, especially the *Nation,* books, maps, illustrations and other similar material, into which he went in detail. He hoped that the people would read and learn from the books and other sources, 'instead of drinking, smoking and card playing'. He was sure that over-indulgence in drink had almost been conquered and that the other vices would follow suit. Tobacco was a 'fatal and foolish habit'. It was also 'a filthy habit, injurious to your health, fatal to your industry, and incompatible with your cleanliness and comfort'. He begged his readers to give it up and, by so doing, have more money to educate their children and be able to buy things that would prove of much greater value. Above all, he wanted integrity from the Irish people and he was outraged when a rumour was heard that a mob wrecked a shop at Kilkenny belonging to one of the jurors in the O'Connell trial. 'If we are to carry Repeal, if this is not to be another of these damnable failures that have disgraced our intellect and our character – there must not be one other popular crime. The Irish people deserve to rot in slavish poverty if they will not keep the discipline under which they enlisted.'[38]

With the Association virtually at a standhill, Davis could only try to bring some realism into any fond expectations the people still held as to a quick granting of Repeal. It should be said with some justification that he, or someone else with authority, was obliged to do so in the wake of Clontarf and the imprisonment of so many of the major leaders. Thus he told them that Repeal was neither certain to come about, nor would it come soon in any event. The people had to persevere in gaining knowledge and in savouring the independence they possessed and the Protestants had to stand with them in the struggle. To him 'Conciliation of all sects, classes, and parties who oppose us, or who still hesitate, is *essential* to moral force,' and he repeated his old theme, 'Feud! Feud! Feud! that is our history, From the hill-side to the library, before assembled men and at the altar of God, Irishmen keep trampling on each other.' To the Protestants he addressed himself as few others could ever have done, lacking as they did both the credentials and the courage,

> Poor deluded Irish Protestants! brave! fierce! impotent! You have denied the country for which a race of Protestant patriots – Daniel

O'Neill, Molyneux, Swift, Lucas, Flood, Grattan, Tone, and Saurin
– fought and spoke ... You saw commerce extinguished, manufactures withered, your militia abolished, your parliament
abolished ... Are you men and bear it? Are you fools and cowards?
Or have your hearts grown so base that interest, patriotism, and
vengeance plead alike in vain? and are you content to accept the
degradation of your country as reward enough for your
subserviency to England? ... Where else in Europe is the peasant
ragged, fed on roots, in a wigwam, without education? ... What
other country pays four and a half million taxes to a foreign
treasury, and has its offices removed or filled by foreigners?
Where else are the people told they are free and represented, yet
only one in two hundred of them have the franchise? Where
beside do the majority support the clergy of the minority? In what
other country are the majority excluded from high ranks in the
university? In what place, beside, do landlords and agents extort
such vast rents from an indigent race?[39]

To the degree that they were valid, Davis's questions were all ones that
the condition of Ireland made pertinent and none of them could be
answered to the satisfaction of a just-minded person. Yet, to the extent
that they were not blinded to reality, the majority of the Protestants
acquiesced in a state of affairs they knew cried out for change.
Nonetheless, Davis did not call for radical change through overturning
the existing social order based on a landed aristocracy, although the
whole bent of his mind and character was such that he would
assuredly have come to that stage of thinking had political freedom
been won in his lifetime. Based whether on his background, his
religion, or a sense of cautious prudence in outlook that only
circumstances could change, at the time he seemed to accept that the
Ascendancy would continue to hold their lands in tranquillity, served
by a meek and humble tenantry and peasantry, and that, in some kind
of idyllic state, the landowners would be found 'on terms of friendship
with their tenants, securing to these tenants every farthing their industry
entitled them to, living among them, promoting agriculture and
education by example and instruction, sharing their joys, comforting
their sorrows, and ready to stand at their head whenever their country
called.'[40]

It was a vision of unreality, probably penned by Davis in an attempt
to assuage the fears that members of the Ascendancy had of losing
their lands. Its unreality sat uneasily with Davis's repeated denunciation
of those land – owners whose absence abroad left their lands in the
hands of often unscrupulous agents. Those agents sometimes placed

249

their own interests before those of their masters, to say nothing of the interests of the tenants and the landless people. The *Warder,* Evangelical, Orange and anti – Repeal, put the situation better in 1844. 'Squalid half – starvation is the desperate lot of the Irish peasant – destitution which no exertion of his can relieve; there is no labour too hard for him – he shrinks from no toil or hardship – but employment there is none for him; privation and misery which could not be borne for two days by Englishmen without the riot of insurrection, are here endured from weary month to month with stoical patience.' It was later calculated that, from 1801 to 1846, the loss to Ireland through absentee landlords, rents, taxes and imports from England of goods previously made in Ireland was £230,000,000.[41]

Davis's main problem was that he knew what the situation was like for tenants and peasants but, in his long and vain attempt to win a union between Catholics and Protestants, he at times had to overlook or forget the root causes of disunion and the lines he had written on them. Even when a peasant had work, his life and that of his family was normally one of extreme want. Elizabeth Smith, wife of Colonel Henry Smith who had inherited his estate of 1,200 acres twenty miles from Dublin at Baltiboys near Blessington, described the circumstances of Harry Kiogh [sic] in 1842. His family home on the Smith property was an old cowhouse without windows or chimney. There were no bedclothes, the beds were of straw, there was no pot, but only a plate or two and a basin and spoon. The 'four starved-looking children' were very clean but the mother was ill, having miscarried while carrying turf. Kiogh was grateful for his employment that brought him 30s annually, of which he paid rent of 20s to the Colonel, who was reputedly a good landlord. Elizabeth also gave some idea of the risk run by tenants who favoured Repeal. One of their tenants, John Ryan, attended the Curragh Repeal meeting in 1843. Elizabeth regretted his audacity because it would 'prevent the Colonel from adding to his farm as he intended, as he could not for the sake of example select for such a mark of approbation the only agitator on his property.' From August 1844 to July 1845 the Smiths travelled in the south of France, but they kept abreast of the situation from their agent, John Robinson. The court proceedings involving O'Connell convinced Elizabeth that 'Irishmen are totally unfit for power' and although she had once accepted that he was a patriot, if indeed 'a little mad', she now thought O'Connell to be 'either a dupe or a deceiver' because he knew full well that Repeal could never be carried.[42]

Even more mistaken was Davis's assumption that the Protestant Irish were a united body owing allegiance to England rather than to Ireland. Although they were prepared to be Irish in their own manner and according to the loyalties they had developed over the centuries of Protestant residence, their kind of Irishness meant that they could not bring themselves to become part of the Ireland that many of the Repealers, including Davis, seemed to want. That Ireland was to be one independent of England, in which case the members of the Ascendancy would lose the one safety valve that allowed them to cling to their lands. Without English support they were convinced that they would be despoiled in the same manner as their forefathers had despoiled the Irish since the Reformation. In most senses, however, the large mass of the Ascendancy accepted that they were not English, but Irish. Apart from some fanatics, since 1829 the Protestant Irish in the south had begun to accept the new reality of the Catholic Irish as citizens with rights. The presence of the Catholic Church was a self-evident fact throughout Irish society and it had to be lived with. Even the immense appeal that Davis and his friends were making for a return to the cultural values of the Irish past need not have proved an obstacle to the assimilation of Irish Protestants into the wider spectrum of society. The centuries of residence in Ireland had woven some of those values into the Ascendancy, even if only on the fringes of their conscience. Those in whom Irish cultural values were strong, such as Samuel Ferguson, had become Irish to the core while still asserting the need to maintain the Union. They were not blind to the negative effects of the Union on many levels of Irish life, both economic and social. With it they had lost their local political power in their own Parliament, and they had lost their power over the Catholic majority. All they had left was their land. Yet, without the Union and that sense it gave of belonging to Empire, the Protestant Irish saw themselves as threatened, isolated and ultimately without prospects. No amount of well-meaning affirmations by Davis, O'Connell, Smith O'Brien, Archbishop MacHale of Tuam, and others, of their rejection of a future Catholic Ascendancy would quieten the fears of most Protestants. Davis was not far from making a beginning on the road to those same fears himself.[43]

The first indication that the Catholic Church at its highest level might try to make the attainment of Repeal even more difficult was the circulation of a report, certainly true, that English Catholics had tried to persuade the pope to ask the Irish bishops to withdraw their support for Repeal and that English agents had put pressure on to that end. Rome refused the plea, coming both from Metternich and from London, but did intervene gently with a letter to the archbishop of Armagh. O'Neill Daunt, rightly proclaiming himself as a 'very sincere Catholic', responded on behalf of lay Catholics. At an Association meeting he said, 'the Catholics of Ireland would pursue the Repeal without caring one straw what Rome might say ... (loud cheers). The Repeal was none of the pope's business – it was our business. (renewed cheers).' He stated firmly that, even were the pope to get out a decree against Repeal, 'he would mind it about as much as he would mind a similar decree from the Grand Turk.'[44] Whether Davis took the rumour seriously is unclear, but he said that the pope had 'no secular control in Ireland'. The affair blew over but the warning was already clear that, whatever about unity among the wider spectrum of society, unity even within the ranks of the Repealers may prove difficult to maintain once the religious question was raised. To some degree Davis was prepared to let his own pen stir the embers. In an article in the *Nation* in August he deplored the fact that the 'poor deluded Protestant artisans' of Ireland could become agitated about such matters as 'the supremacy of the pope and the worship of Loretto [sic]', rather than the real causes of their misery which lay at the door of the Union. He was happy to see that many people were becoming wiser and were prepared to leave 'man and his creed to God, thinking it only needful to consider the religious tenets of a man in the influence they have upon his moral and social relations'.[45]

In the same issue he was even more impetuous, although the principles he stood on were entirely sound. A report of flimsy weight had come through from Cork on the case of a Catholic man who, together with his wife and children, had embraced Protestantism and were subsequently subjected to insult and perhaps even physical violence. Without waiting for confirmation of the facts, Davis weighed in heavily. If true, he wrote, the persons responsible were 'guilty of an act of wicked and barbarous intolerance' and it mattered not a whit whether the victims were mere hypocrites or genuine devotees. He upheld the right of the man and his family to act as they did as much as he would uphold the right of a person to turn from Protestantism to Catholicism. Anyone who would not act on that principle was 'an inquisitor at heart.' He called upon all Repealers, to whom 'religious equality' was a fundamental doctrine, to 'instantly denounce and suppress this crime. For it is a great and disgraceful crime – a crime against God – to interfere with the religious creed or profession of any man – a crime against Ireland for it gives meaning to the otherwise worthless calumnies of our foes who regard Ireland as too bigoted and ignorant for freedom.' That, at the time, Davis was feeling threatened on both religious and political grounds is clear from a letter he wrote to Smith O'Brien two weeks later. He said that, if some leading Repealers continued to act with duplicity, he would be 'forced to withdraw silently from the Association' because 'There are higher things than politics and I will never sacrifice my self-respect to them.' He suggested that, once out of prison, O'Connell should tour Ireland, but he wanted O'Brien or another 'strong secular-minded man' to accompany the Leader on his trip as a guarantee against 'excessive ecclesiasticism'.[46]

Meanwhile the prisoners continued to languish in moderate luxury, although their imprisonment meant humiliation and O'Connell, then entering his seventieth year, certainly suffered by it, but he did his best to brave it out. Despite the assurance given by John O'Connell that active agitation would follow the release of his father from prison, there were grave misgivings among the Davis group that he would renew his relationship with the English Whigs, thereby moving back on to the path of a gradual relief of Irish grievances, rather than sticking to Repeal as the main objective. They should have known that his role in Irish life as mediator of reform and as controller of patronage was not one the Liberator would give up lightly. His position depended upon his maintaining a close association with the Whigs, despite the many occasions on which he had been betrayed by them and he corresponded with some Whig leaders during his imprisonment and several Whig papers showed much sympathy for him.[47] Under the circumstances, it is greatly to the credit of the *Nation* group that they persevered against huge odds in keeping the banner of Repeal unfurled when it would have been so easy to give up. Davis himself was fairly sure that things would never be the same and said to Mitchel, 'O'Connell will run no more risks. Even when this judgment shall be set aside, and he will come out in triumph, he will content himself with 'imposing demonstrations'. He will *not* call the Clontarf meeting again – he will *not* summon the Council of Three Hundred; and from the day of his release, the cause will be going back and down.' 'What care the government', he exclaimed with bitterness, 'how many thousands of people may meet peacefully and legally, or in what trappings they dress themselves, or to what tunes they march, or what banners they may flaunt, – while there are fifty thousand bayonets in all our garrisons, besides the Orange Yeomanry?'[48]

Although he could sense that the Repeal Association was a broken weapon, and its Leader a defeated man, Davis would not yield in his pursuit of Repeal. Thus he was put in the situation of desperately seeking a way in which Repeal, even in a diluted form, could be put back on the agenda with the support of O'Connell. However, by mid-1844, Repeal had never been spelt out in anything like sensible details even as to how a Parliament could run Ireland without its own experienced executive and what would happen were the Irish Parliament to give advice on the same matter to the monarch opposite to that of the Imperial Parliament. In the circumstances, it was reasonable to treat federalism, with its similarly unshaped form, with respect and encouragement provided it did not reject Repeal as an ultimate goal. To that end, Davis worded a series of resolutions on the matter for O'Connell's consideration which he forwarded to the Leader through John O'Connell. The essence of the resolutions was that federalists be seen as allies, provided they shared some of the core values of nationality. In that case they should be supported by Repealers if they were otherwise fit candidates for election to Westminster. In any event, it was Davis's wish that there be no contest between 'simple Repealers and Federalists' for seats and, in some measure, he was successful in winning O'Connell's temporary approval of the tactic.[49]

The federal idea had to be postponed because the House of Lords was in a dilemma trying to decide whether the convictions of the 'traversers' were legally valid. The appeal held that the deficiencies in the jury lists, which had resulted in the non-disclosure of those containing Catholics and the rejection of all Catholics from the final panel of twenty-four, as well as non-partisan Protestants, had rendered the whole proceeding invalid. On 4 September 1844, to great surprise and much relief in Ireland, but especially in Richmond prison, three judges, two of whom were Whigs, and Lord Chief Justice Denham, who had once been a Whig, decided, against two of their peers, to uphold the appeal. Denman said that, if what had occurred in Ireland should continue, 'trial by jury would become a mockery, a delusion and a snare'. The Committee of the Association was sitting at Conciliation Hall when the news came of the London verdict. Preparations were made to welcome their friends from prison and there was widespread rejoicing, both in the Association and throughout Ireland. By 6 September, O'Connell and his fellow prisoners were released with the *Freeman's Journal* proclaiming 'We were wronged – we scorned mercy – we got *Justice*.' In the *Nation*, which ran to three editions, Davis was more circumspect. He rejoiced with sincerity, but asked his 'Dear Countrymen' to 'thank God with us, that we owe no gratitude to Victoria, and are bound by no favour to England for our rescued friends'. Even in such circumstances he could not resist being critical on grounds of nationality. It seems that the bands which accompanied O'Connell on his triumphal procession through Dublin played polkas and Scottish reels. Davis was outraged at this display of 'the ball-room trash of our oppressors!'[50]

To Pigot, Davis had already written that the release of the prisoners was 'a great and useful triumph would that it had not come from a triumvirate of English Whigs' and that he was, as usual after success, 'in low spirits'. His unease about O'Connell being grateful to the Whigs, and possibly contemplating doing deals with them was clear when he warned Pigot that he and O'Brien shared 'grave speculations as to the future'.[51] They did not have to speculate at length and Davis's thoughts about what would happen once O'Connell regained his freedom saw their realisation within a few days. The next weekly meeting of the Repeal Association was to welcome the Leader back in command and, in particular, Davis and Smith O'Brien were anxious to know what his new tactics would be as they could scarcely have conceived that he would have evolved anything in the nature of a long-term strategy. All they could hope for was that he would stick firm to Repeal or, if not that, at least take up the federal idea with energy. Davis even tried to get the idea on the agenda by producing a pamphlet by the High Sheriff of Protestant Fermanagh, Grey Porter, in favour of a Federal Union. All present, however, awaited with keen anticipation the words of the Leader.

The amazement and disappointment of the committed Repealers, and those who wanted to continue some form of decisive action, could not have been greater. O'Connell took his audience through the ordeal of trial and appeal and declared that he had to make atonement to the Whigs given the 'great debt of gratitude he and his companions owed' them. To the Whigs, 'under Providence' they owed their escape 'from the fangs of injustice'. He then rambled on about impeaching the cabinet, the Irish attorney-general and the judges of the queen's bench before the House of Lords for misfeasance in respect of his trial, which was a totally unrealistic, if not absurd proposal, given, as Duffy said, that 'impeachment was a process as obsolete as trial by combat.' In effect, O'Connell said nothing constructive but what he did say was destructive of present morale and lacked any clear purpose for the future.[52] A grand banquet was held to try to revive spirits and Davis put the best face on things by saying, for the benefit of those Protestants who thought that their cause had suffered a genuine setback with the overturning of the verdict against O'Connell, 'Never, while life is left, will the Irish patriots tolerate a Catholic Ascendancy.' O'Connell had a few private conversations over the next few days about federalism and wanted the federalists to state publicly their position before making his own move. Davis was optimistic that, were federalism to become a reality it would mean that 'after six month's independence, Ireland would be a great military power, that we set no limits to our nationality, but those imposed by our means of success,' which indicates that he also was losing his grip of reality under the strain of trying to hold aloft a cause that was now leaderless.[53]

John Mitchel said that O'Connell had held a secret meeting of the Committee at which he proposed to dissolve the Repeal Association and reconstitute it in another way. At an Association meeting he certainly moved that the Committee deliberate on the propriety of forming a 'Preservative Society', which was a return to his tactical gymnastics of the past when he had changed the name of his public bodies successively and successfully. The opposition was such that he withdrew the idea.[54] In any case it mattered little because Repeal was a dead letter. There was to be no renewed agitation, no more 'monster meetings', no Council of the Three Hundred. All that remained for O'Connell was to go home to Derrynane with dignity, to be with his friends, to look out on to the waters of Kenmare Bay and to hunt with his pack of hounds. He was especially pleased to be able to report to his closest friend, P. V. Fitzpatrick, that his potato crop was excellent, indeed of such abundance that it would provide for the needs of others as well as for those who grew it. To him that was good, 'as the inhabitants of other districts are deficient in that necessary article of Irish food'. It was as well he could say that in 1844 there was an abundance of potatoes. It would not be said again in his lifetime.[55]

The only surprising aspect of the events of that September is that any of those who had followed O'Connell with such fervour in the past, except the few who relied on him for all they had become in life, continued to give him their allegiance. Davis was the very one who had written about constancy of character and yet he still placed faith in O'Connell. He was not to know that the illness that would cause death was probably already stretching its fingers into his Leader's being. Davis was happy to see him go off for his holiday, happy too that Duffy was to go with him because Duffy had written that he needed to take a month off 'to recruit my health'. Davis insisted that he would continue to run the *Nation* in Duffy's absence, but Smith O'Brien also went down to his family seat so Davis was left almost alone. Generous to the last, he recognised that O'Connell and Duffy, together with the others, were men who had stood trial for their lives and liberty according to the standards of British justice that held sway in the Ireland of their day. They had undergone the ignominy of imprisonment, even if their material circumstances were comfortable, and they now deserved their rest. It was decent of Duffy to write of Davis, 'If rest be the legitimate requital of work, he had more claim to a holiday than any of us ...' Neither he, nor the others, knew how much Davis needed to rest.[56]

References

1. Duffy, *Davis*, pp 202-3. For Davis's proposals on lessening his involvement with the *Nation*, see ibid., pp 204-8. Some of the letters and diary entries referred to in this period can no longer be traced in the original.

2. See Duffy, *Davis*, p. 143 and Henry Riddell Montgomery, *An essay towards investigating the causes that have retarded the progress of literature in Ireland.* Read before the Belfast Historical Society, 25 November 1842 by a member (Belfast, 1843), p. 49. Pamphlet no 10, box 1748, RIA.

3. *The speeches of the Right Honourable John Philpot Curran* (Dublin, 1843). No name accompanied the volume. The edition I worked from, a republication of the original, was published by Jas Duffy, Dublin 1846, with the title *The life of the Right Hon. J.P. Curran*, after 'a plagiarised and mangled edition' had come out 'lately'. Duffy considered it appropriate that the work now be published as a volume of the Library of Ireland series 'of which Mr Davis was the principal originator'. Davis's *Curran* was published in the one volume with D. O. Madden's *The Right Hon. Henry Grattan* (Dublin, 1846). In the next fifty years, Curran's speeches, with Davis's memoir, went through twenty editions. See also Davis to Madden and Madden to Davis, September 1843, in Duffy, *Davis*, pp 143-45.

4. Davis, *Curran*, p. 5. Davis would have had ample opportunity to read Alessandro Manzoni's, *I promessi sposi*, which was first published at Milan in 1827 and republished frequently. The revised, final version came out in 1840.

5. Davis, *Curran*, pp 12, 19. Curran never wrote down his speeches, but went through them in his mind beforehand. He died in London on 14 October 1817.

6. Ibid., pp 7-51. See Nicholas Furlong, *Fr. John Murphy of Boolavogue* 1753-1798 (Dublin, 1991).

7. For the proposed book see 'A volume of notes by Thomas Davis on the United Irishmen', Ms 1791, NLI.

8. Robert Cane to Davis, 7 September 1845, Ms 14056, NLI.

9. Mrs Tone to Dr Gray, 18 December 1843 in ibid.

10. 'Tone's Grave' in Rolleston (ed. with intro.), *Davis: selections from his prose and poetry*, pp 333-4. There was already a monument to Tone in America.

11. Davis to Pigot, 17 April, 23 May 1844 in *Irish Monthly*, vol. 16 (Dublin, 1888), pp 266-7, 268; Tom Dunne, *Theobald Wolfe Tone, colonial outsider: an analysis of his political philosophy* (Cork, 1982), pp 12, 16; Marianne Elliott, *Wolfe Tone* (New Haven, 1989), p. 418.

12. O'Donovan to Davis, n.d. probably early 1844. See Duffy, *Davis*, pp 208-9.

13. See notes for the history in Duffy, ibid., pp 206, 393-4. See Appendix 2 for Davis's outline and sources.

14. *Nation*, 23 March 1844.

15. Even Samuel Ferguson, whom Davis admired greatly, seemed unable to summon up the energy to respond to Davis's plea for contributions to the *Nation*. See Ferguson to Davis, 21 August 1844 in Davis papers, Ms 2644, NLI. Yeats judged Ferguson as 'the greatest Irish poet'. See Terence Brown and Barbara Hayley (eds.), *Samuel Ferguson: a centenary tribute* (Dublin, 1987), p. 3.

16. Duffy, *Davis*, p. 211.

17. Davis to Pigot, 24 March, 8 May 1844 in *Irish Monthly*, vol. 16 (Dublin, 1888) pp 265, 267. For Charlotte, see inscription on the Davis tomb in Mount Jerome cemetery, Dublin.

18. Ibid., Davis to Pigot, 8, 28 May, 9 June 1844, 15 December 1844, pp 267-9, 339. For the information on scarlatina I am indebted to Dr Peter McCullagh, Division of Clinical Sciences, John Curtin School of Medical Research, Australian National University, Canberra.

19. *Nation*, 30 March 1844.

20. Annie Hutton to Thomas Davis, n.d. but 21 August 1845 in Joseph Hone (ed.), *The love story*, pp 1-3. Hone says that a descendant of James Davis, Thomas's

brother, came across six letters from Annie to Thomas written in August and September 1845. The dates of the earlier letters can be ascertained by working back from the last two in September, which are dated.

21. *Nation*, 25 November 1843. It is perhaps not coincidental that this was a period of great turmoil for the Association with the arrests in the aftermath of Clontarf and Davis being forced to take more responsibility for affairs. Mrs Hutton, possibly her husband also, may have then decided that it was time to act.

22. Ibid., 1 June 1844. Davis signed these poems alternatively as 'Mallow', which would have been instantly recognisable to Annie, and as 'Adragool'. Adragool is a small inlet off Bantry Bay which Davis had visited on his trip south and of which he may have spoken to Annie.

23. See Duffy, *Davis*, p. 385.

24. *Nation*, 6 July, 10 August 1844. Also see the same poem in *Thomas Davis: essays and poems with a centenary memoir 1845-1945*. Foreword by Eamon de Valera (Dublin, 1945), pp 236-7.

25. Davis to Pigot, 24 March 1844 in *Irish Monthly*, vol. 16 (Dublin, 1888), p. 265.

26. Davis to Pigot, 9 June 1844 in ibid., p. 270; and Duffy to a 'Private Friend' from Richmond Prison, 15 March 1849 in vol. 2 (Dublin, 1883), p. 491, ibid. See Peter Alter, 'Symbols of Irish nationalism' in Alan O'Day (intro.), *Reactions to Irish nationalism 1865-1914* (Dublin, 1987), p. 16, and G. A. Hayes-McCoy, *A history of Irish flags from earliest times* (Dublin 1979), p. 140. The tricolour was adopted in 1922 after its use in 1916. It became the flag of the Republic in 1949.

27. Davis to Pigot, 9 June 1844 in *Irish Monthly*, vol. 16 (Dublin, 1888), p. 270.

28. For the beginnings of the Committee see *Nation*, 10 February 1844. The full list of reports of the Committee is found in the bibliography to this work. The reports are held in an excellent collection at the Royal Irish Academy, either as pamphlets or annual volumes. I have used the volumes as a source. See also Davis to Pigot, 24 March 1844 in *Irish Monthly*, vol. 16 (Dublin, 1888), p. 265 and *Freeman's Journal*, 14 June 1844.

29. See Thomas Davis, *Report on the Ordnance Memoir of Ireland* (Dublin 1844), pp 54-60.

30. Davis to Pigot, 23 May 1844 in *Irish Monthly*, vol. 16 (Dublin, 1888), p. 268; Robert Kane, *The industrial resources of Ireland* (Dublin, 1844), pp 3, 32, 297, 340-41, 368, 378-401. Chapter 3 is devoted to 'Water power in Ireland'. The book was republished in 1845 with maps and some additional information. See also T. S. Wheeler, 'Sir Robert Kane: life and work', *Studies,* vol. xxxiii (Dublin, 1944), pt. 1, pp 158-168, pt. 2, pp 316-30. Kane's book in a condensed form was presented as a report of the Committee in 1844.

31. *Nation*, 20 July 1843; *Freeman's Journal*, 23 July 1844.

32. Thomas Davis, *On hurrying bills through parliament* (Dublin, 1844), pp 295-7.

33. Thomas Davis, 'On the opening of Post Office letter', in ibid., pp 300-305. See also F. B. Smith, 'British Post Office espionage' in *Historical Studies*, vol. 14 (Melbourne, October 1969-April 1971), pp 189-203.

34. Thomas Davis, *On the attendance of Irish members in Parliament* (Dublin, 1844) pp 308-9, 351-54. See also MacNevin's presentation of these reports to the Repeal Association, *Nation*, 17, 31 August, 7 September 1844. Also *Freeman's Journal*, 5 July, 9 August 1844.

35. Dan Bryan, 'Thomas Davis as a military influence', in *An Cosantóir,* vol. 5, no. 10 (Dublin, 1945), pp 551-58.

36. *Nation*, 28 October 1843, 25 January, 1 February, 29 March, 11 May, 29 June, 6 July, 12 October 1844; 11 January 1845.

37. See *Freeman's Journal*, 19 August 1844 for *Evening Packet*, 17 August 1844. For the expulsion see *Freeman's Journal*, 15 July 1844.

38. *Nation*, 17 August, 21 September, 1844, 21 March 1845. Duffy, *Davis*, pp 218-9.

39. Davis notes in Ms 1791, NLI; Duffy, *Davis*, pp 219-220.

40. Ibid., pp 221-2.

41. See Waller for 5 October 1844 in William Joseph O'Neill Daunt, *Eighty-five years of Irish history 1800-1885*, vol. 2, pp 68, 139.

42. See David Thomson and Moyra McGusty (eds.), *The Irish journals of Elizabeth Smith 1840-1850* (Oxford 1980), pp 53-4, 61, 63, 69.

43. Jennifer Ridden's paper, 'Union, Empire and the Irish Ascendancy in the early nineteenth century', presented at the Imperial History seminar, London, 7 February 1994, contains a valuable assessment of the role of the Ascendancy.

44. *Nation*, 29 June 1844; See also John F. Broderick, *The Holy See and the Irish movement for the repeal of the union with England 1829-1847* (Rome, 1951), pp 162, 179, 184.

45. *Nation*, 3 August 1844. The Loretto (sic) refers to the belief, held by some Catholics, that the home of Jesus, Mary and Joseph of Nazareth had been transferred miraculously to Loreto in Italy. The Church, understandably, remained silent on the matter.

46. Ibid., Davis to Smith O'Brien, 20 August 1844, Ms 435 NLI.

47. See Michael Tierney, 'Repeal of the Union' in Michael Tierney (ed.), *Daniel O'Connell: nine centenary essays* (Dublin, 1949), p. 167 and Duffy, *Davis*, p, 235.

48. Davis to Mitchel, n.d. but 1844, in Mitchel, *Last conquest*, p. 56.

49. Duffy, *Davis*, pp 224-5; *Nation*, 14 September 1844 where Davis expresses pleasure in the growth of the federal movement, while making it clear that he is not personally committed to it. See also Kevin B. Nowlan, 'The meaning of Repeal in Irish history', in *Historical Studies* (London, 1963), p. 5.

50. *Freeman's Journal*, 6 September 1844; *Nation*, 7, 14 September 1844.

51. Davis to Pigot, n.d. but 4 September 1844. In *Irish Monthly*, vol. 18, part 2 (Dublin, 1890), p. 336.

52. *Nation*, 14 September 1844. Duffy, *Davis*, pp 243-4. Duffy was especially sarcastic about asking the House of Lords, 'where our cause had not so much as one solitary representative' to undertake the process of impeachment.

53. *Nation*, 21 September 1844.

54. See Mitchel, *The history*, vol. 2, p. 374 and *Nation*, 28 September 1844.

55. O'Connell to Fitzpatrick, 3 October 1844 in O'Connell (ed.), *Correspondence*, vol. vii, p. 273.

56. For Duffy to Davis from Lismore, see his letter of 18 September 1844 in *Nation*, 18 September 1844. Duffy on Davis's claim to a holiday is in Duffy, *Davis*, p. 244.

TONE'S GRAVE.

BY THOMAS DAVIS.

I.

In Bodenstown Churchyard there is a green grave,
And wildly along it the winter winds rave;
Small shelter I ween are the ruined walls there,
When the storm sweeps down on the plains of Kildare.

II.

Once I lay on that sod—it lies over Wolf Tone—
And thought how he perished in prison alone,
His friends unavenged, and his country unfreed—
"Oh, bitter," I said, " is the patriot's meed;

III.

For in him the heart of a woman combin'd
With a heroic life, and a governing mind—
A martyr for Ireland—his grave has no stone—
His name seldom nam'd, and his virtues unknown."

IV.

I was woke from my dream by the voices and tread
Of a band, who came into the home of the dead;
They carried no corpse, and they carried no stone,
And they stopp'd when they came to the grave of Wolfe Tone.

Chapter 12

New wine in old vessels

With the waning of Repeal as an objective, the purpose of the Association lost its edge even though its activities seemed outwardly to increase. No Monday passed without the usual meeting, no break was taken for summer and the harangues by John O'Connell, who assumed the mantle of his absent father, became longer and more pointless. The substance of the Association now consisted in its role as a vehicle for education through the reading rooms and the issuing of the reports on government business by the Committee, on which Davis continued to be the anchorman. Even among the English members of Parliament on both sides of the House, the reports were being read with increasing interest and Smith O'Brien thought that his 'notion of making the Repeal Association an introductory legislature has been completely realised'.[1] It was one thing however to draw up the reports, no matter how praiseworthy and weighty their contents, but it was another to have them acted upon and the Association was incapable of bringing that about. The euphoria felt with the release of O'Connell and the other prisoners soon dissipated and little was left but the hard grind of giving reality back to a movement that was, increasingly, both purposeless and leaderless.

Under the circumstances, it was almost inevitable that the vacuum left by the loss of the ideal of Repeal would be filled with elements threatening the stability of the Association. Before his imprisonment, the will and words of O'Connell were law. Since his release, it was as if around him a space had been created for new leadership that would give obeisance to him while he lasted, but would be ready to step into his shoes at any moment. John O'Connell was convinced that he stood as rightful heir to a father whose gifts so far outshadowed his own that everyone but John, and perhaps the father in his love, saw the gap between them. Nonetheless, to say that he did not rank with his father as a leader is not to deny his intelligence and labour. Indeed he was an indefatigable worker. However, a contemporary who knew both father and son, T. C. Luby, wrote that 'Narrow, sordid, poor-souled John O'Connell is the evil genius of his sire.'[2] Such an opinion, and there were many similar to it, would not be worth repeating had it not been for the fact that John played a significant role in the final events of Davis's life. With his customary openness to everyone, Davis seems to have maintained a relationship of some warmth with, and confidence in, John until the end, but none of his friends felt the same way. Perhaps Davis was impressed by John's considerable capacity in financial and commercial matters as proven by his book, *An Argument for Ireland*, published in 1844. The text runs to 40 pages, but the appendices take up another 350. Like his father, John saw success coming from 'the noble, peaceful struggle in which she [Ireland] is engaged'.³ The more important person with whom Davis had a close relationship was Smith O'Brien who was noble-hearted, generous and fully committed to Repeal. He gave full proof of his integrity at Ballingarry in 1848, during his later trial at which he was sentenced to be hanged, drawn and quartered, and throughout the years of his lonely exile as a convict in Van Diemen's Land. Yet he did not have the final stuff of leadership and he knew it. Only Davis of them all seemed to measure up, but he was young, committed still to O'Connell despite all the frayed edges of the older man's charisma and seemingly lacking the ambition necessary to place himself at the head. They were dangerous days for the crumbling Association with O'Connell and the others absent and no one at the helm.

Despite his work load, or perhaps because it softened the intensity of his grief over Annie which had not lessened with the passing months, Davis seemed in reasonable spirits and did not object to Smith O'Brien, from his country retreat, urging him to attend all the Committee meetings in his absence. He wrote to Pigot encouraging him to visit Derrynane, where O'Connell expected him and where he would meet Duffy and O'Hagan. He had received letters from William Eliot Hudson who told him that he had heard, in Wales, 'The March of the Men of Harleck' played by 'an old, blind beggar who was also drunk'. Hudson had concluded that Welsh was a Celtic language, so Davis felt moved to say to Pigot, 'Hurray for my ancestors, and for yours, and you, and myself, and, as poor Tone I think says, hurrah generally.'⁴ He kept himself 'as busy as a swallow' and was delighted that Duffy had enjoyed his visit to Munster. 'I am proud of my own dear, dear Munster having pleased you so much. I love it almost to tears at the thought.'⁵ He was never to visit it again.

Duffy's offer of returning to the *Nation* in order to permit him to take a holiday in the autumn was refused by Davis on the persuasive grounds that he had to be available to attend the marriage of his brother, yet he seemed almost possessed by the demon of work. His brother James was to marry his cousin, Charlotte Eliza Atkins, at the residence of her aunt Mrs Bennett at Monaquil, where they had all passed so many happy holidays together so that the wedding was also to be a family reunion of a kind that Davis could not be absent from. He told Duffy that 'the *Nation* is easy to me, and will grow easier', but he was anxious about the reading rooms which he wanted O'Connell to foster so as to make them more widespread and with the necessary materials made available in them. The old adage that had ever been his guiding force, 'Educate that you may be free', had not diminished and he wrote 'Damn the ignorance of the people – but for that we should be lords of our own future; without that, much is insecure.' When Duffy replied he made it clear that he was not convinced of Davis's happiness and peace of mind. He probably wanted to remind Davis of his human frailty and his need for companionship in life by referring to the impending marriage of his brother, 'I wish it was your brother's brother that was getting married – I fancy it would promote his happiness, and put a waistcoat upon discontents which shake the peace of Jupiter in his seclusion.' Seemingly, Duffy did not realise how much Davis wanted to marry and how his wish to do so was thwarted by factors over which he had no control.[6]

Into the happy and relaxed atmosphere at Derrynane, an event intruded that had profound effects on the relationship between the young men and their elders in the Repeal Association. Those effects dogged Davis for his few remaining months and the others, especially the Catholics in the *Nation* circle, for the rest of their lives. Tedious perhaps in detail, but shot through with passion, the series of charges and rejections, of suspicion and innuendo helped to embitter men who had hitherto managed to preserve their harmony with each other, despite the obstacles they encountered almost daily. Perhaps characteristically, given his refusal to remain uninvolved in the main arena while standing always on the sidelines issuing sage prescriptions, it was Madden who was the first to stir the waters, and he had forewarned Davis that he was about to do so. His contribution, a book called *Ireland and its Rulers*, was part philippic, part warning and part sound sense. He asked Davis to foreshadow the book in the pages of the *Nation*. Recognising that the contents would be attacked, Madden still wanted the notice run and, if possible, on 14 October 1844, perhaps as some kind of a birthday present to the acting editor because he told Davis to look at a section that contained material of personal interest.[7] Madden took a vastly different attitude to Davis than he did to other figures in the Repeal movement, and especially to its Leader. He was intensely critical of O'Connell and it is unnecessary to repeat his calumnies on him, but one is sufficient to give something of the flavour, 'O'Connell a regenerator! His statesmanship is that of a smuggler.'[8] It says much for the total involvement of O'Connell in his devotion to the people of Ireland that many commentators could not distinguish between his person, his great gifts, his generous disposition and his cause. To them, the man was the cause and, in rejecting the cause, they rejected the person. On the other hand, it is striking how frequently apologists for Davis, including Madden and Samuel Ferguson, were able to make a distinction between Davis the indefatigable proponent of Repeal, with whom they disagreed, and Davis the person they loved and admired so greatly. The distinction was a flimsy one and uncomplimentary to Davis because his longing and striving for the independence of Ireland was part and parcel of both his person and personality.

The holiday-makers at Derrynane, where Duffy and John O'Hagan had also arrived, read the section of the third part of Madden's *Rulers* which contained Madden's sketch of a person called 'Dormer' who was unquestionably Davis. The subject was immediately recognisable to informed readers, and especially to the company at Derrynane. In Madden's judgement, Davis had brought entirely unique qualities to 'the cause of the Irish multitude', by which he meant those who attended or applauded the purpose of the monster meetings. With some perception he judged Davis to be 'a man of military intellect', but fell into a misjudgement when he said that he 'looked at men in masses and scientifically calculated the best mode of shaping events by large combinations'. Madden softened this opinion by adding that Davis was also 'a democrat but not of sentiment like Emmett and Fitzgerald' and that he was 'learned profoundly in the history of his own country, and well acquainted with that of other nations ...' Moreover, he had 'the powers of a poet of high promise', which he used admirably in the turmoil of his day-to-day life. Despite his involvement 'in a gangrened state of political society like that of Ireland', he was able to keep intact his gifts of an 'unsullied character', 'a noble disregard of self', and 'a love of fair play' that would never permit him to 'be guilty of the characteristic faults of the Corn Exchange'. Madden fulsomely eulogised Davis as 'An Irish patriot, without the taint of vanity; an Irish democrat loathing those vile arts which have made the word "agitator" synonymous with much of what is abominable; an Irish popular leader without hypocrisy, servility, or meanness – such is the spirited and generous Dormer [Davis].' Madden's conclusion was that, despite his great gifts, Davis 'will fail, but he will splendidly fail', because 'he fancies that the people around him are made of the same materials as himself.' Even more fatally, 'He persists in turning his eyes from all that is paltry, weak, and ridiculous in that side of Irish politics to which he has devoted himself.' Madden's prayer was that Davis may be saved from being 'its most lamented martyr'. In contrast to the men of Conciliation Hall, Madden praised the men of the *Nation* because their foremost political dogma was that Ireland had to have 'an age of action' and they saw their present role as preparing people for that age. At the same time he could have sport with them. 'Young Germany dreams – Young France quarrels – Young England says prayers – Young America swindles – and Young Ireland sings.' From Madden's idle remark the nickname 'Young Ireland' arose and stuck subsequently to the group about Davis.[9]

Despite the trenchant criticism of Repeal and O'Connell in the book, O'Brien displayed his lack of either sensitivity or prudence by telling Davis how delighted he was with it. At Derrynane, no comment was made except that, according to Duffy, the section on 'Dormer' was thought to be 'clever and generous'. He did not say whether others besides himself and O'Hagan considered it to be so. There can be no doubt but that O'Connell was appalled and probably troubled at the contrast drawn between himself and Davis, which was as explicit as Madden could make it. He wrote to Davis and said that 'there never lived a more odious and disgusting public writer' than Madden and that 'I have often felt amongst *some* of the Liberal Protestants I have met with, that there was not amongst them the same *soundness* of generous liberality as amongst the Catholics.' For his part, John O'Connell possibly saw a rival to his own ambitions to become leader of the movement after his father and it is likely that the 'Dormer' episode was discussed between father and son. Davis was manifestly aghast at the sketch in which Madden had 'puffed [him] frightfully', although he thanked him for 'the affection that misled you into it'. He wanted to be regarded as merely one of many who were resolved 'to lift the English rule from off Ireland and give our country a career of action and thought'. To achieve that aim, 'Action, even in a military sense, is not mere cutting, firing and charging. Organisation, leadership, obedience, union, are all action ... Our work is only beginning.' He refused to comment on the 'bitterness' of Madden's attack on O'Connell and advised him to write no more on his 'Irish political contemporaries for some years to come'. Perhaps his admonition to Madden partly stemmed from MacNevin's words to him on the third part of the book as 'insolent trash ... vague assertion, independent self-sufficiency, and underbred kitchen pertness'.[10]

The repercussions from Madden's mischievous book did not end with a mutual decision to let the past bury its dead. In a certain sense they set the pattern of the immediate future and thus clouded the remainder of Davis's life with suspicion, hostility and recrimination. The breach, unsurprisingly, was not widened on strictly political issues but on religious grounds because in such matters there was much more room for disagreement. There is no doubt that, whatever about the strength of Davis's faith in his own Church, he was assuredly a Protestant in the sense that he accepted the usual Protestant reservations concerning Rome and the papacy, religious orders, vows and celibacy. To be a Protestant did not mean that he was anti-Catholic, just as O'Connell was not anti-Protestant. Indeed, Davis was in full agreement with the attitude which the Liberator had expressed as early as 1813. 'Every religion is good, every religion is true to him who in due caution and conscience sincerely believes it. There is only one bad religion: that of a man who professes a faith in which he does not believe.'[11] Understandably, however, Davis, and in some measure Smith O'Brien also, not only saw Catholic beliefs and Catholic practices with Protestant eyes, but they also unfavourably judged the behaviour of some Catholics in the secular sphere when they thought that it was based on Catholic beliefs. Furthermore, Davis had been reared in his home and in his university in a long tradition of Irish Protestantism which looked askance at the Catholic majority in Ireland, deplored their alleged superstitions, doubted their degree of civilisation and recoiled frequently at behaviour which they judged as lacking in good, clean, Protestant virtue. While Davis mixed with university-educated Catholics he could stand aloof from the practices of the Catholic multitude. Once he became part of the Repeal Association he had perforce to associate with those masses and their leaders. At times he found cause for complaint.

In the beginning the cloud was small, but Duffy was subsequently convinced that it was part of a concerted plan by O'Connell and his son, John, to discredit Davis and thus render him politically ineffective. The best method of achieving that objective was to paint Davis as anti – Catholic, 'a point on which the people were naturally sensitive and ready to take alarm', said Duffy, adding that charging Davis with being anti-Catholic was as unreasonable as charging him with being 'anti-Irish', given that 'He was a Protestant with the most generous and considerate indulgence for the opinions of the bulk of his country-men.'[12] In any case, while Davis was in control of the *Nation* during Duffy's holiday he had rejected parts of a poem submitted by Edward Walsh, a teacher in the national system who had been dismissed some time previously by the Board of Education. Walsh was convinced his dismissal was because of 'some sweet simple verses' he had contributed on former occasions to the *Nation*. Duffy and Davis had shown great kindness to Walsh by finding employment for him, initially with the *Monitor* and then at Conciliation Hall. In a letter to the *Wexford Independent*, Walsh said that Davis had censored him because of the Catholic context in which the verses were couched. The accusation, certainly baseless, was made more ungracious because of the past generosity by Davis to Walsh, but perhaps the latter had come under different influences since beginning to work at Conciliation Hall where John O'Connell was in control.[13]

In the meantime, a more serious matter arose. Davis had reviewed Madden's book in the *Nation* with a degree of moderate warmth. He thought that the book 'was more likely to serve those it corrects and those it praises, than any book on Ireland we can call to mind'. Nonetheless, the use of genius and love of the beautiful, which the author possessed in abundance, was put to no good end with its 'sneers' and 'unjust charges'. As for the words on 'Dormer', Davis did not know whether he should resent the praises that Madden so freely poured out, 'at our country's expense'. In short, the review was fair but very cautious.[14] Shortly afterwards, Dr Murray, a priest who taught dogmatic theology at Maynooth, reviewed the book in the *Dublin Review* for September and mentioned that Madden had left Catholicism for Protestantism, which could cast doubt on whatever he wrote '*against* the Catholic priests and the Catholic religion'.[15] Davis reviewed Murray's article and agreed with his final conclusion on O'Connell that 'he is one of the greatest minds of the earth, one that will be eminent over time, and dear to men when his faults and failures, his enemies and friends are forgotten.' Davis then went on to the offensive. 'Neither he, [O'Connell] nor we, nor any of our party will stand tamely by and see *any* man threatened or struck by hand or word for holding or changing his creed. If this were allowed (we say it in warning) events would be made that would indeed change the destinies of Ireland.' Davis did not elaborate on the meaning of his last sentence, but it seemed to imply that intolerance would not be permitted to continue without dire consequences for the unity he longed for in Ireland. He finished on a peaceful note with the remark that Murray's sentence on Madden's change of religion was no more than a passing reference by a critic 'justly vexed by the incivilities of the author'.[16]

The same edition of the *Nation* in which Davis reacted to Murray was its anniversary number. It was the last under Davis's charge before the return of Duffy to his editorial desk and Davis gave himself free rein. His editorial, 'A Second Year's Work', was one of the best he ever wrote in that, despite the evil days that had befallen Repeal, he seemed full of hope and confidence. At the same time, he gave a hostage to fortune in some of the things he said about religion. 'Religion has been for ages so mixed with Irish quarrels that it is often hard to say whether patriotism or superstition was the animating principle of an Irish leader, and whether political rapacity or bigotted [sic] zeal against bigotry was the motive of an oppressor.' Thus the *Nation* had decided to leave 'sacred things to consecrated hands' and to preach 'a nationality that asked after no man's creed', because mingling politics and religion in Ireland blinded men 'to their common secular interests, to render political union impossible, and national union hopeless'. As a result of their work, the men of the *Nation* had gained 'a *practical* as well as a verbal admission' that 'religion is a thing between man and God – that no citizen is to be hooted, or abused, or marked down, because he holds any imaginable creed, or changes it any conceivable number of times.' They were propositions which, if admirable in themselves, were likely to cause misgivings to a theologian or bishop who held that the Church in union with the See of Peter in Rome was the Church founded by Christ. Archbishop MacHale of Tuam was an example saying, 'There is but one true religion according to Catholic belief: there is one royal road marked out by God.' Furthermore, in respect of Murray's remarks on Madden, the point has been well made that Protestants could be relaxed about the fewness in members of their faith becoming Catholics but, given the number of Catholics who had become Protestants in the eighteenth century in Ireland, many of them for material gain, Catholics were unable to take a similarly detached view of the matter.[17]

In a small piece on a criminal trial then being held in Dublin, Davis had the throw-away lines, 'A Roman censorship prevents immoral and impious books, but it destroys liberty of discussion,' and the same edition of the paper ran a favourable review of William Carleton's *Traits and stories of the Irish peasantry* which had just been put out in a new edition. There was nothing offensive whatever in the review, except to those who had never forgiven Carleton for his criticism of the Catholic clergy in the distant past, despite the way he had eulogised the same clergy in his '*The Poor Scholar*' in a later period. A lengthy editorial on 'The Presbyterians' could have given offence to a theologian ill-prepared to accept its purpose, or unable to comprehend its minor intricacies. The purpose of the piece was to persuade the Presbyterians to forget the battle of the Boyne and join with their fellow countrymen for their 'common redemption as a people' and to 'consolidate nationality by unity, holiness, and peace'. In all, the editorial was without fault unless a reader were to quibble with the praise heaped on the Presbyterians because 'They have cast the old slough crusted in profligacy, and walked forth purified and sparkling, and mirroring back to Heaven its simplest and boldest truths.' The writer clearly had in mind Anglicanism, not Catholicism, as the matrix from which Presbyterianism arose and departed. Nonetheless, there were several statements in the one issue of the *Nation* with which a

Catholic theologian, could, if so motivated, disagree or argue while a Catholic bigot could probably have found a good deal to be offended at.[18]

Dr Murray, under the title 'An Irish Priest' was quick to reply in a letter to Staunton's *Weekly Register* which was an offshoot of the *Morning Register*, the demise of which it had survived. Citing the examples referred to, and judging them with the mentality of a nineteenth-century theologian, he accused the *Nation* of teaching anti-Catholic doctrines, spoke of its 'un-Catholic and infidel spirit', 'its un-Catholic sneers and sarcasms' and of the 'unChristian principles put forward constantly' in its pages. He called the writers 'the masked infidels of the *Nation*', and was horrified that Carleton, 'this Monaghan apostate, and cruel reviler of the Catholic priesthood, and people, and religion' could be praised in its pages. As for the article on the Presbyterians, Murray asked, 'Is it to propagate such Calvinisms among the people that the *Nation* is so very anxious to have Repeal reading-rooms established in every parish in the kingdom?' Finally Davis, although unnamed, was summed up as 'this little self-constituted Committee for the protection of the slanderers of the priests and the church' and called a 'poor, little, puffed-creature.'[19]

Leaving aside the invective, a case could be made for Murray's disquiet at some of the contents of the paper of 12 October, but the fact remains that none of it, individually or collectively, amounted to, or even bordered on, infidelity or heresy. Furthermore, in religious matters, the paper had unquestionably maintained a Christian spirit and any criticism it ran of the Catholic Church was fair dealing. For Duffy and Davis to have followed a strictly Catholic line in their paper would have run counter to their overall purpose, and that of the *Nation*, of uniting all segments of Irish society in a common cause. Moreover, such a line would have been tantamount, whether for Davis or Duffy, to admitting that Repeal was a strictly Catholic affair and that its organ, the *Nation*, was a mouthpiece of the Catholic Church. In the event, Davis was unable to reply to Murray as he had set out for Belfast and the north on 19 October, but he was primarily responsible for the edition of 12 October, which Duffy now had to defend.[20]

It is certain that, with the possible exception of the material on the Presbyterians, which may have been written by John Mitchel, Davis was the author of the articles that so disturbed Murray. The fact that, in his reply to Murray on 26 October, Duffy said that all that had been complained of was written by 'men I trust, esteem, and love,' indicates that there was more than one author, unless he is to be accused of deliberate deception. Duffy also said that he was in complete agreement with all that had been written. He admitted that the article on the Presbyterians was by a Protestant who was not writing as a theologian, but as a political journalist who was trying to persuade the Presbyterians to join the national cause. He defended his own record as a Catholic journalist and concluded that 'my fellow labourers [on the *Nation*] are equally incapable of prostituting the press to so abominable a purpose' as propagating infidelity.[21] The argument dragged on with a reply by Murray to Duffy that again showed his high competence in polemics. A Dublin priest, who was a friend of Duffy, wrote publicly that most of the clergy regretted Murray's 'unwarranted and untenable assertions' and that no one in Rome was at all troubled by the contents of the *Nation*. Finally, the *Belfast Vindicator*, with a degree of smug unction, made it plain that it would have no truck with the *Nation*, given its 'insidious insinuation of irreligion'. To this, MacNevin weighed in with a reply that did not confront the main issue, but insisted that the young men had not chosen the name of Young Irelanders. He was almost too fulsome in his defence of Davis. 'It is true that Mr Davis is a Protestant, and woe, woe to the country wherein could be found a single tongue to slander so pure, so upright, so earnest a man' who, without thought of self, had devoted all his energy, intelligence, and enthusiasm to 'the elevation of Ireland'. The *Pilot* had a final word in an editorial against 'indifferentism in religion'. It was an 'iniquity' that had to be struck from the Catholic body.[22]

As Duffy saw the affair, a golden opportunity had been presented to John O'Connell who had long resented the prominence and achievements of the newcomers to the cause. With 'at least the tacit sanction of his father', the 'Young Liberator', as John had become known, rapidly managed to circulate the opinion among priests throughout Ireland that there was 'a dangerous spirit in the *Nation*, hostile to religion'. It was an accusation of vast potential harm to the men connected with the *Nation*, as well as to the paper itself, but Duffy saw no need to refute it forty-five years later. His reason was that so few of those accused were still alive and that their lives had given sufficient proof of its emptiness.[23] At the time, however, Davis reacted with vigour. To Duffy, he wrote from the north that, unless O'Connell could stop 'the lies of bigot journals' and 'prevent bigots from interfering in religious liberty', he would 'withdraw from politics; as I am determined not to be the tool of a Catholic ascendancy, while apparently the enemy of British domination'. He wrote to John O'Connell asking him to enlist his father's support in dampening down the fires. John's cautious reply left the matter up to his father, but he seemed, sensibly and genuinely, more concerned with Davis's health. 'I am very sorry indeed to gather from your letter that neither your bodily health nor spirits are what I sincerely wish them. Take care you do not overwork both, as I strongly think you have done, especially the physical vigour.'[24] In a letter to O'Brien, Davis said that he would not be 'the conscious tool of bigots' and that he would not strive 'to beat down political, in order to set up religious, ascendancy'. He told O'Brien that, 'we Protestants must ascertain whether we are to have a religious liberty.' In his reply, as an older man with greater experience, O'Brien tried to calm Davis down by reminding him that they were Protestants living in the midst of a Catholic majority and that divisions and differences would necessarily arise but that 'Unity is essential to our success, and therefore division at present would be madness.'[25]

Davis did not seem to realise that he was laying himself open to a charge of interfering with the freedom of the press. As he saw the matter, he was asking for his own, and others', freedom to express their opinions on religious matters to be respected, without their being accused of irreligion. He remained unmollified and much agitated so he fired off a broadside to Staunton at the *Weekly Register* saying that he would never yield to such an 'Inquisition' and 'You must now see that the very existence of a Repeal party is perilled, and I trust that *solely on public grounds* you will put an end to so hazardous a quarrel.'[26] O'Connell was chagrined and offended at the accusations made by Davis and he wrote to him from Derrynane on 30 October, 1844. His letter is not in his own hand, except for the last paragraph which is very uncertain and perhaps indicates that he was unwell at the time. After referring to Davis's letter to John O'Connell as a 'Protestant philippic from Belfast', O'Connell denied firmly that he or any of his had anything to do with the attacks on the *Nation*. He turned Davis's resentment on its head and, in a most able fashion, made the young man seem both a bigot and an aggressor. In so doing he tended to forget the extreme pressure that had led Davis to be over-zealous and to show a facet of his humanity that his normal control of his composure rarely revealed. O'Connell asked Davis to 'lessen a little your Protestant zeal' and swore that he would 'most bitterly regret that we lost you by reason of any Protestant monomania'. He also expressed his pride in, and desire for, the prosperity of the *Nation* and hoped that it would be able to continue to '"pioneer the way" to genuine liberty, to perfect liberality, and entire political equality for all religious persuasions.' Avowing that he hated 'bigotry of every kind – Catholic, Protestant, or Dissent' he said that Catholics '*require* cooperation, support, combination, but we do not *want* protection or patronage'.[27]

In its own genre, O'Connell's letter was both noble and generous and the whole course of his life bears testimony to its sincerity. Nonetheless, it did nothing to clarify the main point at issue as to whether a campaign of vilification of Davis had been initiated. A quirk of fate, or a rare failing in Post Office efficiency, resulted in the important letter not getting to Davis for some weeks so that he remained unaware that O'Connell had written to him on so crucial a matter at such an important time in their relationship. He returned from the north on 30 October and, unaware of the letter, wrote to O'Brien on 3 November with some spleen and foreboding. He was not concerned about himself but about the cause, which he was sure would be ruined unless harmony were made to prevail. He had concluded that what was happening was the beginning of an assault on 'the growth of secular education and free discussion' as well as on 'independent lay opinion'. The question at issue was 'one of religious liberty', which he would not sacrifice his right to 'for *any* consideration'. With some degree of flamboyance he asserted, 'I would prefer a military to a theocratic government,' which at least begged the question as to what kind of a government Ireland already had, given the vast military presence there.[28]

The affair was later seen as a kind of 'clerical vendetta with Young Ireland', stemming in some measure from Davis's 'neurotic suspicion of popery'.[29] Maurice O'Connell, the editor of his ancestor Daniel's massive correspondence, has judged the behaviour of Duffy as a cover-up for Davis, whom history has now revealed as the 'culprit' in the whole affair. Davis is blameworthy because he wrote all the damaging material and never admitted to it, so that he 'allowed himself to be protected at the expense of his friends'. Duffy was guilty of suppressing the truth, in order to protect Davis, by implying that there was more than one author, and the way in which Duffy recounted the episode in his writings casts 'additional doubt on his reliability as an historian'. Furthermore, of the young men, only Davis attributed the attack on the *Nation* to 'religious bigotry and intolerance', but it was nonetheless right to conclude that Davis was not a bigot. In order to explain his '*apparent* bigotry' recourse must be made to 'emotional disturbances in his personality and by a measure of vanity', stemming from his self-righteousness and his 'exaggerated sense of his own political impor-tance'. Finally, the charge is made that, had Davis been courageous, or honest, enough to admit that he wrote the offensive material, the Catholics among the Young Irelanders would not have been censured. Because of Davis's silence and Duffy's cover-up, the young men had to spend the rest of their lives as 'suspect' Catholics.[30]

Even were it the case that Davis wrote all the material, which is unproven, there was no reason for Davis and Duffy to depart from the common practice adopted by the *Nation* from its origins of not publicly ascribing material to individual authors. On the other hand, had any of the Catholic members of the *Nation* group been offended by the material, disagreed strongly with it, or demanded that Davis come forward and shift the burden of suspicion away from them, the matter would rest in a different light. There is no proof that any of them reacted in such ways. On the contrary, they all seem to have been fully behind Davis and resented bitterly the attack which they saw as directed specifically at him. It is surely unreasonable to expect that Davis would descend to cheapening the *Nation*, and the material it had run, by proclaiming his Protestantism and authorship. To have done so would have been tantamount to begging the public to judge what he wrote as merely the product of Protestant ignorance or bigotry, rather than as examples of Catholic infidelity or indifference. Finally, given that the Catholics associated with Davis were regarded as 'suspect' in Ireland for the rest of their lives, there must be some grounds to suspect that there was indeed a concerted attack made on the whole *Nation* group in the person of Davis. A letter to Duffy by John Frazer, who wrote for the *Nation* as Jean de Jean, summed up one attitude to the imbroglio. He was disgusted at Murray's attack 'on a great national cause under cover of an attack upon an individual's opinion'. He concluded that, if those who held to the opinions expressed in the paper were stigmatised 'as *professing Catholics and disguised infidels*', the result would be that the 'the people's voluntary education of themselves [would] be rendered not national, but Roman Catholic, not broad and general but narrow and one sided.' At the same time Leigh Hunt, who claimed Irish blood, had written to Duffy begging him not to provoke war between the young men and O'Connell and to tone down the temper of the *Nation*. Hunt thought that O'Connell was 'manifestly achieving' a victory '*because* of bloodlessness' and his example was one 'which it would be a million pities if the world were to lose.'[31]

Dr. Murray ranks with Davis as a leading actor in the whole affair. Were it not for its importance it would be better to leave unsaid his own denouement of his role, because his thought and language rank him with Madden in the attitude he finally adopted to the O'Connells, meaning the circle, led by John O'Connell, who surrounded the Leader in Conciliation Hall. In 1847, John Dillon wrote to his wife, Adelaide, telling her that he had met Dr Murray on a train. The priest delighted him greatly with the way he talked of Conciliation Hall as 'that abomination'. Dillon said that Murray had written 'some very able letters against the *Nation*' in 1844, convinced that the paper was 'established and conducted with a deliberate view to undermine the faith of the Irish people'. Murray had then discovered, through private sources, that he was mistaken in his judgement and he went to Duffy to tell him how much he regretted his attack. Since then, Murray had 'lost no opportunity to repair any damage he may have caused'. Dillon was much impressed with Murray as 'a person of great and well cultivated powers ... quite free from eccentricities' and he took special pleasure in telling his wife that Murray 'abominates the O'Connells chiefly, he says, because they are doing all that such reptiles can do to damage the Catholic faith and to render it odious to all virtuous and reflecting minds'.[32]

Dr Charles William Russell, appointed, before ordination, to the chair of humanities at Maynooth at the early age of twenty-three in 1835 had taken a cool attitude to the affair. He was convinced that the *Nation* was 'a most powerful organ for good or for evil' so he had successfully got close to Duffy, with whom he maintained a life-long friendship, in an attempt to help keep the paper 'within proper bounds'.[33] However, the reaction to the attack on Davis and his friends in some Protestant circles was wonderment that they could continue to support the cause of Repeal. There was also contempt for the methods used against them, even to the degree of crudely, but perhaps understandably in the circumstances, comparing them to those of the Inquisition. Samuel Ferguson was horrified at the degradation brought on the Irish people by 'populist nationalism sharpening philistine, provincial culture and sectarian strife'. Apparently Ferguson connected none of this with Davis, whom he sat near at a meeting of the Royal Irish Academy. The proceedings must have been of little interest to him because he wrote a poem on the back of a ballot paper and passed it to Davis. It was entitled 'To the Gentlemen of the *Nation* Newspaper', and it began by making it plain that Ferguson still remained strongly in favour of the Union with England. Nevertheless he wanted to tell Davis and his friends how he was sure,

> How loving – brave, with manly minds erect
> Ye toil to give the people self-respect
> And therefore now, when in fanatic zeal
> Bigots assail you, that the stake and wheel
> Ye love not, I would cheer you so attack'd

He concluded,

> But let him who would see all hates undone
> And Erin's day of happier note begun
> With you teach national self-confidence.[34]

All this disruption took place in the midst of a more serious political argument about the possibility of supporting the concept of federalism. Davis had already seriously considered the idea, but always saw it as a temporary expedient. On the other hand, while O'Connell was resting at Derrynane, he mulled over federalism and its prospects and was increasingly warm. He hesitated about giving a lead because he did not know with whom he had to deal. A wide spectrum of diverging attitudes had come increasingly together with a push to federalism. The problem was that they lacked cohesion, they had no leadership, no voice in the press and fundamentally little idea of what they wanted. Federalism, in short, was a compromise between Union and no union and, like all compromises, it was difficult to define. The importance of the storm in the ranks of the Association over federalism is that, at least since Clontarf, it revealed how emphatically O'Connell had relinquished the pursuit of Repeal. It also showed how Davis came to accept federalism because he saw it as a kind of a half-way house to independence. He also hoped that it would bring some liberal-minded Protestants, possibly including the Hutton family given that Annie's uncle, Robert Hutton, was a leading federalist, closer to nationality. Finally, Duffy proved how clear-sighted he was with his rejection of the whole idea. Indeed, to the benefit of future generations, it is the one instance in the relationship between Davis and Duffy in which Duffy took the lead and Davis followed. In the admittedly unlikely event that federalism had been accepted by England in the 1840s, or later, Ireland would have been inexorably welded further into an economic, political and, more importantly, cultural union with England that would have rendered the struggle for nationality and independence fruitless.

In the solitude of Derrynane O'Connell became either anxious about his leadership or irritated because no response had been forthcoming to the bait he had thrown out to the federalists after his release from Richmond prison. At the Association meeting in Dublin on 7 October 1844, a lengthy statement from him was read. The Liberator, who had proclaimed 1843 as Repeal Year, said, 'For my own part, I will own, that since I have come to contemplate the specific differences, such as they are, between simple "Repeal" and "Federalism", I do at present feel a preference for the Federative plan as tending more to the utility of Ireland and to the maintenance of the connection with England than the mode of simple Repeal.' He awaited that 'plan for a Federative Union before I bind myself to the opinion I now entertain'.[35] Thus spoke the leader who had rallied the vast majority of Catholic Ireland to Repeal of the Union. In the long run, O'Connell could not think of Ireland without the British connection but he still wanted some form of legislative independence for Ireland. What he could not see was Davis's dream of a free and independent nation embracing all the Irish.

By late 1844, O'Connell's political judgement had led him to conclude that mere speechmaking and crowd-gathering were not going to bring about Repeal and that, in any event, the English were not going to concede it. Provided he could gain the backing of the powerful Protestant federalists in the north and south, he thought that there may be some chance to persuade the men across the water to listen to a plea for a federal system.

Meanwhile, Davis was in Belfast trying to drum up support for federalism and to bring about some form of cohesion between Dublin and Belfast on the question. While there, he read O'Connell's statement but did not take the same degree of umbrage at it as Duffy had done. Duffy was alone, with both Davis and Dillon away, but he knew instinctively that 'O'Connell's surrender might be fatal to the national cause by killing popular confidence, and that even as a stroke of policy it was a mistake.'[36] Davis could not be expected to do an about face, given his current negotiations, so Duffy wrote a letter in his own name to O'Connell and published it as a leader in the *Nation*. He repudiated O'Connell respectfully but forthrightly on the grounds that, in commonsense terms, a system of federalism between the two countries was 'an impractibility', that the Repeal Association would lose its purpose and that a federal system would 'perpetuate our moral and intellectual subjection to England'. Underlying his words was the accusation that, without consulting anyone, O'Connell had taken a stand potentially fatal to an Association of which the members, in good faith, had joined to achieve the specific objective of Repeal.[37]

Davis, on his return to Dublin, after discussions with Duffy and O'Brien, had no hesitation in accepting Duffy's stand. Were it the case that, even in part, federalism had attracted him for personal reasons in that it brought him closer to the world inhabited by his own family and that of Annie, he was both courageous and generous when he wrote, 'Let the Federalists be an independent and respected party; the Repealers an unbroken league – our stand is with the latter.' He was not so much repudiating federalism as he was trying to undo the damage caused by O'Connell. The old fascination with, loyalty to and love for the Leader would never die. He wrote to O'Brien to explain his apparent ambivalence, 'He is too closely bound up with Ireland for me ever to feel less than the deepest concern for his welfare and reputation.' They remain some of his finest lines.[38]

O'Connell smarted over the repudiation of his federalist stand, but tried to put a good face on things. In a letter to the *Kerry Examiner*, he still held that federalism may be the best way to make 'the connection with the British crown more strict, permanent and inviolable' but he would talk about it no more until the federalists said what they wanted.

At his first Association meeting on 25 November, he opened with 'Hurrah for Repeal', attacked the 'young gentlemen who began to exclaim against him' and, to the relief of the *Nation* men said 'Federalism is not worth that' and snapped his fingers.[39] All this had taken place at exactly the same time as the onslaught, for alleged infidelity, on the paper, and on Davis. Very few observers at the time doubted that the challenge to O'Connell's authority over federalism was directly responsible for the campaign of vilification against the *Nation*, but Davis refused to make any connection because his main motive remained that of saving the cause. What mattered was the ending of discord among the leaders and that Repeal was back on the agenda. Davis wrote, 'we will carry the Repeal organisation into every parish, and wait until our leaders tell us we are organised enough, united enough, and educated enough to use the first opportunity.' What first opportunity he expected to get, unless through the use of force, Davis never made clear.[40]

Some sections of the press rejoiced in O'Connell's discomfort and tried to widen the breach further between him and the young men. *Tait's Magazine* was especially forthright in summing up the situation in terminology that surely rankled with O'Connell and his close associates of old. The writer led off with the words 'The Agitator has ceased to be master of the agitation ... He cannot now do what he will with his own.' The reason given was that, behind him, stood a powerful group with even greater influence than his. O'Connell's turnabout on federalism was put down to the influence of 'the young gentlemen' who were praised as having 'talent, sincerity and mental independence'. From now on Repeal, with its own life, would be independent of O'Connell's 'influence or control'. He would still be 'followed and submitted to, but always under the condition that he leads in the right direction'. Although there was some truth in the foregoing, the way it was expressed was surely triumphalistic in the fall of an erstwhile hero, if not malicious, and the potential it contained for real harm was manifest. What it overlooked was the genuineness of the young men's desire to follow and submit to their Leader, while standing on their own right to stick fast to their principles. As Duffy said, they did not expect O'Connell to come out and admit that he had been in error. All they wanted was that he return to wholehearted dedication to Repeal and, insofar as personal relations were concerned, they were not going to be permitted to obscure the main objective. To some degree they revealed that their maturity was greater than that of their Leader's and certainly far greater than that of some of his lieutenants such as John O'Connell.[41]

For O'Connell it was not easy to feel secure unless he knew that he had a man's loyalty, and he made that plain in a petulant way even to his long-standing ally O'Neill Daunt who stood against him on federalism. Davis, however, was happy to write to Madden to say 'I have been walking between two craters, O'Connell and the bigots, but for the present I have succeeded.' He knew in his heart that among his Leader's failings there was no trace of bigotry. He had not received O'Connell's letter and, given the silence, the older man must have wondered where they stood. O'Connell wrote to Smith O'Brien on 9 November and said he thought he had lost all influence with Davis who was 'in *no good temper* with him' over the Murray affair, but 'what can I do?' he asked plaintively. He also thought that Davis was 'quite led away by his fondness for Church and State connection and State control'. It was a strange thing to say about Davis by O'Connell who had scarcely departed from the stand he took in 1825 when he was asked before a Lord's Committee whether he was in favour of state payment of clergy. He replied in the affirmative and said further that he was 'quite convinced that the object of the Catholic clergy and laity in Ireland is sincerely and honestly to concur with the government in Ireland so as to consolidate Ireland with England completely ...' Davis's attitude to the state, as well as to consolidation with England, was far removed from that of O'Connell. Nonetheless, the older man need not have worried. He would never lose his influence over Davis.[42]

There was still much work to be done and one project to which Davis turned his energies was the formation of a National Club. His background in a military family, his comparative youth, perhaps even the emotional strain under which he was living and the mores of the times probably explained his enthusiasm. Another explanation is that, at the time, there was little else to do at Conciliation Hall but, above all, he was determined to use any means to press on with the development of nationality. During their incarceration in Richmond Brideswell, the prisoners discussed an idea, probably initiated by a barrister, Matthew Moriarty, that a National Club should be formed.[43] The Club was to be named the '82 Club in memory of the Volunteers of 1782 and a communication to prospective members issued forth from the prison stating its object as 'the promotion of the principles of nationality' by commemorating 'the more important events of Irish history, in connection with the establishment of a free Parliament'. Subscriptions would be one guinea and a 'handsome' uniform would be worn at its three annual functions, as well as at the annual ball. The list of initial members was impressive, including O'Connell and the other state prisoners, as well as Davis, Smith O'Brien and Henry Grattan.[44]

Davis took to the idea as he thought it would appeal to men with little interest in Repeal, and even to those who positively turned away from the cause, which they thought was mere O'Connellism. He also hoped that the Club would help to reawaken the spirit of nationality in his Protestant brethren. He said that the Volunteers 'presented the finest spectacle that any people ever looked upon', and that 'they were the children and the champions of the state'. He asked,

> And who were these men? They formed the Protestant nationality of Ireland. They were the embodied wealth and intellect and valour of Irish Protestantism. And let it not be forgotten that when the arms of freedom resounded in Dungannon, and when men's eyes were dazzled with approaching liberty, the Protestant Volunteers proclaimed aloud that it was not for a sect alone they had drawn their swords, but for a People. They would not ask nor take freedom for themselves alone – they thought their Catholic countrymen as worthy of its blessings. [As for the Catholics] they are now this moment engaged with some of the best of the Irish Protestants, in a glorious effort to restore the work of the Irish Volunteers, and to rebuild that edifice of freedom so ruthlessly and foully overturned in 1800.[45]

Davis thought that the Club could replace the unrealised Council of Three Hundred and, even more to the point, he saw it as the beginning of a national militia because 'without popular arms, popular liberty' was always unsafe. He thought that 'The youth of Ireland will flock to the new standard. Before a year has passed one thousand men will belong to the unarmed national army. The new organisation will form an obstacle graver than England has ever yet met with in Ireland.' He rejoiced that, of the five vice-presidents three were Protestants, and in order to jealously guard the membership he moved that admission be gained only by ballot.[46] In Dublin Castle, the idea of a national militia, with its overtones of the French Revolution, was probably a source of alarm, but real concern was premature because no one except Davis seemed to know what the functions of the Club were to be. He did his best to drum up membership and the first meeting was held with O'Connell as president. Davis wrote telling Madden that he must join the Club and he entreated Denny Lane to get as many Corkmen as possible to join because 'This club can do all we want, if it be earnestly and resolutely supported.' In a firmly-worded response, Lane posed strong objections to the shape and spirit of the Club. He thought that it would weaken Repealers and strengthen no one else. Furthermore, he was sure it would have no appeal in Cork where the people hated uniforms and not even the town councillors wore robes. His explanation for their attitude was 'the morbidly keen sense of the ludicrous which Cork men generally possess'. To further make his point on the good taste of Corkmen and their abhorrence of 'the old Irish fanfaronade', Lane said, 'Tom Steele could not live a week in Cork.'[47]

Thus, Davis had begun to search with great intentness of purpose for other avenues to achieve the objective to which he had devoted his adult life. Nationality, to the extent that it had looked to Repeal for its development and implementation, was a broken reed that only time and patience could again make strong. The methods already in place through education and culture, including the attempt to revive interest in the Irish language, were the path set out on by Davis and he had given his all to them. Yet, unless some steps could be taken towards the formation of a militia, even if at first unarmed, all would be lost at the moment the English decided again to force their will on Ireland by arms, or even by the threat of arms. Clontarf was the most recent reminder of that painful fact, but it would not be a simple thing for the English to go on repeating Clontarf, especially were it possible to attract Protestant elements to the Club in sufficient numbers and of the requisite standing to command respect both in Ireland and in England. Davis, therefore, saw the Club as the beginning of a resistance movement in Ireland even if, as yet, his fellow members had not seen its potential.

His next step was to turn his attention to the design and price of the uniform the Club members would wear, given that he thought it would 'serve as a model for the uniform of the next national army'.[48] He wrote to tell O'Brien all about his quest. The details of this affair of the uniform reveal Davis's determination to ensure that the appropriate icons were adopted for the public image of the Club. As he told O'Brien, he went around the Dublin shops pricing material because some young men had 'strongly objected' to a cost that would go beyond twelve guineas for the uniform. He found that lace and embroidery were dearer in Dublin than London, which surely did not surprise him. Lace was 10s a yard, buttons 8s a dozen, while two embroidered shamrocks would cost 6d. He drew the design himself, paying particular attention to the collar, cuffs and flaps, on each of which there were to be shamrocks. 'A heavy flap would be very ugly,' he thought and he wanted the cuffs to be 'hussar fashion' because 'The common cuff embroidered is thick and weighty looking.' The design pleased him because it promised to be 'novel, gentlemanly and handsome'. All in all, with pantaloons and cap, the uniform came to £12.1.0, which made it come in slightly under the twelve guineas.[49]

Apart from a further measure of Davis's industry, his meticulous attention to detail and his determination to bring to its best possible

'82 Club uniform (courtesy of National Museum of Ireland).

conclusion whatever he set his hand to, this episode proves that he was sure he had a new instrument of nationality in his hands and he was not prepared to let mere details bring it to risk. The Club met for its first large gathering in the form of a banquet at the Rotonda on 16 April 1845. Over a hundred uniformed members sat down to the banquet while 'About three hundred ladies shed a grace upon that scene, and a galaxy more fair never graced the banquet hall of heroes.' O'Connell was in the chair as President and the conviviality of the evening indicates that the shadows of division in the Association had not yet clouded friendships. Proceedings began at 6.30 with a toast by O'Connell to the Queen, in which he said that 'the sincerity and reality of our allegiance to the throne, and our attachment to the connexion through the crown of Great Britain with that country is not to be doubted and will never be diminished.' There were toasts to the Volunteers, to 'the Legislative Independence of Ireland', to 'the memory of Grattan and Flood', and to Moore. MacNevin rose to great heights of oratory while toasting the memory of Molyneux, Swift and Lucas and Dr Cane, whose responsibility was 'The memory of Griffin, and Banim, and the fame of the living novelists of Ireland', addressed himself to the 'Brothers of the green parliament', meaning the gentlemen who sat before him.[50]

Nonetheless, more practical matters were toasted, in the selection of which Davis may have had a hand. Among them were 'the agricultural interests of Ireland', 'the revival of Irish trade and manufacture', ably proposed by John O'Connell, and 'the men who have made science illustrious in Ireland', during which there was much satisfaction taken in that there were now 'seven complete medical schools' in Dublin. Toasts to the Irish stage and to music followed separately and towards midnight, Davis was called upon to propose the thirteenth toast, 'To the advancement of the Fine Arts in Ireland'. He was reluctant to do other than simply propose it without engaging in 'oratory', given the lateness of the hour. O'Connell would have none of it and insisted warmly that he 'go on 'till one' which Davis did, being listened to 'with rapt attention', thereby helping to establish his reputation as an orator. He began with, 'There is a close connexion between national art and national independence. Art is the born foe of slavery, and of the friends of slavery – of ignorance, sensuality, and cowardice ... but it never flourished under a foreign rule ... Its highest conceptions seem denied to provinces, like progeny to the imprisoned eagle.' He then argued that it was not necessary for a country to be large to foster high art, but that 'meanness of spirit' was the true barrier to its development and he asked 'how can he who never heard the shout of freemen – never looked on the "sight entrancing" of citizens arranged in arms for freedom ... how can he reach the rank of a national artist?' Davis concluded that the Irish temperament and the 'romantic and believing minds' of the people, coupled with the beauty of Ireland, 'more variable and suggestive than any in the world' meant that high art could, and indeed must, flourish among them,' and that Ireland could compete with Europe in the field.[51] Yeats who, as a poet, wanted to be one with 'Mangan, Davis, Ferguson', looked back to the writings and speeches of Davis as the seedbed of his own intellectual quest and the fulcrum for 'the arts we have begun the making of' and Davis's speech was his own finest testimony to his role in making the future possible. However, despite the high oratory of Davis and others, the '82 Club and all the dreams Davis had for it, came to nothing. It died quietly after the split in the Repeal ranks in 1846 because no splendid uniform, even embroidered with shamrocks, could have clothed the skeleton of Repeal after Clontarf. More to the point it died because he who inspired and led it was already dead.[52]

Throughout all this period, the *Nation* had continued to develop its own lines of thinking, many of which diverged from the attitude of O'Connell. In the words of *Tait's Magazine*, the paper had constantly proved that it was 'not a mere O'Connellite, nor a mere Catholic organ. It has a life of its own.' Especially on 'the morality of war' they hold their own opinions and regard O'Connell's 'little doctrine' on war as a. mere 'crotchet', but they respect in him what they would reject in anyone else. Furthermore, 'This war section of the Repeal party are as practical and business-like a set of men as the pacific O'Brien section,' which was an interesting distinction given that O'Brien had been accepted as the chief during O'Connell's imprisonment and had never objected to the policies of the so-called 'war section'. *Tait's* analysis that it was always nonsense to talk war and have no means to wage it was certainly consistent with Davis's thought. Even when he urged government control of the railways, he appeased the possible fears of some of his readers that England could use the railway as a weapon of war by writing, 'A single night would render it incapable of use' and that it was good to see it built because 'it would be our's directly.' This kind of mild sedition probably caused *Tait's* to exaggerate in the statement 'We doubt whether the British Empire contains within its limits a set of more dangerous enemies to its integrity and power ... than this war section of the Irish Repealers.' Perhaps there was a feeling that a rising in Ireland would cause similar risings around the world against British power. In any case, it all meant that the *Nation* continued to be read with great interest throughout Ireland, as well as in the inner chambers of Dublin Castle and probably even at Westminster itself.[53]

It is possible that O'Connell's loathing of private vendettas which thrived in the atmosphere of Whiteboyism, Ribbonmen and similar bodies, was partially responsible for his rejection of violence in any form. Davis stood four square with his Leader in rejecting private acts of vengeance, which he considered one of the most shameful aspects of Irish agrarian life, but he made a distinction that could not have been lost on O'Connell. When, through acts of agrarian violence, six lives were lost in November 1844 in north Munster, Davis called them acts of 'mad and wicked murders', and asked 'is injustice to be remedied by blood?' He appealed to those responsible by reminding them that the Repeal Association was seeking justice for tenants, and adding, 'We have another claim on their faith. We are none of those who, when the worst wrongs are inflicted, and other means fail, would shrink from war,' which again must have been uneasy reading for his Leader.[54]

There was a difficulty also between the *Nation* and O'Connell on the question of slavery in America. O'Connell had set his face in the most determined manner against slavery, which he regarded as abhorrent, and this attitude was made even plainer in respect of Texas, 'the voluntary Botany Bay of America', which, by annexation, would simply increase the number of slave states. It is possible that O'Connell's attitude to slavery had been strengthened by some of the material he read. Joseph Sturge and Thomas Harvey published their *The West Indies in 1837* in 1838. Sturge sent an advance copy to O'Connell on 12 December 1837 and parts of the book are graphic in their description of the evils of slavery.[55] Money that came from the Irish Repeal bodies in America to the Association in Dublin was seen by O'Connell as tainted with the blood of slaves and therefore to be rejected. His son, John, finally said about the contributions that came from American-based Repeal bodies, 'Perish the vile trash.' In the end, O'Connell seemed to become almost paranoiac about America, and finally antagonised practically all organised support for Repeal there by telling England that, were justice done to Ireland, she would come to England's aid to 'pull down and humble the proud American eagle in the dust'.[56] As in practically all that he had stood for in his life, there was also much nobility in O'Connell's stand on slavery, although he had not refused to accept American donations to the cause in the days of Emancipation. There is also some possibility that the inflexibility of his attitude to slavery was closely linked to his determination to distance himself from America in order to appease Whig unease at his alliance with potential enemies of the Empire.

At the same time, there was some good sense in the contrary argument mounted by Davis, even if it smacks of opportunistic pragmatism as it has since been judged.[57] To him, Repeal in Ireland, not slavery in America, was the paramount issue for the members of the Association, and he held that Repeal, because it was for all the Irish, was a greater ideal to aim at than Catholic Emancipation had been and therefore support from America should also be accepted to achieve Repeal. In their own private role, the members of the Association could hold as strong a set of anti-slavery views as they wished, but it was not a matter on the agenda of the Association and therefore should not be canvassed or used as an argument to condemn all Americans. Personally, Davis said he was antislavery and 'I would hail [its] abolition as a great boon to humanity and freedom,' but 'We court, and are most grateful for the sympathy of America.' Therefore, he regarded it as futile to arouse American antagonism and jeopardise the reception of funds from America by strident condemnations of slavery.[58] Only a rash judgement would reject Davis's stand as unprincipled even though, in retrospect, greater dignity lies in O'Connell's.

At the same time as these disagreements were taking place, on other and more dangerous grounds, the *Nation* had started to take a differing stand to O'Connell. Several strands were mixed together in the response of the Leader to a group of initiatives that the Tory government had started to make to the benefit of Ireland. Religion, never far from the centre of Irish life, entered into many of them and O'Connell, whose genuine devotion and loyalty to his Church had grown stronger with his passing years, increasingly saw questions pertaining to religion through Catholic eyes. Politics also could never be far away, because it was almost axiomatic in the thinking of O'Connell that the only good that could come to Ireland would be through the Whigs. He had much justification for his adverse attitude to the Tories because Peel wanted to divide Catholics by a carefully selected set of conciliatory acts and thus break their unity, although he accepted that the system of favouring landlords and Protestants, thereby continuing their monopoly of land and power, was unjust and dangerous, 'but above all it is utterly impractical.'[59]

On the other hand, even the Catholics among the young men, whatever about the strength of their personal adhesion to the Church, did not share the same kind of loyalty to, and enthusiasm for, Catholic causes as O'Connell, at least in the immediate sense. Their whole striving in the political and cultural spheres was for nationality and to Davis, who had constantly made plain his thirst for justice for Catholics, nationality was increasingly assuming a religious tonality. When a rumour went about that the queen was to visit Ireland in 1845 he wrote, 'let her not be falsely made to hope that the Priests of Nationality shall stop their anthems because a Monarch has come in.' He added, 'Let her come, and right welcome, but sooner may the sod wither from our land, and bare the bones of our martyrs to our famished eyes, than Ireland, for courtesy or favour, halt in her march to Independence.'[60] The young men felt no allegiance whatever to either Tory or Whig, whether in Ireland or in England and they were like Archbishop MacHale, who all his life had striven for much the same ends as Davis and his friends, and wanted 'no compromise with Whigs, or Tories, or with any political party whatever'. Furthermore, they neither expected nor hoped for favours in the way that O'Connell had done for years from his political allies in England. Their one concern was the good of Ireland and justice for its citizens, Catholic or Protestant. Thus they were not inclined to scrutinise with the same keenness as O'Connell, nor turn to the bishops for a judgement, on any measure that bore upon Catholic interests that they deemed to be consistent with justice.[61]

As a first measure towards either justice or division, the Peel government decided in 1844 to bring forward a Charitable Bequests bill that would give the Catholics representation on the Bequests Board, which in that year had forty-nine Protestants to one Catholic. The Board would henceforth consist of thirteen persons, five of whom had to be Catholics, including three bishops. The bill also proposed to reform the giving of donations and bequests so that the Board could have property vested to it in trust for the maintenance of Catholic clergy and churches. On the face of it, the bill seemed a just step but O'Connell attacked it with vigour and the O'Connellite press denounced it as 'hellish', 'treacherous', 'insidious' and so forth.[62] Within the Association there was disquiet, especially among the young men, at O'Connell's attack on the bill. The *Nation* decided to take a neutral stand but much work was done to get up a report on the bill by the committee of the Association, which finally came down largely in favour. Davis was distressed by O'Connell's refusal to accept the report, which he judged as a means of trying to impose his own opinion on the question and he saw clearly that the Leader was now allowing himself to be led by bishops such as MacHale of Tuam and Cantwell of Meath. The latter had gone as far as to threaten with excommunication any Catholic in his diocese who tried to make use of the new provisions entailed in the bill. Davis was concerned that O'Connell and his allied bishops were 'doing *horrible* injury to our cause' and wanted O'Connell to quieten MacHale down. It was too late to stop MacHale, 'the lion of the West', whose loudest roar was that 'no ecclesiastic, possessed of the least regard for the interest of religion, would ever consent to becoming an agent in working a Bill of such infernal machinery,' because any measure taken by the Tories was almost inexorably 'hostile to our holy religion'. MacHale, despite his sincerity, proved his own lack of prudence and judgement when it came to matters that emanated from England, and O'Connell, who reserved his deepest suspicions for anything that came through Tory hands, did the same by aiding and abetting him.[63]

The end result was exactly as Peel wished because O'Connell had played into the hands of the Tories. The bishops were divided, as was the Catholic laity, and when three bishops, including Murray, archbishop of Dublin, and Crolly, archbishop of Armagh and primate of all Ireland, decided to serve on the Board, Peel saw it as 'signal triumph over O'Connell and MacHale' while Eliot, chief secretary for Ireland, wrote to him from Dublin Castle, with some exaggeration to say that, as a result of the new Board, 'The "Roman Catholic party" as such has ceased to exist. O'Connell can no longer rely on the support of the Church.' It was an exaggeration because there had never been a Roman Catholic party, unless one was in process of being formed since Clontarf, and at no time was it the case that, at least in the person of Murray, and several other bishops, the Irish Church was in any sense united behind O'Connell even if the aged pope in Rome always showed a keen interest in the progress of Repeal. Nonetheless, it is true that Repeal had been discredited even further because O'Connell had been discredited. He had seen himself as 'one of the body-guards of the bishops', but they had decided they could do without his protection from 'the wily serpent' in Dublin Castle.[64]

In early 1845, a previous rumour on Maynooth was made concrete when Peel offered to treble the annual grant to the College, from £8,928 to £26,360, together with a capital grant of £30,000. The Protestant outcry throughout England, as well as in Ireland, was such as to cause the queen herself to be appalled because it was 'not honourable to Protestantism to see the bad and violent and bigoted passions' that were being aroused.[65] Peel saw the advantages accruing from the bait he held out in that a hierarchy that accepted his liberality with gratitude would have to show restraint in matters of Irish nationality. There was no way in which O'Connell and his followers in Conciliation Hall could oppose the measure, even though it was brought forward by their worst enemies in London, so that they had to receive it with public approbation. Davis judged the 'doctrine of the Maynooth measure' to be 'religious equality', which pleased him greatly. He also took pleasure in the outrage of its opponents in Dublin who, as was customary, revealed their own deep-seated bigotry while enjoying the benefits of an endowed Church and University, the latter, according to Davis, being one of the richest in Europe. Thus, while Trinity educated 'the clergy of 850,000 Episcopalians', Maynooth had to educate 'the clergy of 6,500,000 Catholics on £8,000 a year!' he wrote.

He told Lane in March 1845 that 'The events at Maynooth will greatly weaken our enemies' and added that he was 'nearly recovered from the cold winter' and from the effects of reading a very long series of essays on Repeal for which the Association had offered prizes. He went on, 'I am left too much without affections; but I am coldly happy and dutiful.'[66]

The last months of 1844 had proven too much for Davis who had not had a holiday since 1843 and whose burden of work was immense. The atmosphere in his home had not become more cheerful with a son whose prospects in life were, in their eyes, being frittered away on a cause that, to them, was an anathema, although his sister continued to support him as best she could. Above all, the continued silence from Annie, still out in Italy with her mother, with the ever-increasing prospect that their separation would be permanent, had tended to bring him to despair. At the same time, O'Connell, despite the joyous days with his friends and his hounds in the South West at Derrynane had felt the loneliness of a man whose strength was ebbing away, whose finances were in disarray and whose heart was unmoved by human love, except for his family and a few close friends. It was good for Davis and O'Connell that, despite their differences on the Bequests Bill, they were at last able to come together on a related matter. It arose because the bill had given no redress to the Jesuits and to the members of other religious orders in Ireland. They were unable to benefit from the bill, if interpreted strictly, because they were still subject to a law that rendered them liable to banishment for life and, if found to be in Ireland three months later, they were to be transported for life, even though the law (10 Geo. 1V., c. 7, 1829) had never been enforced.

At an Association meeting on 24 February 1845 O'Connell rose to present a petition to Parliament for 'the emancipation of the religious orders' in Ireland.[67] Davis was present and seconded the motion 'as a citizen and a Protestant'. He praised O'Connell, and called him 'that good man who is beside me – whom I shall ever honour and never flatter.' He said the law was 'disgraceful and insolent' and merely 'a remnant of the old ascendancy', it 'disgrace[d] Protestantism and postpone[d] independence'. Therefore, on Protestant grounds, he sought the abolition of an 'impotent law' which could 'only excite and insult without ever rising to the woeful dignity of oppression'. Without much point in the circumstances, except to stress that he stood on principle, he reiterated his opposition to 'monastic institutions in this age' and said that, while he may be wrong, his 'conscientious Protestant conviction [was] against religious vows ... but I dislike oppression more.' Possibly thinking of the inhabitants of Elm Park, who stood between him and Annie, he returned to his old task of wooing the Protestants to nationality and concluded with 'Perhaps it is sectarian vanity; but I believe that were the Protestants of Ireland to devote themselves to her service they would hold the foremost place, so highly do I think of their energy and training. They are sacrificing their rank, their wealth, their honour, and their country to a traditionary quarrel.' His words illustrated what a heavy toll the attack on the *Nation* had taken on him. As never before, he had begun to talk in Protestant terminology tinged with ancient phobias of monks and vows and to exaggerate the future role of the Protestant minority, rather than, as he had always done, to see the strength of Ireland being achieved through the unity and equality of all traditions. The aberration was brief, but telling, because Thomas Davis was tired with a tiredness that had seeped into his spirit.

References

1. See O'Brien to Davis, n.d. mid 1844 in Duffy, *Davis*, p. 214.
2. T. C. Luby, *The life and times of Daniel O'Connell* (Glasgow, c. 1880), p. 536.
3. John O'Connell, *An argument for Ireland* (Dublin, 1844), p. 40.
4. Smith O'Brien to Davis, 1 October 1844, William Eliot Hudson to Davis, 30 September 1844, Davis papers, Ms 2644, NLI; Davis to Pigot, 29 September 1844, in *Irish Monthly*, vol. 16 (Dublin, 1888), p. 338.
5. Davis to Duffy, 21 September 1844 in Ms 5756, NLI.
6. Ibid. Duffy to Davis, undated, early October 1844, in Duffy, *Davis*, pp 246, 249; the wedding was reported in the *Nenagh Guardian*, 23 October 1844.
7. Madden to Davis, 3 July, 6 October 1844, Ms 2644, NLI; Daniel Owen Madden, *Ireland and its rulers since 1829*, 2 vols (London, 1843, 1844). Volume 2 contained the third part of the work.
8. Madden, *Ireland*, vol. 1, pp 300-1. In Madden's favour it should be noted that he also wrote an able pamphlet, *The impolicy and injustice of imprisoning O'Connell* (London, 1844).
9. See Madden, *Ireland*, pt. iii, pp 227, 233, 253-255.
10. O'Connell to Davis, 30 October 1844, Ms 129, NLI; Davis to Duffy, 21 September 1844, Ms 5756, NLI; Davis to Madden, n.d. October 1844, Duffy to Davis, n.d. October 1844 in Duffy, *Davis*, pp 246, 248-9; MacNevin to Davis, n.d. probably October 1844 in Ms 2644, NLI. Maurice O'Connell, 'Young Ireland and the Catholic clergy in 1844: contemporary deceit and historical falsehood', in *Catholic Historical Review*, vol. lxxiv (Washington, D.C., 1988), p. 200, judged Madden's book as 'probably the most scurrilous book ever written on Irish politics'.
11. See O'Connell in O'Faolain, *King of the beggars*, p. 70.
12. Duffy, *Davis*, p. 269.
13. Ibid., pp 269-70; Edward Walsh to Duffy, 19 July, 19 October 1844 in Ms 5756. He lays the blame squarely on Davis's shoulders for sneering at his poem 'O'Donovan's daughter' and suppressing two stanzas from another poem, unmentioned but probably 'Song of the penal days'. See *Nation*, 16 September, 19 October 1844.
14. Ibid., 14 September 1844.
15. O'Connell had helped found the *Dublin Review*. He bought it out in 1836, continued to help it financially and consistently supported it. Although a religious

journal, it was never apolitical. See Joseph L. Althoz, 'Daniel O'Connell and the *Dublin Review*' in *The Catholic Historical Review*, vol. lxxiv (Washington D.C., 1988).

16. See Davis's review in *Nation*, 12 October 1844.
17. Ibid.; Maurice R. O'Connell, 'Young Ireland', p. 206; MacHale in Bernard O'Reilly, *John MacHale Archbishop of Tuam*, 2 vols (New York 1890), vol. 1, p. 640.
18. *Nation*, 12 October 1844; Maurice O'Connell, 'Young Ireland', pp 199-207.
19. *Weekly Register*, 19 October 1844. Murray's letter was reproduced in the O'Connellite organ, *Pilot*, 21 October 1844. Murray was incorrect about Carleton's origins. He was born in Tyrone in 1794. See entry for Carleton in Anne M. Brady and Brian Cleeve, *A biographical dictionary*.
20. Davis to O'Brien, 18 October 1844 in Ms 434, NLI. He had just returned from a brief trip to Tipperary and was to leave for the north on the next day. No detailed record exists of these trips.
21. *Weekly Register*, 26 October 1844. *Pilot*, 28 October 1844. Maurice O'Connell, 'Young Ireland', p. 200, says that, in his opinion, the Catholics in the *Nation* group, 'with the possible exception of Charles Gavan Duffy', were neither anti-Catholic nor anti-clerical but of 'a sturdy independence.' He did not explain why he excepted Duffy.
22. *Nation*, 2, 9, 23 November 1844; *Pilot*, 8, 20, 25 November 1844. The quote from the *Vindicator* of 26 October 1844 is in Maurice O'Connell, 'Young Ireland', pp 210-11 and MacNevin's reply was printed in the *Nation*, 2 November 1844.
23. Duffy, *Davis*, p. 271.
24. The original letters are no longer traceable. Davis to Duffy is in ibid., pp 271-2, while John O'Connell's reply is on p. 274.
25. Davis to O'Brien, 27 October 1844 in Ms 435, NLI. O'Brien's reply is in Duffy, *Davis*, pp 272-3.
26. Davis to Staunton, n.d. but end of October 1844. In ibid., pp 273-4. The letter was marked 'Strictly private and confidential'.
27. O'Connell to Davis, 20 October 1844, Ms 129, NLI.
28. Davis to O'Brien, 3 November 1844, Ms 434, NLI. At the time, Duffy was unaware of O'Connell's letter to Davis. He probably came across it in Davis's correspondence forty years later when he was preparing the materials for his biography. See Duffy, *Young Ireland*, p. 227.
29. Oliver MacDonagh, 'The politicisation of the Irish Catholic bishops, 1800-1850' in *Historical Journal*, xviii, i (Cambridge, 1975), p. 52.
30. O'Connell, 'Young Ireland' where the title for pp 218-25 that contain the charges against Davis, and to a lesser extent Duffy, is 'The Culprit Discovered'.
31. Leigh Hunt to Duffy, 25 September 1844; John Frazer to Duffy, 21 October 1844, Ms 5756, NLI.
32. John Dillon to Adelaide Dillon, n.d. no later than 1847, in John Blake Dillon papers, Ms 6455/34, Trinity College, Dublin.
33. Russell to H. R. Bagshawe, editor of the *Dublin Review*, 16 March 1845 in Ambrose Macaulay, *Dr Russell of Maynooth* (London, 1983), p. 57.
34. Seamus Deane, 'Irish national character 1790-1900' in 'The writer as witness: literature as historical evidence'. *Historical Studies*, xvi, Cork, 1987, p. 108; Samuel Ferguson's poem is in 'Thomas Davis: cuttings and notes compiled by R. D. Walshe', c. 1915, Ms 14056, NLI.
35. *Nation*, 12 October 1844.
36. Duffy, *Davis*, pp 260-61.
37. *Nation*, 19 October 1844.

38. *Nation*, 2 November 1844. Davis to O'Brien, n.d. November 1844 in Duffy, *Davis*, p. 264.
39. O'Connell's letter of 30 October to the *Kerry Examiner* is in *Nation*, 9 November. For O'Connell's repudiation of federalism see ibid., 30 November.
40. Ibid., 16 November 1844.
41. For *Tait's Magazine* see Duffy, *Davis*, p. 267.
42. Davis to Madden, n.d. November 1844, Ms 5756 NLI; O'Connell to O'Brien, 9 November 1844, John O'Connell to O'Brien, 11 November 1844, Ms 434, NLI. For O'Connell in 1825 see William J. Walsh, *O'Connell, Bishop Murray and the Board of Charitable Bequests* (Dublin, 1916), appendix L, p. 39.
43. See Charlotte M. Kelly, 'The '82 Club' in *Studies*, xxxiii (Dublin, 1944), pp 257-62.
44. See communication dated 30 August 1844, Ms 435, NLI.
45. *Nation*, 19 April 1845.
46. Ibid.
47. Ibid.; Davis to Madden and Lane, n.d. November 1844 in Duffy, *Davis*, pp 251-3.
48. Thomas Davis, *History and proceedings of the '82 Club: Dublin 1845, by a member of the press*, Dublin, 1845, p. 7.
49. Davis to O'Brien, n.d. except Thursday night, probably late 1844 Ms 432, NLI.
50. *Nation*, 19 April 1845.
51. Ibid.; Davis, *History ... of the '82 Club*, pp 7-8; Charlotte M. Kelly, 'The '82 Club' p. 262. Carlyle had another view of the Irish, 'The Irish national character is degraded, disordered ... Immethodic, headlong, violent, mendacious; what can you make of the wretched Irishman?' Quoted in Seamus Deane, 'Irish national character', p. 99.
52. See Yeats in ibid. *Nation*, 19 April 1845; Robert Maunsell, *Recollections of Ireland* (London, 1865) summed up one powerful strand of opinion on Repeal. He said O'Connell's movement 'was ridiculous, and ended in a bubble', p. 104.
53. *Tait's Magazine* quoted in *Nation*, 6 July 1844, Davis, 'Control over Railways', ibid., 13 July 1844.
54. Ibid., 9 November 1844.
55. See report of John O'Connell's speech at the Repeal Association, 19 May 1844. John always spoke with the approval of his father. *Nation*, 25 May 1844. See also Joseph Sturge and Thomas Hardy, *The West Indies in 1837* (London, 1838). See inscription by Strurge to Daniel O'Connell on the fly leaf of the book in author's possession kindly given to me by Dr Maurice Bric. The book had passed into the keeping of John O'Connell.
56. *Nation*, 26 July, 9 August 1845.
57. See Maurice O'Connell, 'O'Connell, Young Ireland and Negro slavery', in *Thought*, vol. lxiv (Fordham, 1989), pp 130-6. The fact that Mitchel, as a resident in America later was pro-slavery does not detract from the anti-slavery stand taken on principle by the *Nation* in the early 1840s.
58. *Nation*, 5, 19 April, 9 August 1845.
59. See Peel's memo to Cabinet, 17 February 1844 and Peel to Lord Heytsbury, 8 August 1844 in Charles Stuart Parker (ed.), *Sir Robert Peel; from his private correspondence*, 3 vols (London, 1899), vol. 3, pp 106-77, 116-7.
60. *Nation*, 5 April 1845.
61. See MacHale's words in Bernard O'Reilly, *John MacHale*, vol. 1, p. 529.
62. See MacDonagh, *O'Connell*, p. 541 and Walsh, *O'Connell*, p. 541. Walsh was later Catholic archbishop of Dublin. He found it 'curious' that such an 'odious' and 'infernal' measure had worked so well for 71 years, without ever interfering with the rights of the Church, p. 3.

63. Davis to O'Brien, undated letter but probably of early 1845, Ms 432, Davis to O'Brien, 13 November 1844, Ms 434, line 3, vol. 1, NLI; MacHale in Walsh, *O'Connell*, pp 8-9; Bernard O'Reilly, *John MacHale*, vol. 17, p. 500.
64. Peel to Croker, 17 December 1844, Eliot to Heytsbury, December 1844, in Parker, *Sir Robert Peel*, pp 130-32; O'Connell in Walsh, *O'Connell*, p. 52. Walsh, mindful of his role as Murray's successor, wrote that O'Connell never 'attempted to make good the offensive imputations which he had so recklessly cast upon Dr Murray, nor did he withdraw them'. Ibid., p. 144.
65. Queen Victoria to Peel, 15 April 1845 in Parker, *Sir Robert Peel*, p. 176.
66. See MacDonagh, *O'Connell*, pp 542-3; *Nation*, 19 April 1845; Davis to Lane, n.d. c. March 1845 in Duffy, *Davis*, p. 285.
67. *Nation*, 1 March 1845.

Chapter 13

Parting of the ways

In October 1844 Davis had turned thirty. For at least eight years, the burning passion of his life had been Ireland, its independence and its destiny. His love for, and loyalty to, his family, achieving some kind of a station in life befitting his personal qualities, wanting to widen his horizons by travel on the continent, and his love for Annie Hutton had all been, in varying degrees, part of the mosaic of his visionary Ireland. Despite the waning of the Repeal Association, there had been no lessening in his drive towards nationality and the continued success of the *Nation* gave him a perfect vehicle and the confidence to persevere. The obstacles he had encountered, whether in his personal life or on the public stage, had made him more determined to press on because, with every passing week, he became increasingly convinced that only by independence would the Irish be ever a nation. Davis longed for the day when his people would claim their nationality with pride. Thus the dawning of a New Year gave him renewed hope. The false exaltation of the 1843, 'Year of Repeal', and 1844, the year of defeat, were behind him.

Daily, Davis saw the signs of growth in nationality about him in the 'incessant progress in literature'. The publication and widespread acceptance of the Irish ballads, songs and articles in *The Spirit of the Nation* and in *The Voice of the Nation,* to both of which he had contributed a preface, was enough to prove to him that he was right. He rejoiced that 'A Press, Irish in subjects, style and purpose has been formed ...' There was now 'a National Literature' for the wealthy classes written by scholars such as George Petrie (1789-1866), Eugene O'Curry (1796-1862) and John O'Donovan (1809-1862) who had all worked together on the Ordnance Survey. In archaeology, history, topography, antiquities and the Irish language they were unsurpassed in their day. Others such as the brothers John and Michael Banim, Gerald Griffin, William Drennan, Jeremiah John Callanan, Thomas Furlong, and Samuel Ferguson, had also written ballads and other literature that were 'true to Ireland' and everywhere there were signs of spring in the spirit of the people. The work of some of the writers was often found in the pages of the *Dublin University Magazine*, where it reached an audience among the intellectual elite of the island.[1] In July, the first in the series that was to comprise 'The Library of Ireland' came out. It was Thomas MacNevin's *The History of the Volunteers of 1782*, and Charles Gavan Duffy edited *The Ballad Poetry of Ireland* which also came out in July. Three works by Carleton and *The Annals of the Four Masters* translated by Bryan Geraghty appeared about the same time while John O'Donovan's monumental edition of the same work was in process. The publisher and collector, John Daly had seen what was happening in educated circles and opened a bookshop in Dublin to sell 'new, rare and second hand Works Relating to Ireland and the Irish Language.' It is unthinkable that this flowering could have taken place three years previously and a good deal of it was a direct result of the message of nationality that Davis and the *Nation* had incessantly preached.

There were, however, ominous signs. During the winter of 1844-45, Davis's health had begun to deteriorate and at Christmas he told Pigot that he was 'deaf and breathless almost with a heavy cold, and dispirited over many things'. Nonetheless the very pressure of his concerns, he said, would force him 'to get well and fierce'. By February he was feeling better and with a flash of the old spirit he said how much he wished Pigot could be in Dublin to share the work, 'Committees are excuses, men are everything.'[2] He remained convinced that the best medicine he could take was exercise and he continued to walk regularly or to ride or drive, but even when so engaged his mind remained restless as it sought the source of nationality. He told Mitchel that, when he added on 'the quantity of exercise to keep me fit' to his other responsibilities, there was little time left for writing. As he seemed to be writing the greater part of the paper at this period, exercise was badly needed, even had he been in good health.[3]

Davis often took his exercise in Phoenix Park, going 'from one gate to the other by a winding road, through clumps of trees'. He had heard that the road was to be straightened, requiring many trees to be knocked down, and a 'new monster, the Police Barracks, has been thrust under our noses.' Again, the blame lay, as customary, in other than Irish hands. 'Has each dyspeptic pauper who comes over here to misrepresent the Queen a privilege to mutilate and destroy?' he asked of the viceroys. He demanded that 'these butchers of the picturesque' permit the Irish to still enjoy 'The hour of glory in the grass, and nature in the flower', but he could not end without asking 'Who has the dominion of the Park?' With his usual confidence he asserted, 'We know that if a National Government had it, the Park might be made the handsomest ornament that any city in Europe could boast, filled from end to end with attractions for the People of the town.'[4]

By March, he was able to tell Pigot that the weather had turned suddenly and had become 'as soft as Munster', which delighted him because 'the long windy parching cold has sickened everyone.' His warm supporter and committed nationalist, Dr Robert Cane of Kilkenny, sensing perhaps that Davis was wavering in how to make further progress with the cause, wrote an appealing and strong letter in which he said, 'You but half serve your country while your services are confined to the pen only. You have capabilities, if you had the *courage* of serving her as a speaker. Why not do it? Your usefulness and influence would be tenfold increased once you took up that position. Why not do it?' Cane pointed out that 'Some other man may soon occupy ground that should be yours, ground which he may occupy for mischief to the cause as effectively as you would have done it for the public good.' He asked Davis not to take offence, but to accept that not only his own destiny was involved but 'what is of still deeper import, the destiny of a country we both love and would die for' and he pleaded with him to 'act as becomes the man, the *time* and the circumstances'.[5] Perhaps as a result of Cane's letter Davis began to attend the meetings of the Association more often and even chaired a couple of them. On one occasion, he had to stop speaking because of a 'horrid sore throat' and on another he found his voice 'so wearisomely weak' that he turned to 'his friend' Maurice O'Connell, the finest of Daniel's sons, and asked him to speak for him. It is possible that he had reached a stage of such debilitation by mid-1845 that he was no longer able to speak publicly on any regular basis, even had he been so inclined.[6]

Nonetheless, there is no record of his having ever spoken publicly outside Dublin and, in the city, it was only within the confined circle of Trinity and the Repeal Association that he did so. There can be no question of his courage, which he had proved consistently to be a major virtue with him. He clearly had no personal ambition except to serve Ireland and going on to the public stage as a politician, and therefore required to attend at Westminster, would have been totally unacceptable to him at the time. The old conviction remained that he could best serve with the pen and perhaps the number of competent speakers in which the Association abounded, irrespective of whether they talked good sense, deterred him. Finally, there was the example of Ireland's finest orator, O'Connell, who had spent most of 1843 speaking for Repeal without furthering the cause one wit. All the 'monster meetings' and the demonstrations, Davis said to Mitchel in late May, 'are ruining us; they are *parading* the soul out of us.' Davis may have concluded that the time for speeches was over and it was now necessary to prepare on another level. He gave Mitchel a volume of

The Artillerist's Manual and told him '*that* was what we must all study now.'[7]

Despite the better weather, his weakened constitution did not allow him to regain his strength and Frederic Burton wrote to say how sorry he was to hear that he had been 'so ill' and hoped that he would be '*green* and fresh again'. Burton was also distressed because he could not accept Davis's teachings on nationality, bound up as they were with Repeal. He said that he wanted to separate 'the pure and abstract beauty and justice which I know lies at the bottom of *some hearts* from the poverty of spirit, the falsity, the selfishness, the *weakness* – the in every way degraded conditions that are mingled with the efforts now being made. It is saddening to see such opposed feelings linked together – it rots the tap root.' Although Burton asked Davis to 'forgive my plain talking', Davis surely continued to grieve that he was unable to win to his side at least a handful more of his Protestant compatriots. In particular, he longed to see the Orangemen of the north join with the Repealers in a common bond for the land they all lived in and loved. He had always admired their tenacity of purpose, spirit of independence and courage in adversity, all shown so clearly at the end of the eighteenth century, and he looked for the faintest evidence that again the Orangemen would turn back from religious feuding and be one with the men of the south. An article in the *Dublin Evening Mail* seemed to hold out the hope that the Orange and Green would unfurl a common banner and 'a new-born nation' would be born in unity. Davis was quick and eager to read the signs and wrote, 'Here it is at last – the dawning. Here, in the very sanctuary of the Orange heart, is a visible sign of nationality.' His ballad, 'Orange and Green will carry the day', set to the air of 'The Protestant Boys', expressed his joy,

> No surrender!
> No pretender!
> Never to falter and never betray –
> With an Amen
> We swear it again,
> Orange and green shall carry the day!

His joy was premature, how premature can scarcely be calculated, but hope was a virtue that Davis never lost.[8]

Already a member of the Royal Dublin Society, early in 1843 Davis had been elected to membership of the Royal Irish Academy where he soon began to play a role on its committees. With typical forthrightness he wished to see dropped 'these royalties' because, at the very least, no one was interested in them. He also pointed out that the spheres of concern of the two Societies were overlapping, giving as examples eight areas that could be divided among them to the benefit of both.[9] His pleasure in the foundation of the Irish Celtic Society was unbounded and it was his hope that Irish would be introduced into the national schools of the West and he expected the Society to foster that aim. He and Duffy were members of the provisional committee of the new Society and Davis wrote the prospectus that ran, 'to preserve the evidence and landmarks of a distinct Nationality by means of a more enlarged cultivation of the Language, History, Antiquities,' of a country that was 'the noblest *Relique* of the *language spoken* by the great Celtic family'.[10] With the years his knowledge of, and enthusiasm for, the language grew stronger and when he reviewed O'Donovan's *A Grammar of the Irish Language* that came out in 1845, he was sure that things were combining in such a way as to 'make this age the founding-time or epoch of the restoration for the Gaelic language'. Despite his enthusiasm, he had little success in persuading his friends to form a class to study the language, nor was he able to win their ready approval for the revival of the old Irish names for places in instances in which they had been anglicised. He had never lost the conviction that the language was 'the vehicle of history, the wings of song, the soil of their genius, and a mark and guard of nationality' and, given his attempt to master Irish history and the Irish language it was unfair to write that his knowledge was 'superficial and inexact' and that he 'knew no Irish, although retrospective piety has credited him with a wish to remedy that defect'.[11]

O'Donovan and O'Curry, acknowledged specialists in the field and the latter said to be 'probably the greatest native Irish scholar who ever lived', had come to Davis's aid when he and John Pigot insisted that proper names in the ballads and songs in *The Spirit of the Nation* be turned into Irish.[12] This almost caused 'an insurrection of the bards' who had written the originals in the *Nation* and now had to revise them, where needed, to fit the new metre and rhythms. Only their friendship with Davis could induce them to comply, but they did so with grace and much banter. Denis MacCarthy despaired and threatened to write no more because if he wrote the lines,

Let us go down
To pretty Kingstown,

Davis would be as likely to change them to,

Let us go down
To pretty Dunleary[13]

General Post Office, Dublin. Departure of the Crawling Coaches, 30 May 1893. The head pacificator calming the people.

and Richard Dalton Williams, a prolific contributor whose poems were collected and edited in 1894, sent back his corrected proofs with the words,

Lord save us
From Alaric Davis![14]

Duffy was prescient when he said that, instead of changing the names in *The Spirit*, it was better 'to await the possible future when the honourable members for Mallow and Fermoy [Davis and Pigot] will introduce a bill making the authentic spelling compulsory in official documents and national school-books' which is what eventually happened. He even had to struggle with Davis to prevent him from adding an introductory, and explanatory, verse to his noble ballad on Owen Roe O'Neill which would have spoilt its majestic opening entirely. All of this Duffy set down later in a delightful chapter in his *Young Ireland* entitled 'Recreations of the Young Irelanders'. In it the wit and erudition of the young circle of friends, using their highly competent, indeed profound knowledge of the English language, are apparent. Their good spirits, even in adverse times, were maintained but Davis was always the more serious member of the group and they delighted in making quiet fun of him.[15]

The Repeal Association had settled to a routine of fortress-holding throughout the early months of 1845 and the rifts that had arisen in the ranks in the previous year between the young men and the O'Connell group seemed smoothed out. In pursuance of a conscious deter- mination to make concessions to Ireland that would steal a march on the Whigs, while at the same time cause further dissension in Catholic ranks, Peel's government introduced a measure for higher education that envisaged the setting up of university colleges which would be open to all male Irish, irrespective of religion. They succeeded in the latter aim beyond even their highest hopes. In retrospect it is at first sight puzzling that matters regarded essentially by John Mitchel as of little moment, indeed as trash, should have so impinged on the committed members that the Association was rent asunder and its alleged objective, Repeal, made temporally to fade into insignificance. The fact was that the question of higher education was bound to cause dissension, given the attitude taken by most 'practical' Catholics, as O'Connell called them, that demanded some form of control over education by the Church.[16] The attempt made by Protestantism in earlier decades to woo Catholics from their allegiance to Irish nationality, so as to make them more acceptable, and useful, members of the British Empire had not been forgotten. Thus, any scheme that seemed to open the way to proselytism among the wealthier and more influential Catholics was bound to cause suspicion. The government's proposal was, therefore, potentially divisive, coming as it did at a time when, on the side of O'Connell, the objective of Repeal had become secondary. The men associated with Davis and the *Nation* could only look upon the proposal with acceptance of the principle but with deep dismay, bending every sinew as they were to keep the principal cause of Repeal alive.

Once it was known that the move towards colleges was afoot, O'Connell, who had wavered from one stand against mixed education to another of favouring it since the 1830s, said at a committee meeting of the Association in the autumn of 1844 that 'I have been for years and still am an advocate for mixed education.' He did, however, want to see the parents free to decide whether they wanted their children educated in a mixed or separate system and made the strange statement, in a body that was supposed to be undenominational, that the Catholic bishops should be consulted on the matter and he would do all he could to enforce whatever a majority of them decided. Possibly influenced by his son John, who was utterly against mixed education, by February 1845, O'Connell had changed sufficiently to tell MacHale that his opinion was 'decidedly favourable to the education of Catholics being exclusively committed to Catholic authority'. MacHale was never of any different opinion, but what brought O'Connell to take that stand in 1845 is unclear. Davis, however, had long been an advocate of mixed education for the youth of Ireland, and especially at tertiary level, given that the generality of Catholics, and indeed of the Protestants, had no opportunity to receive a higher education as Trinity was the only university in Ireland. Apart from the benefit accruing to Ireland from higher education, Davis was convinced that national unity would be greatly fostered by the close intermingling of young students during the formative years of their lives. It is scarcely surprising that he welcomed the proposal of the Tories to establish three colleges which would probably be located in Belfast, Cork and Galway. The colleges would be endowed by the state and they would offer a form of secular education that would not cross traditional religious boundaries. With customary vigour Davis demanded that there be 'guarantees against proselytism' by any one denomination.[17]

There was a considerable body of support in Ireland for the proposal on the colleges by almost half of the Irish hierarchy, together with nearly all the liberal and Repeal members of Parliament, the young men of the *Nation*, as well as the middle and upper classes of all religious persuasions. The problem for O'Connell was that bishops like MacHale of Tuam were nearly all his own followers and supporters in public matters and it was difficult for him to take a stand that would alienate them. In March 1845, O'Connell himself said that he would have remained neutral on the Bequests Bill, 'as he was on the education question', but that MacHale and Cantwell 'threatened to withdraw from the Repeal movement' had he not taken an anti-stand. The same pressure was probably also applied on the education question.[18] Furthermore, there was almost common consent that, with some modification on details such as the appointment of professors and the provision of chaplains for non-resident students, the proposal could be made acceptable to all but its intransigent opponents. To take a stand against the colleges therefore would line O'Connell up as a supporter 'of narrow and bigoted doctrines', but it was a risk he seemed prepared to run.[19] That it would also put him in direct opposition to a large and influential section, led by Davis, within the Repeal movement did not appear to cause him great concern.

Even before the bill was introduced into Parliament it had become clear that the O'Connells were prepared to make the issue one of old, Catholic Ireland and its concerns for denominational education, as well as a matter on which loyalty to the leadership was to be demanded. There is, moreover, every likelihood that they thought, were a breach to occur, it would be welcome in that everyone would then know where they stood so that the Association could revert to its old position without the irritant of unruly and subversive elements in its ranks. While Davis stood firmly by the rights of Catholics to justice in the matter of education, he had reached a position regarding religion in its place in education that made his public stand on the colleges ambivalent. He was not concerned with the arguments in themselves about the colleges, provided they did not affect the situation within the Association adversely. His purpose was to see the young men of Ireland, especially the disadvantaged Catholics, given an opportunity for higher education in a system that did not jeopardise their faith.

Davis wrote to John Mitchel in the midst of the turmoil within the Association and, although he said that his words were 'a very abstract way of suggesting my religious position', his meaning was clear. 'We are not likely to agree on Education or Religion. I have deep faith in mere Truth, and in informal humanity; and, moreover, I feel that an artificial education prevents that faith from being still deeper and more practical.' In other words, he preferred to see a system enshrined in the colleges in which no religious education whatever was officially imparted. Davis was not implying to Mitchel that he had become an atheist. He merely thought that education, with the pursuit of truth as its goal, was the ideal and that a person without religious faith, and therefore a part of 'informal humanity', could still pursue 'mere Truth'.

When an education was based on a religious faith, the pursuit of truth was likely to become artificial or constrained, with the result that religion, education and truth could all suffer. It was not a view shared by many in Ireland in the 1840s and Davis was wise not to enunciate it publicly were he to avoid further charges of atheism. As for Mitchel, he took a less complicated stand in that he was against the colleges, which he 'detested as much as the Archbishop of Tuam, but for a different reason, – not that they were "godless," but that they were British.'[20]

The furore that followed within the Association on the colleges left its mark on Davis and very probably contributed to his death. Even by some of his own closest intimates one aspect of his behaviour in the matter was criticised, while O'Connell's most recent biographer accused Davis of precipitating the 'scene' that led to the final denouement. The episode deserves, as a matter of justice, to be treated fully to illustrate the profound nature of the division between those who held to the tradition of 'old Ireland' and those who wanted that same tradition to blend with others in the making of a new nation. As MacDonagh notes, the question was one of religious liberty and he then went on, 'Looked at in one light, it was the 1940s challenging the 1970s; looked at in another, it was the opening skirmish in a campaign which grips Ireland still.'[21] The literature on the affair is extensive but the single, most in-depth study was done by Denis Gwynn. He was strongly critical of Davis, whom he claimed to have been arrogant, self-righteous, frequently 'the chief source of discord' and 'quite definitely anti-Catholic'. He regarded it as 'the tragedy of Davis that he could not appreciate or make allowance for the traditional Catholic view'.[22] Without entering into the matter of Davis's other alleged failings, it ought to be noted that the Catholic archbishops of Dublin and Armagh did not hold to the alleged 'traditional' Catholic view on the colleges.

The principal O'Connellite organ, the *Pilot*, under Barrett's editorship, had already decided that Catholics had to have 'purely Catholic Colleges' for their youth and that the bill was an 'Academic Education Fraud' intended to wean Catholics away from their faith.[23] On the other hand, the Association debated the matter at its meeting on 12 May 1845 and O'Connell said that he would oppose the bill with as much 'negative opposition' as he could, called the whole scheme 'absurd' and agreed with Sir Robert Inglis, who had condemned mixed education at Westminster by defining it as 'a gigantic scheme of Godless education', which words passed down to posterity, even among Catholics in far-off Australia. O'Connell also spoke of the immense patronage that would accrue to those who made appointments of 'crouching, snivelling, shuffling, half-Catholic, half-nothing renegade' professors in the colleges. He refrained from putting a motion forward on the grounds that there was 'some difference of opinion on the matter' and remarked that Peel, while he was 'bidding against me for old Ireland', was nonetheless trying to do good, but was misguided. To all this there was 'vehement applause' and Dillon Browne, M.P., showed his unfamiliarity with, or contempt for, proper procedures by seconding the motion that O'Connell had not put forward. Browne, whom Duffy later called 'a marplot in Conciliation Hall', said that mixed education was 'incompatible with the spirit of the Roman Catholic religion', castigated the *Nation* roundly and showed that he, at least, intended to join battle with the young men by quoting, irrelevantly but provocatively, from a letter in which the author rejected any weapon but 'reason' to achieve Repeal. O'Connell interjected, asking who was the writer of the letter and Browne replied that it was from Smith O'Brien who was absent from the meeting. To this, there was loud applause that 'lasted several minutes'.[24]

In case any of the young men had misread the situation, John O'Connell launched into a verbal onslaught on 'the abominable scheme for education'. He said that he could not conceive of any 'physical calamity that could befall Ireland that he would not think preferable to this present scheme of education, for it would bring everlasting ignominy and dishonour on the country, and do more to uproot religion and morality than a thousand penal laws (hear, hear).' Davis had arrived late and was unprepared to speak, but he did so at length and was constantly interrupted. He gave it as his judgement that the people wanted academical education, 'no matter from where it came (no, no, no)', and saw its acceptance as an instalment instead of a compromise. He gave 'positive and deliberate adhesion' to the principle of mixed education because in any country it tended 'to secure the union of men ... but in Ireland – in Ireland whose peculiar curse was religious dissension – that principle was invaluable.' While he would not surrender the appointment of professors in the new colleges to 'an anti-Irish government' and he protested against all English administration 'on the broad principle on which he demanded nationality for his country', he would not call the proposed system of education 'execrable' or 'dangerous to Ireland'. Rather, he thought that the principle of the bill was 'sound and wholesome', but insisted that the religious instruction of Catholics in the colleges be done by Catholics and that of the Protestants by Protestants. Finally, he was against the exclusion of Trinity from becoming part of a national university because he wanted to have 'the education of Roman Catholics level with the education of the Protestants – he as a Protestant demanded for Irishmen admission to the scholarships, professorships and fellowships of Trinity.' Present throughout this interchange of 'opinion' was Michael

George Conway who spoke of the prospects for Repeal in the north of Ireland. O'Connell was impressed and called him 'my friend Mr Conway', as he also called Davis.[25]

As an editor of a newspaper, Duffy, no longer able to attend meetings of the Association, decided not to let the matter of 'Academical Education' rest and wrote a hard-hitting editorial on the question which was run in the same edition of the *Nation* as the report of the debate. Duffy opened by saying that Sir Robert Inglis was 'a blockhead and a bigot' who, being a 'preposterous fanatic', even demanded the repeal of the Emancipation Act of 1829. Duffy was convinced that the great blight on Ireland was ignorance and he could not understand why the system of national education could be supported and the same system of mixed education so bitterly opposed at tertiary level. He wanted to 'knit the sects of Ireland in liberal and trusting friendship', and the new colleges seemed a step in that direction. However, if the government insisted on nominating the professors, Duffy was opposed to the bill. It is undeniable that, in the 1860s, both Duffy in Australia and Dillon in Ireland, who had stood firmly for mixed education in the mid-1840s, had changed their minds on mixed education for Catholics. By then, both men had changed in that they were politicians dependent on Catholic support but, more importantly, the Church had changed in Rome, Ireland and Australia. Under a changed Pio Nono, with the increasing loss of his papal states and the prescriptions of the Syllabus of Errors, the world of liberalism and all that it stood for, including mixed education, had become the enemy. In Ireland, Cardinal Cullen had become as intransigent as the pope, while in Australia his appointees to most of the bishoprics there echoed his, and the papal, attitude.[26]

In Ireland in 1845, there can be no doubt that the government had gone about the measure in a manner little calculated to appease those, whether in Ireland or in England, who thought with the *Times* that, 'When the student enters the pompous portico of the Academy at Belfast, or the lyceum at Cork, he will leave Christianity behind.'[27] The proper and sensible course that ought to have been taken by Peel was to have initiated private consultations with the Irish bishops before making public the details of the proposed measure. In such a way some form of agreement could have been reached with the less intransigent members of the hierarchy, such as Murray and Crolly. Once out in the open, the unacceptable details, as distinct from the 'principle' of mixed education had to be opposed by the bishops, so that the inevitability of the overall measure being rejected became well-nigh certain.[28]

Ironically, the relative importance of the debate on the colleges to other matters pressing on Ireland, and perhaps illustrative of Mitchel's irritation with such a degree of concentration on 'godless colleges and other trash', came in the same number of the *Nation* in which the first debate on the colleges was reported. It ran a review, probably by Davis, of a newly-released book by Thomas Willis, *Facts connected with the social and sanitary conditions of the working classes in the city of Dublin*, that gave the results of an inquiry into the living conditions of the workers in the city. In one parish north of the Liffey, St Michan's, there was an average of 16.51 inhabitants in each house, most houses had no sanitation with perhaps a dozen in 1,381 having water closets, and less than one in ten had any form of a water supply.[29] Perhaps the committee of the Association felt that other things besides education also needed attention, even if it could go no further than trying to show some degree of unity within its large membership of about eighty. At the next general meeting, O'Connell presented the report on the Land Question and Davis, who had worked hard with O'Connell on it, seconded O'Connell and spoke at length. He asked his hearers to 'look at the foul and fetid lanes in which the great mass of the population lived ... huddled together in filthy rooms', while the peasants couldn't even eat what they grew. In the past, the peasants were able to eat bread and potatoes, but now the absentee landlords enjoyed the first fruits of the land which meant that, without change, an agrarian war was inevitable. He asked those present 'Did they know what lumpers were?' and went on to tell them how he had entered 'a peasant's house, wearied with mountain toil, and hungry as ever man was, and he protested he could not, even under such circumstances, eat the potato on which his countryman was forced to live, it was so bitter and unpalatable.' His editorial on 'The State of the Peasantry' was a forceful appeal to justice and reason. He began tenderly with, 'In a climate soft as a mother's smile, on a soil fruitful as God's love, the Irish peasant mourns', but he then changed his pitch and said to the Ascendancy that, unless they acted, they would be 'a doomed race'. Davis concluded, 'Once more, Aristocracy of Ireland, we warn and entreat you to consider the State of the Peasantry, and to save them with your own hands.'[30]

Davis's tactical wisdom had sensed the danger of a complete split in the ranks of the Association and he had proposed a truce, which O'Connell accepted, until the bishops made their attitude public. The truce was futile as it only applied within the meetings of the Association, leaving both sides free to say what they liked in the press and elsewhere. Davis and others wrote in favour of the colleges in the *Nation* and O'Connell put the opposite case in the *Freeman's Journal.* The bishops met and agreed that, as the proposal stood, the colleges would certainly be a danger to faith and morals, but that 'fair and reasonable terms' should be worked out by the government and then they would co-operate. They did not insist that the only form of higher education they would accept would be one based on the denominational principle of separate, rather than mixed, institutions, although the traditionalist group wanted that outcome. The bishops were clear that they could not give their 'approbation' to the bill as it stood, but that they would send their suggested amendments to the lord lieutenant for presentation to the government. There is nothing in the bishops' statement to imply that, as a body, they were not prepared to accept mixed education, próvided the safeguards they wanted were put into place. Archbishop Murray, as chairman of the meeting, signed their 'Resolutions and memorial' and Archbishop Crolly moved the suggested amendments to the bill. MacHale accompanied Murray and Crolly to the Castle to present the memorial and he then leaked the document to the press to ensure that the government would place itself in the untenable position of seeming to give way under episcopal pressure were it to accept the bishops' amendments.[31]

This left the Association free to debate the matter on 26 May. Smith O'Brien opened by approving the bill with modifications and said that, as he had always been in favour of mixed tertiary education, it would be odd were he to oppose it now. In a speech lasting two hours, O'Connell began with the magisterial statement, 'I now as a Catholic, and for the Catholics of Ireland, unhesitatingly and entirely condemn this execrable bill.' He then thanked the bishops for condemning 'this abominable bill', which they had not done, either in whole or in part, in such unequivocal terms as he had used. Finally, he insisted that the colleges be rejected as dangerous to faith and morals and that there should be separate colleges for Catholics, Protestants and Presbyterians with, presumably, the government footing the bill for each of them. His son John followed with a virtual invitation to a parting of the ways by saying that he didn't want 'peace or reconciliation', gave his own interpretation of what the bishops had said, attacked Davis and the *Nation* and concluded with scarcely little less majesty than his father, 'I call upon the people of Ireland to decide between us.'[32]

Michael Joseph Barry, a member of the inner group of the *Nation*, gave support to the bishops' memorial in clear terms saying, 'I am indifferent whether the education which that memorial approves be called separate or mixed ... I am in favour of such a system as that memorial approves.' He went on to tell the meeting that he and the *Nation* group had put a document before the Liberator in which 'we avowed our determination to oppose any system of education which did not amply provide for the religious instruction of the people'. Thus, 'We advocated then, what we approve now,' meaning that they accepted the bill, provided it was modified according to the bishops' wishes. With astonishing simulation O'Connell said that he had 'conceived that document [of the *Nation* group] had been private', which leaves open the interpretation that he had not seen it as an olive branch, but that he had ignored it in order to achieve his ends of opposing the bill and destroying his opponents.[33] On the reasonable assumption that Davis had been party to the composition of the document, it makes hollow any accusation that he was not prepared to recognise the claims of the ancient tradition of Catholicism in Ireland to justice in the area of education. When Barry finished, several members rose to their feet, including Davis and Steele, asking permission from Matthew Moriarty, chairman on this occasion, to speak. Michael George Conway had come in late so that he had only heard Barry, but he was chosen by the chair to reply. Conway had been a contemporary of Davis at Trinity and his youthful promise was such that his tutor held he would outshine Davis in later life. He lacked the application, and perhaps the integrity, for a successful career and, according to Duffy, had 'fallen out of men's esteem'. Nevertheless, he had applied for membership of the 'Eighty-two Club', to find that he was blackballed, despite the fact that O'Connell had publicly referred to him warmly as 'my friend'.[34] It was an injudicious step to have rejected Conway, and one for which Davis had to pay in full.

Motivated either by revenge or a heightening of Catholic zeal, Conway opened by saying that St Patrick was 'no friend of, or patron of, masked infidelity – of mixed education'. He accused Barry of making 'a most Jesuitical speech (applause). He is for the bill and against the bill. There is an imbecility about him characteristic of his party and his principles ... My learned friend has said that on some matters connected with this question he is "utterly indifferent". Utterly indifferent! What a sentiment for a Catholic.' Barry rightly demurred at this false accusation, but to no avail. Conway then asserted that all the Irish people, including the Protestants, were with him and that 'every man who has any faith in Christianity, is resolved that it shall neither be robbed nor thieved by a faction made up of people who did not comprehend "the Irish character in the Irish heart (cheers)". Turning to the audience he said, 'Oh! you are not prepared to yield up old discord nor its sympathies to the theories of Young Ireland.' Finally, speaking as 'a Catholic and an Irishman', he said that he would resist any attempt at a Protestant ascendancy. This tirade of bigotry and false accusations, including the implication that the young men were 'masked' infidels and lacking faith in Christianity, would have deserved nothing but contempt from any fair-minded audience. Yet it was cheered to the echo, mainly because O'Connell applauded every sentence uttered by his ally and culminated his approval by taking off his cap and waving it over his head in triumph.[35]

Davis was the next speaker and, if his opening remarks are interpreted as insincere, bigoted or both, his customary detachment and unswerving fairness must have been unbalanced by the person of Conway and by the method of his attack. Based on his reputation for sincerity, there is, however, another interpretation of Davis's words that is also plausible. Davis referred to Conway's speech as 'useful, judicious and spirited', and to Conway himself as 'my old college friend – my Catholic – my very Catholic – friend'.[36] The description of Conway's speech was surely ironical, but it did not transgress the normal behaviour of opponents in a debate. However, given the Leader's reception of the speech and Davis's determination to maintain his reverence for O'Connell, as well as to keep the debate at a high level, there need be no reason to suppose that the description of Conway himself was insincere. That Conway and Davis had been acquaintances, perhaps even friends, at Trinity could account for the 'old college friend' remark. That Conway had been a Catholic in his student days, and was still a Catholic, was undeniable. Moreover, the intervention of Conway had been based on his avowed adhesion to his Catholicism and Irishness, so that to call him a Catholic was surely not to insult him, nor was it an insult to put him among those who were, in this particular instance, revealing themselves as the most Catholic of the Catholics, indeed more Catholic than several of the leading bishops of Ireland. To call Conway 'very Catholic' was descriptive rather than offensively sarcastic, but perhaps it was too close to the truth for some present in Conciliation Hall.

O'Connell chose to interpret Davis in the worst light possible. He interjected with the remark, 'It is no crime to be a Catholic, I hope,' which surely begged the question as to whether it was acceptable to be a Catholic bigot and accuse another of not being a Christian at all, as Conway had implied of Barry and of those who stood with him on the colleges' question. Davis replied, 'No, surely no, for –' and O'Connell again interjected with, 'The sneers with which you used the word would lead to the inference.' There was immediate outrage and consternation among those present who had never had occasion to question Davis's sincerity and John Dillon tried so hard to restrain his rage that he burst a blood vessel. Davis, however, remained calm and addressed himself to O'Connell with an avowal of his lack of bigotry, his love for his friends, for his country and his dismay at the prospect that a lack of unity would again destroy Ireland,

> No! sir, no! My best friends, my nearest friends, my truest friends, are Catholics – I was brought up in a mixed seminary, where I

learned to know, and, knowing, to love my countrymen, a love that shall not be disturbed by these casual and unhappy dissensions (hear, hear). Disunion, alas! has destroyed our country for centuries. Men of Ireland, shall it destroy it again (no, no)?[37]

While O'Connell, who was close by, 'maintained a running comment to disturb and frighten me and to rouse the people',[38] Davis proceeded to express his 'strong approval of the memorial of the Catholic bishops' and of the proposals they had made to render the colleges acceptable to Catholics. His main argument was that the bishops had accepted the principle of mixed education, otherwise they would have rejected the colleges outright. In other words, the bishops had not asked for a separate system, run by the Church and financed by the state, in which Catholics would be educated. The fact that the modifications they had requested were likely to be rejected cannot be construed as a deliberate act intended to provoke a reaction which they could then reject but rather as a basis for genuine discussion and, hopefully, some suitable agreement. Within the Church, as within the Association, there were those prepared to accept mixed education as a principle. Davis stood firmly with those who did, while the O'Connells stood equally firmly with those who rejected it.[39] It is difficult to see how Davis can be accused of going on 'to further provocation, claiming, in a passage of perverse and contorted reasoning, that he and the Irish bishops were at one in their objections to the colleges bill'.[40] Davis was fully aware that some of the bishops were against the bill in toto, but he was entitled to base his argument on the memorial that had come from the bishops as a body. A fair reading of it establishes that the bishops did not reject the principle of mixed education.

O'Connell was immensely vexed with Davis. He had had his fill of his young allies whose provocation he was not prepared to tolerate further, and the occasion was on offer to clarify the situation. He accused Davis of perverting the meaning of the bishops' memorial, and asserted that the bishops had stood for Catholic education, which meant they rejected a mixed system. After a sideswipe at the *Nation*, 'a newspaper professing to be the organ of the Roman Catholic people of this country, but which I emphatically pronounce is no such thing', he directed himself at the wider target,

The section of politicians styling themselves the Young Ireland party, anxious to rule the destinies of this country start up and support the measure. There is no such party as that styled 'Young Ireland' (hear, hear). There may be a few who take that denomination on themselves (hear and cheers). I am for old

Ireland (loud applause). 'Tis time that this delusion should be put an end to (hear, hear, and cheers). Young Ireland may play what pranks they please. I do not envy them the name they rejoice in. I shall stand by Old Ireland (cheers). And I have some slight notion that Old Ireland will stand by me (loud cheers).[41]

O'Connell then sat down and Steele jumped to his feet to express his opinion on 'this iniquitous, delusive, and perfidious bill' and to prevent Davis replying. While Steele was speaking, Davis leant across Henry Grattan and told O'Connell that he was 'mistaken in supposing us a separate party, or that we ever called ourselves Young Ireland. It was a nickname given and used in jest.' In fact, realising that the name could serve as a pretext for dissension within the Association, they had attempted to disclaim it as soon as Madden had coined it in his book. O'Connell rose again and withdrew his use of 'Young Ireland' as applied 'to these gentlemen' and apologised 'in the most ample manner for any unpleasantness the allusion may have created'. He could scarcely have been unaware that, withdrawn or not, his statement that there was a party within the Association 'anxious to rule the destinies' of Ireland and, by clear implication, at odds with his own leadership, made public a division that nothing now could hide or heal. His profession of adhesion to old, Catholic Ireland, an adhesion that was always part of his being, did him credit for honesty and loyalty, but further complicated his leadership of a cause that depended upon unity among all the Irish for success.[42]

Patching up the broken peace was uppermost in Davis's mind when he rose to his feet again. Throughout the previous four years he had never given any grounds to anyone to suspect that his loyalty to O'Connell, as well as his affection for him, were anything other than genuine. Part of that loyalty depended on his courageous opposition to his leader when he deemed him mistaken. To have acted otherwise would have been to rank him with Steele and the assorted toadies who jumped to O'Connell's every beck and call. He now proceeded to state both his loyalty and affection, having rejoiced that 'the assumption that there are two parties in the association' had been dispelled because he and his friends 'were bound to work together for Irish nationality'. He said that he had often expressed his affection for O'Connell in his 'most private correspondence – the dearest and closest I ever had' and for it he 'would have been ridiculed, such was its intensity'. At that moment Davis was moved to tears, lost his voice and sat down. Overcome also with emotion at Davis's words and tears, O'Connell was immediately on his feet and, with largeness of heart, thanked and embraced him.[43]

Davis had always been aware that, by joining the Repeal Association, he would have to work in a hard-headed atmosphere in which rhetoric, emotionalism, loyalties to old friends and day-to-day alliances would, at times, control events and policies. He had accepted that way of conducting affairs, but in the matter of the colleges he had been unable to compromise. The fracas at least gave him the opportunity to enunciate what could be regarded as his last will and testament to those with whom he had worked, as well as to the people of Ireland for whom he had spent himself. He also proved his continued faith in God. To the gathering in Conciliation Hall he said,

> I have only now to hope that whatever disagreement may have occurred here – whatever strength of language may have been used elsewhere – for I am as liable to fall into it with my pen as others with their tongue – it will leave no sting behind. If there has been any harshness of feeling – if any person has made use of his private influence to misrepresent us to each other and to foster dissension, as adverse to the interests of our country, as productive of unhappiness to ourselves -if any person has done so, I don't know whether I can forget it, but I forgive him, trusting that it will never be repeated; and I now sit down with a prayer to Almighty God, that the people of this country and the leaders of the people may continue united in that pursuit of liberty in which they were so often defeated at the moment of its apparent fruition before – and with a prayer to that God that we may not be defeated again.[44]

The meeting would not permit Davis to apologise for what he recognised as his 'miserable weakness' but the reason for his weakness, apart from his health, was one he could not have made clear in public. His 'dearest and closest' correspondent, to whom he had spoken so highly of O'Connell, had been Annie, as he made plain to Pigot, without referring to her by name. The realisation that the correspondence was in the past, with no likelihood that it would ever be renewed, also helped to unman him for a moment, as perhaps did his knowledge that by remaining loyal to O'Connell he had helped to endanger his future with Annie.

The reaction among Davis's friends to the attack made on him was strong and, according to Duffy, 'left behind poisonous seeds of distrust and division'. It is difficult to disagree with MacDonagh's version of Conway as 'a glib but disreputable young journalist' who had jumped on the 'Catholic bandwagon' but why he chose this moment to jump is unclear unless he saw advantage to himself in so doing.[45] Madden thought that Davis's speech was 'excellent' except that he should have 'struck harder at Conway (whoever he is)'. William Griffin wrote to Davis to say 'how truly I deprecate [Conway's] conduct and how totally every thinking and intelligent Catholic [in Limerick] differs from him – nothing could betray the utter hypocrisy of his pretensions to patriotism more than the recklessness with which he cast the seeds of discord among the members of the Association, the audacity with which he attacked a party who have done more to create a feeling of Nationality and self-respect in Irishmen than even the oppression of the centuries, and the undisguised meanness of his servility, and sycophancy to Mr O'Connell.' On the other hand, unaware of its causes, Denny Lane and MacNevin were critical of Davis's emotional lapse. The latter wrote to O'Brien asking, 'What was there in the vulgar assault made on himself and his friends to authorise these pearly drops or this quivering emotion?', while Lane told Davis, 'Your conduct at the Hall, except "the tears", was unimpeachable,' but went on to warn him that he had to try to be 'a little less overbearing in committee meetings'. Davis accepted Lane's criticism of his demeanour, but said that he was prone to 'lose patience with the lying, ignorant, and lazy clan who surround' the Leader, so much so that 'I have to maintain a perpetual struggle to prevent myself from quitting politics in absolute scorn; but my heart melts, when I think it possible for a union of brave, patient men to lift up the country in more ways than politics.'[46]

Barrett, in the *Pilot*, was not prepared to adopt the conciliatory line that was needed if the Association were to remain intact. He wrote of the 'party of young men, activated by a morbid self-esteem, who have latterly been assuming an unearned and fancied importance amongst us, had, by way of aspiring to ascendancy in the councils of Repealers, the folly to make it [mixed education] their *cheval de bataille* for the day'. He rejoiced that they had been checked and chastised and asked his readers to recognise that the question was now decided for reasons which they would see proved in the speeches of O'Connell and 'his talented and religious son' John.[47] O'Connell kept silent on the question at the Association but he continued to deprecate Young Ireland and called for three cheers for Old Ireland at a public meeting in Cork. The audience, perhaps not taking his point, made no response. John O'Connell maintained the infidelity and godlessness refrain and Archbishop MacHale became almost frenzied in a letter to Peel, calling the proposal a 'Pagan plan' which was 'demoralising', and was also 'full of inexorable empirics.' Davis said no more in the Association, but he and his friends got up a petition in favour of mixed education which lay at the Commercial Building in Dame Street, Dublin, and was signed by a strong body of supporters, including all the *Nation* writers, as well as Matthew Moriarty who had chaired the unhappy meeting, and

Thomas Hutton. Davis remained unrepentant and wrote an editorial, 'Differences in the Association', that laid down his position with firmness. He insisted that differences were 'signs of health and manhood' and gave some illustrations. He recognised that some members of the Association held that liberty was not worth 'a drop of human blood' while others were equally of the opinion that, 'like religion, property and sanctity of the home', liberty was worth the sacrifice of life. Davis did, however, accept that the Association was bound to use only moral and legal means to achieve its objectives. Some, again, held that to accept financial assistance from American slave owners was wrong while others, who also strenuously condemned slavery, denied that it was Ireland's duty to 'redress all the wrongs of mankind'. Finally, the education question had caused dissension but 'we repeat that we prefer the existence and avowal of honest differences to a servile or stupid unanimity, and we do not dread the consequences'. In the midst of all this seriousness, some slight relief may have been afforded to the young men when Duffy was fined 40s because the *Nation* called an advertisement appearing in another paper 'a quack advertisement'. The advertisement was for a pill guaranteed to cure consumption and to rescue people from the 'actual grip of death'. There were many offers to pay the fine, which Duffy refused, but the support of the *Dublin Medical Press* was appreciated.[48]

Perhaps in order to make it plain that he took no sides in a denominational sense on the education question, Davis demanded that Trinity College, instead of remaining strictly a Protestant institution to the degree that Catholics who won scholarships to it had to receive the Anglican communion or be deprived of their scholarships, be opened on an equal footing to men of all religious affiliations. While repeating that the 'sweetest days of his life' had been passed there, he said that 'nothing can save or serve Trinity College but speedy reforms', in the religious and educational spheres and he went so far as to demand that 'practical and industrial education' be undertaken there. Finally, whether caused by strain, the lack of a holiday, his emotional disturbance or his overall ill health, Davis's normal degree of prudence and common sense seemed to snap under the continued provocation of O'Connellite 'political lackeys' such as Captain Broderick. He was so insulted by some expressions that Broderick had used that he consulted Barry about whether he should call Broderick out 'in the manner then usual' of a duel. Barry advised him 'to take no further steps in the transaction'.[49]

Before departing to London with his son John for the debate on the colleges bill, O'Connell went as far in committee as to attempt forcing those in favour of mixed education to secede from the Association.

Davis wrote to O'Brien, already in London, to say that, 'to avert disaster from our cause and country' none of them had done so, nor would they 'under *any* circumstances short of impending expulsion'. When he spoke in the House, O'Connell admitted that he once had thought 'the plan of a mixed education' proper, but was now opposed to it. Peel had hoped to modify the bill so as to meet some of the objections of the bishops, but O'Connell was determined to defeat the measure and remained convinced that the Ministry, as he told MacHale, would yield if the bishops stood their ground on 'Church sanctions relative to Catholic education'. All that was a pipe dream, if not arrant nonsense, designed to placate MacHale and, given Protestant opposition in England to any watering down of the original plan, O'Connell finally realised that there was an overwhelming majority in favour of 'any measure opposed by the *old Irish*'. Peel, despite some good intentions, was thus forced to see the bill through to its fruition without any genuine modification. O'Brien wrote from London to tell Davis that 'The Irish public will now become fully convinced of the folly of asking Irish members to come here in the vain hope of amending bad legislation' and said that he had thrown down the gauntlet to the government by formally declining to serve on any parliamentary committees, a decision for which he was briefly imprisoned. He advised Davis that the only proper course for 'the friends of Irish freedom' was to oppose the proposed new system of higher education in toto, because 'it gives to this Govt a powerful engine of corruption', as well as the means to drive a deeper wedge into both the Association and the Catholic clergy. The wedge however was already there and nothing either side could, or was prepared to do, was able to alter the reality of deep division. Duffy wrote in 1890, 'two generations of young Irishmen have paid the penalty of mistakes on both sides which rendered futile a beneficent design', but Archbishop Walsh said in 1897 that 'the costly, fantastic scheme ... of education in the new Colleges [was] utterly at variance with Catholic principles.' His remained a long-lived conviction among many of the Catholic hierarchy so that further generations continued to pay the penalty. As for Davis, he never departed a whit from his adherence to the principle inherent in the measure of mixed education but, as with the others of both convictions, his purpose was rendered nugatory. Nonetheless he had come to the conclusion, long since held by Mitchel, that any advantages to be derived from the Bill were not worth 'even a moment's division amongst us'.[50]

Surprisingly, given that John O'Connell represented Kilkenny at Westminster, a form of support for Davis came from the local paper. The *Kilkenny Journal* noted that, with all the Young this and that in

France, Germany, Italy, England and Ireland, 'a new order of things' was the cry. The young men who formed those bodies were worthy of much praise except in their excessive tolerance to 'irreligion'. In Ireland itself they had said things that 'fell with a heavy weight on the *Catholic* conscience of Ireland'. The paper did not specify exactly what the Catholic conscience of Ireland was, nor whether it encompassed those who disagreed with its own attitude to mixed education such as the respective archbishops of Ireland's two major sees, Armagh and Dublin. It went on, however, to say that, despite his faults,

> We could not well spare from our ranks the head and heart of Thomas Davis, and, the less, that he is a Protestant. He who wept at suspicion, like a tender woman, has a fund of virtue in his breast of which his country could not want the service, without loss. We admire his talents – we have been stirred by his poetry – we believe in his patriotism – and with Mr O'Connell, shake him by the hand as a brave, and affectionate and faithful brother Irishman.[51]

What Davis made of this kind of praise is uncertain, especially when John O'Connell continued to virtually rave about the 'infidel education bill' and asked his audience at an Association meeting to 'point out to him one man among the advocates of the godless education scheme, who had proved himself the steady and steadfast friend of Ireland'. Davis told Madden, 'If I had to deal only with O'Connell we would never fall out; but he is surrounded by sycophants who lie away against every man whose honesty they fear.' To O'Brien he was even more trenchant. 'Between unaccounted funds, bigotry, billingsgate, Tom Steele missions, crude and contradictory dogmas, and unrelieved stupidity, any cause and any system could be ruined.' He still hoped that, with a ' sincere and numerous people, a rising literature, an increasing staff of young, honest, trained, men', something good would come about, but 'it is character, honesty, high principles and clear, consistent designs the Association wants – power it has in abundance.' The painful fact was that there could no longer be a meeting of the ways and the Leader, for such he still remained in Davis's eyes, seemed determined to make matters worse. He repeated his words about pulling down and humbling 'the proud American eagle of the American republic' and even pleaded with England to bribe Ireland with favours so that England and Ireland could then 'stand against the world'. His words also give some grounds for wondering whether O'Connell, while doubtless sincere in his rejection of slavery, was not also prepared to use any pretext to oppose America so as to make it seem that he stood with England. It is also possible that the excessive nature of some of his behaviour may have stemmed from the fact that he had suddenly aged after his imprisonment, that his nerves were badly shaken and that he now wanted little more than compromise. In any case, such public utterances by O'Connell almost entirely ruined the Repeal cause in America and Davis claimed that 'but for the *Nation* there would not now be one Repeal Club' there. Without American aid, there were good reasons for concern about the finances of the Association. By July the Rent was down to £319-18-1 and, in mid-September, it had fallen to £173-2-11. The customary cheers at the announcement of the Rent were not forthcoming on the latter occasion.[52]

In the midst of all this controversy an event of passing moment had occurred but Davis, as one of its instigators, seemed to take great pleasure and pride in it, publicly at least. The anniversary of the imprisonment of the 'martyrs' of Richmond prison had come around and a national levee was held at the Rotonda on 30 May 1845. The assembly in the great Round Room included the 'martyrs', led by O'Connell, Repeal delegates, mayors and aldermen from most of the towns of Ireland, the '82 Club resplendent in their green and gold uniforms and about fifty trades with their bands and banners. Later, they and others took part in a huge procession through the streets of Dublin. Both events drove Davis to the heights of fanciful warning and prophecy. The procession alarmed the authorities in the Castle and they took measures to prevent what they assumed could turn into a rising by parading the Dublin garrison through the streets with their arms at the ready, while the viceroy himself watched proceedings from an upper window in Sackville (O'Connell) Street. Of the levee, Davis wrote to Pigot that it was 'the most imposing scene he had ever witnessed'. On behalf of all present in the Round Room, O'Brien proposed 'Ireland's oath' not to give up Repeal 'I was close to O'B., and his breast heaved and his eyes clouded, and his voice gurgled with passions,' Davis wrote and concluded, 'The day was really great, and the effects will be serious.' His words illustrated his ability to divorce his private thoughts from his public utterances because it was this same procession that Davis had in mind when he told Mitchel on the following day that such manifestations 'are ruining us'. Davis was sitting in his study at Baggot Street with Mitchel where they 'were intent on some exquisite German engravings which he had just received'. He was so full of good spirits that Mitchel had to provoke him to get a response on the previous day's proceedings by making fun of Tom Steele. Davis replied, 'Why, the Mayor and Corporation of Kilkenny have gone home, satisfied that Kilkenny at least has done its *duty*; that if Ireland do not gain her independence this year, it is not Kilkenny's fault; for what could scarlet robes and gold chains do more?' To the representative of English power in Dublin Castle he had words in a more serious vein, 'Viceroy of the alien, your precautions were cowardly against us as we were [unarmed], and would have been vain had we been what you assumed us [armed]. Your troops would have perished in our streets, like a rivulet among sands ... Dear Liberty! Liberty for which Sarsfield fought, and Tone organised! Liberty gained at Clontarf and Dungannon – lost by division.' Switching to a tone bordering on John the Evangelist in his Apocalypse, except that freedom took the place of the Redeemer, he exclaimed, 'Come! – come quickly! – we are athirst for Freedom!'[53]

Very few of his friends were aware how badly Davis needed a rest, although neither he nor they had reason to suspect the potential gravity of his situation were he to keep up the pace that he had sustained for the past several years. At the time he must have felt well himself and in July he wrote to Pigot, who was still studying in London, telling him that Duffy was better than he had ever been while 'Myself in good health of body and in a *calm* mood after a storm'. He was full of plans for the future and delighted that Ray and John O'Connell had reached an agreement with him on the development of the reading rooms. He said, 'I never despair of doing anything I can get rightly at, nor do I fail, save from laziness or passion. The world is very obedient and good.' With all his calmness and the evident control he had reached over his emotions since the breakdown at the Association meeting, he could not resist the urge to give Pigot some brotherly advice on how he should go about organising his life,

> I am *equally* glad of your health and your hard reading. Vigorous habits, power equal to your needs and position, and something over for adornment and benevolence, are the conditions of happiness. I sometimes, when I see fine spirits, like rudderless ships, drifting to ruin, think to be a teacher and to guide individual minds, but end by returning to my public mission. Ever toil at your sober duties. If great opportunities, lightning inspirations come, be the man of the hour and act and create it.[54]

Some of his friends thought that one way of getting him out in the public eye and giving him a change from the grinding routine of the *Nation*, and also from the need to attend the depressing meetings of the Association, was to persuade him to use his law degree and go on circuit. Dillon was 'greatly annoyed' and strongly opposed to the idea because it would seem as if Davis had been driven from the political arena which would be 'ruinous' to the cause. Instead, Dillon wanted him to be present at public dinners in Galway and Sligo. If he refused to attend both functions, Dillon wanted him at the Sligo one and thus close to Mayo. His reason was that Davis's presence was much needed, given that, in Mayo, the Repeal cause was practically extinct, due mainly to 'the universal rottenness of all classes, gentry, priests and people'. Lane, who was the only one of Davis's correspondents to address him as 'My dear Tom' rather than simply 'Dear Davis', told him that it was a good idea for Davis to go on circuit because it would acquaint him 'with the provincial mind of Ireland' which he thought was more powerful than that of the 'metropolis'. Lane did not believe that Dublin was truly a metropolis because it had 'no theatre, no periodical literature, no gathering of artists – no great merchants, above all, no legislative assembly gathering into a focus every ray of intellect and enterprise in the country'. Davis, whose whole formation as a private and public person had taken place in Dublin, had already done much towards filling the gaps that Lane mentioned, and the attainment of the 'legislative assembly' was a focal point of all his activity. It says much for the unsullied idealism of Lane, and perhaps Davis, that they looked to such a body as the centre of 'intellect and enterprise'.[55]

In the event it was not possible for Davis to go anywhere except out to Dundrum, where his family had taken up residence for the summer. He was happy to go daily to the *Nation* office because he had strong, personal reasons for remaining in Dublin through the late summer and autumn but, at the time, he told them to no one. Yielding to Davis's insistence that he could manage things alone, Duffy took off for a holiday with Mitchel to go through Roscommon, Armagh, Fermanagh and Tyrone and was away for five to six weeks. Dillon, although he had recovered from the burst blood vessel, was not in a position to contribute to the paper so that Davis, once again, was left practically alone. He wrote to Pigot, 'Duffy and everyone gone to the country, and I am alone, anxious for various reasons; but in work, and that is a shield for most assaults on the mind.' With joy he told Pigot, 'I have just this minute been looking at my niece who is two hours old, and a very pretty little Irishwoman. Do you or don't you mean to marry young? If I'm ever married, which is not likely, our wives will, I suppose, be inseparable gossips, and with that interesting prophesy I am as ever yours, T. D.'[56]

References

1. See Davis's editorial, 'The Library of Ireland' in *Nation*, 28 June 1845.
2. Davis to Pigot, 31 December 1844; Davis to Pigot, 17 February 1845 in *Irish Monthly*, vol. 18, pt. 2 (Dublin, 1890), pp 339-40, 341.

3. Davis to Mitchel, 7 July 1845 in Mitchel, *The last conquest*, p. 88.
4. *Nation*, 15 March 1844.
5. Davis to Pigot, 22 March 1845 in *Irish Monthly*, vol. 18, pt. 2 (Dublin, 1890), p. 340. Cane to Davis, 14 March 1845 in Ms 2644, NLI.
6. *Nation*, 28 June 1845.
7. See John Mitchel, *The last conquest*, pp 87-9.
8. Burton to Davis, 11 May, 5 June 1845 in Ms 2644, NLI. *Nation*, 26 July, 16 August 1845; Mitchel, *The last conquest*, pp 85-6.
9. *Nation*, June, 5 July 1844. Davis was a member of the Royal Irish Academy's committee entrusted with the purchase of art works.
10. Ibid., 6, 13 September 1945.
11. Ibid., Flanagan, v, p. 498, 30 December 1843, 23 August 1845; Duffy, *Davis*; Thomas, 'Literature in English, 1801-91', in Vaughan, *A new history*.
12. *The Spirit of the Nation: or ballads and songs by the writers of the Nation'*, reissued in quarto form with music, illustrations and including a preface by Thomas Davis (Dublin, 1845). For the quote on O'Curry see A. A. Ward and A. R. Walker (eds.), *The Cambridge history of English literature*, vol. xii, p. 400.
13. Dunleary is now rendered Dun Laoghaire. For the foregoing account of the banter over Davis's insistence on the use of Irish, see Duffy, *Young Ireland*, part 1, pp 207-8.
14. Ibid., p. 208.
15. Ibid., pp 204-12.
16. See O'Connell to MacHale, 19 February 1845 in O'Connell (ed.), *Correspondence*, vol. vii, pp 306-7.
17. Davis to Lane, n.d. June 1845 in Duffy, *Davis*, p. 302; *Nation*, 16, 30 November, 1844, 8 February 1845; Geraldine Grogan, 'The Colleges Bill 1845-49' in Maurice R. O'Connell (ed.), *O'Connell, education, church and state*, pp 27-8; O'Connell (ed.), Correspondence, vol. vii, p. 303; O'Connell to MacHale, 19 February 1845. ibid, pp 306-7. See also Duffy, *Davis*, p. 302.
18. See O'Connell to William Walsh, bishop of Halifax in Desmond Bowen, *The protestant crusade in Ireland 1800-1870* (Dublin, 1978), p. 24.
19. See O'Connell to MacHale, 19 February 1845 in O'Connell (ed.), *Correspondence*, vol. vii, pp 306-7.
20. Davis to Mitchel, n.d. but April or May 1845 in Mitchel, *The last conquest*, p. 89 and ibid for Mitchel.
21. MacDonagh, *O'Connell*, p. 550. For a pro-Davis account see Duffy, *Davis*, pp 287-8.
22. Denis Gwynn, 'O'Connell, Davis and the Colleges Bill' in *Irish Ecclesiastical Record*, fifth series, vol. lxix, January to December (Dublin 1947) and vol. lxx, 1948, pp 28, 29, 669, 1063. The articles were later reprinted as *O'Connell, Davis and the colleges bill* (Oxford, 1948).
23. *Pilot*, 24 February, 19 May 1845.
24. *Nation*, 17 May 1845; Duffy, *Young Ireland*, vol. 1, p. 291.
25. *Nation*, 17 May 1845. The matter of Trinity's position in university education continued to be a bone of contention into the next century. See Thomas J. Morrissey, *Towards a national university: William Delany SJ (1835-1924.) An era of initiative in Irish education* (Dublin, 1983).
26. See John N. Molony, *The Roman mould of the Australian Catholic Church* (Melbourne, 1969) and P. Mac Suibhne, *Paul Cullen and his contemporaries*, 3 vols (Naas, 1961-65).

27. *Times*, 2 June 1845.
28. Ibid.
29. *Nation*, 17 May 1845. The book reviewed was Thomas Willis, *Facts connected with the social and sanitary conditions of the working classes in the city of Dublin* (Dublin, 1845).
30. *Nation*, 24 May 1845.
31. See *Freeman's Journal*, 24, 26 May for the meeting of the Synod. See also 'Resolutions and memorial of the Catholic Bishops on the Colleges Bill' in Duffy, *Young Ireland*, p. 288; for MacHale see Donal A. Kerr, *Peel*, pp 303-4.
32. *Nation*, 31 May 1845.
33. Ibid.
34. Ibid. For Conway, see Duffy, *Davis*, p. 292. Duffy later wrote of Conway in a way that would have displeased Davis, given the latter's attitude to the right of anyone to change their religion. Duffy said, 'the pious Mr Conway finally confessed himself a convert to Protestantism to obtain the wages of a proselytizing society.' Ibid., p. 294; O'Reilly, *MacHale*, p. 642, said that Conway was 'the Richard Pigot of that day, the infamous spy and apostate.'
35. *Nation*, 31 May 1845; *Freeman's Journal*, 27 May; Duffy, *Davis*, p. 293. MacDonagh, *O'Connell*, p. 550 does not report Conway's speech, nor O'Connell's approval of it, but says that Conway 'lauded denominational university education to the skies.'
36. *Nation*, 31 May 1845.
37. Ibid.
38. Davis to Pigot, 28 May 1845 in *Irish Monthly*, vol. 16 (Dublin, 1888), pp 344-5.
39. *Nation*, 31 May 1845.
40. MacDonagh, *O'Connell*, p. 551.
41. *Nation*, 31 May 1845.
42. Davis to Pigot, 2 June 1845 in Duffy, *Davis,* pp 298-99; *Nation,* 31 May, 1845; Duffy, *Young Ireland*, p. 257; MacDonagh, *O'Connell*, p. 551.
43. *Nation*, 31 May 1845; Davis to Pigot, 2 June 1845 in *Irish Monthly,* vol. 16 (Dublin, 1888), p. 345.
44. *Nation*, 31 May 1845.
45. MacDonagh, *O'Connell*, p. 550.
46. Davis to Pigot, 2 June 1845 in *Irish Monthly*, vol. 16 (Dublin, 1880, p. 345; Griffin to Davis, 2 June 1845, Madden to Davis, 3 June 1845, Lane to Davis, 16 June 1845, MacNevin to Davis n.d. but June 1845, Ms 2644, NLI.
47. *Pilot*, 28 May 1845.
48. Lane to Davis, 11 June 1845 in Ms 2644; *Freeman's Journal*, 11 June 1845; *Nation*, 28 June, 5 July 1845; Duffy, *Davis*, p. 304.
49. *Nation*, 28 June 1845. Duffy, *Davis*, p. 304.
50. Davis to O'Brien, 15 June 1845, Ms 432, NLI; *Nation* 28 June 1845; *O'Connell* to MacHale, 21 June 1845 in O'Connell (ed.) *Correspondence*, p. 321; O'Brien to Davis, 1 July 1845, Ms 2644, NLI; William J. Walsh, *The Irish university question – the Catholic case* (Dublin, 1897), p. 32.
51. *Kilkenny Journal* in *Nation*, 7 June 1845.
52. *Nation*, 26 July, 6, 13 September 1845; Davis to Madden, n.d. but early June 1845, in Duffy, *Davis*, p. 310; Davis to O'Brien, 26 July 1845, Ms 432, NLI. On O'Connell's health see Raymond Moley, quoting Lecky, in *Nationalism without violence* (New York, 1974), pp 169-70.
53. Davis to Pigot, 2 June 1845 in *Irish Monthly*, vol. 16 (Dublin, 1888), p. 346; *Nation*, 31 May 1845; Mitchel, *The last conquest*, p. 87.

54. Davis to Pigot, n.d. July 1845, and another Tuesday, but again July 1845 in *Irish Monthly*, vol. 16 (Dublin, 1888), pp 346-7.
55. Dillon to Davis, 22 July 1845, Ms 2644; Dillon to Duffy, July 1845 in Duffy, *Davis*, p. 312; Lane to Davis, 16 June 1845 in Ms 2644, NLI.
56. Davis to Pigot, 5 August 1845 in *Irish Monthly*, vol. 16 (Dublin, 1888), p. 348.

A NATION ONCE AGAIN.

BY THOMAS DAVIS.

I.

WHEN boyhood's fire was in my blood
  I read of ancient freemen,
For Greece and Rome who bravely stood,
  THREE HUNDRED MEN and THREE MEN.*
And then I prayed I yet might see
  Our fetters rent in twain,
And Ireland, long a province, be
  A NATION ONCE AGAIN.

II.

And, from that time, through wildest woe,
  That hope has shone, a far light;
Nor could love's brightest summer glow,
  Outshine that solemn starlight;
It seemed to watch above my head,
  In forum, field, and fane,
Its angel voice sang round my bed,
  "A NATION ONCE AGAIN."

III.

It whispered, too, that freedom's ark
  And service high and holy,
Would be profan'd by feelings dark,
  And passions vain or lowly;
For freedom comes from God's right hand,
  And needs a godly train;
And righteous men must make our land
  A NATION ONCE AGAIN."

IV.

So, as I grew from boy to man
  I bent me to that bidding—
My spirit of each selfish plan
  And cruel passion ridding;
For, thus I hoped some day to aid—
  Oh, can *such* hope be vain?—
When my dear country should be made
  A NATION ONCE AGAIN.

---

* The Three Hundred Greeks who died at Thermopylæ, and the Three Romans who kept the Sublician Bridge.

Chapter 14

Ireland's son

In September 1845, Thomas Davis was a few weeks short of his thirty-first birthday. He had kept good health throughout the years of his manhood, but the hard years since 1842 had taken their toll on his physique. He had never ventured far from his mother's home, where he had lived since childhood. From 67 Lower Baggot Street to Trinity College, from the Law Courts to the office of the *Nation*, from the reading rooms of the Royal Irish Academy to those of the Royal Dublin Society, in and out of book shops, enjoying the wit and banter at dinners and on visits to the homes of his small circle of closest friends, such had been his life. His excursions to other parts of Ireland had been all too rare and he had only once ventured beyond her shores. Since the fleeting years of early childhood at Mallow, Dublin had nurtured him and he knew and loved his city which had etched itself into his being during his vigorous and regular walks. The Liffey, where it ran down to the sea close to the Corn Exchange, the muffled tolling of vessels' bells in the fog, the fading glories of Dublin's Georgian past, the ever-present mountains with their annual reminder that all things pass, whether cities or men, all these things had helped to make Davis. Above all, he was shaped by the ballads, the folk myths, the language and the antiquities of Ireland and her age-long struggles. He was Ireland's son in flesh and spirit.

Davis had come through the turmoil of the past months daunted, but not bowed. His unshakeable conviction that Ireland had to win her independence had never wavered, but he now saw with burdensome clarity how long and hard the road to that goal was as it stretched into an indefinite future. Yet, there was also rich advantage in the postponement of freedom, provided the time was used for the formation of the minds and wills of the Irish people. In that way they would be able to use their freedom, once achieved, with benefit and dignity. Thus, he never ceased trying to find and develop means of formative value that would, over time, uplift and educate the people. The organisation of the masses was to Davis a thing of practical consequence, but he knew that it was passing. He feared any form of activity based merely on exhortation and emotional stirring, because little remained behind in the form of conviction among the masses once the objective had been achieved or tactics had dictated that it be changed. For Davis, one properly equipped and regularly used reading room was worth more than a dozen meetings. One sound article in the *Nation* surpassed in value any number of harangues in the Conciliation Hall. He was no enemy of democracy, because he never worked for a society shaped by elites who would try to construct it according to their own blueprint. On the contrary, he was essentially a democrat in that he respected the value of the human person whom he wanted to see recognised as the fundamental ground of every society. Thus, his whole striving was for the formation of individuals through education, respect and trust. Were Ireland ever to be independent and able to take her rightful place among the nations, the essence of her democracy had to flow from the integrity of the individuals who made up the whole. For Davis, that was a work to be undertaken over painstaking years and one which would never see its full realisation because it began again and again. In short, democracy was an ideal to be striven for constantly and could never be achieved in a perfect form in any given era. Democracy was born, day by day, not in parties or in masses, but in individuals. In that concept lay the genesis of Davis's Ireland of the future. Its great truth, and even greater simplicity, was that it could begin the moment an individual acted upon it.

Idle antiquarianism or playful romanticism were of no interest to Davis who was a realist with a clear-cut purpose. The past was not there simply for its own sake, but for the enrichment and enlightenment of the generations that followed. How much time and energy was yet to be expended, how many more defeats and minor victories had to be endured and savoured, how many friends and enemies would be made in the struggle, when would the divisions between the old traditions and the new ideals be healed and internal unity be achieved in Ireland? Davis knew nothing of the future. He only knew that it was his bounden duty to persevere in his chosen task. Meanwhile, he had the *Nation* to direct and, for the greater part, write. It was of small moment to him that Duffy and the others had left him alone, because nothing would divert him from ensuring that, week by week, it came out and that its contents remained at the highest possible level. The fact that the proceedings at Conciliation Hall, with O'Connell absent at Derrynane and his son John in charge, whom Dillon called an insolent 'little frog', from whose venom 'no man or country [is] safe', made the continuation of the *Nation* imperative if any vestige of the quest for nationality were to survive.[1]

The personal burden of anxiety that had consumed him in those long months since he had vowed his heart to Annie Hutton never left him for a moment. While at Baggot Street there had been incomprehension at the way he had given his life to achieve an objective towards which there was much hostility, he nonetheless still remained a beloved son and brother. In the Hutton home, Elm Park, at Drumcondra, Annie's father could not share the outlook and convictions of one who saw England as the ancient enemy and wanted Ireland to make a clear break with her. Her mother had made her attitude to O'Connell, and all those who stood with him, very plain from the start. There remains no record of Annie's estimate of Davis's involvement with a cause and persons who were alien to her upbringing, but the fact that, before they were parted, she had loved Davis and wanted to be his wife, indicates that she accepted the high purpose of his life. She had not loved him for fame or fortune, but for his warmth and gentility, his enormous energy, his far-ranging intellect, his resoluteness and generosity and such things spelt promise for the future.

In March 1845, Annie and her mother returned from Italy and, by late July, Davis must have known that there was some possibility of a reunion being permitted. Who the intermediaries were, and what persuasive reasons were given that made the opening to a reunion possible, are unknown. Thomas Hutton's association with Davis on the federalist issue may have helped to persuade him that his prospective son-in-law was, after all, more moderate in his views than had been thought to be the case. Frederic Burton, who so loved Davis that he 'could refuse him nothing', may have intervened on Davis's behalf with the Huttons, with whom he was very close.[2] In any case, Davis was aware that something had changed and he had indicated his anxiety to Madden without specifying its cause. 'I have been for some time, and am likely to continue for a while in a state of feverish anxiety on a subject purely personal, and which I hope I am yet able to talk of to you.' Madden replied from London on 4 August, 'I am the more sorry for whatever is troubling you as I cannot be of assistance, but I hope that whatever it is, it will soon be over and that you will not be disappointed.' Pigot also wrote to say that something he had heard about Annie had made him think 'there is at least an even chance', but he also was not specific.[3]

On 13 August 1845, after an absence of over a year, Davis was again welcomed into the Hutton home. The welcome was doubly warm because it took place on the understanding, and acceptance by her parents, that Annie and Thomas would marry, but no date was set because, for the good of her health, she and her mother were to go out to Italy again over the Irish winter. Annie was overjoyed, although she could scarcely speak when they met and appeared 'sadly cold' but her true feelings were otherwise. She wrote to Davis on the next day, a Thursday, to say 'I have perfect confidence in you; you are everything that is noble and good. Oh, I am very happy, a happiness above all that I ever dreamt of.' She said that her mother was 'so good to us' and that she 'showed me all your letters, and gave me back all my poetry'. For the first time she told him of 'that sad Sunday that your first letter came and she thought I must give you up. I gave her all you had ever given me, and in the bitterness of my grief, wondered if ever I should be happy again as I was before.' Annie asked him why he feared that she might change and said, 'have you less confidence in me than I in you, you will have more temptations, for all admire *you*.' Finally, she assured him that 'my soul shall be yours as my heart is (i.e *nearly*!), bye and bye it will be all.' On the next Monday she wrote to invite him to breakfast at Elm Park 8.30 a.m. on Wednesday and said that her letter was disjointed because she was 'a little mad' at the thought of seeing him sooner than she had expected. He had recently received the proof of his first few pages on Tone, which was to come out as the third volume in the 'Library of Ireland' series, and Annie was longing to hear him talk about 'this great rebel', which he had promised her he would do on the previous Sunday. She and her mother were leaving for the continent in three weeks time, but Annie was determined not to grieve, given how much there was 'to look forward to after a time'. Davis had said to her how much he liked to hear her say she loved him, so she wrote, 'May I write it, Oh! how dearly, passionately I love you. Somehow I am afraid to say it when you are by, but I will the next time you come.' She signed the letter, 'Ever your Annie.'[4]

In a few days a pattern was set of a visit on Sunday when breakfast was at 9 a.m. rather than at 8.30 a.m. He went again every Wednesday and there were regular letters in between. The thought of having to part so soon after their reunion weighed heavily on them both, but Davis was able to escape into his work which had to go on, whereas, to divert herself, Annie only had the quiet routine of Elm Park, the playing of Irish airs, which she asserted she could play rather than sing, and reading. Davis started to write poetry for her which she read and re-read. He also advised her on wider reading with a concentration on Irish topics. Other authors were Carlyle and Ruskin, as well as some European thinkers, including Freidrich von Schlegel, whose *Philosophy of History* had come out in English in 1835 and J. G. Fichte's *Addresses to the German Nation*. The Catholic von Hugel had said of Fichte that he was 'iron-willed, violently ethical' and had a 'heroic character and mind' which description Annie thought fitted Davis as well.[5] The normality of the relationship they quickly established, as if there had never been a break between them, stemmed from the combination of Davis's maturity and Annie's almost hero worship of him. Nonetheless, Annie's own character was such that she attracted Davis by its strength and she had no intention of being treated by him as less than the woman she was. One letter, evidently found by Duffy in the Davis papers, but not deposited with them at the National Library of Ireland, reveals much of her character,

> How shall I tell you how happy I was to get your dear, dear letter, for which I love you twenty times better than before, for now you are treating me with confidence, not like a child whom it pleases you to play with. Do you know that was (but it is nearly gone) the one fear that I had, that you would think of me as a plaything, more than as a friend; but I don't think you will since last night.[6]

They shared, too, a love for the physical beauty of Ireland which she expressed to him in the same letter,

> I had such a lovely drive all round Howth yesterday, and at the most beautiful part was alone, which I was very sorry for; I like to have someone to enjoy beauty with, not to talk about it, but just quietly to enjoy. It was very beautiful, Killiney all brilliant in the sunlight, with white-sailed boats dancing merrily over the water, and then the Dublin and Wicklow Mountains behind frowning blackly, as if jealous that they had no sun, and Bray Head, the Grey Stones, and Wicklow Head stretching out farther and still farther away. And there wasn't a sound to be heard.[7]

Clearly, Duffy suffered no qualms of conscience at leaving Davis alone in Dublin because he had been assured that he had his own good reasons for remaining there through the summer, reasons which had at last found their fulfilment. Duffy was enjoying himself so much on his tour that he told Davis he had 'lived a year, not an hour less, since I saw you', but he expected to be back by early September. In reply, Davis chided his absent friends playfully in the 'Answers to Correspondents' section of the *Nation* because they 'seem to have glutted themselves with summer fruits and gone to sleep'. Although he expected they would wake up as 'refreshed giants' he thought their 'conduct vile in the extreme' and he wished he could 'make the hills wetter, and the inns dirtier, their talk dull, and their tea indigestible for such treachery'.[8] The banter, however could not hide the seriousness of the situation with which he had to contend. MacNevin, in a letter to Duffy, wrote, 'Dillon is sick of the abomination of desolation on Burgh quay. It never opens its sooty mouth on the subject of Repeal now. By the way, where *is* the Repeal Agitation? Is it hunting at Derrynane? ... I am glad that Davis does not go to the Association.' MacNevin said that he would work with Duffy and Davis, 'but no more with the base melange of tyranny and mendicancy' that reigned in the Hall.⁹

John O'Connell was still in complete charge and he took every opportunity to rail at 'those base Americans', to the discomfort of even the sturdiest anti-slavery advocates. He had turned Conciliation Hall into 'a revivalist bethel', where politics mixed with religion, misplaced zeal with imprudence and confusion prevailed over order. On the grounds that 'We are bound to show both England and our own country that we have men in our ranks capable of performing any functions connected with the government of a great Kingdom,' O'Brien pleaded with Davis to attend and speak as often as possible at the meetings, but he rarely went to Conciliation Hall and he could only hope that better times would come once the Liberator returned to take charge. From Derrynane O'Connell sent a series of resolutions, some of which were admirable as objectives to be striven for such as vote by ballot, and others about which there was much disagreement like the abolition of the Poor Law, which, once adopted, the Association would have been bound to uphold. O'Brien, whose innate conservatism was not shaken or changed by his dedication to Irish nationality, was perturbed by the contents of the resolutions, which he regarded as extreme, and thus 'fatal to the cause', in that, if agreed upon by the Association, any fruitful appeal to Irish conservatives would become so much harder. He was also much displeased because the usual practice of discussing such matters in committee, before bringing them to a public meeting, was not followed. Any such quibble by O'Brien and his allies was pointless because normal behaviour on Burgh Quay was now over, but Davis took the matter seriously and saw the resolutions as likely to sow further seeds of discord within the Association. They had come at the exact time when he had hoped that some minimal unity may have been achieved with the cessation of open hostilities on the education question. To him, slavery in America or liberal measures on the political level had to remain secondary to the main objective, Repeal. The harsh truth was that the usefulness of Conciliation Hall, of Repeal itself as either reality or slogan, of the leadership of O'Connell, O'Brien or anyone else, were all in the past. All that remained was the *Nation*, where Davis stayed at the helm.¹⁰

His editorial, 'The Twelfth of August', noted that there were 1,580,000 Protestants in Ireland and 6,620,000 Catholics. He begged them all to rally to the Orange and Green flag, to think only of 'Nationality' and 'to resolve to be governed by native laws and native rulers'. O'Brien wrote him, 'I am delighted with the article in yesterday's *Nation* respecting the prospect of a union between Orange and Green, It makes me for a moment believe that the dream of my life is about to be realised.' He had ample time to dream that vain dream in his subsequent exile at the convict hole called Port Arthur in Van Diemen's Land.[11] At the time, O'Connell, to Davis's outrage, was insisting that Federalists and Whigs who were wavering on nationality, whether candidates for Parliament or sitting members, should take the Repeal pledge or lose any support from the Association. O'Brien had agreed with this measure and Davis wanted him to repudiate his support, as well as to persuade O'Connell to postpone it. 'I must say that, except for Catholicising the Association, I know of nothing so mischievous to our causes as these *premature mob pledges.*' He had immediate proof of his fears because the Orangemen were quick to reply to O'Connell's provocation. Meeting at Inniskillen, they resolved to reorganise their own system and to support only candidates for Parliament who joined it. Almost in despair and in ominously prophetic tones, Davis could not resist warning them that they were playing into the hands of those in the Association, he meant O'Connell and his followers, who 'believe you incurably blind fanatics; and who, if they could, would induce us all to compromise with Peel and accept franchises, establishments, and office from the British Ministry under a British Parliament'. He told them that such men would make the Union even stronger and ensure that Catholicism became the ruling institution in Ireland in the same way as Presbyterianism was in Scotland and Episcopalianism in England. The reason for the actions and aspirations of the men in question was that 'they despair of nationality, because they despair of your becoming true Irishmen.' On the other hand, if he and those who thought like him despaired of the Orangemen, the words of the others 'would be eagerly believed; the voice of men like us, who would strive, while we "had a ditch of our country left to die in" (as William said), would be drowned, the compact made, and you would become a despised, petty faction – politically extinct. By purposeless fanaticism you do run this danger.' He little realised the pathetic truth his words prophesised.[12]

Recurring once again to 'First Principles', Davis wrote that 'There is another striking cause of misery in England to be found in the manufacturing despotism, the tyranny of accumulation.' He was convinced that manufacturers were 'the greatest oppressors, the most ruthless extortioners. Masters of the market of labour, by their command of capital they can dictate their own terms to the laborious poor.' While he had no difficulty in agreeing with Burke on the 'great horrors' of the French Revolution, he saw that Burke was 'blind to the vast benefits which were to spring from that bold recurrence to first principles'. In respect of mixed education he did not withdraw his stand, while admitting that the 'mode of introducing the Bill was offensive, the details clumsy, some of them dangerous, one of them despotic'. Archbishop Crolly, at a meeting held in Armagh to petition that a college be situated there, had said that, because mixed education was going well in the schools, there was no reason why the same could not take place in the colleges if it were 'managed in the same Christian spirit'. He also said that he and several of his fellow bishops agreed on the matter, that for his part he was determined to give the colleges 'a fair trial' and that as far as he was concerned the Bill was 'calculated to afford general satisfaction'. The fanaticism of some of those who opposed mixed education, as well as the truth of Davis's later remark to O'Brien on 'mad bigotry' was well illustrated by the O'Connellite paper, the *Pilot*, which mounted an attack on Crolly in much the same way as it had attacked Davis. Unable to refute the archbishop directly, the first attempt to discredit him came in the form of a rumour that he was about to become a Protestant, which was reinforced by remarking that his mother had been a Presbyterian. That attempt to discredit Crolly having failed, the paper announced on its main page that 'He was incapable of attending the meeting of bishops at Maynooth owing to the unsound state of his mind ...' In fact, Crolly, at the time, was presiding at the bishops meeting and was in sound mental and physical health. Any reputation for integrity the paper had ever possessed was forthwith lost and its editor, Barrett, entirely discredited. However, given the primate's attitude, Davis regretted that there was no chance now to amend the Bill, something he was sure could have happened had they remained united. He concluded with his own reason for endorsing the new system, 'Yet we can never treat knowledge as an enemy, no matter how allied,' meaning that, even in the new colleges with all their shortcomings, there would still be an opportunity for young Irishmen to gain knowledge. He wrote to O'Brien at the same time saying that he would not 'in any wise co-operate with the mad bigotry which has since shewn its obstinacy and exhibited greater virulence and vice than ever. If I am driven to it I shall rather secede from the Association, or even quit the country.' Hindsight heightens the pathos of his concluding words, 'I see little chance of my getting from town; though I pine for the country. Still I am in iron health.'[13]

His last words went back to the themes that he had sustained almost since the days when, in his young manhood, he had seen nationality as the lodestar of his existence. He regretted that so many flocked to the reading rooms, 'to enjoy and not to study – to worship eloquence or laugh at wit; and not to labour for the higher enjoyment of intellectual power'. The reason was that there are 'no people in the world whom, after all, it is so difficult to lead in the slow and sure path of useful learning as the Irish. Of a quiet perception, and most riotous facilities of acquisition, they are apt to spurn the difficult control of a steady education.' Now, however, they had to get on with 'useful learning' and their foremost duty was to study the history of Ireland. In Ireland there had always been a thirst for freedom and education but 'the Norman and the Saxon, the freebooter and the fanatic' had hated 'Irish arts, letters and civilisation' and tried to eradicate them all. In the silence that followed such destruction, an immense amount of falsehood and calumny had been created and called 'history' but, despite that, the love of the beautiful, the noble and the virtuous had lived on 'in the heart of Ireland, unwatched and unfed'. It was alive again and 'when she shall stand forth strong and free, it will still be the heart of the old isle animating a frame of greater sinew, proportion and beauty.' Davis concluded, 'The Irish people have learnt to feel the ambition of a great nation – they appreciate the true position they occupy, and their importance in the European system ... It was because they were ignorant that they were wretched. With enlightenment they will grow prosperous and powerful.'[14] The love of the language that he had so diligently tried to learn from native speakers, including the scribe Ó Longáin, O'Donovan's collaborator and 'member of a great family of Munster poets', was with him still. He never saw in print his last words on the language. 'No country possesses more abundant resources for a National Literature than Ireland: but, unfortunately, they have long been locked up in a language with which, to our shame be it spoken, the intellectual minds of the nation are nearly all unfamiliar.' In a few short years, the Commissioners for National Education would say, 'the National Schools are quietly but certainly destroying the national legends, the national music and the national language of our country'.[15]

The summer had passed, the wet days had come and the light was beginning to draw in at evening time in the streets around the Liffey, but Davis was happy. He was doing what he knew how to do best by persevering with the main objective of his life. Unlike the past, when uncertainty clouded his future, he now had sure grounds for believing that he and Annie would face life together. He continued his visits to Elm Park and they were in regular correspondence between visits. She wrote to him on 26 August asking him not to be as 'grave' when he came tomorrow as he had been on his Sunday visit, or else she would begin to fear that he had begun to regret his decision to marry her. She said, 'If you are glad of my love, don't you think I am far more proud of yours, to have the privilege of making one like you happy, oh! that it may ever be so.' There was a verse in a poem he had given to her on Sunday that she wanted changed as it seemed to imply that she may not continue to love him. 'You *must* not doubt me, you *must not* dream of my casting away the happiness before me.' She promised him that she would take the poem, together with all else he had given her, with her to Rome and 'when I read them it will be as if you were talking to me.' Annie accepted that they would have 'a long, long parting, but we must not think of that, we must look forward to a joyous return'. He must have given her some glimmer of how he had suffered throughout his life, with no one in his home, except Charlotte, to pour out his heart to on the things he held most dear. 'I long to hear the history of your life,' she wrote, 'and were you so very lonely?' She was sorry that he had not been able to tell his feelings to others and, even when he had done so, they did not understand him. They were to meet on Thursday, 4 September when she promised to talk to him about his worries and she concluded, 'Yes, dearest, I will take care and be so well and strong when I come home, that perhaps you won't know me. That would be a most desirable consummation!'[16]

Duffy was back in his editorial chair by 1 September 1845 and found Davis 'in vigorous health and exuberant spirits, except when the talk fell on the calamities at Conciliation Hall', but he 'was still full of projects for the far future'. On 6 September, Davis wrote to Mitchel to ask him to jot down anything he remembered hearing from Reverend Mr Thackeray of Dundalk on Wolfe Tone and 'especially anything as to his manner and views of future events in Ireland'. He visited Elm Park on the next day, a Sunday, but did not appear at the *Nation* office two days later. His life of constant toil, worry, incomprehension by those whom he most loved, financial uncertainty combined with reticence to pursue a career with greater economic prospects than journalism, and recurring bouts of scarlatina finally weakened his constitution and struck him down. He wrote a short note to Duffy telling him, 'I have had an attack of some sort of cholera, and *perhaps* have slight scarlitina [sic].' He told Duffy that he could not have visitors and asked him not to be alarmed, but added that he wasn't up to writing anything for the present. The handwriting was not in its usual bold manner, but appeared shaky. When Duffy heard that he had written it from his bed, neither he nor the others were alarmed. Davis also wrote to O'Brien and, under the circumstances, there was a certain sadness in that to his colleague and friend he used the uncustomary salutation 'My dear Sir', probably occasioned by their disagreement over the pledge exacted of parliamentarians. 'I have got scarlitina [sic] and cannot attend the Committee for a few days.' He must have felt that his recovery would be rapid because he said that he would 'willingly report on whatever they refer to me'. On hearing of his condition, MacNevin wrote a note full of his customary banter to assure him that, as he had such an 'unpatriotic' ailment as 'English' cholera he would soon be well given his 'Celtic constitution'. MacNevin also asked for a list of books to consult as he was about to start writing a volume on the Ulster Plantation for the 'Library of Ireland' series.[17]

The news of the illness quickly reached Elm Park through Davis's doctor, William Stokes, who was a friend of the Huttons, of Burton and Petrie and a lover of the old past of Ireland. Annie had been wondering why she had not heard from him and wrote on 10 September saying that she had thought of twenty things that would have stopped him writing, but not of illness. She insisted that he neither write to, nor visit her until he was well and that her mother would prohibit a visit until Dr Stokes, who was giving them a twice-daily bulletin, pronounced him well. Annie concluded, 'Remember dearest all you have said to me about care, act upon it now and I shall feel much happier. My dear, dear love, ever your heart and soul. Annie.'[18]

Davis's next note to Duffy was in a worse hand. He explained that he had had a 'bad attack of scarlitina [sic], with a horrid sore throat.' He begged Duffy not to mention his illness 'to *any* one for a very delicate reason I have', which probably means that he was hoping that Annie would not be told about it. Nonetheless, he must have been feeling better because he concluded, 'In 4 days I hope to be able to look at light business for a short time.' As he also asked Duffy to attend to some editorial matters, his friends were still not worried because he was clearly able to think about his work, and they thought that they knew the strength of his constitution. Duffy immediately replied saying that he could not keep the illness secret because he had already told O'Hagan and others. O'Hagan had even joked about the illness saying that 'by dying at this minute'. Davis could rival Mirabeau, who had died at the height of his influence in France in 1791, but O'Hagan begged him not to be 'tempted by the inviting opportunity'. Stokes was 'a physician in the first rank of his profession', but probably without his permission Davis went out walking on Thursday. On his walk he met John O'Connell, whom he told that his work 'was telling against him', returned home and relapsed.[19]

On Friday morning Annie wrote again hoping he was better. Stokes had told her that he had not been 'quiet enough', so she asked him to be patient. Oblivious of any danger, she made light of things by telling him that she and her mother were sorry that he had not used Osborne as his first name in preference to Thomas, 'which is so ugly and which I have heard since I was born!' The last week had proved to her how hard the parting and the long sojourn in Rome would be, 'for I didn't know how much I loved you, till you were prevented coming'. She wanted to hear from him on Sunday, but only if he were fit enough to write. On Sunday, Stokes gave a good report and even on Monday there was no great fear, but that night Mr Hutton said, 'I am very uneasy, it really seems a precarious state!' Still thinking of the future and impatient at being unable to return to work, Davis spent a restless night on Monday in the company of his mother and sister who had been constantly attentive to him. Towards dawn he was alone with Neville, who had been in the employ of the family for many years. Noticing that he was weakening, Neville took him in his arms. A month short of his thirty-first birthday, Thomas Davis died at his mother's home, 67 Lower Baggot Street, Dublin, at dawn on Tuesday, 16 September 1845.[20] A soul had gone out from Erin.

Duffy went to the home where 'lay the man whom I loved beyond any on earth, a pallid corpse'. He returned to the office to write letters to the others. Within a few days he was at the deathbed of his own wife, Emily, who was twenty-five. The word of Davis's death spread rapidly but, as in life, so too in death, there was disunity over him. Duffy and his friends wanted him to be buried in Glasnevin so as to lie with the patriots of the land. The Davis family determined on the Protestant cemetery of Mount Jerome, near to where the villa stood in which the Catholic leader, John Keogh, had met Wolfe Tone to discuss how to unite the 'jarring creeds' in a common pursuit of the good of all Ireland. To discourage mourners, the family had also decided that the funeral would be an early morning one at 8 a.m. and that the route through the city would not be published. Their discouragement was to no avail because Dublin, and most of Ireland, knew that their own was being buried. Politics no longer mattered and, on Thursday 18 September, as the hearse passed from the home at Baggot Street, through Merrion Square, College Green, close to offices of *Nation* on Trinity Street, Sackville Street, Dame Street, Grafton Street, Harcourt Street and along the canal to Harold's Cross, thousands watched from the streets and windows of the city he had loved. Among the chief mourners were Duffy, Pigot and Webb, together with the servants of the household. As was customary, the women of his home mourned privately but Mrs Davis, whose mother's heart was surely stricken, did not lessen her rejection of Thomas's aspiration to Irish nationality one whit. She was prepared to acknowledge her son's work, but she could not bring herself to agree in any sense with his objectives, although she graciously remarked later to the warders of the Repeal Association in London that 'we know that he was ever ardent, direct and persevering in pursuit of what he thought to be right, whilst a forbearing spirit tempered that pursuit in the moments of its greatest fervour.'[21]

In the procession walked the Committee of the Repeal Association, the lord mayor and the members of the Corporation of Dublin, the 'Eighty-two Club, green-uniformed as he would have wished, members of the Royal Irish Academy, the Irish Celtic Society, the Irish Library Association, the artists of the Royal Hibernian Academy, members of Parliament, representatives of Trinity College and of all the scholarly bodies of Ireland, together with a throng of the humble. In the Liberties, the ballad singers sang their own lament. At the cemetery, Reverend Mr Quinton read the service. Duffy, Pigot, Webb, O'Hagan, John Mitchel, Thomas Devin Reilly, Samuel Ferguson, George Petrie, John O'Donovan, William Carleton, William Wilde, and many others whose names rang on in Irish history, stood nearby as they laid him to rest. Thomas Hutton was there in his own right, as well as to represent the broken girl at Elm Park. The coffin bore the words, 'Thomas Osborne Davis, Esq.; died September 16, 1845, aged 30 years.' The last line of the epitaph he had written years earlier was later put on the headstone,

Be my epitaph writ on my country's mind
He served his country and loved his kind.[22]

Davis's friends were stricken as one man, and, in the manner of the followers of Owen Roe O'Neill, they became like,

Sheep without a shepherd
When the snow shuts out the sky.

Dillon, as one struck by 'a dagger', sorrowed so much that he was tempted to be out of this world himself. He could not attend the funeral because he was suffering a recurrence of his lung complaint and was forced to go to Madeira to recover. O'Brien was constrained, but his grief was long-lived and he still sorrowed for Davis and for Ireland during his years in Van Diemen's Land. Brilliant, brittle, vivacious MacNevin was in Galway when he heard and he lamented that the 'bond of union' which had held them all together was broken by the loss of the 'noble, gentle creature'. He mourned that 'bright, pure, manly spirit!' and wrote to Mitchel, 'The more I think of his death – and day by day it grows even more terrible – the more I am afraid to look its effects on the country and on ourselves in the face.' He said that Ireland could have spared a million lives rather than that of Davis, unaware that the million lives were already in jeopardy because the same issue of the *Nation* that mourned Davis ran an article on the 'Disease in the Potatoes' that had just begun to show its first effects in

PRICES OF IRISH STOCKS

PRICE OF SHARES

ENGLISH STOCKS—London Sept. 17.

FOREIGN STOCKS—London, Sept. 11.

THE NATION.

"To create and to foster public opinion in Ireland, and to make it racy of the soil."—CHIEF BARON WOULFE.

REMEMBER THE 30TH MAY, '44.

DUBLIN, SATURDAY, SEPTEMBER 20, 1845.

OUR PROSPECTS

Thomas Davis

Edition of *The Nation*, 20 September 1845, mourning the death of Davis (courtesy of Royal Irish Academy).

the land. MacNevin never recovered from the loss of the one by whom he was 'possessed', lost his faculties and spent his remaining years in a hospital for the mentally ill. Madden told Duffy that 'he never loved any man as much', but with his usual practicality immediately turned to devising ways of recording Davis's life and suggested a biography by Duffy, as the one among them whose mind and will were most closely identified with Davis. Every page of the *Nation* of 20 September, 1845 was bordered in black, which was entirely fitting for it was his chief, public mourner and Davis's highest love in the form of the printed word. Duffy could only manage a few lines to ask his readers to, 'Work as he worked, to live beloved, and to die honoured.' The longer obituary was left to John O'Hagan who paid fitting tribute to one with whom his young manhood had been joined in lasting friendship at Trinity. O'Hagan did his task well. He spoke of Davis who 'has died in his youth, before his matured understanding and his ripened knowledge have poured their wealth upon the world' and went on,

> Of his acquirements it were almost as vain to speak as of his genius. They ranged through all the walks of human thought and speculation, they were as profound as they were various. But of his own people – of their annals, their statistics, their topography, their literature – his knowledge was especially remarkable. No man of his years – we believe no man of his generation – had achieved so full an insight into these things.[23]

Samuel Ferguson, who never ceased to hold loyally to the union between England and Ireland, had admired Davis since they began to know each other in the late 1830s. He said that Davis was 'a poet, a judge and lover of art and elegant literature' who became 'the friend and favourite of the *elite* of the intellectual world of Dublin.' The 'young mind of the country' had listened to him because he 'had sounded the intellectual reveille of a whole people, and, if they had slept long, they awoke refreshed.' He also admired Davis because 'he had all along abjured his party's pretended abhorrence of a recourse to arms', and had taken up Repeal as a thing desirable in itself, rather than as a means to force concessions from the British government. Ferguson was convinced that Davis had done a great deal to get rid of the stage-Irish-buffoon character and had proved that 'accuracy of language, and consistency of ideas were no longer irreconcilable with an Irish style'. Moreover, Davis had stimulated a love of art because he had a gift for 'the perception of beauty and could excite it in the minds of others', but his great and essential service was 'the diffusion of amicable feelings among those who differed in politics and religion'.

Ferguson was also bedridden when he heard of the death. It may have been as well for he spent his time writing the finest of all the elegies that poured from pen after pen in the following days and weeks. His words are not mere praise of Davis. They are also a prayer for Ireland.

I walked through Ballinderry in the springtime,
      When the bud was on the tree;
And I said, in every fresh-ploughed field beholding
      The sowers striding free,
Scattering broadcast forth the corn in golden plenty,
      On the quick seed-clasping soil,
Even such, this day, among the fresh-stirred hearts of Erin,
      Thomas Davis, is thy toil!

I sat by Ballyshannon in the summer,
      And saw the salmon leap;
And I said, as I beheld the gallant creatures
      Spring glittering from the deep,
Through the spray, and through the prone heaps striving onward
      To the calm, clear streams above,
'So seekest thou thy native founts of freedom, Thomas Davis,
      In thy brightness of strength and love!'

I stood on Derrybawn in the autumn,
      And I hear the eagle call,
With a clangorous cry of wrath and lamentation,
      That filled the wide mountain hall
O'er the bare deserted place of his plundered eyrie,
      And I said, as he screamed and soared,
'So callest thou, thou wrathful-soaring Thomas Davis,
      For a nation's rights restored!'

And, alas! to think but now, and thou art lying,
      Dear Davis, dead at thy mother's knee;
And I, no mother near, on my own sick-bed,
      That face on earth shall never see:
I may lie and try to feel that I am not dreaming,
      I may lie and try to say 'Thy will be done' –
But a hundred such as I will never comfort Erin
      For the loss of the noble son!

Young husbandman of Erin's fruitful seed-time,
      In the fresh track of danger's plough!

Who will walk the heavy, toilsome, perilous furrow
		Girt with freedom's seed-sheets now?
Who will banish with the wholesome crop of knowledge
	The flaunting weed and the bitter thorn,
Now that thou thyself art but a seed for hopeful planting
	Against the resurrection morn?

Young salmon of the flood-tide of freedom
		That sweeps round Erin's shore!
Thou wilt leap against their loud oppressive torrent
		Of bigotry and hate no more:
Drawn downward by their prone material instinct,
	Let them thunder on their rocks and foam –
Thou has leapt, aspiring soul, to founts beyond their raging,
	Where troubled waters never come!

But I grieve not, eagle of the empty eyrie,
		That thy wrathful cry is still:
And that the songs alone of peaceful mourners
		Are heard today on Erin's hill:
Better far, if brother's wars be destined for us
		(God avert that horrid day I pray!)
That ere our hands be stained with slaughter fratricidal
	Thy warm heart should be cold in clay.

But my trust is strong in God Who made us brothers,
		That He will not suffer those right hands,
Which thou hast joined in holier rites than wedlock,
		To draw opposing brands.
Oh, many a tuneful tongue that thou mad'st vocal
	Would lie cold and silent then;
And songless long once more should often-widowed Erin
	Mourn the loss of her brave young men.

Oh, brave young men, my love, my pride, my promise,
		'Tis on you my hopes are set,
In manliness, in kindness, in justice
		To make Ireland a nation yet.
Self-respecting, self-relying, self-advancing
	In union, or in severance, free and strong –
And if God grant this, then, under God, to Thomas Davis
	Let the greater praise belong![24]

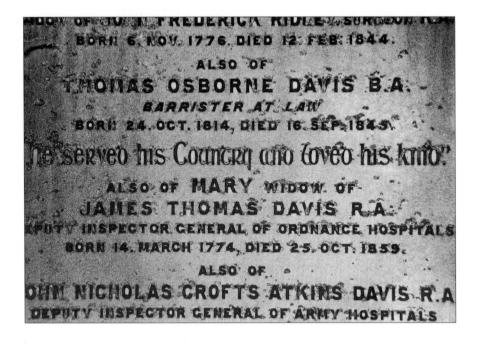

...DOW OF JOHN FREDERICK RIDLEY SURGEON R...
BORN 6. NOV. 1776. DIED 12. FEB. 1844.
ALSO OF
THOMAS OSBORNE DAVIS B.A.
BARRISTER AT LAW
BORN 24. OCT. 1814, DIED 16. SEP. 1845.
"he served his Country and loved his kind."
ALSO OF MARY WIDOW OF
JAMES THOMAS DAVIS R.A.
...PUTY INSPECTOR GENERAL OF ORDNANCE HOSPITALS
BORN 14. MARCH 1774, DIED 25. OCT. 1859.
ALSO OF
...OHN NICHOLAS CROFTS ATKINS DAVIS R.A
DEPUTY INSPECTOR GENERAL OF ARMY HOSPITALS

HANNAH HUTTON
DIED 11TH OCTOBER 1837.
DAUGHTERS OF DANIEL HUTTON

ANNIE HUTTON
DIED 7TH JUNE 1853 AGED 28.
DAUGHTER OF THOMAS HUTTON

SARAH HATCH
DIED 18TH JANUARY 1863 AGED 8.

Grave-slabs of Thomas Davis and Annie Hutton.

The blow that fell on the household at Elm Park on that Tuesday morning was intense and made much the worse for Annie in that she had no suspicion that matters would come to such a final pass. She did not even know whether Thomas had been able to read the letters she sent to him and wondered whether he had feared for her or 'thought that he should not see her again.' Mrs Hutton decided to take her on the proposed trip to the continent and they departed within days. She regained some strength and her cough was almost gone by early October. She and her mother 'fondly hoped the happiness and sunshine of the soul, reflected from the love of that noble spirit which had breathed joy around her, had brought life and healing on its wings.' Annie told Mrs Davis how 'profoundly' she had loved Thomas, but that she tried to 'think of all he has been spared. No woman's love could have saved him from bitter disappointment, no care of mine could have prevented his glorious spirit from being bruised, crushed, by the unworthiness of those he had to deal with.' Finally, she asserted that, 'if I were to live through an eternity of grief, I would not give up that short month of happiness' she had with her beloved. On her return to Dublin in the spring of 1846, she wanted Charlotte Davis to regard her as a sister and to come to visit her at Elm Park 'that he loved so well' and asked 'is it not enough to make us love God to think he lent the world such a mind to shew us what our nature is capable of?' Although she felt the spirit of Davis was close to her, she wished for death in order to 'come to the end and be united' with him, but she was determined to fulfil his wish that she translate from the Italian a book published in Florence in 1844 dealing with Archbishop Rinuccini, who had been the papal envoy in Ireland during the fateful years 1645 to 1649. She laboured at the task and, when the work was almost at the end she could do no more. The book was finished and edited by her mother. Annie died, unmarried, and was buried in St George's cemetery near to her home at Elm Park. Her tombstone bore the simple words, 'Annie Hutton died 7th June, 1853 aged 28'.[25]

The protagonist of Davis's final years was not John O'Connell, who stooped to revile his memory in 1848. Daniel the father, the Liberator and the Leader was the other conductor of the spirit of Ireland and when word came to Derrynane of the death of Ireland's son his great heart, soon itself to be stopped in death, mourned deeply. He wrote a letter to Ray to be read at the next meeting of the Association. On this occasion, O'Connell could rightly claim to speak for all the Irish and thus he deserves the last word. It is fitting that it should ring with the tones of grief of a disconsolate father at the loss of a beloved son,

My mind is bewildered and my heart afflicted. The loss of my beloved friend, my noble-minded friend, is a source of the deepest sorrow to my mind. What a blow – what a cruel blow to the cause of Irish nationality! He was a creature of transcendent quality of mind and heart; his learning was universal, his knowledge was as minute as it was general. And then he was a being of such incessant energy and continuous exertion. I, of course, in the few years – if years they be – still left to me, cannot expect to look upon his like again, or to see the place he has left vacant adequately filled up; and I solemnly declare that I never knew any man who could be so useful to Ireland in the present stage of her struggles. His loss is indeed irreparable. What an example he was to the Protestant youths of Ireland. What a noble emulation of his virtues ought to be excited in the Catholic young men of Ireland! And his heart too! It was as gentle, as kind, as loving as a woman's. Yes, it was as tenderly kind as his judgment was comprehensive and his genius magnificent. We shall long deplore his loss. As I stand alone in the solitude of my mountains, many a tear shall I shed in the memory of the noble youth. Oh! How vain are words or tears when such a national calamity afflicts the country ... I can write no more – my tears blind me – and – after all, 'Fungar inani munere.'[26]

******

The voices of the dead of yesterday's century are long stilled and, with few exceptions, their names are unknown. In the wake of Davis's death, the famine wreaked its havoc and brought Ireland and so many of her people to their knees. O'Connell grieved with them because he loved them to the last. On his way to Rome, he died at Genoa on 15 May 1847. Duffy worked on, revived the *Nation* that had been suppressed in 1848 and became a member of Parliament until 1855 when he left Ireland for Australia in despair. He became premier of the colony of Victoria and tried to reform land legislation there with his series of laws called the Duffy Acts and became an unsung father of Australian federation. He accepted a knighthood for his labours from the queen he had once looked at with cold reserve, retired to Nice and fulfilled the long promise with his biography of Davis whom he had never ceased to love. Duffy died in 1903. John Dillon, his life in jeopardy, fled Ireland for America after the minor insurrection of 1848. He returned to Ireland in 1855 and became a Member of Parliament for a time. Dillon never lost the high estimate in which he was held by all those who knew him. He died in 1866 and again the pages of the *Nation* were black bordered. By the 1860s, the Repeal Association was

342

long since forgotten, the men of Young Ireland were scattered around the globe, and many of the places where they were heard were silent. In time, Conciliation Hall was no more and the heartland of so much Irish history in the Corn Exchange became a derelict barn.

In Ireland, Davis was not forgotten and Denny Lane, who loved him as much as Duffy or any of the others, summed up his influence in 1893, the year of his own death. To a group from the National Literary Society of Ireland, on a visit to his home city of Cork, he said,

> I stood on the outer margin of the group of devoted Irishmen of whom my dear friend Thomas Davis was the centre and inspirer. From him, as from some great organ of life, radiated all those currents that then coursed through the frame of Ireland, and back to him again converged, from the remotest extremities of the land, and from the furthest outposts of our race, those counter-currents which helped to revive our country into warmth and into life. Then indeed 'a soul came into Ireland'. By the touch of a magic wand, the sleepers were awakened.[27]

It is not the role of the historian to speculate about the future, even of a future that is now in the past, but based on his convictions and his actions, it is legitimate to ask the question where Davis would have stood in the struggles that lay ahead. Without giving an inch he would have helped Duffy and the others to maintain the *Nation* as the single, most powerful and effective weapon they then possessed in the struggle for nationality and for educating the masses. He would have remained true to O'Connell, even though John O'Connell and others continued to attack the *Nation,* but he would have refused an alliance with the Whigs on their return to power in 1846. Finally, he would have been forced, in company with O'Brien, Duffy, Meagher, Mitchel and others, to secede from the Repeal Association. He may have persuaded them to give way to O'Connell and his son on the issue of the use of violence, but the very thought of giving up Repeal, as O'Connell was prepared to do, was a step he would never have contemplated. Based on his conviction that violent conflict could never be ruled out as an ultimate choice in the struggle for independence, there can be little doubt but that Davis would have chosen that road if its inevitability had become clear in his lifetime. Nonetheless, his military bent, his knowledge of tactics and his conviction that armed struggle was useless, unless thoroughly and lengthily prepared for, would have made him refuse to countenance the gesture of insurrection by Smith O'Brien and the others in 1848.

The reform of land tenure and the loss of an established Church were already among his objectives. Short of full independence, Home

Rule, as a step towards that goal, and the total and thorough reform of land holding in Ireland would have been welcomed and worked for by Davis. The revival of the Irish language, the birth of a national theatre, the growth of an Irish literature in prose and poetry, whether in Irish or English; all these would have been a passion to him. A divided Ireland was so unthinkable that it was not seen as possible, scarcely thought as a hidden thought by Davis, because to him Ireland was a unity of land and people that he could not have suffered to see broken. An Ireland, shattered in its unity and mangled in its integrity, with the loss to it of the people of the north and the great richness they could bring to their country, would have broken Davis also. The priceless richness of an Ireland in which a Protestant minority, acting throughout its totality as a peaceful protest against religious and cultural homogeneity, rather than confined to a few northern counties, would have been precious to Davis. So precious in fact that, to preserve or restore its unity, Davis would have given life itself. When his life, his works, his spirit and his love for Ireland and all its people, regardless of origin or religion, are thought about, it may be that, from the well-springs of nationality that Davis drew from and expanded, re-union and reconciliation can flow in a united Ireland. He fully recognised the right, based on generations of residence, of the Protestant people of the north to live there in peace and happiness and his words to them on reconciliation still echo over the decades since his death,

> Surely our Protestant brethren cannot shut their eyes to the honour it would confer on them and us if we gave up old brawls and bitterness, and came together in love like Christians, in feeling like countrymen, in policy like men having common interests. Can they – ah! tell us, dear countrymen! – can you harden your hearts at the thought of looking on Irishmen joined in commerce, agriculture, art, justice, government, wealth, and glory?

Arthur Griffith wrote in 1914, 'When the Irish read and reflect with Davis, their day of redemption will be at hand.'[28]

Through the years many have written, sung and spoken of his legacy. The ancient bardic saying, 'Tháinig anam in Éirinn', 'A Soul came into Ireland', was fulfilled in Thomas Davis because he became part of the conscience of the Celt. The achievement and development, in its finest flowering, of the nationality of his people was the mission of his life. The spirit he breathed was one of love and respect, of the need for the uplifting and creative development of individuals. That spirit lives wherever democracy truly breathes. Davis's legacy was not of a creed, party or organisation, because such things can never be more than instruments of good. His legacy was that of the infinite capacity of the individual person for good, for justice, truth and beauty. From that source all that is precious, and can ever be precious in the long march of humanity, alone flows.

References

1. Dillon to Davis, n.d. but July 1845 in Duffy, *Davis*, pp 315-6.
2. See Joseph Hone (ed.), *The love story*, pp ix, xii. Burton was later the Director of the National Gallery in London.
3. Davis to Madden 31 July in Duffy, *Davis*, p. 355; Madden to Davis, 4 August 1845, Pigot to Davis, 9 August 1845 in Ms 2644, NLI.
4. Annie Hutton to Davis, 16, 20 August 1845 in Hone, *The love story*, pp 1-5. T. Caldwell [printer] to Davis, 20 August 1845 in Duffy, *Davis*, p. 353. Davis's letters to Annie have not been traced.
5. Hone, *The love story*, pp x, xi.
6. Annie Hutton to Davis, n.d. but early September 1845 in Duffy, *Davis*, pp 359-60.
7. Ibid.
8. Duffy to Davis, 14 August 1845 in Ms 2644, NLI; *Nation*, 30 August 1845.
9. MacNevin to Duffy, n.d. but summer 1845, in Duffy, *Davis*, p. 316.
10. *Nation*, 9 August 1845; O'Brien to Davis, 3, 23 August 1845 in Ms 2644, NLI. Duffy, *Davis*, p. 314 misdates O'Brien's second letter to 23 July 1845; O'Faolain, *King of the beggars*, p. 321.
11. *Nation*, 2 August 1845; O'Brien to Davis, 3 August 1845, Ms 2644, NLI.
12. Davis to O'Brien, n.d. late August 1845, Ms 432, NLI, *Nation,* 16 August 1845.
13. Ibid., 16, 23 August 1845. *Freeman's Journal*, 18 August 1845; Davis to O'Brien, n.d. late August 1845, Ms 432, NLI. Duffy, *Young Ireland*, part 1, pp 280-81.
14. *Nation*, 30 August, 6 September 1845.
15. See *Thomas Davis: essays and poems*, p. 45; *Nation*, 20 September 1845; Report of the Commissioners for National Education, 1855, XXVII, in Marilyn Kelly, "The silence of the tongues, the clamour for souls'. M.Phil. Irish Studies, University College Galway, p. 46, Ó Cathaoir, *Dillon*, p. 26.
16. Annie Hutton to Davis, 26 August, 2 September 1845 in Hone, *The love story*, pp 5-8.
17. Davis to Duffy, n.d. but 9 September, 1845 in Ms 12 P 19, RIA; Davis to Mitchel, 6 September 1845 in Mitchel, *The last conquest*, p. 89; Davis to O'Brien, n.d. 9 September 1845 in Ms 432, NLI; MacNevin to Davis, n.d. 10 September, 1845 in Duffy, *Davis*, p. 364.
18. Annie Hutton to Davis, 10 September 1845 in Hone, *The love story*, pp 9-10; on Stokes see Jeanne Sheehy, *The rediscovery*, p. 24.
19. Davis to Duffy, 10 September 1845, Ms 12 P 19, RIA; Mrs Hutton to Mrs Davis, from Frankfurt, 8 October 1845, in Ms 5758, NLI. Duffy to Davis. n.d. but 11 September 1845 in Duffy, *Davis*, p. 365. Duffy strongly hints that Davis visited Elm Park on Sunday, 14 September, but such could not have been the case. The account of Davis meeting John O'Connell is in *Freeman's Journal*, 17 September 1845.
20. Annie Hutton to Thomas Davis, 12 September 1845 in Hone, *The love story*, pp 11-13; Mrs Hutton to Mrs Davis, 8 October 1845 in Ms 5758, NLI; Duffy, *Davis*, pp 365-6; *Nation*, 27 September 1845.

21. Ibid., 20 September 1845; *Freeman's Journal*, 17, 18, 19 September 1845; Duffy, *Davis*, pp 367-9; Mrs Davis to the ex-Repeal wardens of London, 1 November 1845, Ms 5756, NLI. Davis had intervened, vainly, on behalf of the ex-wardens who had been relieved of their positions so as to accommodate the debts of William John O'Connell, a kinsman of Daniel O'Connell, who served as inspector-general of the London wardens. See Duffy, *Davis*, pp 351-2 and for William John O'Connell, derisively called 'Lord Kilmallock', see W. R. Le Fanu, *Seventy years*, pp 140-44; *Nation*, 20 September 1845; *Freeman's Journal*, 17, 18, 19 September 1845; Duffy, *Davis*, pp 367-9.

22. *Nation,* 20 September 1845; *Freeman's Journal*, 17, 18, 19 September 1845; Duffy, *Davis*, pp 367-69; Loma Kellett, 'The *Nation* in mourning' in MacManus, *Davis and Young Ireland*, pp 32-7. Davis's remains lie in an unkempt vault with those of his mother, his brothers, an aunt and a sister-law.

23. Dillon to Duffy, 18, 24 September 1845; MacNevin to Duffy, 18 September 1845, Ms 5756, NLI; Madden to Duffy, n.d. September 1845 in Duffy, *Davis,* pp 366-7; *Nation*, 20 September 1845.

24. Samuel Ferguson, 'Our portrait gallery: Thomas Davis' in *Dublin University Magazine*, vol. xxix, January-June 1847 (Dublin, 1847), pp 190-99; Duffy, *Davis*, p. 372; Duffy, *Young Ireland*, vol. 1, p. 282.

25. Mrs Hutton and Annie to Mrs Davis, from France and Frankfurt, 8, 9 October 1845, Ms 5758, NLI; Annie Hutton to Charlotte Davis, 27 March 1846, in Hone, *The love story*, pp 13-17, G. Aiazzi (ed.), *Nunziatura in Irelanda di Monsignor G. B. Rinuccini ... negli anni 1645 a 1649* (Florence, 1844); Annie Hutton, *The Embassy in Ireland of Monsignor G. B. Rinuccini Archbishop of Fermo – in the year 1645-1649* (Dublin, 1873). The volume runs to 598 pages. Among the subscribers to its publication were Duffy, Gladstone, J. Anthony Froude, John O'Hagan, William Wilde, Robert Kane, Professor Mahaffy and Talbot of Malahide. St.George's cemetery is situated off Whitworth Road near to Elm Park. See introduction to 'Letters of Thomas Davis' in the *Irish Monthly*, part 2, vol. 16 (Dublin, 1888), p. 336. Annie's grave later became part of the Hutton tomb on which a family headstone now stands. Her father's inscription reads, 'Thomas Hutton of Elm Park, Esq. J.P. D.L. [deputy-lieutenant] died 12 November 1865 aged 78'. The mother's is 'Margaret Hutton died 11 January 1877 aged 79'.

26. O'Connell to Ray, 17 September 1845 in Maurice O'Connell (ed.), *The correspondence*, vol. vii, p. 342. The Latin is Horace, 'My task is fruitless.'

27. See Denis Gwynn, 'Denny Lane and Thomas Davis' in *Studies*, vol. 38 (Dublin, 1949), p. 28.

28. For Davis see Rolleston (ed.), *Prose writings*, p. 254; Griffith is in Arthur Griffith, *Davis*, p. xiv.

Appendix 1

Irish Historical Paintings
(From Davis, *Prose writings*, 155-7)

The Landing of the Milesians. — Keating, Moore's Melodies.

Ollamh Fodhla Presenting his Laws to his People. Keating's, Moore's, and O'Halloran's Histories of Ireland. — Walker's Irish Dress and Arms, and Vallancey's Collectanea.

Nial and his Nine Hostages. — Moore, Keating.

A Druid's Augury. — Moore, O'Halloran, Keating.

A Chief Riding Out of his Fort. — Griffin's Invasion, Walker, Moore.

The Oak of Kildare. — Moore.

The Burial of King Dathy in the Alps, his thinned troops laying stones on his grave. — McGeoghegan, 'Histoire de l'Irlande' (French edition), Invasion, Walker, Moore.

St. Patrick brought before the Druids at Tara. — Moore and his Authorities.

The First Landing of the Danes. — See Invasion, Moore, etc.

The Death of Turgesius. — Keating, Moore.

Ceallachan tied to the Mast. — Keating.

Murkertach Returning to Aileach. — Archaeological Society's Tracts.

Brian Reconnoitring the Danes before Clontarf.

The Last of the Danes Escaping to his Ship.

O'Ruarc's Return. — Keating, Moore's Melodies.

Raymond Le Gros Leaving his Bride. — Moore.

Roderic in Conference with the Normans. — Moore, McGeoghegan.

Donald O'Brien Setting Fire to Limerick. — McGeoghegan.

Donald O'Brien Visiting Holycross. — McGeoghegan.

O'Brien, O'Connor, and McCarthy making Peace to attack the Normans. — McGeoghan, Moore.

The Same Three Victorious at the Battle of Thurles. — Moore and O'Conor's Rerum Hibernicarum Scriptores.

Irish Chiefs leaving Prince John. — Moore, etc.

McMurrough and Gloster. — Harris's Hibernica, p. 53.

Crowning of Edward Bruce. — Leland, Grace's Annals, etc.

Edgecombe Vainly Trying to Overawe Kildare. — Harris's Hibernica.

Kildare 'On the Necks of the Butlers.' — Leland.

Shane O'Neill at Elizabeth's Court. — Leland.

Lord Sydney Entertained by Shane O'Neill.

The Battle of the Red Coats. — O'Sullivan's Catholic History.

Hugh O'Neill Victor in Single Combat at Clontibret. — Fynes

Moryson, O'Sullivan, McGeoghegan.

The Corleius. — Dymmok's Treatise, Archaeological Society's Tracts.

Maguire and St Leger in Single Combat. — McGeoghegan.

O'Sullivan Crossing the Shannon. — Pacata Hibernia.

O'Dogherty Receiving the Insolent Message of the Governor of Derry. — McGeoghegan.

The Brehon before the English Judges. — Davis's Letter to Lord Salisbury.

Ormond Refusing to give up his Sword. — Carte's Life of Ormond.

Good Lookers-on. — Strafford's Letters.

Owen Conolly before the Privy Council, 1641. — Carey's Vindiciae.

The Battle of Julianstown. — Temple's Rebellion, and Tichbourne's Drogheda.

Owen Roe Organising the Creaghts. — Carte, and also Belling and O'Neill in the Desiderata Curiosa Hibernica.

The Council of Kilkenny. — Carte.

The Breach of Clonmel. — Do.

Smoking Out the Irish. — Ludlow's Memoirs.

Burning Them. — Castlehaven's Memoirs.

Nagle before the Privy Council. — Harris's William.

James Entry into Dublin. — Dublin Magazine for March 1843.

The Bridge of Athlone. — Green Book and Authorities.

St Ruth's Death. — Do.

The Embarkation from Limerick. — Do.

Cremona. — Cox's Magazine.

Fontenoy. — Do.

Sir S. Rice Pleading against the Violation of the Treaty of Limerick. — Staunton's Collection of Tracts on Ireland.

Molyneux's Book Burned.

Liberty Boys Reading a Drapier's Letter. — Mason's St Patrick's Cathedral.

Lucas Surrounded by Dublin Citizens in his Shop.

Grattan Moving Liberty. — Memoirs.

Flood Apostrophising Corruption. — Barrington.

Dungannon Convention. — Wilson, Barrington.

Curran Cross-examining Armstrong. — Memoirs.

Curran Pleading before the Council in Alderman James's Case.

Tone's First Society. — See his Memoirs.

The Belfast Club. — Madden's U. I., Second Series, vol. i.

Tone, Emmet, and Keogh in the Rathfarnham Garden.

Tone and Carnot. — Tone's Memoirs.

Battle of Oulart. — Hay, Teeling, etc.

First Meeting of the Catholic Association.

O'Connell Speaking in a Munster Chapel. — Wyse's Association.

The Clare Hustings. — Proposal of O'Connell.

The Dublin Corporation Speech.

Father Matthew Administering the Pledge in a Munster County.

Conciliation. — Orange and Green.

The Lifting of the Irish Flags of a National Fleet and Army.

Appendix 2
(From Duffy, *Davis*, pp. 393-4)

Irish History
Political, Social and Military History, from 1692 to 1829

Books, &c. | College Library | Marsh's Library | 22 pts. | Rolls office. | British Museum
    | Paris
Governors of Ireland | Plowden | Thorpe papers | Ormond.
Write to priests for anecdotes of Penal laws.
Statutes | Journals of Commons | Walker's Magazine.
Cox's Magazine | Dalrymple | Swift's Works | Mason's State P^{hs} to W.W.'s, Dublin |
    King & Harris MS.
Tone's life | Madden | Lucas' Works | Flood's Life and Letters.
Grattan's Memoir & Speeches | Curran's | Pamphlets.
Baratiana | Travels in Ireland, see College Library.
Edgeworth, Morgan, Griffin, Banim, Campbell's L. of Ireland.
Arthur Young on Manners.
Dublin Society's Labours | Wyse and reports.
Curry's Life, Parnell's, O'Connor's, Howard's, Scully's.
MS. notes on Penal laws. Sir J. F^{gd} the fair of Cashell, Pipers | Sheehy | fee simples
    O'Sull^n (Thierry as a model) recruiting for the Brigade (see papers).
Music, Bunting, Squire Jones | Dr. M'Donnell.
Local Hist^{ries} Hardiman, Macgregor, Smith, Mason, Windele Dutton, (Rowley Lascelles)
    An^m Hy., Wilson's Volunteers | Teeling, Hay, Graham, Musgrave, Holt, Lord E. Fit^d
    diff^t States in diff^t Provinces.

Chr^l table	Financial tables.
Catalogue of Pamphlets, books,	Pop^{tion}.
etc. used, & criticisms on	Surface & dis^{ons}.
them & papers.	Tables of gov^{rs}.
————	Ch^{rsn} Ministers.
Arts & lit^{re} during this time,	Arch.bps. & bps.
costume. ————	Provosts.
Society, arch^{re}.	Parliaments.
Trade (Spain, Engl.)	List of Absentees.

He estimated, at the same time, the space the separate periods would occupy.

Intro^n & Rev^n	50	— to Cath^c Com^e	30
(clear and highly wrought).		Lord Fitz^m	20
First effect of Rev^n	20	U.I.	30
Molyneux	5	Insur^{tn}	50
— to Swift	15	Union	50
Swift	50	To 1812	30
Lucas	30	To 1817	20
Flood	50	To 1829	50
Grattan	50		580

The grave-stone of Thomas Davis in Mount Jerome cemetery, Harold's Cross, Dublin.

Bibliography

Primary Sources
National Library of Ireland, Dublin
Davis papers.
Davis to Duffy, letters, 1840-45.
Davis to William Smith O'Brien, letters.
Davis, collection of material of Irish balladry.
Davis's notes for a book on Wolfe Tone.
Davis. Two lectures to the Historical Society; notes for a book on the English invasion of Ireland; a leading article on 'Justice in Tipperary' and 'Origin and Writers of the *Nation*'.
Davis Testimonial proceedings.
Davis's lists of officers in Irish regiments in France.
Davis centenary papers 1945.
Davis, Carolan's airs.
Davis, 45 Irish Song Sheets of Irish Street Ballads.
Charles Gavan Duffy, cuttings relating to Anglo-Irish balladry.
Charles Gavan Duffy, collection of miscellaneous scraps.
Charles Gavan Duffy, correspondence.
Count Plunkett papers, including a manuscript by Davis.
F. S. Bourke collection, including a letter by Davis to James Finn.
Remarks on the Index to the *Spirit of the Nation* sent to Davis by Eugene O'Curry.
Daniel O'Connell, letter to Davis.
List of signatories for Repeal 30 May 1845.
Items relating to Gavan Duffy and others.
William Smith O'Brien papers, including letters by Davis 1844-5.
Walshe, R. D. Cuttings and notes relating to Thomas Davis.
Tasmanian Journal of William Smith O'Brien.
Thomas Wyse, papers.
Kathleen McKenna, Napoli papers.
Thomas Davis commemoration lists, 1945.

Genealogical Office, Dublin.
Davis, KK, John Nicholas, Croft Atkins, 'Pedigrees'.

Royal Irish Academy
Two notebooks of Thomas Davis.
Davis's letter to John Windele.
Davis and others' letters to Duffy and Davis diary fragments.
Book of Autographs and MSS of the Young Irelanders and many of their contemporaries.
Davis and others' letters in Songs and Nursery Rhymes.

Papers read at the Thomas Davis and Young Ireland centenary.

R. R. Madden papers.

Haig, Mr. An index to articles of the *Dublin University Magazine* vols. 1-55 January 1833-June 1860 dated 1 July 1864 with a handwritten introduction by Richard Robert Madden.

Trinity College Dublin
John Blake Dillon papers.

University College Dublin
Irish Folklore collection. Department of Irish Folklore, University College Dublin.

Newspapers and Journals
An Consantóir (Dublin)
Anglo-Irish studies (Cambridge)
Catholic historical review (Washington, D.C.)
Canadian historical review (Toronto)
Canadian journal of Irish studies (Vancouver)
Citizen (1839-41) then *The Dublin Monthly Magazine* (1841-43)
Dublin Evening Post
Dublin Journal
Dublin Review (London)
Dublin University Magazine
Dublin University Review
Eighteenth-century Ireland (Dublin)
Éire-Ireland (Minnesota)
English historical review (Harlow)
Etudes Irlandaise (Lille)
Freeman's Journal (Dublin)
Gentleman's Magazine (London)
Hermathena (Dublin)
History Ireland (Dublin)
Historical journal (Cambridge)
Historical studies (London)
Historical studies (Melbourne)
Irish Book Lover (London)
Irish ecclesiastical record (Dublin)
Irish economic and social history (Belfast)
Irish historical studies (Dublin)
Irish Monthly (Dublin)
Irish Times (Dublin)
Journal of the Galway archeological and historical society (Galway)
Morning Register (Dublin)
Nation (Dublin)
New Ireland Review (Dublin)

Pilot (Dublin)
Studies (Dublin)
Studia hibernica (Dublin)
The Bell (Dublin)
The Other Clare (Shannon)
Thought (New York)
Threshold (Dublin)
Times (London)
Transactions of the Royal historical society (London)
Ulster folklife (Belfast)
Vindicator (Belfast)

DAVIS'S WORKS (including those edited by others)
The reform of the Lords by a graduate of the Dublin University, Dublin, 1837.
An address read before the Historical Society, Dublin, on the 26th of June, 1840, Dublin, 1840.
Essays: literary and historical essays by Thomas Davis, Dublin, 1845 and 1945.
Golden words of Thomas Davis, Dublin, 1845.
A member of the Irish press; history and proceedings of the '82 Club, Dublin, 1845.
The life of the Right Hon. J. P. Curran, Dublin, 1846.
The poems of Thomas Davis: now first collected, Thomas Wallis (ed.), Dublin, 1846.
Letters of a Protestant on Repeal, edited by T. F. Meagher, Dublin, 1847.
History and proceedings of the '82 Club. Edited by a member of the press. To be continued quarterly, nos 1 and 2, Dublin 1845.
Irish national ballads, songs and essays, edited by Thomas Wallis, Dublin, 1848.
Poems, with notes, historical illustrations, etc., introduction by John Mitchel, New York, 1854.
National and historical ballads, songs, and poems, edited by Thomas Wallis, Dublin, 1869.
Prose writings: essays on Ireland by Thomas Davis, edited by T. W. Rolleston, London, 1899.
Canada. Parliament and Senate. Select committee on resources of territory between Labrador and the Rocky Mountains, edited by Captain Ernest J. Chambers, Ottawa, 1906.
National and other poems, edited by Thomas Wallis. Dublin, 1907.
Thomas Davis: selections from his prose and poetry, edited by T. W. Rolleston, London, 1914.
The patriot parliament of 1689 with its statutes, votes and proceedings, edited with an introduction by the Hon. Sir Charles Gavan Duffy, London, 1893.
Our national language, Dublin, 1914.
Thomas Davis: Essays and poems with a centenary memoir 1845-1945. Foreword by Eamon de Valera, Dublin, 1945.
Thomas Davis: the thinker and teacher. The essence of his writings in prose and poetry, Arthur Griffith (ed.), Dublin, 1914.

Sinn Féin poems of Thomas Davis, Dublin, n.d. 1930s.
Songs, ballads and poems by famous Irishmen: Thomas Davis, Dublin, 1945.
The battle eve of the Brigade. Words by Davis. Music by P. J. Ryan, Dublin, n.d.
Clare's Dragoons. Words by Davis, arranged by T. D. Ryan, Dublin, 1941.
Davis, T.D. *Sheet music,* words by Davis, Dublin, 1964.

Davis's reports to the Parliamentary sub-committee of the Loyal National repeal Association

Arms (Ireland) returns, Dublin, 1844.
Army estimates for 1844-45, Dublin, 1844.
First report of the sub-committee on the Estimates for 1844-45, Dublin, 1844.
Commissariat estimates 1844-45, Dublin, 1844.
Correspondence between Lord Wicklow and the Loyal National Repeal Association, Dublin, 1844.
Militia estimates for 1844-45, Dublin, 1844.
Navy estimates 1844-45, Dublin, 1844.
Ordnance estimates, 1844-45. Dublin, 1844.
Ordnance memoir of Ireland, Dublin, 1844.
The attendance of Irish members in Parliament, Dublin, 1844.
The hurrying of Bills through Parliament, Dublin, 1844.
The opening of Post Office letters, Dublin, 1844.
Tenants' Compensation Bill, Dublin, 1845.
Valuation (Ireland) Bill, Dublin, 1845.
Bill to enable town councils to establish museums of art, Dublin, 1845.

Contemporary Sources

Books, pamphlets, articles and works of reference, including works published later but of contemporary provenance.

'A Batch of "Young Ireland" Letters', in *The Irish Monthly*, vols 11, 12, 14, 16, Dublin, 1883, 84, 86, 88.

A Catholic Priest. *Thoughts on academical education, ecclesiastical and secular*, Dublin, 1845.

Aiazzi, G. (ed.), *Nunziatura in Irelanda di Monsignor G. B. Rinuccini...negli anni 1645 a 1649,* Florence, 1844.

Armstrong, John Simpson, *A report of the proceedings on an indictment for a conspiracy in the case of the Queen v Daniel O'Connell*, Dublin, 1844.

Barrington, Daines, *Observations upon the statutes, chiefly the more ancient, from Magna Carta to twenty-first James the First*, London, 1766, 2nd. ed., Dublin, 1767.

Barry, Michael Joseph, *Ireland as she was, as she is and as she shall be.* First Prize Repeal Essay, Dublin, 1845.

___ (ed.), *The songs of Ireland*, 2nd. ed., Dublin, 1846.

Battersby, W. J., *The repealer's manual*, Dublin, 1833.

Beranger, G., *Beranger's views of Ireland*, with text by Peter Harbison, Dublin 1991.

Bourke, Ulick J., *The life and times of the Most Rev. John MacHale, Archbishop of Tuam and Metropolitan*, 2nd. ed., Dublin, 1882.

Carleton, William, *Traits and stories of the Irish peasantry*, D. J. O'Donoghue (ed.), London, 1986.

Cooper, P. (Rev.), *Letters on education addressed to the Catholic prelates*, Dublin, 1845.

Dalton, John, *Letter on the Irish Colleges Bill and on academic education generally*, Dublin, 1845.

Daunt, Alice O'Neill (ed.), *A life spent for Ireland: being selections from the journals of the late W. J. O'Neill Daunt*, London, 1896.

Daunt, W. J. O'Neill, *Personal recollections of the late Daniel O'Connell, M.P.*, 2 vols, London, 1848.

___, *Ireland and her agitators*, Dublin, 1867.

___, *Eighty-five years of Irish history: 1800-1885*, 2 vols, London, 1886.

___, *Ireland since the Union*, Dublin, 1888.

Dawson, Edward, *First letter to the tradesmen and labourers of Ireland on the repeal of the Union*, Dublin, 1845.

De Beaumont, Gustave, *L'Irlande sociale, politique et religieuse*, 2 vols, Paris, 1839.

De Jean, J., *Poems for the people*, Dublin, 1845.

Dillon, John, *An address read before the Historical Society, Dublin Institute, at the close of the session 1840-41*, Dublin, 1842.

Dillon, William, *Life of John Mitchel*, 2 vols, London, 1888.

Doheny, Michael, *The felon's track*, Dublin, 1918 edition.

Dublin University Calendar, Dublin, 1836, 1837.

Duffy, Charles Gavan, *Thomas Davis: Literary and historical essays*, Dublin, 1846.

___, *Young Ireland: A fragment of Irish history, 1840-1845*, Dublin, 1884.

___, *Young Ireland; Part 2 or four years of Irish history, 1845-1849*, Dublin, 1887.

___, *Thomas Davis: The memoirs of an Irish patriot, 1840-1846*, London, 1890.

___, *Short life of Thomas Davis 1840-1846*, London, 1895.

___, *My life in two hemispheres*, 2 vols, London, 1898.

___, *The ballad poetry of Ireland*, Charles Gavan Duffy (ed.), facsimile of the fortieth edition, 1869, New York, 1973.

Dunkley, R., *Report of the Great Protestant commemoration ... for the Dublin Protestant Operative's Association*, Dublin, 1845.

Ellis, Hercules, *Memoranda of Irish Matters: 'Ireland is our Party'*, Dublin, 1844.

Ferguson, Lady, *Sir Samuel Ferguson in the Ireland of his day*, 2 vols, Edinburgh, 1896.

Ferguson, Samuel, 'Our portrait gallery: Thomas Davis' in *Dublin University Magazine*, vol. xxix, January-June, Dublin, 1847.

Fichte, Johann Gottlieb, *Addresses to the German nation*, R. F. Jones and G. H. Turnbull (trans.), Conneticut, 1979.

Fine Arts in Ireland 1840-41: Second annual report, Dublin, 1842.

Fine Arts in Ireland 1843: Royal Irish Art Union, Dublin, 1844.

Fine Arts in Ireland 1844. Fifth annual report of the Committee of selection of the Royal Irish Art Union, Dublin, 1845.

Foster, John, *Essays in a series of letters to a friend*, 2 vols, 3rd. ed., London, 1806.

Glynn, P., 'Biographical Sketches no iii. Thomas Davis' in *The Dublin Journal*, February, 1887.

Griffith, Arthur (ed.), *Meagher of the sword: speeches of Thomas Francis Meagher in Ireland 1846-1848*, Dublin, 1917.

Hall, Mr and Mrs S. C., *Ireland: its scenery, character, etc.* vol. i, London, 1841, vol. ii, London, 1842, vol. iii, London, 1843.

Hall, Mrs. S. C., *Tales of Irish life and character*, London, 1913.

Herve, Edouard, *La Crise Irlandaise*, Paris, 1885.

Hickey, Michael P., 'Nationality according to Thomas Davis', in *The New Ireland Review*, Dublin, May 1898.

Holmes' defence of the 'Nation': a special report of the proceedings in the case of the Queen v. Charles Duffy Esq ... on an indictment for seditious libel. Dublin, 1846.

Holmes, Robert, *The case of Ireland stated*, 2nd. ed., Dublin, 1847.

Hone, Joseph (ed.), *The love story of Thomas Davis told in the letters of Annie Hutton.* Dublin, 1945.

Hutton, Annie (trans.), *The embassy in Ireland of Monsignor G. B. Rinuccini, Archbishop of Fermo in the years 1645-1649*, Dublin, 1873.

Kickham, Charles J., *Knocknagow, or, the homes of Tipperary*, Dublin, 1870.

Larkin, Emmett (trans. and ed.), *Alexis de Tocqueville's journey in Ireland July-August, 1835*, Dublin, 1990.

Le Fanu, W. R., *Seventy years of Irish life: being anecdotes and reminiscences*, 3rd. ed. Dublin, 1894.

Levy, John (ed.), *A full and revised report of the three days' discussion in the Corporation of Dublin on the Repeal of the Union*, Dublin, 1843.

Luby, T. C., *The life and times of Daniel O'Connell*, Glasgow, c. 1880.

McCarton, Michael, *Instructions for Young Ireland how to conciliate the Protestants and repeal the Union ... addressed to Daniel O'Connell*, Dublin, 1845.

MacDermott, Martin (ed.), *The new spirit of the Nation*, London, 1894.

MacHale, John, *The letters of the Most Rev. John MacHale ... Archbishop of Tuam*, 2 vols, Dublin, 1888.

MacNevin, Thomas, *The lives and trials of ... eminent Irishmen*, Dublin, 1846.

Madden, Daniel Owen, *Ireland and its rulers since 1829*, 2 vols, London, 1843, 1844.

___, *The impolicy and injustice of imprisoning O'Connell*, London, 1844.

Madden, Richard Robert, *The connexion between the Kingdom of Ireland and the Crown of England*, Dublin, 1845.

Maunsell, Robert, *Recollections of Ireland*, London, 1865.

Mitchel, John, *The last conquest of Ireland (perhaps)*, Dublin, 1861.

___, *The history of Ireland*, 2 vols, Dublin, 1869.

Mitford, Mary Russell, *Recollections of a literary life*, London, 1859.

Molyneux, William, *The case of Ireland's being bound by Acts of Parliament in England stated*, Dublin, 1698.

___, *The case of Ireland stated by William Molyneux*, with intro. by J. G. Simms and afterword by Denis Donoghue, Dublin, 1977.

Montgomery, Henry Riddell, *An essay towards investigating the causes that have retarded the progess of Literature in Ireland Read before the Belfast Rhetorical Society, 25 November, 1842*. Belfast, 1843.

Montgomery, R. Martin, *Ireland before and after the Union with Great Britain*, London, 1843.

Mulvany, Annabella, *Letters from Professor Thomas J. Mulvany R.H.A. 1825-1845*, n.p. n.d.

Nemo, *A few words on the new Irish colleges*, London, 1845.

O'Callaghan, John Cornelius, *The Green Book or gleanings from the writing-desk of a literary agitator*, Dublin, 1841.

O'Connell, John, *The Repeal dictionary*, Part One, Dublin, 1845.

___, *An argument for Ireland*, Dublin, 1844.

O'Connell, Daniel, *Letters on the repeal of the legislative union, between Great Britain and Ireland*, Dublin, 1830.

___, *An historical memoir of the Irish, Native and Saxon, addressed to Her Majesty Queen Victoria*, vol. 1, 1172-1660, Dublin, 1843.

___, *The twenty-two unanswerable objections of Daniel O'Connell to the Bequests Bill*, Dublin, 1845.

O'Donohoe, Patrick, *Irish wrongs and English misrule or the repealers' epitome of grievances*, Dublin, 1845.

O'Hagan, John, 'Thomas Davis', in *The Irish Monthly*, vol. 19, Dublin, January 1891.

Parker, Charles Stuart (ed.), *Sir Robert Peel: from his private papers*, 3 vols, vol. 1, London, 1891, vols 2 and 3, London, 1899.

Pettigrew and Oulton, *Directory*, Dublin, 1835.

Porter, John Grey. *Some calm observations upon Irish affairs*. London, 1845.

___, *Ireland*, 3rd ed., London, 1844.

Ramsay, George, *A proposal for the restoration of the Irish parliament*, Dublin, 1845.

Ray, Thomas M., *Repeal reading rooms*, Dublin, 1845.

Reports of the parliamentary committee of the Loyal National Repeal Association, Dublin, vol. i, 1844, vol. ii, 1845, vol. iii, 1846.

Reports of the committee and sub-committees of the Loyal National Repeal Association 1844-45 (as follows):

Bianconi, Charles, *Lunatic Asylums of Ireland*, Dublin, 1845.

Barry, Michael, *Papers relating to Science*, Dublin, 1844.

Brady, Francis, *Borough franchise*, Dublin, 1844.

___, *County franchises of Ireland*, Dublin, 1844.

___, *Borough's electors manual*, Dublin, 1844.

Crean, Martin, *The glass duties,* Dublin, 1844.

Doheny, Michael, *The Irish municipal amendment Bill*, Dublin, 1844.

Fitzgerald, J. L., *Petit juries: County Tipperary*, Dublin, 1844.

___, *General Grand Jury laws of Ireland*, Dublin, 1845.

Kane, Robert, *The industrial resources of Ireland*. Dublin, 1844.

Molloy, Brian Arthur, *On the report of the Council of the Chamber of Commerce, Dublin, for 1844*, Dublin, 1845.

Mullen, Robert, *The removal of the Irish Poor from Ireland*, Dublin, 1844.

O'Connell, Daniel, *First and second reports on the Land Question*, Dublin, 1845.

___, *Bill for the perpetual endowment of Maynooth*, Dublin, 1845.

O'Connell, Maurice, *Irish Fisheries*, Dublin, 1844.

O'Brien, William Smith, *First General Report of the Parliamentary Petitions Committee*, Dublin, 1844.

___, *Petition to the House of Commons praying for an enquiry into the State Trials,* Dublin, 1844.

___, *Second General Report of the Parliamentary Petitions Committee,* Dublin, 1844.

O'Dowd, James, *Service of Process Bills for England and Scotland*, Dublin, 1845.

Reynolds, John, *Joint Stock Banking in Ireland*, Dublin, 1844.

___, *Issue of Bank Notes in Ireland*, Dublin, 1845.

Second report of the sub-committee on the removal from England of poor persons born in Ireland, Dublin, 1845 [This is the last of the reports].

Rossetti, William Michael (ed.), *The poetical works of Thomas Moore*, London, 1870.

Scully, Denys, *A Statement of the penal laws, which aggrieve the Catholics of Ireland,* Dublin, 1812.

Selection of Irish national poetry: from the landing of the Milesians to the present time, Dublin, 1846.

Sillard, P., *The life and letters of John Martin*, Dublin, 1893.

Smyth, Alfred P., *Faith, famine and fatherland in the Irish midlands: perceptions of a priest and historian, Anthony Cogan, 1826-1872*, Dublin, 1992.

Smyth, Patrick James (ed.), *Thomas Francis Meagher*, Dublin, 1867.

Staunton, Michael, *Speech of Michael Staunton, Esq: on the state of Ireland*, Dublin, 1843.

Sturge, Joseph and Harvey, Thomas, *The West Indies in 1837*, London, 1838.

Sullivan, A. M., *New Ireland: political sketches and personal reminiscences,* 2 vols, 5th ed. London, 1878.

The treble almanack for the year 1825, Dublin, 1824.

*The spirit of the **Nation**,* Dublin, May 1843 with a preface by Thomas Davis; 2nd ed. September, 1843; part 2, November, 1843 with a preface by Thomas Davis.

*The spirit of the **Nation**: or ballads and songs by the writers of the 'Nation',* reissued in quarto form with music, an artistic page by Thomas Burton, illustrations and a preface by Thomas Davis, Dublin, June 1844. Reprinted 1845. 50 editions by 1877, again, 1882, 1911, 1934.

*The Voice of the **Nation**: A manual of nationality, by the writers of the **Nation** newspaper,* Dublin, 1844. Preface by Thomas Davis.

Thom's official directory of the United Kingdom of Great Britain and Ireland, Dublin, 1844.

Thompson, David, and McGusty, Moyra (eds.), *The Irish journals of Elizabeth Smith, 1840-1850,* Oxford, 1980.

Urban, Sylvanus, 'James Thomas Davis', in *The Gentleman's Magazine,* vol. lxxxiv, London, 1814.

Venedey, Jacob, *Ireland and the Irish during the Repeal year, 1843,* trans. with notes by William Bernard MacCabe, Dublin, 1844.

Waller, John Francis (ed.), *Imperial dictionary of universal biography,* vol. 2, London, 1863.

Wiggins, John, *The 'Monster' misery of Ireland: a practical treatise on the relation of landlord and tenant,* London, 1844.

Wilde, Lady, *Poems by Speranza,* new ed., Dublin, 1907.

Willis, Thomas, *Facts connected with the social and sanitary conditions of the working classes in the city of Dublin,* Dublin, 1845.

Secondary Sources
Books, articles, etc.

Aalen, F. H. A. and Whelan, Kevin (eds.), *Dublin city and county: from prehistory to present,* Dublin, 1992.

Adam-Smith, Patsy, *Heart of exile,* Melbourne, 1986.

Ahern, J. L., with an intro by Alan Downey, *Young Ireland: its founder and his circle,* Waterford, 1945.

Akenson, Donald Harman, *Irish Catholics and Irish Protestants, 1815-1922: an international perspective,* Toronto, 1981.

Alter, Peter, 'Symbols of Irish Nationalism' in Alan O'Day (intro.), *Reactions to Irish Nationalism 1865-1914*, Dublin, 1987.

Althoz, Joseph L., 'Daniel O'Connell and the Dublin Review', in *The Catholic historical review*, vol. lxxiv, Washington D.C. 1988.

Archer, J. R., 'Necessity and ambiguity: nationalism and myth in Ireland" in *Éire-Ireland*, Minnesota, no. 19, 1984, pp 23 -27.

Aspinall, A., *Politics and the press: 1780-1850*, London, 1949.

Atkinson, Sarah, *Essays*, Dublin, 1895.

Bardon, Jonathon, *A history of Ulster*, Belfast, 1992.

Bartlett, Thomas, *The rise and fall of the Irish nation: the Catholic question, 1690-1830*, Dublin, 1992.

___, 'The Catholic question in the eighteenth century', in *History Ireland*, vol. 1, no. 1, Dublin, 1993.

Bartlett, Thomas; Curran, Chris; O'Dwyer, Riana; Ó Tuathaigh, Gearóid (eds.), *Irish studies: a general introduction*, Dublin, 1988.

Beames, Michael, *Peasants and power: The Whiteboy movements and their control in pre-famine Ireland*, Sussex, 1983.

Beckett, J. C., *Confrontations: studies in Irish history*, London, 1972.

___, *The Anglo-Irish tradition*, London, 1976.

___, *The making of modern Ireland, 1603-1923*, London, 1966.

Beresford Ellis, P. *A history of the Irish working class*, London, 1989.

Biggs-Davison, John and Chowdharay Best, George, *The cross of St Patrick and the Catholic unionist tradition in Ireland*, Buckinghamshire, 1984.

Black, R. D. Collison, *Economic thought and the Irish question 1817-1870*, Cambridge, 1960.

Blake, Lord (intro.), *Ireland after the Union*, Oxford, 1989.

Bolton, G. D., *The passing of the Act of Union*, Oxford, 1966.

Bolton, Walter, *Thomas Davis (1814-1845)*, Dublin, 1930.

Bowen, Desmond, *The Protestant crusade in Ireland, 1800-1870*, Dublin, 1978.

Boyce, D. George, *Nineteenth-century Ireland: The search for stability*, Dublin, 1990.

___, *Nationalism in Ireland*, Dublin, 2nd ed. 1991.

Boylan, Henry, *Theobald Wolfe Tone*, Dublin, 1991.

___, *A dictionary of Irish biography*, 2nd ed. Dublin, 1988.

Bradshaw, Brendan, 'Nationalism and historical scholarship in modern Ireland', in *Irish Historical Studies*, vol. xxvi, Dublin, 1988-9.

Brady, Anne M., and Cleeve, Brian, *A biographical dictionary of Irish writers*, Mullingar, 1985.

Bryan, Dan, 'Thomas Davis as a military influence', in *An Cosantóir*, vol. 5, no. 10, Dublin, 1945.

Broderick, John F., *The Holy See and the Irish movement for the repeal of the union with England 1829-1847*, Rome, 1951.

Brown, Malcolm, *The politics of Irish literature: from Thomas Davis to W. B. Yeats*, London, 1972.

Brown, Terence and Hayley, Barbara (eds.), *Samuel Ferguson: a centenary tribute*, Dublin, 1987.

Buckley, David N., *James Fintan Lalor: radical*, Cork, 1990.

Buckley, Mary G., 'Thomas Davis: a study in nationalist philosophy' Ph.D. thesis, National University of Ireland, Cork, 1980.

Búrca, Seamus de, *The love story of Thomas Davis and Annie Hutton*, Dublin, 1962.

Burke, Edmund (ed. with intro. by Conor Cruise O'Brien), *Reflections on the Revolution in France*, London, 1986.

Burke, Helen, *The people and the Poor Law in 19th-century Ireland*, West Sussex, 1987.

Burtchaell, George Dames and Sadlier, Thomas Ulick, *Alumni Dublinensis*, London, 1924.

Byrce, James, *Two centuries of Irish history*, Dublin, 1987.

Campbell, Flann, *The dissenting voice: Protestant democracy in Ulster from plantation to partition*, Belfast, 1991.

Canny, Nicholas, 'Early Modern Ireland' in R. F. Foster (ed.), *The Oxford illustrated history of Ireland*, Oxford, 1989.

Casway, Jerrold I., *Owen Roe O'Neil and the struggle for Catholic Ireland*, Philadelphia, 1984.

Cecil, Algernon, *Queen Victoria and her prime ministers*, London, 1953.

Clarke, Randall, 'O'Connell and the Young Irelanders', in *Irish Historical Studies*, vol. iii, Dublin, 1942-3.

Collins, Kevin, *The cultural conquest of Ireland*, Dublin, 1990.

Connell, K. H., *The population of Ireland 1750-1845*, Oxford, 1950.

Connolly, S. J., *Priests and people in pre-famine Ireland, 1780-1845*. New York, 1982.

Corkery, Daniel, 'Davis and the national language', in M. J. MacManus (ed.), *Thomas Davis and Young Ireland*, Dublin, 1945.

Cosgrove Art (ed.), *Dublin through the ages*, Dublin, 1988.

Cronin, Seán, *Irish nationalism: A history of its roots and ideology*, Dublin, 1980.

Cullen, L. M., *An economic history of Ireland since 1660*, London, 1978.

Daly, Mary E., *Dublin, the deposed capital: a social and economic history 1860-1914*, Cork, 1984.

___, 'An alien institution? Attitudes towards the city in nineteeth- and twentieth-century Irish history', in *Etudes Irelandais*, no. 10, Lille, December, 1985.

___, *The Famine in Ireland*, Dundalk, 1986.

D'Arcy, Fergus, 'The artisans of Dublin and Daniel O'Connell, 1830-47: an unquiet liaison' in *Irish Historical Studies*, vol. xvii, 1970.

Davis, Richard P., *The Young Ireland movement*, Dublin, 1987.

___, 'The violence of poetry: O'Connell, Davis and Moore', in *Threshold*, no. 37, Dublin, 1986/7.

___, 'Patrick O'Farrell and Irish secular nationalism – a reconsideration,' in *Tasmanian Historical Research Association*, vol. 20, no. 4. Hobart, December, 1973.

___, 'William Smith O'Brien as an imperialist' in *Irish-Australian studies: papers delivered at the seventh Irish-Australian conference, July 1993*, Sydney, 1994.

Deane, Seamus, 'The writer as witness: Literature as historical evidence', in *Historical Studies*, xvi, London, 1987.

de Paor, Liam, *The peoples of Ireland*, Indiana, 1986.

de Tocqueville, Alexis, *Alexis de Tocqueville's journey in Ireland July-August. 1835,* translated and edited by Emmett Larkin, Dublin, 1990.

Dickson, David, *New foundations: Ireland 1660-1800*, Dublin, 1987,

___, (ed.), *The gorgeous mask: Dublin 1700-1850*, Dublin, 1987.

Dillon, T. W. T., 'Thomas Davis; 1815 (sic) – 1845', in *The Bell*, vol. x, Dublin, 1945.

Donnelly, James S., Jr., *The land and the people of nineteenth-century Cork*, London, 1975.

Dunne, Tom, *Theobald Wolfe Tone: colonial outsider. An analysis of his political philosophy.* Cork, 1982.

___, 'Haunted by history: Irish romantic writing 1800-1850', in Roy Porter and Mikulas Teich (eds.), *Romanticism in national context*, Cambridge, 1988.

Edwards, Owen Dudley; Evans, Gwynfor; Rhys, Ioan; MacDiarmid, Hugh, *Celtic nationalism*, London, 1968.

Edwards, R. Dudley, *Ireland and the Italian risorgimento*, Dublin, 1960.

___, 'The contribution of Young Ireland to the development of the national idea', in S. Pender (ed.), *Feilsribhinn Torna: essays and studies presented to Tadgh Ua Donnachadha (Torna)*, Cork, 1945.

Eglinton, John (W. F. Magee), *Bards and saints*, Dublin, 1906.

Elliott, Marianne, *Wolfe Tone*, New Haven, 1989.

Ellis, Steven G., 'Historiographical debate: Representations of the past in Ireland: whose past and whose present?' in *Irish Historical Studies*, vol. xxvii, Dublin, 1991.

Ellmann, Richard, *Oscar Wilde*, London, 1988.

Farrell, Brian (ed.), *The Irish parliamentary tradition*, Dublin, 1973.

Fennell, Desmond, *The revision of Irish nationalism*, Dublin, 1989.

Fitzpatrick, David, 'The disappearance of the Irish agricultural labourer, 1841-1912', in *Irish economic and social history*, vol. vii, Belfast, 1980.

Fitzpatrick, W. J. *The life of Charles Lever*, 2 vols., London, 1879.

___, (ed. with notes), *Correspondence of Daniel O'Connell*, 2 vols, London, 1888.

Flanagan, Thomas, 'Literature in English, 1801-91', in W. E. Vaughan (ed.), *A new history*, vol. v, Dublin, 1989.

Fogarty, L., *Father John Kenyon: A patriot priest of forty eight*, Dublin, 1921.

Foster, R. F., *Modern Ireland: 1600-1972*, London, 1988.

___, *The Oxford illustrated history of Ireland*, Oxford, 1989.

___, 'History and the Irish Question' in *Transactions of the Royal Historical Society*, London, fifth series, vol. 33, 1983.

Freeman, T. W., *Pre-famine Ireland*, Manchester, 1957.

___, 'Land and people, c. 1841'; in W. E. Vaughan (ed.), *A new history*, ch. xi, vol. 5, Dublin, 1989.

Garvin, Tom, *The evolution of Irish nationalist politics*, Dublin, 1981.

Gleeson, Dermot, F., 'Father John Kenyon and Young Ireland' in *Studies*, Dublin, vol. xxxv, 1946.

Green, Alice Stopford, *Irish nationality*, London, 1911, reprinted 1922.

Grogan, Geraldine F., *The noblest agitator: Daniel O'Connell and the German Catholic movement 1830-50*, Dublin, 1991.

___, 'The Colleges Bill 1845-49' in Maurice R. O'Connell (ed.), *O'Connell, Education, Church and State*, Dublin, 1992.

Gwynn, Denis, *O'Connell, Davis and the colleges bill*, Oxford, 1948.

___, 'O'Connell, Davis and the Colleges Bill', in *The Irish Ecclesiastical Record*, vols lxix and lxx, Dublin, 1947, 1948.

___, 'Father Kenyon and Young Ireland', parts 1 and 2 in *ibid*, vol. lxxi, 1949.

___, 'Denny Lane and Thomas Davis', in *Studies*, vol. 38, Dublin, 1949.

___, 'John F. Pigot and Thomas Davis', in ibid.

___, '*Thomas Francis Meagher*', O'Donnell lecture delivered at University College Cork, 17 July, 1961, Dublin, n.d.

Hachey, Thomas E. and McCaffrey, Lawrence J., *Perspectives on Irish nationalism*, Kentucky, 1989.

Hayes-McCoy, G. A., *A history of Irish flags from earliest times*, Dublin, 1979.

Hill, Jacqueline R., 'Nationalism and the Catholic Church in the 1840s: views of Dublin repealers.' in *Irish Historical Studies*, vol. xix, no. 76, Dublin, 1975.

Hincken, Pamela (told to), *Seventies years young: memories of Elizabeth Countess of Fingall*, London, 1937, Dublin, 1991.

Hogan, Daire, *The legal profession in Ireland 1789-1922*, Naas, 1986.

Hone, J. M., *Thomas Davis*, London, 1934.

Hoppen, K. Theodore, *Elections, politics and society in Ireland, 1832-1885*, Oxford, 1984.

___, *Ireland since 1800: conflict and conformity*, Essex, 1989.

Hutchinson, John, *The dynamics of cultural nationalism: the Gaelic revival and the creation of the Irish nation state,* London, 1987.

Inglis, Brian, *The freedom of the press in Ireland 1784-1841,* London, 1954.

Jupp, P. J., 'Irish J. P.s at Westminster in the early nineteenth century', in *Historical Studies*, vii, London, 1969.

Kable, K. J., 'Fulton, Henry (1761-1840)' in Douglas Pike, ed., *Australian Dictionary of Biography*, vol. 1, Melbourne 1966.

Kee, Robert, *The green flag: the most distressful country,* London, 1989.

Kellett, Lorna, 'The *Nation* in mourning' in M. J. MacManus (ed.), *Thomas Davis and Young Ireland*, Dublin, 1945.

Kelly, Charlotte, M., 'The '82 Club', in *Studies*, vol. xxxiii, Dublin, 1944.

Kelly, James, *Prelude to union: Anglo-Irish politics in the 1870s*, Cork, 1992.

Kelly, Marilyn Josephine, 'The silence of the tongues, the clamour for souls', M.Phil. thesis, Department of Irish Studies, U.C.G. Galway, 1993.

Kennedy, Brian, A., 'Sharman Crawford and the repeal question 1847', in *Irish Historical Studies,* vol. 6, Dublin, 1948-49.

Kennedy, Dennis, '1798 rebellion seen as a political disaster,' *Irish Times,* Dublin, 21 September, 1981.

Kerr, Donal A., *Peel, priests and politics: Sir Robert Peel's administration and the Roman Catholic Church in Ireland, 1841-1846,* Oxford, 1982.

Kerrigan, Colm, *Father Mathew and the Irish temperance movement,* Cork, 1992.

Kiely, Benedict, *Poor scholar: A study of the works and days of William Carleton (1794-1869),* Dublin, 1947.

Kiernan, C. G., 'The emergence of a nation' in C. H. E. Philpin (ed.), *Nationalism and popular protest in Ireland,* Cambridge, 1987.

King, Bolton, *The life of Mazzini,* London, 1912.

Kirwin, Bill, 'The radical youth of a conservative: D'Arcy McGee in Young Ireland' in *Canadian Journal of Irish Studies,* vol. x, no. 1.

Vancouver, June 1984.

Knowlton, Steven R., *Popular politics and the Irish Catholic Church,* New York, 1991.

___, 'The politics of John Mitchel: a reappraisal' in *Éire – Ireland,* Minnesota, summer, 1987.

Lampson, Locker, G., *A consideration of the state of Ireland in the nineteenth century,* London, 1907.

Langer, William L., *Political and social upheavel 1832-1852,* New York, 1969

Lecky, William E. H., *A history of England in the eighteenth century,* 8 vols, London, 1878.

___, *Leaders of public opinion in Ireland,* 2 vols, London, 1903.

Lefevre, G. Shaw, *Peel and O'Connell: a review of the Irish policy of parliament from the act of Union to the death of Sir Robert Peel,* London, 1887.

'Letters of some interest', M. R. (ed.), in *Irish Monthly,* vol. 36, Dublin, 1908.

Lyons, F. S. L. and Hawkins, R. A. J. (eds.), *Ireland under the Union: essays in honour of T. W. Moody,* Oxford, 1980.

McCaffrey, Lawrence, J., *The Irish Question 1800-1922,* Lexington, 1968.

McCartney, Donal (ed.), *The world of Daniel O'Connell* , Dublin, 1980.

___, 'The world of Daniel O'Connell', in *The world of Daniel O'Connell,* Dublin, 1980.

___, *The Dawning of Democracy: Ireland 1800-1870,* Dublin, 1987.

___, 'The writing of history in Ireland 1800-30', in *Irish Historical Studies*, vol. x, Dublin, 1956-7.

Macaulay, Ambrose, *Dr Russell of Maynooth*, London, 1983.

McCracken, J. L., 'Irish parliamentary elections, 1727-68' in *Irish Historical Studies*, vol. v, Dublin, 1946-7.

MacDonagh, Oliver, *The life of Daniel O'Connell 1775-1847*, London, 1991.

___, *Ireland*, New Jersey, 1968.

___, *Ireland: The Union and its aftermath*. London, 1977.

___, *States of Mind: A study of Anglo-Irish conflict 1780-1980*, London, 1983.

___, 'Time's revenge and revenge's time: A view of Anglo-Irish relations', in *Anglo-Irish Studies*, iv, Cambridge, 1979.

___, 'The politicization of the Irish Catholic bishops', in *Historical Journal*, vol. xviii, Cambridge, 1975.

___, 'Ambiguity in nationalism – the case of Ireland', *Historical Studies*, vol. 19. 1981.

___, 'Ideas and institutions, 1830-45; 'The economy and society, 1830-45' in W. Vaughan (ed.), *A new history of Ireland*, vol. 5, chs ix, x, Dublin, 1989.

___, with Mandle, W. F., and Travers, Pauric (eds.), *Irish culture and nationalism, 1750-1950*, London, 1983.

___,with Mandle, W. F. (eds.), *Ireland and Irish-Australia*, London, 1986.

McDowell, R. B. (ed.), *Social life in Ireland, 1800-1845*, Dublin, 1957

___, *Public opinion and government policy in Ireland 1801-1846*, London, 1952.

McDowell, R. B. and Webb, D. A., *Trinity College Dublin 1592 -1952: an academic history*, Cambridge, 1982.

Macgrath, Kevin, 'Writers in the *Nation*, 1842-5', in *Irish Historical Studies*, vi, Dublin, 1949.

McHugh, Robert (ed.), *Davis, Mangan, Ferguson: tradition and the Irish writer*. Dublin, 1970.

McHugh, Roger, 'Thomas Davis' in *The Irish Ecclesiastical Record*, vol. 66, Dublin, 1945.

MacIntyre, Angus, *The Liberator Daniel O'Connell and the Irish Party 1830-1847*, London, 1965.

MacManus, M. J., *Thomas Davis: nation builder*, Dublin, 1945.

___, (ed.), *Thomas Davis and Young Ireland*, Dublin, 1945.

___, (ed.), *Book Fair:Thomas Davis and Young Ireland*, Dublin, 1945.

MacMillan, Gretchen, *State, society and authority in Ireland*, Dublin, 1993.

MacSweeny, Patrick, M., *A group of nation builders: O'Donovan, O'Curry, Petrie*, Dublin, 1913.

MacSuibhne, P., *Paul Cullen and his contemporaries*, 3 vols, Naas, 1961-65.

Mahler, F. C., 'The general strike of 1842' in R. Quinault and J. Stevenson (eds.), *Popular protest and public order, London 1790-1920*, London, 1972.

Mannin, Ethel, *Two studies in integrity: Gerald Griffin and the Rev Francis Mahony ('Father Prout')*, London, 1954.

Mansergh, Nicholas, *Ireland in the age of reform and revolution*, London, 1940.

Maxwell, Constantia, *Country and town in Ireland under the Georges*, Dundalk, 1949.

Maxwell, G., *A history of Trinity College Dublin, 1591-1892*, Dublin, 1946.

Mazzini, Joseph, *The duties of man and other essays*, London, 1907.

Moley, Raymond, *Nationalism without violence*, New York, 1974.

Molony, John N., *The Roman mould of the Australian Catholic Church*, Melbourne, 1969.

___, *Eureka*, Melbourne, 1984.

Moody, T. W., 'In Memory of Thomas Davis.' *Irish Times*, Dublin, 7 September, 1945.

___, *Thomas Davis 1814-45, A Centenary address*. Dublin, 1945.

___, 'Thomas Davis and the Irish Nation' in *Hermathena*, no. C111, Dublin, 1966.

___, and Beckett, J. C., *Queens, Belfast: the history of a university*, 2 vols, London, 1959

Morrissey, Thomas J., *Towards a National University: William Delany SJ (1835-1924). An era of initiative in Irish education*, Dublin, 1983.

Mulvey, Helen, F., 'Nineteenth-Century Ireland, 1801-1914', in *Irish Historical Studies*, vol. xvii, no. 65, Dublin, 1970.

___, 'Sir Charles Gavan Duffy: Young Irelander and imperial statesman', in *The Canadian Historical Review*, vol. 33, Toronto, December, 1952

Murphy, Brian, The Canon of Irish cultural history: some questions concerning Roy Foster's *Modern Ireland* in *Studies*, summer, Dublin, 1993.

Murphy, Maura, 'The ballad singer and the role of the seditious ballad in nineteenth-century Ireland. Dublin Castle's view.' in *Ulster Folklife*, vol. 25, Belfast, 1979.

Nolan, William, 'A Clareman in Van Diemen's Land: the Tasmanian journal of William Smith O'Brien', in *The Other Clare*, no. xxi, Shannon, April 1992.

Noonan, John D., 'The Library of Thomas Davis', in *The Irish book lover*, vol. v, Dublin, October 1913.

Norman, Edward, *A history of modern Ireland,* London, 1971.

___, 'The Maynooth question of 1845', in *Irish Historical Studies*, vol. xv, Dublin, 1966-7.

Nowlan, Kevin B., *Charles Gavan Duffy and the Repeal movement*, Dublin, 1963.

___, *The politics of Repeal: a study in the relations between Great Britain and Ireland, 1841-50*, London, 1965.

___, 'The meaning of repeal in Irish history' *Historical studies*, iv, London, 1963.

___, 'Writings in connection with the Thomas Davis and Young Ireland centenary, 1945', in *Irish Historical Studies*, vol. v, Dublin, 1946-7.

___, 'The Catholic clergy and Irish politics in the eighteen thirties and forties' in *Historical Studies*, ix, 1974.

O'Brien, Connor Cruise, *Passion and cunning: Essays on nationalism, terrorism and revolution,* New York, 1988.

O'Brien, Gerard, 'Charles Gavan Duffy 1816-1903: rebel and statesman' in G. O'Brien (ed.), *Nine Ulster lives,* The Ulster Historical Foundation, Belfast, 1992.

O'Brien, R. Barry, *Fifty years of concessions to Ireland 1831-1881,* 2 vols., London, 1893.

___, (intro.), *Studies in Irish History*, Dublin, 1903

O'Brien, William, *The influence of Thomas Davis*, Cork, 1915.

O'Broin, Leon, *Charles Gavan Duffy – patriot and statesman – the story of Charles Gavan Duffy, 1816-1903*, Dublin, 1972.

Ó Buachalla, Breandán, 'Poetry and politics in modern Ireland', in *Eighteenth-century Ireland*, vol. 7, Dublin, 1992.

___, 'A speech in Irish on Repeal', in *Studia Hibernica*, no. 10, Dublin, 1970.

O'Cathaoir, Brendan, *John Blake Dillon, Young Irelander*, Dublin, 1990.

___, 'An Irishman's Diary,' in *Irish Times*, 4 June, Dublin, 1993.

___, '"*Nation*", created vision of a pluralist Ireland' in ibid., 14 October 1992.

O'Connell, Maurice R. (ed.), *The correspondence of Daniel O'Connell,* 8 vols, Dublin, 1972-80.

___, (ed.), *Daniel O'Connell: political pioneer*, Dublin, 1991.

___, (ed.), *O'Connell, education, church and state*, Dublin, 1992.

___, 'Daniel O'Connell; income, expenditure and despair.' *Irish Historical Studies*, vol. xvii, Dublin, 1970-71.

___,'Thomas Davis: a destructive conciliator', *Irish Times*, Dublin, 6 August, 1974.

___, 'O'Connell reconsidered.,' in *Studies*, vol. lxiv, Dublin, 1975.

___, 'Daniel O'Connell and religious freedom', in *Thought*, vol. 50, Fordam, N.Y., 1975.

___, 'O'Connell, Young Ireland, and violence', in ibid., vol. 50, 1977.

___, 'Irish constitutionalism: a rescue operation', in *Studies*, vol. 75, Dublin, 1986.

___, 'Young Ireland and the Catholic clergy in 1844: contemporary deceit and historical falsehood', in *The Catholic historical review*, Washington, D.C., lxxiv, 1988.

___,'O'Connell, Young Ireland, and Negro Slavery: an exercise in romantic nationalism', in *Thought*, vol. lxiv, Fordam, N.Y., 1989.

O'Connor, Emmett, *A labour history of Ireland 1824-1960*, Dublin, 1992.

Ó Corráin, Donnchadh, 'Nationality and kingship in pre-Norman Ireland', in *Historical Studies*, vol. xi, London, 1978.

O'Day, Alan (intro.), *Reactions to Irish nationalism, 1865-1814*, Dublin, 1987.

O'Faolain, Seán, *King of the beggars: a life of Daniel O'Connell,* Dublin, 1970.

O'Farrell, Patrick, *Ireland's English question: Anglo-Irish relations 1534-1970*, London, 1971.

O'Flaherty, Eamon, 'Ecclesiastical politics and the dismantling of the penal laws in Ireland, 1774-82', in *Irish Historical Studies*, vol. xxvi, Dublin,1988-9.

O'Ferrall, R. F. B., 'The growth of political consciousness in Ireland: 1823-1847. A study of O'Connellite politics and political education', Ph.D. thesis, University of Dublin, 1978.

Ó Gráda, Cormac, *Ireland before and after the famine: explorations in economic history 1800-1925*, 2nd. ed., Glasgow, 1993.

___, *A new economic history 1780-1939*, Oxford, 1994.

___, 'Poverty, population, and agriculture, 1801-1845' and 'Industry and communication, 1801-45' in W. E. Vaughan (ed.), *A new history*, vol. 5, Dublin, 1989.

___, '"For Irishmen to Forget?" Recent research on the Great Irish Famine', in *Crises in the Past,* Hakkinen, Antii (ed.), Helsinki, 1992.

___, 'The Lumper Potato and the Famine', in *History Ireland*, vol. 1, no. 1, Dublin, 1993.

O'Hegarty, P. S., 'Note' in *The Irish book lover*, vol. xxx, February, London, 1947.

O'Neill, Patrick, 'The reception of German literature in Ireland, 1750-1850', in *Studia Hibernica,* part 1, no. 16, 1976, part 2, nos 17-18, Dublin, 1977-8.

O'Neill, Timothy P., *Life and tradition in rural Ireland,* London, 1977.

O'Reilly, Bernard, *John MacHale: Archbishop of Tuam,* 2 vols, New York, 1890.

O'Riordan, Michelle, *The Gaelic mind and the collapse of the Gaelic world,* Cork, 1990.

Ó Siodhacháin, Donal (ed.), *Glimpses of old Ireland,* Cork, 1990.

O'Sullivan, T. F., *The Young Irelanders,* Tralee, 1944.

Ó Tuathaigh, Gearóid, *Ireland before the famine 1798-1848,* Dublin, 1972.

___, 'Gaelic Ireland, popular politics and Daniel O'Connell*'* in *Journal of the Galway Archaeological and Historical Society,* vol. 34, Galway, 1974-75.

___, 'Nineteenth century Irish politics: the case for normalcy', in *Anglo-Irish studies,* vol. 1, Cambridge, 1975.

Pearse, P. H., *The spiritual nation,* Dublin, 1916.

Pender, Seamus (ed.), *Feilscribhinn Torna: essays and studies presented to Tadgh Ua Donnchadha (Torna),* Cork, 1947.

Phelan, Josephine, *The life and times of Thomas D'Arcy McGee,* Toronto, 1951.

Porter, Roy and Teich, Mikulas (eds.), *Romanticism in national context,* Cambridge, 1988.

Patrick, Ross and Heather, *Exiles undaunted: the Irish rebels Kevin and Eva O'Doherty,* Brisbane, 1989.

Pearl, Cyril, *The three lives of Gavan Duffy,* Sydney, 1979.

Pelan Rebecca, *Papers delivered at the seventh Irish-Australian conference, July 1993,* Sydney, 1994.

Philpin, C. H. E. (ed.), *Nationalism and popular protest in Ireland,* Cambridge, 1987.

Poirtéir, Cathal (ed.), *The great Irish famine,* Cork, 1995.

Powell, Frederick, W., *The politics of Irish social policy, 1600-1990,* New York, 1992.

Pretty, Graeme L, 'Wakefield, Edward Gibbon, 1796-1862' in Douglas Pike (ed.), *Australian dictionary of biography,* vol. 2, Melbourne, 1967.

Price, Glanville (ed.), *The Celtic connection*, Buckinghamshire, 1992.

Quarton, Marjorie, *Renegade* (London, 1991).

Quigley, Michael (ed.), *Pictorial record: centenary of Thomas Davis and Young Ireland*, Dublin, 1945.

Quinault, R, and Stevenson, J. (eds.), *Popular protest and public order: 1790-1920*, London, 1972.

Raifeartaigh, T. Ó, *The Royal Irish Academy: a bicentennial history 1785-1985*, Dublin, 1985.

Ridden, Jennifer, 'Britishness, Protestantism, and citizenship in early nineteenth-century Ireland and Australia', Paper presented at Imperial history seminar, London, 1993.

Roche, Kennedy, F., 'The relations of the Catholic Church and the State in England and Ireland, 1800-52' in *Historical Studies*, iii, London,1961.

Romeo, Rosario, *Vita di Cavour*, Rome, 1984.

Sigerson, George, *Bards of the Gael and Gall: examples of the poetic literature of Erinn*, London, 1907.

___, *The last independent parliament of Ireland*, Dublin, 1918.

Schenk, H. G., *The mind of the European romantics*, London, 1966.

Sheehy, Jeanne, *The rediscovery of Ireland's past: the Celtic revival 1830-1930*, London, 1980.

Siodhacháin, Donal Ó (ed.), *Glimpses of Old Ireland*, Cork, 1970.

Simes, Douglas, 'A voice for Irish conservatism: the *Dublin University Magazine* 1833-41. Paper delivered at the Australasian Victorian Studies Association, Auckland, 1993.

Simms, Katherine, 'Bardic poetry as a historical source', in *Historical Studies*, xvi, 1987.

Simms, J. G., *Colonial nationalism 1698-1776*, Cork, 1976.

___, *William Molyneux of Dublin*, Blackrock, 1982.

Sloan, Barry, 'The autobiographies of John Mitchel and Charles Gavan Duffy: a study in contrasts', *Éire – Ireland*, Minnesoata, summer, 1987.

Smith, F. B., 'British Post Office espionage, 1844', in *Historical Studies*, Melbourne, vol. 14, 1969-71.

Stephen, Leslie and Lee, Sidney (eds.), *The dictionary of national biography*, vol. v, London, 1959.

Sullivan, Eileen, *Thomas Davis*, New Jersey, 1978.

Talmon, J. L., *Romanticism and revolt: Europe 1815-1848*, London, 1967.

The Thomas Davis and Young Ireland Centenary Commemoration 1945, Dublin, 1945.

Tierney, Michael, 'Politics and culture: Daniel O'Connell and the Gaelic past', in *Studies*, vol. xxvii, Dublin, September 1938.

___, (ed.), *Daniel O'Connell: nine centenary essays*, Dublin, 1949.

___, 'Repeal of the Union' in ibid.

uí Ógáin, Rionach, 'Folklore on Daniel O'Connell', Unpublished manuscript, Department of Irish Folklore, University College Dublin.

Vaughan, W. E. (ed.), *A new history of Ireland: Ireland under the union 1801-70*, vol. v, Oxford, 1989.

Walsh, William, J., *The Irish university question: the Catholic case*, Dublin, 1897.

___, *O'Connell, Archbishop Murray and the Board of Charitable Bequests*, Dublin, 1916.

Ward, A. W. and Waller, A. R. (eds.), *The Cambridge history of English literature*, New York, 1932.

Wheeler, T. S., 'Sir Robert Kane: Life and Works', parts i and ii in *Studies*, vol. xxxiii, Dublin, 1944.

Whelan, Kevin, 'Opening the doors on Grattan's Parliament', in *Irish Times*, Dublin, 10 April, 1993.

___, 'Pre and post-famine landscape change', in Cathal Poirtéir (ed.), *The great Irish famine*, Cork, 1995.

White, Hayden, *The historical imagination in nineteenth-century Europe*, Baltimore, 1973.

Whyte, J. H., 'Daniel O'Connell and the repeal party', in *Irish Historical Studies*, xi, Dublin, 1958-9.

___, 'The influence of the Catholic clergy on elections in nineteenth-century Ireland', in *English historical review*, vol. lxxv, Harlow, 1960.

White, Terence de Vere, *The parents of Oscar Wilde*, London, 1967.

Wilson, Philip, 'Ireland under Charles II' and 'Ireland under James II', in R. Barry O'Brien (intro.), *Studies in Irish history 1649-1774*, London, 1903.

Woodham-Smith, Cecil, *Queen Victoria: her life and times*, vol. 1, London, 1972.

Yeats, W. B., *Tribute to Thomas Davis*, Denis Gywnn (intro.), Cork, 1947.

Zimmerman, George-Denis, *Irish political street ballads and rebel songs*, Geneva, 1966.

THE WEST'S ASLEEP.

BY THOMAS DAVIS.

I.

WHEN all beside a vigil keep,
The West's asleep, the West's asleep—
Alas! and well may Erin weep,
When Connaught lies in slumber deep.
There lake and plain smile fair and free,
'Mid rocks—their guardian chivalry—
Sing oh! let man learn liberty
From crashing wind and lashing sea.

II.

That chainless wave and lovely land
Freedom and Nationhood demand—
Be sure, the great God never plann'd,
For slumbering slaves, a home so grand.
And, long, a brave and haughty race
Honoured and sentinelled the place—
Sing oh! not even their sons' disgrace
Can quite destroy their glory's trace.

III

For often, in O'Connor's van,
To triumph dash'd each Connaught clan—
And fleet as deer the Normans ran
Through Coirrslabh Pass and Ard Rathain.*
And later times saw deeds as brave;
And glory guards Clanricarde's grave—
Sing, oh! they died their land to save,
At Aughrim's slopes and Shannon's wave.

IV.

And if, when all a vigil keep,
The West's asleep, the West's asleep—
Alas! and well may Erin weep,
That Connaught lies in slumber deep.
But—hark!—some voice like thunder spake :
" *The West's awake, the West's awake*"—
Sing, oh! hurra! let England quake,
We'll watch till death for Erin's sake!

---

* Vulgarly written Curlews and Ardrahan.

Index of Places

377

Index of Institutions/Persons

Cullen, Paul, 128-9
Curran, John Philpot, 233-4
Curry, John, 28-9

Dalcassian, 200
Daly, John, 294
Danes, The, 200
Daunt, William Joseph O'Neill, 94, 121, 127, 145, 153, 217, 251, 278
Davies, Sir John, 28
Davis, Charlotte Mary, 2, 5, 24, 93, 119, 239, 332, 341
Davis, James, 262
Davis, James Robert, 2, 5
Davis, James Thomas, 2, 4, 144
Davis, John Nicholas Atkins, 2, 5, 24, 75, 93, 119, 144
Davis, Mary (née Atkins) 2, 4, 5, 24, 74, 93, 119, 239, 341
de Jean, Jean, 273
de Beaumont, Gustave, 46-7, 51-2, 62, 101
de Courcy, O'Brazil, 239
de Tocqueville, Alexis, 14, 41-2, 160
Defenders, The, 120
Demosthenes, 89
Denham, Sir John, chief justice of the king's bench, 254
Desmonds, The, 247
Dickson, Thomas, 48
Dillon, John Blake, ix, xi, 13, 38, 59, 62-4, 66-7, 71-4, 77-9, 88-92, 94-6, 100, 104, 106-7, 125, 127, 137, 145, 172, 177, 185, 194, 208-10, 217, 228, 238, 243, 273-4, 276, 308, 317-8, 324, 327, 335, 342
Dillon, Luke, 59
Doheny, 217, 243
Doheny, Michael, 153
Doran, John, 195
Drennan, William, 293
Druids, The, 149
Drummond, Thomas, 30, 47, 67
Dublin Castle authorities, 201
Dublin Evening Mail, 296
Dublin Evening Post, 48, 63-4, 84
Dublin Medical Press, 313
Dublin Review, 166, 267
Dublin University Magazine, 124, 294
Dubliners, 72

Duffy, Charles Gavan ix, x, xi, 13, 16, 18, 24-5, 37, 54, 74, 80, 83-4, 90-5, 99-107, 112, 125, 127, 137, 139, 141, 145-6, 149, 152, 155-6, 172-3, 186-8, 191, 194-5, 208, 210, 215, 217, 233, 237-9, 242-3, 247, 255-6, 262-4, 266-7, 269-77, 294, 299, 307, 311, 313, 317-8, 324, 327-8, 332-5, 337, 342-3
Duffy, Emily (wife of C. G. Duffy), 239, 334
Duffy, George Gavan, 304
Duffy, James, 143
Dunne, Tom, 142
Dupin, Charles, 246

Edgeworth, Maria, 130
Eighty-two, Club, 307, 335
Eliot, chief secretary of Ireland, 287
Eliot, Lord, 152
Elizabeth I, 10, 14, 29, 114, 151
Emmett, Robert, 11, 99, 122, 264
Engels, Friedrich, 7
Evening Freeman, 95
Evening Herald, 63
Evening Mail, 94
Evening Post, 94, 172

Federalists, The, 16
Fenians, The, 156
Ferguson, Sir Samuel, xi, 251, 274, 283, 293, 335, 337, 338
Fermoy, Roche, 239
Ffrench, Lord, 179
Fichte, 187, 326
Fitzgerald, 234
Fitzgerald, Lord Edward, 264
FitzGerald, Sir John, 186
FitzGeralds, The, 28, 55
Fitzpatrick, P.V., 256
Fletcher, Alexander, 138
Flood, Henry, 115, 249, 282
Foster, R.F., 25
Frazer, John, 273
Freeman's Journal, 60, 66, 71, 94, 95, 112, 146, 196, 209, 214, 245, 254, 305
Fulton, Henry, 5
Furlong, Thomas, 293

Gaelic Society of Dublin 1807, 26
George II, 221

George III, 17, 235
George IV (the Fat), 17, 93, 169
Gladstone, 128
Goldsmith, Oliver, 11
Grand Turk, The, 252
Grattan, Henry, 42, 48, 68, 86, 89, 115, 125, 179, 187, 249, 278, 282, 310
Gray, Dr, 71, 92, 95, 196, 215, 235
Green Book, The, 94
Gregg, Rev, 170
Grey, Porter, 255
Griffin, Gerald, 194, 282, 283
Griffin, William, 312
Griffith, Arthur, 244, 344
Grogan, 86
Gwynn, Denis, 302

Hallam, Henry, 29, 51
Hardiman, James, 185, 186
Harvey, Thomas, 284
Hebrews, The, 74
Herder, 25
Historical Society, 27, 38, 40, 41, 45, 88
Hogan, John, 188, 190, 192
Hogan, xi
Holy See, The, 129
Hone, J.M., 90, 240
Hottentots, The, 83
Howards, The, 4
Hudson, William Eliot, 13, 45, 143, 262
Hughes, Terence McMahon, 94, 104, 145
Hume, 29
Hunt, Leigh, 273
Hutton, Annie (Anna Maria), 226-9, 233, 240, 241, 242, 262, 288, 293, 311, 325-7, 331-3, 340, 341
Hutton family, 275
Hutton, Margaret, 226, 228-9, 240, 242, 288, 341
Hutton, Robert, 86, 226, 275
Hutton, Thomas,71, 226, 228, 313, 325, 334, 335
Huttons, The, 218, 229, 333

Inglis, Sir Robert, 302, 304
Ingram, John Kells, 173, 208, 219
Irish Archaeological Society, 72
Irish Book Lover, The, 119
Irish Celtic Society, 233, 297, 335
Irish History Society, 72

Irish Library Association, 233, 335
Irish Record Commission, 26
Irish Volunteers, 80
Italians, The, 101

James I, 31
James II, 31,111-17,120
Johnson, Samuel, 132

Kane, Robert, 244
Kearney, Francis, 13, 38
Kearney, Nick, 139
Kenealy, Edward, 180
Keogh, John, 83, 334
Keogh, William ,13
Kerry Examiner, 276
Kilkenny Journal, The, 314
King, Archbishop, 102
Kiogh Harry, 250

L'Estrange, 29
Lalor, James Fintan, 141
Lamennais, 53, 76
Landor, William Savage, 43, 45
Lane, Denny, 13, 187, 193, 279-80, 288, 312, 318, 343
Le Fanu, Joseph, 172, 174
Le Fanu, W. R., 201
Lecky, William, 112
Leinster, duke of, 10
Leland, 29
Lessing, 39
Lloyd, Bartholomew, 12
Locke (moral philosopher), 40
Lord Lieutenant, 163
Loyal National Repeal Association, 59, 66
Loyal Repeal Association, 73
Luby, T.C., 261
Luby, Thomas, 10-1
Lucas, 115, 249, 282

Macauley, 154
MacCarthy, Denis Florence, 13
MacCarthy, Eugene, 297
MacDonagh, 26, 302, 311
MacDonagh, Oliver, 123
MacHale, John, archbishop of Tuam, 180, 251, 268, 286-7, 300-2, 306, 312, 314
MacManus, Henry, 91, 106
MacManus, Terence Bellew, xi, 91